The Memory of the World

Cary Wolfe, Series Editor

70 *The Memory of the World: Deep Time, Animality, and Eschatology*
Ted Toadvine

69 *Hermes I: Communication*
Michel Serres

68 *Nietzsche's Posthumanism*
Edgar Landgraf

67 *Subsurface*
Karen Pinkus

66 *Making Sense in Common: A Reading of Whitehead in Times of Collapse*
Isabelle Stengers

65 *Our Grateful Dead: Stories of Those Left Behind*
Vinciane Despret

64 *Prosthesis*
David Wills

63 *Molecular Capture: The Animation of Biology*
Adam Nocek

62 *Clang*
Jacques Derrida

61 *Radioactive Ghosts*
Gabriele Schwab

60 *Gaian Systems: Lynn Margulis, Neocybernetics, and the End of the Anthropocene*
Bruce Clarke

59 *The Probiotic Planet: Using Life to Manage Life*
Jamie Lorimer

58 *Individuation in Light of Notions of Form and Information* Volume II. *Supplemental Texts*
Gilbert Simondon

57 *Individuation in Light of Notions of Form and Information*
Gilbert Simondon

56 *Thinking Plant Animal Human: Encounters with Communities of Difference*
David Wood

55 *The Elements of Foucault*
Gregg Lambert

(continued on page 330)

The Memory of the World

Deep Time, Animality, and Eschatology

Ted Toadvine

posthumanities 70

University of Minnesota Press
Minneapolis
London

The University of Minnesota Press gratefully acknowledges the financial assistance provided for the publication of this book by the Office of Research and Graduate Studies in the College of the Liberal Arts at The Pennsylvania State University.

Publication History on pages 319–20 gives original and previous publication information for the writings compiled in this book.

Copyright 2024 by the Regents of the University of Minnesota

All rights reserved. No part of this publication may be reproduced, stored in a retrieval system, or transmitted, in any form or by any means, electronic, mechanical, photocopying, recording, or otherwise, without the prior written permission of the publisher.

Published by the University of Minnesota Press
111 Third Avenue South, Suite 290
Minneapolis, MN 55401-2520
http://www.upress.umn.edu

ISBN 978-1-5179-1599-5 (hc)
ISBN 978-1-5179-1600-8 (pb)

A Cataloging-in-Publication record for this book is available from the Library of Congress.

Printed on acid-free paper

The University of Minnesota is an equal-opportunity educator and employer.

Contents

Acknowledgments	vii
Abbreviations	xi
Introduction	1

PART I. DEEP TIME

1 *Chronopoiesis: A Phenomenology of Natural Time*	29
2 *The Elemental Past*	43
3 *Recursive Reflection and the Music of Nature*	63

PART II. ANIMALITY

4 *Beyond Biologism: Evolution as Alteraffection*	87
5 *The World of the Bee*	111
6 *Animal Memories*	137
7 *Extinction and Memory: From Biodiversity to Biodiacritics*	153

PART III. ESCHATOLOGY

8 *Apocalyptic Turns: The Chiasm of Cosmic Imagination*	175
9 *The Elements at the End of the World*	201
10 *Climate Change and the Temporal Sublime*	235
11 *Future Fossils: The Anthropocene and the Earth*	257

Notes	281
Bibliography	293
Publication History	319
Index	321

Acknowledgments

My sincere thanks to Cary Wolfe, founding editor of the Post-humanities series, and Douglas Armato, director of the University of Minnesota Press, for their enthusiasm for this project and their support in bringing it to fruition. Editorial assistant Zenyse Miller and the rest of the team at the University of Minnesota Press have been a pleasure to work with throughout the publication process. Many colleagues and students have shaped my thinking over the years in ways that have left their mark on these pages. I am especially grateful to Alia Al-Saji, Bryan Bannon, Renaud Barbaras, David Baumeister, Carla Bengtson, Bettina Bergo, Robert Bernasconi, Étienne Bimbenet, Brendan Bohannan, Brett Buchanan, Megan Burke, Mauro Carbone, Ed Casey, Tim Christion, Claire Colebrook, Adam DeHeer, Lowell Duckert, Annabelle Dufourcq, Russell Duvernoy, William Edelglass, Lester Embree, Fred Evans, Lu Feng, Anthony Fernandez, Martina Ferrari, Rob Figueroa, Matthias Fritsch, Stephen Gardiner, Mercer Gary, Sam Gault, Paul Guernsey, Ryan Gustafsson, Ben Hale, Shannon Hayes, Sara Heinämaa, Juho Hotanen, Dale Jamieson, Galen Johnson, Ben Jones, Richard Kearney, Irene Klaver, Mérédith Laferté-Coutu, Don Landes, Kwok-ying Lau, Rawb Leon-Carlyle, Susanna Lindberg, Rebecca Longtin, Phil Lynes, Kym Maclaren, Laura McMahon, T. S. McMillin, Briana Meier, Jérôme Melançon, Eduardo Mendieta, Nicolae Morar, Marie-Eve Morin, David Morris, Brook Muller, Barbara Muraca, Ann Murphy, Michael Naas, Thomas Nail, Anne O'Byrne, Kelly Oliver, Tano Posteraro, Scott Pratt, Joel Reynolds, Jacob Rogozinski, John Russon, Emmanuel de Saint Aubert, Jason Schreiner, Lucy Schultz, Dan Smith, Bryan Smyth, Henry Somers-Hall, Peter Steeves, Jeremy Swartz, Allen Thompson, Brian Treanor, David Vessey, Steve Vogel, Nicolas de Warren, Molly Westling, Keith Whitmoyer, Kyle Whyte, Rafael Winkler, Jason Wirth, David Wood, and Dan Zahavi. My debt is all the greater to those whom I have unwittingly failed to acknowledge here.

I thank Amy Allen, former head of Philosophy, and the late Susan Welch, former Dean of the College of the Liberal Arts at Penn State, for their encouragement and support of this project. I also thank the Centre for Research in Modern European Philosophy at Kingston University for hosting me as a visiting researcher in Spring 2018, which made possible my trip to Lyme Regis and other sites of significance for researching this book. I am also grateful for the opportunity to present portions of the draft manuscript at its colloquium series and for the generous feedback from its faculty and students. Peter Osborne and Stella Sandford deserve special thanks for their hospitality during my visit.

Earlier versions of portions of this book were presented at conferences or as invited lectures hosted by the American Philosophical Association, the Canadian Philosophical Association, the Canadian Society for Continental Philosophy, the Centre for Continental Philosophy at the University of London, the Centre for Phenomenology in South Africa, Charles University, the Chinese University of Hong Kong, the Collegium Phaenomenologicum, the Danish Institute for Advanced Study, DePaul University, the Helsinki Collegium for Advanced Studies, the International Association for Environmental Philosophy, the International Merleau-Ponty Circle, Laurentian University, Loyola Marymount University, the Phenomenology Roundtable, the Society for Phenomenology and Existential Philosophy, the State University of New York at New Paltz, Stony Brook University, Tsinghua University, the University of Alberta, and the University of Regina. I am grateful to these venues for their hospitality and to the colleagues who attended my lectures for their insights, suggestions, and critical feedback.

I owe a special debt to Corinne Lajoie, who read a rough version of this manuscript in a substantially different form. Their incisive suggestions were transformative as this project took shape. I am equally indebted to Benjamin Décarie-Daigneault for his thoughtful suggestions on the penultimate draft and his encouragement through the final stages of revision.

My philosophical path has been profoundly shaped by two incredible teachers, Jerome A. Miller and Leonard Lawlor. Jerry had faith in me before I had faith in myself, and he has shown me what it means to approach philosophy as a genuine vocation. I am immensely lucky to count Len as my mentor, colleague, and friend, and I cannot thank him enough for all of the ways that he has supported me over the years. Jerry and Len have not only been amazing teachers and friends but they are also original thinkers whose works continue to teach me what it means to think.

This book would not have been possible without all that I have learned from Jay Fiskio, my partner in life's adventures. You give meaning to the world.

Abbreviations

A Derrida, Jacques. 2006. *L'Animal que donc je suis.* Paris: Éditions Galilée. Translated by David Wills as *The Animal That Therefore I Am* (New York: Fordham University Press, 2008).

AF Meillassoux, Quentin. 2006. *Après la finitude.* Paris: Éditions du Seuil. Translated by Ray Brassier as *After Finitude: An Essay on the Necessity of Contingency* (London: Continuum, 2008).

AFEC Nancy, Jean-Luc. 2012. *L'Équivalence des catastrophes (Après Fukushima).* Paris: Éditions Galilée. Translated by Charlotte Mandell as *After Fukushima: The Equivalence of Catastrophes* (New York: Fordham University Press, 2015).

AFT Nancy, Jean-Luc. 1990. *Une pensée finie.* Paris: Éditions Galilée. Translated as *A Finite Thinking,* edited by Simon Sparks (Stanford, Calif.: Stanford University Press, 2003).

ATP Deleuze, Gilles, and Félix Guattari. 1980. *Mille Plateaux.* Paris: Éditions de Minuit. Translated by Brian Massumi as *A Thousand Plateaus* (Minneapolis: University of Minnesota Press, 1987).

BS2 Derrida, Jacques. 2010. *Séminaire: La bête et le souverain, Volume II (2002–2003).* Paris: Éditions Galilée. Translated by Geoffrey Bennington as *The Beast and the Sovereign, Volume II* (Chicago: University of Chicago Press, 2011).

BSP Nancy, Jean-Luc. 1996. *Être singulier pluriel.* Paris: Éditions Galilée. Translated by Robert Richardson and Anne O'Byrne as *Being Singular Plural* (Stanford, Calif.: Stanford University Press, 2000).

C Nancy, Jean-Luc. 2008. *Corpus.* Bilingual ed. Translated by Richard Rand. New York: Fordham University Press.

CC Gasquet, Joachim. 1926. *Cézanne.* Paris: Bernheim-Jeune. Translated by Julie Cochran as *Conversations with Cézanne,* edited by Michael Doran (Berkeley: University of California Press, 2001).

CD Merleau-Ponty, Maurice. 1996. "Le doute de Cézanne." In *Sens et non-sens,* 13–33. Paris: Gallimard. Translated as "Cezanne's

xii *Abbreviations*

CE Bergson, Henri. 1959. *L'Évolution créatrice*. In *Oeuvres*. Paris: Presses Universitaires de France. Translated by A. Mitchell as *Creative Evolution* (Mineola, N.Y.: Dover, 1998).

Doubt," in Maurice Merleau-Ponty, *The Merleau-Ponty Reader*, edited by Ted Toadvine and Leonard Lawlor, 69–84 (Evanston, Ill.: Northwestern University Press, 2007).

CN Bataille, Georges. 1976. "Les conséquences du non-savoir." In *Oeuvres complètes*, vol. 8. Paris: Gallimard. Translated by Annette Michelson as "Un-knowing and Its Consequences," *October* 36 (1986): 80–85. Alternate translation by Michelle Kendall and Stuart Kendall as "The Consequences of Nonknowledge," in Georges Bataille, *The Unfinished System of Nonknowledge*, edited by Stuart Kendall, 111–18 (Minneapolis: University of Minnesota Press, 2001).

CW Nancy, Jean-Luc. 2002. *La création du monde ou la mondialisation*. Paris: Éditions Galilée. Translated by François Raffoul and David Pettigrew as *The Creation of the World or Globalization* (Albany: State University of New York Press, 2007).

EE Levinas, Emmanuel. 1947. *De l'existence à l'existant*. Paris: Fontaine. Translated by Alphonso Lingis as *Existence and Existents* (Pittsburgh, Pa.: Duquesne University Press, 2001).

EM Merleau-Ponty, Maurice. 1964. *L'Œil et l'esprit*. Paris: Gallimard. Translated by Carlton Dallery as "Eye and Mind," in *The Merleau-Ponty Reader*, edited by Ted Toadvine and Leonard Lawlor, 351–78 (Evanston, Ill.: Northwestern University Press, 2007).

FCM Heidegger, Martin. 1983. *Die Grundbegriffe der Metaphysik: Welt—Endlichkeit—Einsamkeit*. Frankfurt am Main, Germany: Vittorio Klostermann. Translated by W. McNeill and N. Walker as *The Fundamental Concepts of Metaphysics: World, Finitude, Solitude* (Bloomington: Indiana University Press, 1995).

FW Uexküll, Jakob von. 1956. *Streifzüge durch die Umwelten von Tieren und Menschen*. Hamburg, Germany: Rowohlt Taschenbuch. Translated by Joseph O'Neil as *A Foray into the Worlds of Animals and Humans* (Minneapolis: University of Minnesota Press, 2010).

G Derrida, Jacques. 1987. "La main de Heidegger (*Geschlecht* II)." In *Psyché: Inventions de l'autre*, book 1, 415–52. Paris: Éditions Galilée. Translated by John P. Leavey Jr. as "*Geschlecht* II:

Heidegger's Hand," in *Deconstruction and Philosophy,* edited by John Sallis, 161–96 (Chicago: University of Chicago Press, 1987).

HPC Scheler, Max. 1949. *Die Stellung des Menschen im Kosmos.* Munich, Germany: Nymphenburger. Translated by Max Frings as *The Human Place in the Cosmos* (Evanston, Ill.: Northwestern University Press, 2009).

I Nancy, Jean-Luc. 1992. "L'Indestructible." *Cahiers Intersignes,* nos. 4–5. Translated by James Gilbert-Walsh as "The Indestructible," in Jean-Luc Nancy, *A Finite Thinking,* edited by Simon Sparks, 78–88 (Stanford, Calif.: Stanford University Press, 2003).

IdII Husserl, Edmund. 1952. *Ideen II.* Husserliana IV. The Hague: Martinus Nijhoff. Translated by Richard Rojcewicz and Andre Schuwer as *Ideas II* (Dordrecht, Netherlands: Kluwer, 1989).

IP Merleau-Ponty, Maurice. 2003. *L'Institution, la passivité.* Tours, France: Belin. Translated by Leonard Lawlor and Heath Massey as *Institution and Passivity* (Evanston, Ill.: Northwestern University Press, 2010).

LB Maeterlinck, Maurice. 1905. *La vie des abeilles.* Paris: Bibliothèque Charpentier. Translated by Alfred Sutro as *The Life of the Bee* (Mineola, N.Y.: Dover, 2006).

N Merleau-Ponty, Maurice. 1995. *La nature.* Paris: Éditions du Seuil. Translated by Robert Vallier as *Nature* (Evanston, Ill.: Northwestern University Press, 2003).

O Agamben, Giorgio. 2002. *L'Aperto: L'Uomo e l'animale.* Torino, Italy: Bollati Boringhieri. Translated by Kevin Attell as *The Open: Man and Animal* (Stanford, Calif.: Stanford University Press, 2004).

OS Derrida, Jacques. 1987. *De l'esprit.* Paris: Éditions Galilée. Translated by Geoffrey Bennington and Rachel Bowlby as *Of Spirit* (Chicago: University of Chicago Press, 1989).

OT Derrida, Jacques. 2000. *Le toucher, Jean-Luc Nancy.* Paris: Éditions Galilée. Translated by Christine Irizarry as *On Touching—Jean-Luc Nancy* (Stanford, Calif.: Stanford University Press, 2005).

P Derrida, Jacques. 1987. *Psyché: Inventions de l'autre.* Book 1. Paris: Éditions Galilée, 2007. Translated as *Psyche: Inventions of the Other,* vol. 1, edited by Peggy Kamuf and Elizabeth Rottenberg (Stanford, Calif.: Stanford University Press, 2007).

PA Claudel, Paul. 1929. *Art poétique*. Paris: Mercure de France. Translated by Renée Spodheim as *Poetic Art* (New York: Philosophical Library, 1948).

PM Merleau-Ponty, Maurice. 1969. *La prose du monde*. Paris: Gallimard. Translated by John O'Neill as *The Prose of the World* (Evanston, Ill.: Northwestern University Press, 1973).

PP Merleau-Ponty, Maurice. 1945. *Phénoménologie de la perception*. Reprinted 2005; Paris: Gallimard. Translated by Donald Landes as *Phenomenology of Perception* (London: Routledge, 2012).

R Derrida, Jacques. 2003. *Béliers*. Paris: Éditions Galilée. Translated by Thomas Dutoit and Philippe Romanski as "Rams: Uninterrupted Dialogue—Between Two Infinities, the Poem," in *Sovereignties in Question*, edited by Thomas Dutoit and Outi Pasanen, 135–62 (New York: Fordham University Press, 2005).

S Merleau-Ponty, Maurice. 1960. *Signes*. Paris: Gallimard. Translated by Richard McCleary as *Signs* (Evanston, Ill.: Northwestern University Press, 1964).

SB Merleau-Ponty, Maurice. 1942. *La structure du comportement*. Paris: Presses Universitaires de France. Translated by Alden Fisher as *The Structure of Behavior* (Boston: Beacon Press, 1963).

SW Nancy, Jean-Luc. 1993. *Le sens du monde*. Paris: Éditions Galilée. Translated by Jeffrey Librett as *The Sense of the World* (Minneapolis: University of Minnesota Press, 1997).

TI Levinas, Emmanuel. 1971. *Totalité et infini*. 4th ed. The Hague: Martinus Nijhoff. Translated by Alphonso Lingis as *Totality and Infinity* (Pittsburgh, Pa.: Duquesne University Press, 1969).

VI Merleau-Ponty, Maurice. 1964. *Le visible et l'invisible*. Paris: Gallimard. Translated by Alphonso Lingis as *The Visible and the Invisible* (Evanston, Ill.: Northwestern University Press, 1968).

Introduction

One damp and chilly weekend in February 2018, I had the opportunity to visit Lyme Regis, a small coastal town in West Dorset, England, with a reputation for being one of the best fossil collecting locations in the world. Dating from Saxon times and contoured around a thirteenth-century harbor, the quiet seaside resort is now one of the major attractions along the ninety-five-mile stretch of the "Jurassic Coast," an area designated as a World Heritage Site since 2001, where the eroding cliffs reveal a 185-million-year span of nearly continuous geological deposits from the Triassic, Jurassic, and Cretaceous periods. Visitors are regularly reminded of the town's most famous paleontologist, Mary Anning, who owned a downtown fossil shop in the 1820s, around the same time that the term *paleontology* was first coined. Despite her discovery of dozens of scientifically significant specimens now featured in major museums, including the first identified ichthyosaur and plesiosaur skeletons, she was excluded from the scientific circles of her day and only recognized for her contributions years after her death. The collecting of fossils is now carefully regulated in many areas, but because of the constant and rapid erosion of the local cliffs, amateurs as well as professionals are encouraged to continue in Anning's footsteps and glean freshly exposed specimens, both common and rare, before they are destroyed or washed out to sea. Fossils of many species are regularly discovered as the cliffs weather away, and among the most popular are the spectacular coiled ammonites, a species of cephalopods related to the living octopus and squid that vanished from the earth some sixty-six million years ago. These ubiquitous fossils received the name "horns of Ammon" from Roman naturalist Pliny the Elder, in his first-century *Naturalis historia,* with reference to the ram's-horn shape associated with the Egyptian god. Today, the streetlamps of Lyme Regis sport the ammonite ram's horn spiral, and an ancient graveyard of thousands of impressive shells, many more than two feet in diameter, can be visited during

2 *Introduction*

low tide, encrusted in the limestone ledge that juts out below the cliff face west of town.

On the rainy afternoon of my arrival, I set out walking east along the coast toward Charmouth in the shadow of cliffs of the Blue Lias formation, layers of limestone and shale deposited between 195 and 200 million years ago. On the sandy stretch of beach near town, what first caught my eye were the many shards of old pottery and bits of beach glass deposited at the tide line. Hardly ancient fossils! Yet some fragments of porcelain decorated with antique motifs reminded me of the long inhabitation of these shores—Neanderthal, Neolithic, Roman, medieval, Victorian—and the inevitable accumulation of human vestiges now on the way to becoming geological deposits in their turn. Some minutes farther along, while combing through the pebbles at the shoreline, I found my first pyritized ammonite—three-quarters of an inch in diameter, dark copper in color, and heavy like a coin. Just as the cold rain began in earnest, I decided to take a seat right there on the wet rocks to rake and sift through the fine pebbles in the vicinity for more ammonites. A second copper spiral appeared, and then a pair joined together. Caught up in the joy of the search, I removed my soaked-through gloves and continued bare-handed, paddling in widening circles until my fingers were completely numb from the cold. Only after I had gathered a small fistful of diminutive ram's horns did I realize that my hands were bleeding. Strewn among the beach pebbles were sharp hunks of rusty iron and other relics of apparent human origin. When I later paid a visit to the Lyme Regis Museum, built on the former site of Mary Anning's home, I learned that the town's garbage dump, dating from the Victorian period, had been located at the top of a cliff east of town. A landslip in 2008 had deposited several centuries' worth of human refuse onto the same stretch of beach where Mary Anning had discovered the first complete ichthyosaur skeleton. Since then, seekers of antique collectibles and curios have "fossicked" alongside fossil hunters whose finds have never before been seen by human eyes.

Although any beachcomber might notice a striking pattern on a pebble or a pottery shard, when the sought-for prize is a fossil or an antique button, it helps to know what to look for. At Lyme Regis, tour guides compete for the opportunity to train beginners to spot crinoids, belemnites, and coprolites. Nevertheless, just *knowing* what to look for is not enough, because the search relies more on what the senses notice than on what the mind knows. In this respect, scouring the beach for fossils reminded me of foraging for mushrooms in the forests of Oregon's Cascades Range. Veteran morel seekers speak of the need to regain their "mushroom vision" each season, because the elusive mushroom blends so well with its habitat. As they tune in again, mushroomers often report finding themselves surrounded by bounty that remained invisible moments earlier. Learning to spot an ammonite or a morel is an embodied practice, one that involves opening your senses to a specific solicitation by adopting the bodily comportment and perceptual rhythms that this call requires. This is comparable to the body-world dialogue involved in perceiving the figure in an impressionist painting or picking out an autostereogram's hidden image, which require that we take up a certain bodily attitude and adjust our senses to respond to the question that has been posed to us by what offers itself to be perceived. Searching for a particular pattern or shape among the pebbles thereby exemplifies the perceptual event that phenomenologist Maurice Merleau-Ponty describes as a "certain type of symbiosis, a certain manner that the outside has of invading us, a certain manner that we have of receiving it" (PP 373/331). Emphasizing the bidirectional exchange of question and response between our senses and the world, Merleau-Ponty describes perception as a "language that teaches itself," which is "why it can be said that our senses literally interrogate the things and that the things respond to them" (375/333).

And yet, beyond this sensory attunement and dialogue, my experience at Lyme Regis suggests another dimension of embodied perceptual engagement. Searching for an antique or a fossil also involves our bodies in a *temporal* dimension, because it requires the proper resonance not only with the *what* that we seek but also with its *when*. Things present themselves to our glance or touch as a material memory of their endurance through time, as the sensible, embodied expression of their age. Whether searching for beach glass or fossils, one's sensory rhythms take up an orientation toward things *as* the reified memories of a specific temporal framing or duration, from the antique to the unfathomably ancient. On the shore at Lyme Regis, my perceptions shifted seamlessly between vastly incommensurable temporal scales—from two years to two

4 *Introduction*

hundred to two hundred million. This occurs prior to any explicit conceptual knowledge or mental representation; it is more fundamental than any thematic belief about the precise age of the object in my sight or in my hand. This is not at all to deny that my understanding of ammonites as fossil remains dating from the Devonian period depends on contemporary scientific knowledge, and certainly this knowledge infuses and informs what and how I perceive. My point is rather that we do not simply affix a past date to a present perception by some cognitive process of association. Instead, we directly *perceive* the ammonite *as* immemorially ancient, as beyond the scale of comprehensible historical time. When searching the shoreline for fossils, I take up the very sensory rhythms of something more ancient than my mind can grasp. This is possible because my body and mind are also temporal events within the unfolding happening of innumerable durations, including those of the distant and ancient past. Of course, the sand and pebbles, the very geomaterial stuff of the shoreline itself, are also ancient beyond human measure. But the fossil stands out precisely as the trace of a once-living individual, of the singular event of an unrepeatable life. It is, as Jacques Derrida (2002, 130–31) says of an insect preserved in amber, the "archive of a singular event." This ancient individual lived its life within an entire primeval world that has subsequently vanished. As the trace of another life and another world separated from my own by an unimaginably vast temporal abyss, the fossil both invites and eludes my sensory explorations, and I register this invitation and escape in a corporeal way, as the very experience of what it means to perceive a fossil as such. It is undoubtedly true that a centuries-old relic of a bygone human world invites a parallel encounter of invitation and escape. Yet we have richer means for mediation, both conceptual and imaginative, between our world and earlier moments of human history than is the case for a creature whose kind has been extinct for millions of years.

My visit to Lyme Regis illustrates the challenges of understanding how our human experience of "lived" time overlaps, intersects, and entangles with innumerable temporal durations, extending not only across intergenerational and historical horizons of human time but also to the incomparably vast expanses of "deep" time at evolutionary and geological scales. As the example of Mary Anning and the history of paleontology reminds us, the scientific discovery of deep scales of time is still comparatively recent in Western intellectual history. It is only for two centuries that we have known that species can go extinct, and we did not discover until the 1980s that a series of mass extinction events over the last 450 million years has repeatedly eliminated the majority of living species and reset the evolutionary process, often requiring millions of years to rebound (Brannen 2017). Such discoveries dramatically reshape how we imagine the future of our planet and our role in that future, even if the philosophical and ethical implications of our entanglement in these temporal scales are only beginning to register. One lesson of this expanded sense of time is that our usual background assumptions about constancy and change are scale-dependent and often grant our own context an outsized importance. For instance, the warm and stable climate of the twelve-thousand-year Holocene epoch, which ushered in the Neolithic revolution and widespread human settlement, is an outlier from the perspective of the earth's climatic history and is expected to be followed by a major ice age. One recent study concludes that the next major glaciation event would have occurred in around fifty thousand years absent human influences but that anthropogenic CO_2 production will defer this ice age by an additional fifty thousand years (Ganopolski, Winkelmann, and Schellnhuber 2016). On one hand, this illustrates the incredible reach of anthropogenic influence across space and time, an influence that may well outlast the human species. On the other hand, this example also makes salient the contingency and precarity of our dependence on geological forces and processes at planetary scales. Grappling with deep time means taking seriously both the geological scale of human impacts and the transience of the world that we take for granted.

The Memory of the World is the first investigation of the relation between human and deep scales of time to draw on the resources of phenomenology, the philosophical tradition that takes as its starting point the description of experience and its essential structures. Deep time has typically been portrayed as incommensurate with, and incomprehensible from, the perspective of human temporal horizons (see Chakrabarty 2021, 83, 171). On this view, there is no experience of deep time as such, and our understanding of the geological or cosmic past is limited to mathematical representations that scientific reconstructions have made possible. In short, deep

6 *Introduction*

time would simply be an extension of the serial order of temporal units familiar from clocks and calendars—abstract, homogenous, and repeatable—but now on a scale so grand as to be incommensurate with our everyday understanding of these temporal units. A phenomenological description of deep time would therefore be both impossible and superfluous, because deep time exceeds our temporal comprehension. *The Memory of the World* proposes that such a view is mistaken both in its conceptualization of deep time and in its assumptions about human temporality. Against this view, I argue that deep time is an essential structure of human temporal experience and that its depths can be understood only in experiential terms. To make this case, I propose accounts of embodied temporality, geomateriality, and interanimality in conversation with the traditions of phenomenology, deconstruction, critical animal studies, speculative realism, and new materialism. I also draw out the implications of this novel understanding of our implication in deep time for addressing contemporary environmental debates over biodiversity, climate change, the Anthropocene, and the contemporary obsession with pending environmental apocalypse. *The Memory of the World* addresses the provocation of deep time in three movements: first, the entanglement of the deep past with the experience of lived time; second, the evolutionary memory that we share with other living beings; and third, our speculative projections of the far future, especially in the form of postapocalyptic fantasies.

The initial inspiration for my phenomenology of deep time is drawn from Merleau-Ponty's descriptions of the anonymous, cyclical time of the sensing body in distinction from the narrative, historical time of personal subjectivity. As I established in an earlier work, *Merleau-Ponty's Philosophy of Nature,* Merleau-Ponty describes the "natural time" of the body as an absolute or immemorial past that has never been present to reflective awareness, even though it grounds our subjective experience of time (see Toadvine 2009, chap. 2, esp. 61–63). This "original" past structures and conditions our conscious temporal experience while withdrawing from our thematic awareness, so that every moment of our lives is haunted by "a past that has never been present" (PP 280/252). In *Phenomenology of Perception,* Merleau-Ponty identifies this immemorial past of the body with the elemental time of nature, although he does not develop the implications of this insight. I take up this task in part I of *The Memory of the World,* where I extend Merleau-Ponty's account to establish a phenomenological basis for understanding the asubjective time of nature, including its deep geological and cosmic durations.

Because our implication in deep time also includes the evolutionary past that we share with other forms of life, part II addresses the phenomenology of animality and its relationship with scientific accounts of evolution and biodiversity. Deep time is typically associated with the geological timescale, reaching back 4.5 billion years to the origins of the earth, but this encompasses the evolution of life, the earliest evidence for which dates back 3.7 billion years. The last universal common ancestor of all forms of life is hypothesized to have been a single-celled organism living in hydrothermal vents and feeding on molecular hydrogen between two and four billion years ago (Weiss et al. 2016; Cooper 2017). That human beings share a common ancestor with other forms of life has been taken as a challenge to the Western tradition's anthropocentrism and insistence that humans are different in kind than other species. Rather than describing this evolutionary heritage in terms of kinship or continuity, however, I explore life as the incarnate memory of billions of years of differential improvisational exchange. As an alternative to the received view of biodiversity, I propose a "biodiacritics" that is modeled on the parallel between life and language as historically evolving webs of differential relations. Biodiacritical configurations embrace the ontological memory of all evolving life. This is again a question of deep time, although now approached from the perspective of organic and evolutionary time, and it has a bearing on how we understand the world of another form of life as well as what is at stake in contemporary efforts to preserve biodiversity and prevent the extinction of other species.

In part III, I turn from the deep past to the far future, especially our fixation on anthropogenic environmental apocalypse. The perspective of deep time has transformed our relationship to the future of humanity and the planet. In particular, our awareness of the deep past has been paralleled by our speculative fictions about the far future and what it holds for us, especially the specter of our own extinction. This is most apparent in our contemporary obsession with postapocalyptic culture, although it also informs scientific claims that we have entered the Anthropocene, which depend on conjectures about the fossils that we are currently leaving behind for posterity. Tracing the history of representations of the unity of the world and the earth, Kelly Oliver (2015, 12) suggests that, in philosophy as well as popular culture, our projections of unity depend on the imagination of destruction, whether by war, nuclear devastation, or technological advancement: "In order to take the world as a whole, we imagine it gone. In order to see the whole earth, we fantasize its obliteration." To this insight, we can add a temporal dimension: in order to understand the earth's deep past, we imagine the very destruction of the world's future. I argue that the horizons of the far future are first opened for us with the discovery of the deep past but that current sustainability efforts risk foreclosing the very future they claim to safeguard. Clarifying our relationship with deep time, both past and future, is therefore essential for critically evaluating the eco-eschatological narrative underlying much of contemporary environmental theory and practice.

As an illustration of burgeoning concern with our "place" in deep time, let us consider in more detail the controversial proposal to name our current geological epoch the "Anthropocene."[1] This designation has been widely adopted beyond its scientific context as a convenient label for the dominant influence of human beings on Earth systems at a planetary scale, with unprecedented impacts on the atmosphere, ecosystems, and biodiversity. Of course, the fact that human beings are altering the planet on a global scale has been extensively documented and discussed for more than a century. Many critics have also pointed out that the "Anthropocene" formulation risks political naïveté insofar as it suggests that the root cause of global environmental problems is *anthropos*, a generalized and abstract version of humanity. This obscures the historical, political, and economic context that has made the disruption of Earth systems possible, enriching some while destroying the lives and livelihoods of others. In this respect, the "Anthropocene" designation replays a common strategy of blaming "human nature," thereby rationalizing and naturalizing colonial and capitalist violence. Summarizing these criticisms, Jeremy Baskin (2015, 23) concludes that, "as a concept, [the Anthropocene] appears overall to legitimate the dominant order, even if unintentionally." It is to address such limitations that a series of alternatives has been proposed: Capitalocene, Plantationocene, and Chthulucene, among others.[2]

There is, however, another reason that the "Anthropocene" label has proven attractive, which is that it suggests a veneer of objectivity by purporting to designate something empirically tractable to "hard" physical sciences, such as geology. In its scientific usage, the Anthropocene refers to the factual prediction that human beings are leaving a trace in the geological record comparable to other traces that mark, for geologists, the transitions between stages on the geological timescale. When geologists agree on a reference point in rock strata that marks such a transition, they designate it as a Global Boundary Stratotype Section and Point (GSSP), colloquially termed a "golden spike."[3] Briefly put, the Anthropocene designation would require international agreement on the specific human-caused traces in geological strata that signal the boundary between the Holocene and the Anthropocene. These traces, comparable to other distinct transitions in the fossil record, would be expected to remain legible into the far future at geological scales of time. Identifying these stratigraphic reference points or golden spikes is the work of the International Commission on Stratigraphy, which has yet to make a formal decision concerning the Anthropocene. Among the reference points that have received serious discussion are radionuclides from atomic bomb testing (currently the leading option), sedimentary evidence of species extinctions and introductions, ice cores marking climatic changes, and artificial "techno-fossils" from human refuse.

What makes the Anthropocene proposal both distinctive and controversial as a scientific claim is its reversal of the temporal perspective from which GSSP designations have been made up to this point. Because claims concerning the Anthropocene are based on prediction rather than on reconstruction of events from the deep geological past, they call for entirely different evidence and methods than with other golden spikes. Provocatively, the proposal essentially involves imagining ourselves from the perspective of a post-Anthropocene future: the prediction that humans *will have* left such a mark of transition between geological stages is essentially a claim about our own future fossils and their legibility for imagined future paleontologists. As Stefan Skrimshire (2017, 141) puts this point, the Anthropocene is about imagining our own fossils under the gaze of far future stratigraphers of another species or from another planet—and imagining how they will remember us. Claire Colebrook (2014, 34) captures this logic quite succinctly: "from [the] capacity to read our own inhuman past, we can imagine an inhuman future that would read our human present."[4] For a popular example, consider this quote from science writer Rachel Brazil (2021) in *Chemistry World*:

> If anyone is around in millions of years to examine the future geological record, they may still find the "techno-fossils" of the Anthropocene. Perhaps, says [environmental scientist Neil] Rose, "whereas we [now] see, for example, an imprint of an ammonite in a rock record, we may [then] see an imprint of a Coke can, CD or Lego brick."

It is worth noting that the Anthropocene proposal is not without its critics within the scientific community, some of whom dismiss these predictions about the legibility of our own fossil record on deep temporal scales. Science writer Peter Brannen (2019) pointedly summarizes this skepticism in *The Atlantic*:

> Perhaps, someday, our signal in the rocks will be found, but only if eagle-eyed stratigraphers, from God knows where on the tree of life, crisscross their own rearranged Earth, assiduously trying to find us. But they would be unlikely to be rewarded for their effort. At the end of all their travels—after cataloging all the bedrock of the entire planet—they might finally be led to an odd, razor-thin stratum hiding halfway up some eroding, far-flung desert canyon. If they then somehow found an accompanying plaque left behind by humanity that purports to assign this unusual layer its own epoch—sandwiched in these cliffs, and embarrassed above and below by gigantic edifices of limestone, siltstone, and shale—this claim would amount to evidence of little more than our own species' astounding anthropocentrism.

For Brannen and the scientists who share his skepticism, the very claim of the Anthropocene is further evidence of our profound hubris, reflecting our inflated sense of our own significance for and influence on the unimaginably long expanse of the future.

Such debates suggest that the Anthropocene is not something scientists have discovered but rather something that they are trying to produce evidence for, like prosecutors in a trial. In fact, proponents of the Anthropocene as a geological designation have been explicit that their motives are not purely or even primarily scientific but rather political. Paul Crutzen and other Earth system scientists who have promoted the idea admit that their aim is to provide a "wake-up call" concerning the self-destructive actions of our species (Crutzen and Schwägerl 2011). In this respect, the "scientific" version of the Anthropocene presents a controversial factual prediction about the far future as justification for a political agenda today. The Anthropocene proposal therefore joins a long history of attempts to influence public opinion around environmental issues by promoting political positions under the guise of scientific claims (see Morar, Toadvine, and Bohannan 2015).[5]

What makes the Anthropocene proposal significant for our purposes is the temporal logic involved, namely, the interpretation and management of the present by means of speculative fantasies about the deep past and far future. By imagining a distant, posthuman future, the narrative of the Anthropocene parallels and borrows much of its rhetorical force from our ubiquitous popular imaginary about pending environmental apocalypse. This eco-apocalyptic imaginary is, in turn, dependent on our knowledge of deep time. In scientific discourse as well as popular culture, it is our awareness of the incomprehensible duration of geological time prior to human existence, not to mention the abundant evidence of past extinctions, that inspires our fantasies and fears about our own future demise. In this respect, the opening of deep temporal horizons first makes possible our eco-apocalyptic imagination as well as political efforts toward sustainability. *The Memory of the World* investigates the understanding of deep time that inspires these fantasies and the desires concerning our relationship to time that they express. The Anthropocene debate challenges us to address these questions by clarifying how the time of our lives relates to deep, geological time, both past and future.

The work of historian Dipesh Chakrabarty has been decisive in making salient the challenges of bridging geological and human time. In his widely cited 2009 essay "The Climate of History: Four Theses," Chakrabarty introduced the idea that anthropogenic climate change collapses the distinction between natural history and human history. His subsequent work on this topic, culminating in *The Climate of History in a Planetary Age* (2021), argues that critiques of capitalism and globalization cannot tell the whole story because they are limited to the perspective of human history, what he terms the "global" perspective (4). To this he contrasts the "planetary" perspective adopted by Earth system scientists, which is concerned not with human history but with geological and evolutionary time. None of this is to deny what postcolonial critique has demonstrated concerning differential contributions to global problems, but the challenge, as Chakrabarty frames it, is precisely to "mix together the immiscible chronologies of capital and species history" (42). With this distinction between global and planetary perspectives, mapping onto a contrast between historical and geological time, Chakrabarty defangs the criticisms levied against the Anthropocene concept for its flattening of human differences and for its failure to recognize the role of capital and colonialism in creating the conditions for a subset of the human population to become drivers of planetary systems. Such criticisms remain enclosed within the global and human perspective and have no bearing on the planetary perspective that now interrupts our lives from an incommensurate "outside."

Chakrabarty expresses this temporal incongruence between human and deep time with a series of striking formulations. The fact that humans have become geological agents collapses "the distance between the two calendars," namely, "geological time and the chronology of human histories" (32). Consequently, "the geologic now of the Anthropocene has become entangled with the now of human history" (36). Or, in different terms, "the wall between human and natural history has been breached" (45). This framing puts the relationship between human and geological time at the center of what we need to learn from the Anthropocene, as two temporal registers, histories, calendars, or chronologies that have become fused, collapsed, entangled, or breached—Chakrabarty uses all of these formulations. The problem that he poses is therefore how to "encounter together" planetary and global forms of thinking that are disparate yet intertwined and that refer to "vastly different and incommensurable scales of time" (86).

As Chakrabarty emphasizes, the stakes of this problem concern not only our environmental future but also how we are to understand humanity as a form of life and in relation to other forms of life. Critics of the language of the Anthropocene have pointed out that to blame environmental destruction on the "human species" risks "universaliz[ing] and normaliz[ing] a small portion of humanity" (Baskin 2015, 15). But, for Chakrabarty (2021, 37), references to the "human species" by proponents of the Anthropocene are connected to the "enterprise of deep history" and planetary thinking, in contrast with human history that emphasizes the global and "critiques of capital." Therefore he defends the language of the human species, if only as a "placeholder for an emergent, new universal history of humans that flashes up in the moment of the danger that is climate change" (45). Tarrying with the language of species in this way opens, he believes, a perspective on the extrahistorical "conditions for the existence of life in the human form" and our relation with "the history of life on this planet" (40).

Chakrabarty does not claim to have solved the problem of mixing the immiscible or of fusing global and planetary thinking with their incommensurable scales of time. Yet by reinterpreting the Anthropocene challenge in temporal terms, he clarifies the stakes of our relation with deep time as well as its paradoxical character. In framing deep time as incommensurable with human history, Chakrabarty draws out the consequences of the subjective biases of philosophical theories of time. Following the influential work of Immanuel Kant, who described space and time as formal features of how we perceive sensible objects, prominent philosophies of time have emphasized time's essential relationship with subjectivity. Accounts of time in the works of Henri Bergson, Edmund Husserl, and Martin Heidegger, for example, rarely address deep time directly. When they do, it is taken as an example of the abstract scientific representation of time that remains secondary to time as a structure of human experience. Extended to deep scales of time, such as those that preceded human life, or indeed any known life in the universe, this approach to time appears paradoxical. It is precisely such quandaries that have inspired Quentin Meillassoux's critique of post-Kantian philosophy as mired in various forms of what he calls "correlationism." Like Chakrabarty's, Meillassoux's critique is motivated by the desire to take seriously deep scales of time that exceed the limitations of human subjectivity and finitude.[6]

Meillassoux's well-known critique, first proposed in *After Finitude* (2006, 2008), has been a major inspiration for the development of

14 *Introduction*

speculative realism and object-oriented ontology. His claim is that all philosophical traditions since Kant have embraced in some form the assumption that thinking and being may be understood only in their relation and never independently of the other, that is, that they may be understood only in terms of their correlation. But Meillassoux objects that this makes it impossible to speak meaningfully about any time anterior to the emergence of thought or life in the cosmos. For the correlationist, statements about "ancestral" time—a time prior to all manifestation—are strictly meaningless. This leaves us, Meillassoux argues, with a "strange feeling of imprisonment or enclosure," because the correlation cuts us off from "the *great outdoors*, the *absolute* outside [*le* Grand Dehors, *le* Dehors *absolu*] of pre-critical thinkers: that outside which was not relative to us, and which was given as indifferent to its own givenness to be what it is, existing in itself regardless of whether we are thinking of it or not" (21–22/7). This absolute Outside would no longer be the correlate of any subject but would remain absolutely indifferent to subjectivity.

Meillassoux does not hesitate to refer to this absolute Outside as a "world"—as "a world without us" (AF 158/114) or "the mathematized world" (160/116). But this could be a "world" only in a very unusual sense. In contrast with the world as we experience it, Meillassoux's Outside would be a "*glacial* world . . . , a world in which there is no longer any up or down, centre or periphery, nor anything else that might make of it a world designed for humans. For the first time, the world manifests itself as capable of subsisting without any of those aspects that constitute its concreteness for us" (159/115). Meillassoux sees the mathematization of nature introduced by Galileo as the historical turning point that makes this decisive break with qualitative experience possible. Mathematical description can, he holds, definitively detach itself from the world of experience to create an independent and ahuman world of its own—although it is not clear what justifies the decision to call this mathematical construction a "world" or what could be meant by a "world" that has nothing in common with this world here, the one that we all inhabit.[7]

Although Meillassoux claims that mathematical description can definitively replace the world as experienced, phenomenologists have long pointed out that mathematical descriptions are themselves founded on embodied experience. Edmund Husserl argued in the 1930s that Galileo's mathematization of nature is ultimately dependent on the world of concrete, lived experience, even though this dependency is obscured by science's technicization, that is, by the historical sedimentation of scientific techniques that covers over their constitutive history and founding assumptions (Husserl 1962; 1970, sec. 9). Merleau-Ponty further developed these insights by arguing that mathematical truths essentially refer to embodied forms of creative expression (see Hass and Hass 2000; Halák 2022). My aim here is not, however, to enter into a defense of correlationism or a detailed critique of Meillassoux's alternative.[8] Instead, I take seriously his challenge to account for "ancestral" time, the time that precedes human experience. I argue that Meillassoux's mathematical version of ancestrality is inadequate for understanding our entanglement in diverse temporal scales and that the resources of phenomenology prove essential for describing the abyssal and vertiginous character of our immersion in deep time. Our lived experience of time is entangled with deep temporal dimensions, including those of the geomaterial elements and of our evolutionary history. The materiality of our bodies embeds us within the asubjective temporal flows of the elements, while our senses and affects entangle us in the generative time of evolution.

Meillassoux does not identify the "glacial" world constructed by mathematics with the planet, but his account has obvious parallels with what this term names for Chakrabarty (2021). Like Meillassoux's "absolute Outside," Chakrabarty's "planet" remains "profoundly indifferent" to human existence (70), and he repeatedly emphasizes its "radical otherness" in relation to human perspectives and experiences (87, 89; cf. 15, 182). This follows, for Chakrabarty, from the fact that the planet is "an entity no one ever encounters physically" and that is inaccessible to direct human experience (79, 47). In parallel, even though we can intellectually comprehend the concept of the human species, we can never "experience it as such," and consequently, "there could be no phenomenology of us as a species" (43). Like Meillassoux, then, Chakrabarty dismisses the contributions of phenomenology as limited to human horizons of experience. For instance, notions of "earth" proposed by Husserl and Heidegger, insofar as they reflect human dwelling, remain attached to the global perspective and cannot accede to the

16 *Introduction*

planetary (68–71, 74, 80, 179–80, 183, 195, 205), because the latter is an essentially comparative perspective for which our planet is only one of many and occupies no special position (75, 79). This is why, for Chakrabarty, the planet is "a new historical-philosophical entity" (3), not a variation on earlier conceptions of world, earth, or globe; it is instead equivalent to the "Earth system" as reconstructed through the methods of Earth system science (4, 70, 84, 172, 193), a science that is itself "made up of observed and simulated data and their analyses" (80).

And yet, while Chakrabarty often seems to follow Meillassoux in rejecting the very possibility of any phenomenology of deep time, his broader argument suggests not only that we *can* relate deep temporal scales to human experience but even that we *must* do so. This follows, first, from Chakrabarty's richer perspective on scientific knowledge of the planet and deep time. Even for Earth system scientists, as he reports, the planet is never strictly reducible to a physical phenomenon mathematically described, because it also becomes an "abstract figure of the imagination" (79) and is haunted by "scientific-poetic intuition," as illustrated by James Lovelock's invocation of Gaia (80). Furthermore, geological time is irreducible to purely mathematical time, even for geologists, because such time retains a "material" dimension (171) and engages our affects as well as our cognitive faculties (162, 171, 173). And furthermore, Chakrabarty recognizes that the very challenge of the planetary and its vast temporal scales precisely concerns the ways that these interrupt lived human reality and everyday understandings of time. This is why the very task of his book is framed in reference to phenomenology. As he writes in the introduction, "we need to connect deep and recorded histories and put geological time and the biological time of evolution in conversation with the time of human history and experience" (7), and this must be accomplished "without ever taking our eyes off the individual human who continues to negotiate his or her own phenomenological and everyday experience of life, death, and the world" (8). Returning to this point in the final pages of his book, Chakrabarty refers to the difficulties of synchronizing planetary and global calendars as a "profoundly phenomenological challenge" (203). In this sense, his call to think together what initially seem to be incommensurable scales of time actually demands of us an investigation of the phenomenology of deep time.

The Memory of the World inaugurates a renewal of the phenomenology of time by taking seriously how our lived horizons of time are entangled with deep temporal dimensions, including those of the geomaterial elements and of our evolutionary history. Scientific discovery has made possible our cognitive representations of deep time, but phenomenology reveals a more fundamental encounter with these durations that outstrip our understanding and imagination, durations that are disclosed through their abyssal interruption of our narrative histories even as they condition from within the possibility of our lived experiences. In part I, "Deep Time," I provide the framework for this phenomenological account of deep time. Before we can appreciate the experiential encounter with deep temporal horizons, we must first complicate the lived experience of time and consider in what sense nature is temporal. As I show in chapter 1, Merleau-Ponty discovers that lived time is not unified but always plural, because the body expresses its own temporal rhythms that remain autonomous from consciousness. The body lives through an anonymous and cyclical "natural" time that for the reflective subject remains an impossible past, so that the personal self forms from the kernel of this immemorial past that makes "my" present possible. The asubjective durations of nature are therefore the quasi-transcendental repressed heart of personal time, which we might call, borrowing a term from Jerome Miller (2020, 161), its "traumatological" condition. This trauma of the immemorial past is what we live from yet what our conscious awareness and philosophical reflection can never equal. Furthermore, drawing inspiration from Paul Claudel and A. N. Whitehead, Merleau-Ponty radicalizes our understanding of nature's own temporal durations, which are not reducible to cyclical repetitions but instead leaven the future with generative difference. In his reading of Whitehead, Merleau-Ponty refers to the "memory of the world" as the asubjective and differential passage of nature from which we emerge and to which we remain liable.

Turning explicitly to the challenge that deep time poses for phenomenology, chapter 2 reopens a 1951 debate that marked the beginnings of the analytic–Continental divide in contemporary philosophy, when Merleau-Ponty sided with Georges Bataille in rejecting A. J. Ayer's claim that the sun existed before human beings. I defend Merleau-Ponty's counterintuitive position against naturalistic and antisubjectivist critics by arguing that the world emerges in the exchange between perceiver and perceived. A deeper challenge is posed, however, by Meillassoux, who argues that the "correlationism" of contemporary philosophy rules out any account of the "ancestral" time that antedates all subjectivity. Against Meillassoux, and taking an encounter with fossils as my guide, I hold that the past prior to subjectivity can be approached only phenomenologically. The paradoxical character of this immemorial past, as a memory of the world rather than of the subject, opens the way toward a phenomenology of the "elemental" past. Drawing on Merleau-Ponty's descriptions of the absolute past of nature and the anonymity of the body, as well as Emmanuel Levinas's account of the elements at the end of the world, I argue that our own materiality and organic lives participate in the differential rhythms of the elements, opening us to a memory of the world that binds the cosmic past and the far future.

In chapter 3, I confront the problem of how to relate the generative temporal *poiesis* of nature, here expressed through the figure of *musica universalis*, with nature's resistance and withdrawal. Drawing on ethologist Jakob von Uexküll's proposal to understand nature as a symphony of ecological niches formed at the confluence of organisms and their environments, I approach the memory of the world here through the perspective of evolutionary time. First, I trace the development of Merleau-Ponty's ontology across his major theoretical works, in conversation with Uexküll, to examine critically the resources that they offer for thinking nature's musicality together with its withdrawal. *The Structure of Behavior* relies on musical structures to propose an architectonic of gestalts as ontologically fundamental but only tacitly accounts for nature's propensity to hide. Merleau-Ponty's sequel, *Phenomenology of Perception*, deepens his investigation of the immemorial past that haunts reflection from within. While each book clarifies one of nature's dual aspects, its musicality or its secrecy, it is only in Merleau-Ponty's later ontology that the principle of nature's dehiscence comes to the fore as the *écart* of the world's flesh. Yet Merleau-Ponty's own disavowal of the ontological significance of music leads us to consider, second, criticisms posed by anthropologist Claude Lévi-Strauss. These point toward a fundamental silence disclosed within the reflexivity of voice and hearing, a silence that marks the time of the world's withdrawal while also opening the horizon of cultural expression and philosophical reflection.

Part II, "Animality," continues our inquiry into evolutionary temporality and its implications for the relation between nonhuman animals and the animal dimension of the human being. Chapter 4 challenges the typical interpretation of our evolutionary relation with nonhuman others in terms of kinship or continuity, which Derrida aligns with the ideology of "biologistic continuism." This problematization of the logic of the human–animal limit holds implications for how we are to understand life in relation to auto-affection, immanence in relation to transcendence, and naturalism in relation to phenomenology. Derrida's abyssal logic parallels the "strange kinship" described by Merleau-Ponty, although only if this strangeness is intensified as "alteraffection" by incorporating death into life. Drawing on Elizabeth Grosz, I locate the creative moment of this abyssal intimacy in the transformative productions of sexual difference. This excess of alteraffection reconciles phenomenology with evolution and offers a figure for thinking the thickening and multiplying of the differences between human and nonhuman, living and nonliving, corporeal and cosmic.

I turn, in chapter 5, to a detailed consideration of the world of the bee, a nonhuman other with whom human beings share a long history but that counts neither as a companion species nor as charismatic megafauna. Philosophers from Plato to Heidegger have privileged the bee as both cipher and foil for human society and human nature. I trace the account of the beehive as an ambivalent double of human society from Vergil through Henri Bergson and Maurice Maeterlinck, finding there an oscillation between two tendencies: the first elevates instinct to self-consciousness within human subjectivity, as a form of becoming-bee, whereas the second insists on the abyssal obscurity of the bee's own perspective for itself. This poses the challenge of whether the bee can be said to "have" a world at all, which we consider in relation to Uexküll's rich descriptions of the bee's *Umwelt* and Heidegger's use of the bee to illustrate the captivation and world-poverty of nonhuman life. For Heidegger, the bee has no world or perspective in the subjective sense, yet his account of the animal's resistance to our efforts to transpose ourselves into its world illustrates a more complex dance of invitation and refusal that constitutes our interanimality. I propose an apian phenomenology that celebrates the heterogeneous multiplicity of life without nostalgia for mutual recognition or translation into the language of reflection.

As the example of the bee illustrates, phenomenology's attention to the theme of animality has typically focused not on animal life as such but rather on the animal dimension of the human and its contested role in human identity. I argue in chapter 6 that phenomenology thereby reproduces Giorgio Agamben's "anthropological machine" by which humanity is constructed through the "inclusive exclusion" of its animality. The alternative to this inclusive exclusion is not a return to kinship or commonality but rather an intensification of the constitutive paradox of our own inner animality, understood in terms of the anonymous, corporeal subject of perception that lives a different temporality than that of first-person consciousness. Our embodied temporality and its evolutionary history entail that nonhuman others speak through our own voices and gaze out through our own eyes. To open this perspective, I first consider the proximity of Merleau-Ponty's early work with that of Max Scheler, who paradigmatically reduces human animality to bare life. Merleau-Ponty differentiates himself from Scheler, in *The Structure of Behavior*, by insisting that life cannot be integrated into spirit without remainder. Merleau-Ponty's later work thinks this remainder as the ineliminable gap and delay in the autoaffection of the body and as a chiasmic exchange that anticipates Gilles Deleuze and Félix Guattari's concept of "becoming-animal." This remainder of life within consciousness is the immemorial past of one's own animality. It follows that our "inner animality" is neither singular nor plural but a pack that speaks through the voice that I take to be mine. Furthermore, in the exchange of looks between me and a nonhuman other, the crossing of glances occurs at an animal level that withdraws from my own reflective consciousness.

In the concluding chapter of part II, I take up the challenge of understanding extinction as the loss of evolutionary memory, which has been misconstrued by the mainstream understanding of biodiversity preservation. Biodiversity has become a central value of conservation biology and a plank of international environmental policy—despite the well-known contestations of the concept's meaning, the de jure problems with its operationalization, and the lack of any empirical evidence correlating it with ecosystem function or other valued features of nature. Yet a deeper problem with biodiversity in the received sense—as a formula for aggregating incommensurable differences within and between life-forms at all scales—is that it aims to maximize present differences without regard for historical configurations and evolutionary memory. I argue that current diversity is inseparable from its contingent history and that the memory of this history is embodied as the differential relations among populations, species, and their biotic and abiotic surroundings. This suggests, as an alternative to biodiversity, a biodiacritics modeled on the parallel between life and language, as networks of difference with synchronic and diachronic axes. The synchronic heterogeneity of current life is the figured memory of its diachronic evolution. Such biodiacritical configurations, insofar as they embody the ontological memory of evolving life, are the source of what we value in threatened and rare ecosystems and species. The intuition that motivates biodiversity conservation, I argue, is better captured phenomenologically as an encounter with the biodiacritically embodied memory of life than as a formula for aggregating present difference.

In part III, "Eschatology," I bring the phenomenology of deep time to bear on the challenge of contemporary apocalypticism and our fantasies of the ending of the world. Chapter 8 traces the transformation of our cosmic imagination away from the eternity, tranquility, and unity described by Gaston Bachelard and toward an immanent and toxic unraveling, as illustrated by long-term radioactive waste disposal projects. This echoes the apocalyptic framing of phenomenology itself, starting from Husserl's famous thought-experiment of world annihilation in *Ideas I* that discloses the sphere of pure consciousness as the fundamental field of phenomenology. I trace here the alternate path that Merleau-Ponty and Levinas take in disclosing both the origin and the dissolution of the world as revealed through works of art. Merleau-Ponty locates in Cézanne's paintings an aesthetic revision of the phenomenological reduction that discloses our inherence in and liability to the very world that we aim to bring to expression. Cézanne's aim to "join the wandering hands of nature" anticipates the touching–touched relationship that would inspire Merleau-Ponty's late ontology of flesh, yet it also discloses anonymous sensation below the perceptual exchange with the world. This return to anonymous sensation finds its parallel

22   *Introduction*

in Levinas's analysis of modern art as unveiling the impersonality of the elements after the end of the world. These studies radicalize our adherence in nature by figuring it as a cosmic chiasm. However, Derrida's criticisms of the role of touch in Merleau-Ponty show that a phenomenology of the end of the world must break with any auto-affective telos, taking more seriously than does Merleau-Ponty the disruptive implications of the immemorial past and reconfiguring the chiasm as a radical alteraffection.

Chapter 9 revisits the classic phenomenological encounter between world and earth to show that the world, as a unifying nexus of significance, is inherently precarious and constitutively destined toward its own unraveling. Here I consider Donn Welton's description of the horrific events of September 11, 2001, as the dissolution of the world alongside Levinas's claim that apocalyptic destruction is the very culmination of the phenomenological conception of the world. This poses the question of how much conflict or illusion "the" world can tolerate and from what perspective one can even imagine the loss of the world as meaningful horizon. I approach this question through Jean-Luc Nancy's notion of the ecotechnical, which hovers ambivalently between, on one hand, the end of the world as *mundus* or *cosmos* that would ground a meaning and orientation for our lives and, on the other, the rediscovery of the sense of world as *this world here,* absent any purpose or meaning beyond its own existence. Similarly, Nancy's conception of the "equivalence of catastrophes," formulated in response to the 2011 Fukushima nuclear disaster, helps to diagnose the figure of temporal interchangeability underlying the apocalyptic imagination. In apparent contrast with Nancy, Derrida repeatedly insists on the seemingly paradoxical formulation that each and every death of a unique living thing is *the* end of the world, absolutely and infinitely, and not merely the end of *a* world or of a living thing *within* the world. For Derrida, this "end of the world" as the withdrawal or liquidation of any sense of a world in common is the very situation of ethics. I suggest that Derrida's final seminars reveal an ambivalence in his approach to the end of the world that converges with the insights of Nancy. Here Derrida recognizes that, rather than the *end* of the world being a phantasm, the phantasm is actually *the world itself,* a phantasm of the world in common that aims to mask the absence of the world. Consequently, our anxieties about the end of the world serve to reinforce our belief in the world's unity. Yet Derrida also concedes another sense of the world, namely, as the common, elemental habitat of living things. Alongside the phantasmic projection of a world in common, we must take into account the persistent geomateriality that grants existence its areal spacing and temporal span. This is less a matter of common habitat, I suggest, than of the essential and constitutive lithic materiality of every living being and of this world here. To rediscover the world's liability to the elements requires forgoing any eschatology that approaches everything within the world and the very sense of the world itself against a background of absolute contingency or nothingness, vulnerable to total destruction. Consequently, eco-eschatology not only deforms our relationship to time but also prevents us from encountering the materiality of each thing in its absolute singularity.

I return to our eco-eschatological imagination in chapter 10 with attention to climate change. It is commonplace to hear climate change identified as the single most important challenge facing humanity. Is this prioritization of climate destabilization as the defining threat of recorded human history justified? Here I investigate the image of time underlying this apocalyptic narrative to show that it depends on, and attempts to manage, the explosion of our horizons of time represented by deep geological timescales. On this basis, I explore a series of questions posed by such apocalyptic narratives: Does this image of time exhaust our possibilities for relating to the sublime dimensions of the deep past and far future? Does it skew our relation to the present? What investments or fears are expressed through this apocalyptic image, and what does it reveal about our responsiveness to and responsibility for the past, present, and future? I proceed first by showing how the transformation of temporal horizons opened by geological scales of time and past extinctions reconfigures the temporal sublime. I turn then to the role of apocalyptic narratives in climate change rhetoric and the image of time that frames these narratives. At stake here is the role that crisis plays as the passage from the corrupt present to a purified future, marked by the transfiguration of time in the crucible of Judgment Day. On this basis, I consider some of the investments and motivations underlying the tragic and comic modes of time that drive climate narratives. These instantiate what Nancy terms "catastrophic equivalence," leveling time into homogenous and substitutable units to facilitate the predictability and manageability of the future. Rather than owning our temporal responsibilities, apocalyptic narratives seek to liquidate our obligations to the past, obscure the singularity of the present, and exert absolute control over the future. I conclude with two alternative figures of temporal justice: Potawatomi philosopher Kyle Powys Whyte's proposal of "spiraling time" as a living dialogue with our ancestors and descendants and artist Roni Horn's installation *Library of Water* in Stykkishólmur, Iceland.

In the final chapter, I turn to debates over the proposal to name our current geological epoch the "Anthropocene," whose proponents revive Bill McKibben's claims concerning the "end of nature" while shifting their valence. McKibben mourned the loss of any autonomous nature as a consequence of climate change, whereas champions of Anthropocene rhetoric call for humanity to embrace its responsibility for managing the planet. I explore how the postnatural logic of the Anthropocene intersects with the social constructionist view proposed by Steven Vogel, who argues that no autonomous and independent nature has existed since the appearance of human beings on the planet. The difference between Anthropocene and social constructionist rejections of nature depends on our temporal scale, because both treat nature as equivalent to what Chakrabarty calls the "planetary," which operates on geological registers of time beyond all human experience, in contrast with the "global" calendar of human history. For Chakrabarty, as we have noted, the central challenge of the Anthropocene is to think the collapse or the breach of these two calendars. I show that Vogel's efforts to replace discourses of nature with those of the built environment are challenged by his own descriptions of the wild and unbuilt processes that human technology takes for granted. What resists the conversion of nature into a purely artifactual environment are nonconstructed elemental processes that function as a quasi-transcendental geomateriality. Chakrabarty, on the other hand, identifies the challenge of the Anthropocene as reconciling the "immiscible chronologies" of human history and geological time, with implications for how we relate the human species to the evolutionary history of all life. Yet Chakrabarty's dual calendars fail to recognize the plexities of our relation to evolutionary and geological pasts. Rather than treating the earth as one planet among many, phenomenology reveals that the unity of humanity and of all earthly life rests on the uniqueness of the earth, not as a scientific representation, but as the memory that is constitutive of our being from within. The emergent universal history of life that Chakrabarty seeks is to be found in our common soil, in the earth as our temporal horizon of horizons and as the ontological memory of the world.

The overarching aims of *The Memory of the World* are threefold: first, to open the horizons of deep time, both past and future, to phenomenological exploration; second, to refocus our relationship with the history of life and with the geomaterial elements in terms of the asubjective and differential memory of the world; and third, to illuminate how our preconceptions about deep time shape our imaginations and desires in the present in ways that threaten to assimilate the future. The pursuit of these aims does not leave the vocation of phenomenology, its methods and aspirations, unchanged. The conditioning of reflection by its immemorial past, the refiguring of autoaffection as alteraffection, and the liability of the world to the elements call us to describe and interpret ourselves and our relation to the earth in a new light. More importantly, appreciating the singularity of each unprecedented moment as it emerges ever anew within the skein of innumerable temporal flows and eddies invites us to open ourselves to a future that we can neither predict nor control.

Part I
DEEP TIME

1

Chronopoiesis
A PHENOMENOLOGY OF NATURAL TIME

French philosopher Maurice Merleau-Ponty was among the first to recognize that understanding the temporality of nature on its own terms, apart from any relationship with subjectivity, poses a radical challenge to the philosophical tradition and to phenomenology in particular. According to the received view that Merleau-Ponty puts in question, nature exists wholly in the present, while the existence of the past and future are a function of human consciousness. He emphasizes these problematic assumptions in his 1956–57 course on the Concept of Nature, in the context of his critique of Jean-Paul Sartre, where he notes that "Sartre, like the whole of the philosophical tradition from Saint Augustine to Bergson, defines matter by instantaneity, the instantaneous present, and conceives memory and the past only by mind; in the things there is only the present, and correlatively, the 'presence' of the past or of the future requires mind or the For-Itself" (N 161/118–19).

Admittedly, however, Merleau-Ponty does not arrive at this critique, or his alternative to it, in one stroke. His appreciation of the challenges posed by a temporality independent of subjectivity develops gradually over the course of his oeuvre and parallels the reformulation of fundamental aspects of his thought. The shift in perspective that distinguishes his last writings is often described as a turn from privileging the lived body as a methodological starting point, as we find in *Phenomenology of Perception,* to the standpoint of an ontology of flesh. Within this later ontology, as we see it emerging in the courses on nature as well as the manuscript of *The Visible and the Invisible,* the human body is a remarkable variant of flesh, but only a variant nonetheless. In other words, the shift from the earlier to the later perspective involves a decentering of human subjectivity, which loses both its status as primary methodological point of access and its cardinal ontological position as the keystone of the perceived world.

This decentering is more than simply a critique of consciousness, which Merleau-Ponty had always considered secondary to our fundamentally corporeal engagement with the world; now it is the intentionally oriented body as well that is asked to relinquish its privileged status. In *Phenomenology of Perception,* Merleau-Ponty could still describe the body as "in the world just as the heart is in the organism," animating and nourishing the "visible spectacle" from within, thereby emphasizing the singularity of this relationship, the essential correlation of body and world, and the dependence of the perceived on its intentional bonds with the human perceiver (245/209). By contrast, as Renaud Barbaras (2001, 37) has noted, the later Merleau-Ponty "suspends subjectivity and becomes interested only in natural being, at the heart of which he discovers a constitutive reference to perception." The starting point is no longer the embodied subject but nature, so that Merleau-Ponty's final ontology illustrates the "mutation in the relationship between man and Being" that he felt was underway in our epoch (EM 63/368).[1]

Temporality is the pivot of this transformation in Merleau-Ponty's philosophical approach. The climax of *Phenomenology of Perception* is the discovery that time is nothing other than the autoaffection of "ultimate" subjectivity (484/446, 487/448). Merleau-Ponty makes an effort to distinguish this subjectivity from individual reflective consciousness, it is true, but only by affirming the pre-thetic correlation of subject and world: "the subject is being-in-the-world and the world remains 'subjective,' since its texture and its articulations are sketched out by the subject's movement of transcendence" (493/454). This is why nature, at the close of the chapter on temporality, can be equated with "the nature that perception shows to me" (PP 496/456). In this work, then, both time and nature retain an essential reference to subjectivity.

But we will see that Merleau-Ponty's later writings tell a different story concerning the relation between time, subjectivity, and nature. *The Visible and the Invisible* speaks of a past that cannot be related to any series of lived experiences *(Erlebnisse),* a past that belongs to a "mythical time, to the time before time" (296/243). Describing the reversal by which the things have us, rather than our having them, Merleau-Ponty speaks of the "Memory of the World," a notion developed in his reading of Whitehead from the first course on nature.[2] There Merleau-Ponty describes a "natural passage of time" that is "not a pulsation of the subject, but of Nature" (N 162/119).

The transformation in Merleau-Ponty's understanding of the relation between subjectivity and nature, as mediated by the concept of time, is nevertheless not as linear as the foregoing suggests, for two reasons that we will develop. First, although Merleau-Ponty generally affirms the correlation of subject and world in *Phenomenology of Perception*, the descriptions of the thing and the natural world in that text already demonstrate a resistance and aloofness of nature that stretches the phenomenological concept of intentionality to its limits. Our everyday, practically oriented perceptions tend to disclose only the familiar presence of things, yet beneath this superficial appearance is hidden a "nonhuman" aspect that remains aloof from the body's perceptual advances. Setting aside our instrumental involvement, we discover the natural thing as "hostile and foreign," "no longer our interlocutor, but rather a resolutely silent Other" (PP 378/336). We note, therefore, that as Merleau-Ponty's writings increasingly recognize a "back side" of nature that exceeds and resists explanation in terms of intentionality (S 227/180), he is following out the implications of the descriptions already registered in this earlier work.

Second, despite Merleau-Ponty's effort to equate temporality with subjectivity in *Phenomenology of Perception*, there is a notion of "natural" time at work in this text that similarly resists intentional explanation. This is not "objective" time, the metrics of clocks, but rather the time of the body insofar as it is anonymous and prepersonal. The body, as we will see, maintains a certain autonomy with respect to the personal and reflective self precisely because it lives a distinctive temporality: whereas the personal self follows a linear and historical time, the anonymous body is like an "innate complex" that lives a cyclical, repetitive time, the rhythm of the heartbeat (113–14/86–87). It is through an account of "radical" or second-order reflection that Merleau-Ponty aims to think the jointure of this cyclical and linear time, revealing that, for reflection, the time of the body remains an impossible time, the past of all pasts, or the immemorial. Radical reflection therefore prepares the path for the alternative account of temporality that emerges in Merleau-Ponty's later works.

To clarify this alternative temporality and the changed relation with nature that it represents, we begin by first tracing Merleau-Ponty's notion of "natural" time as it develops in his early work, and in particular its relationship to the "natural self" of the body. The notion of natural time, we will see, is central to the problematic of reflection on the unreflective. Yet natural time is not restricted to the rhythm of the body, because the body is "connatural" with the world. This leads us, second, to see that the rhythms of the body express immemorial depths of nature as such and that our prereflective lives open onto and are incorporated into this "absolute past" of nature. The significance of this recasting of the relationship between reflection and the prereflective becomes clear only when Merleau-Ponty returns to the problem of reflection on the unreflective in *The Visible and the Invisible*. There we learn that reflection, in its effort to interrogate the antecedent being that precedes it, "remembers an impossible past" and "anticipates an impossible future" (164/123). The disclosure of this absolute past is not an effort to coincide with a lost origin but rather involves the "good error" of expression. Consequently, nature appears as always "at the first day." We will see that this notion of nature "at the first day" is ambiguous, because it may refer either to a bare repetition of the same or to an unending process of productive creation that would grant a wholly different relation between past and future. This alternative account of nature's past as productive creation draws inspiration from Merleau-Ponty's reading of both Paul Claudel and A. N. Whitehead, for whom the insertion of the sensing body into nature catches subjectivity up in "the system of a cosmic time, in a subjectivity of Nature" (N 161/119). Natural time embraces us to the extent that the body is an event within Nature's process, that is, to the extent that our lives participate in the "Memory of the World." The resistance of natural time is no longer to be attributed to its status as prereflective, therefore, but rather to the *poiesis* by which it is continually renewed.

Radical Reflection and the Natural Self

Merleau-Ponty's effort to describe the sensible world as an expressive unity in *Phenomenology of Perception* rests on his account of the body as a "natural myself" that would be the "subject of perception"

(249/213). In this text, he repeatedly and consistently distinguishes between the perspective, on one hand, of the reflective personal self and, on the other hand, of the prereflective anonymous body. The body is not "I," the personal self that makes decisions and creates a situation through conscious acts, but "someone" whom I find already there ahead of me, someone already engaged with the world and taking its side. As Merleau-Ponty writes:

> I would have to say that *one* perceives in me, and not that I perceive. Every sensation includes a seed of dream or depersonalization, as we experience through this sort of stupor into which it puts us when we truly live at the level of sensation. . . . This activity unfolds on the periphery of my being; I have no more awareness of being the true subject of my sensation than I do of my birth or my death. (260/223)

This anonymous *someone (On)* who is the subject of perception can remain aloof from my conscious, personal self and even act autonomously: "each time that I experience a sensation, I experience that it does not concern my own being—the one for which I am responsible and upon which I decide—but rather another self that has already sided with the world, that is already open to certain of its aspects and synchronized with them" (261/224). Of course, this "someone" is none other than my body, my "natural self" in its "synchronization" with the world. This "natural self" of the body is not to be confused with the "objective" body studied by the physiologist; it is not an inert or mechanical object but precisely a manner of existing and of intending a world. It is a "natural mind" that already "sketches out the movement of existence" (302/265, 113/86).

To say that the body is "synchronized" with the world means that it shares the time of the world, what Merleau-Ponty calls "natural time." Here again, "natural" does not mean "objective," as if the time of the body were the mechanical metrics of a clock; natural time is not a "time of things without subjectivity" (PP 517/479). But the subjectivity that lives through natural time is generalized and depersonalized; in Merleau-Ponty's words, this is the "time of our bodily functions, which are cyclical like it, and it is the time of nature with which we coexist" (517/479). This generalized time of nature is an empty repetition; "nothing comes to pass but always identical 'nows'" ceaselessly sketching "the empty form of the genuine event" (202–3/167–68). This is because, in Merleau-Ponty's words, "bodily existence, which streams forth through me without my complicity, is but the sketch of a genuine presence in the world"; it is nevertheless enough to establish "our primary pact with the world" (204/168).

The anonymous body and the personal self therefore live through distinct temporalities that encroach upon each other without coinciding. In a section of *Phenomenology of Perception* titled "Intertwining of Natural Time and Historical Time," Merleau-Ponty describes the effort of the personal self to construct an interpretive narrative about its history. This process is essentially tentative and open-ended because of the debt to natural time. As he writes,

> my voluntary and rational life . . . knows itself to be entangled with another power that prevents it from being completed and that always gives it the air of a work in progress. Natural time is always there. . . . Since natural time remains at the center of my history, I also see myself as surrounded by it. . . . For example, nothing was perceived in intra-uterine life, and this is why there is nothing to remember. There was nothing but the sketch of a natural self and of a natural time. This anonymous life is merely the limit of the temporal dispersal that always threatens the historical present. To catch sight of this formless existence that precedes my history and that will draw it to a close, all I have to do is see, in myself, this time that functions by itself and that my personal life makes use of without ever fully concealing. (404/362)

According to this description, the reflective subject is encompassed and exceeded by natural time, yet when the subject turns inward, it also discovers this time at the very core of its personal history, in the cyclical rhythms of its organs, as near as its own heartbeat. Reflective reconstructions of our personal history never manage to "silence its protests" (403/361). Yet while this time is at the heart of the reflective present, it withdraws to the margin of personal time; it is the time of birth or death, a time that does not represent my own possibilities, an irrecuperable and impossible time. This is why Merleau-Ponty repeatedly refers to natural time as "the opacity of an originary past" (408/366), a "thought older than I am" (409/367), a "pre-history" (287/250, 302/265), an "absolute past of nature" (171/139), and, most famously, "a past that has never been present" (289/252).

Merleau-Ponty emphasizes the tension between these two temporalities when he compares the time of the body to a repression in the psychoanalytic sense of this term. On his interpretation, repression occurs when the subject remains imprisoned within and constantly relives a moment of the past as if it were the present: "One present among all of them thus acquires an exceptional value. It displaces the others and relieves them of their value as authentic present moments" (PP 112/85). And yet this past moment is not itself ever directly given, because "personal time" comes to a halt, and the traumatic moment that is relived stands behind the back of the consciousness that it ensnares—beyond representation or memory. As Merleau-Ponty writes,

> all repression is thus the passage from first person existence
> to a sort of scholastic view of this existence, which is sustained
> by a previous experience, or rather by the memory of having
> had this experience, and then by the memory of having had this
> memory, and so on, to the point that in the end it only retains
> its essential form.
>
> Now, as the advent of the impersonal, repression is a universal phenomenon. It clarifies our condition of being embodied
> by relating this condition to the temporal structure of being
> in the world. . . . Insofar as I inhabit a "physical world," where
> consistent "stimuli" and typical situations are discovered—and
> not merely the historical world in which situations are never
> comparable—my life is made up of rhythms that do not have
> their *reason* in what I have chosen to be, but rather have their
> *condition* in the banal milieu that surrounds me. (112–13/85–86)

The fundamental or originary repression is therefore that of the body itself and the temporality of rhythmic repetition that it constantly adumbrates beneath my personal awareness, providing me with the bare form of temporality on which my personal history is constructed, yet constantly threatening that edifice with the germ of anonymous resistance. Thus my body may be described as a "pre-personal adhesion to the general form of the world, as an anonymous and general existence" that "plays the role of an *innate complex* beneath the level of my personal life" (113/86). So understood, the time of the body cannot be reduced to the correlate of any lived experience; rather, it opens an abyssal dimension straddling both subject and world.

36   *Chronopoiesis*

The tension between these two times—of the body and of reflection—defines the problematic of reflection on the unreflective. Because philosophy, in Merleau-Ponty's words, is "an ever-renewed experiment of its own beginning" and "consists entirely in describing this beginning," it must be "conscious of its own dependence on an unreflected life that is its initial, constant, and final situation" (PP 14/lxxviii). It follows that philosophy's task is to reflect on its own debt to the anonymous life of the body. But if natural time is the repressed of reflection, if it is an immemorial moment that can never be made directly present, then this task can only be achieved through a doubling of reflection that Merleau-Ponty calls "radical" reflection (89–90/63). This doubling is the acknowledgment by reflection of its liability to an unreflective life that it can never equal. Radical reflection must necessarily incorporate its own unreflective history, which is the kernel of natural time at the core of personal time. Consequently, the immemorial reveals itself to reflection as the internal limit or *punctum caecum* of its own constitutive history. In other words, the "nature" of natural time and of the body haunts reflection precisely as the excluded supplement that completes it from within.

We have noted that Merleau-Ponty speaks of the anonymous body as "synchronized" with the world and of the immemorial as the "absolute past of nature." This raises the question of the relation between the natural world as it unfolds before our senses and the immemorial time that haunts reflection. In other words, what is "natural" about natural time? In this connection, it is worth remembering that the anonymous body is described by Merleau-Ponty as "connatural" with the world (PP 262/225), and the "time of our bodily functions" is said to be "the time of nature with which we coexist" (517/479). In other words, nature follows the same cyclical, repetitive time as does the body. This means that nothing new can happen in nature and that it can never rise to the level of a genuine history. This is, in fact, exactly the view of nature that Lucien Herr (1894, 1000) ascribes to Hegel in his entry in *La Grande Encyclopédie,* where he writes that the evolution of nature, in Hegel, is a "logical reconstruction, but not a history of nature." He continues as follows:

> For Hegel, as for Aristotle, nature is at the first day; for as long as it has been, it has been as it is today. Genesis and transmuta-

tion of forms are only dreams: nature is inert and its forms are eternal; philosophy of nature is the system of nature, but not the history of it. (1000, my translation)

I call attention to this passage because Merleau-Ponty returns to it several times in his later investigations of nature. But Merleau-Ponty is interested only in a particular phrase from Herr's discussion, "la nature est au premier jour," nature is at the first day (cf. VI 264/210, 320/267; N 76/49; Merleau-Ponty 1968a, 94; 1988, 133). As Herr intends this phrase, it means that nature never changes, that it involves no genuine *passage*. This sense of the phrase is consistent with an understanding of natural time as empty repetition, as Merleau-Ponty presents it in his descriptions of the anonymity of the body. On this interpretation, then, natural time would be fundamentally ahistorical and consist of nothing more than equivalent, repeatable, and substitutable moments.

There is, however, another, richer manner of understanding the "at the first day" of nature already in *Phenomenology of Perception*. This interpretation discovers a genuine creative newness within each moment of perception and links this newness with the accumulation of perceptual memory. For instance, Merleau-Ponty writes:

When I contemplate an object with no other worry than to see it exist and to display before me its riches, it ceases to be an allusion to a general type and I realize that each perception— and not merely perceptions of scenes that I discover for the first time—begins anew for itself the birth of intelligence and has something of an inspired invention to it. If I am to recognize this tree as a tree, then beneath this acquired signification, the momentary arrangement of the sensible spectacle must begin afresh—*as if at the origin of the vegetal world*—to sketch out the individual idea of this tree. (69/45–46, my emphasis)

We find, then, a creativity that is both natural and historical at the core of each perception. Furthermore, this creative event is linked by Merleau-Ponty with the immemorial time of my own personal history, as when he writes that "my first perception, along with the horizons that surrounded it, is an ever-present event, an unforgettable tradition; even as a thinking subject, I still am this first perception, I am the continuation of the same life that it inaugurated"

(468–69/429–30). This account of the creativity of natural time conflicts with its presentation as empty repetition. What must be understood is precisely the sense in which the passage of nature may yet entail its creative renewal, so that its being always "at the first day" does not deny its establishment of a genuine history. This would seem to be what Merleau-Ponty has in mind when he interprets this phrase in a late working note: "It is a question of finding in the present, the flesh of the world (and not in the past) an 'ever new' and 'always the same.' . . . The sensible, Nature, transcend the past present distinction, realize from within a passage from one into the other" (VI 320–21/267). Our question, then, is how this passage between past and present is to be conceived according to a richer conception of natural time.

Chronopoiesis of Nature

Two sources are indispensable for understanding the broadening of Merleau-Ponty's conception of time. The first of these is Paul Claudel's *Poetic Art,* which Merleau-Ponty cites repeatedly in the manuscript of *The Visible and the Invisible* (VI 140/103, 161/121, 233/179). Years earlier, *Poetic Art* had also provided an epigraph for the "Temporality" chapter of *Phenomenology of Perception*: "Time is the *sense* of life (*sense* as in the direction *[sens]* of a stream, the sense of a sentence, the weave *[sens]* of a fabric, the sense of smell)" (470/432; PA 33/19–20). Here time lies at the intersection of direction, meaning, and sensibility. But whereas Merleau-Ponty's chapter on temporality emphasizes the fundamental equivalence of time and subjectivity, for Claudel, time discloses the creative differentiation of the universe as a whole. This is, in fact, the meaning of his title, a reference to his call for a "new Art of Poetry of the Universe," in the sense of *poiein,* which would be the "autochthonous art used by all that which is born" and which is "practiced before our eyes by nature itself" (PA 50–51/31–32). This poetry of nature is the metaphor, harmony, or proportion by which each thing calls for precisely the completion that it finds in the rest of the universe. As Claudel writes,

> no thing is complete in itself and each can only be completed by that which it lacks. But that which each particular thing lacks is

infinite; we cannot know in advance the complement it calls for. Only through the secret taste of our spirit, do we realize when effective harmony is achieved, that is, the essential and generating fundamental difference. (PA 22/12)

This "essential and generating fundamental difference" may call forth "effective harmonies" among the natural objects that we encounter, as Claudel describes the "green of a maple tree" answering the "appeal of a pine" or as he insists that "the plantation of this bouquet of pines, the shape of this mountain are no more due to chance than the Parthenon or this diamond" (50–51/31–32). More pertinently, what makes nature always appear as "at the first day" is the generative difference of the past. As Claudel explains,

the past is an incantation of things to come, the generating difference they need, the forever growing sum of future conditions. It determines the *sense*, and, in this light, it does not cease existing anymore than the first words of a sentence when the eye reaches the last ones. Better still, it does not stop developing, organizing within itself, like a building, whose role and aspect is changed by new constructions, or like a sentence made clearer by another sentence. In a word, what has been once, never loses its operating virtue; it increases with each moment's contribution. The present minute is different from all other minutes, in that it does not border on the same quantity of past. . . . At every breath, the world remains as new as it was at the first gulp of air out of which the first man made his first expiration. (44–45/27)

The world is, at every moment, entirely new, not because it eternally repeats an unchanging beginning, but because the passage of becoming guarantees the uniqueness of each combination of generating differences. This becoming is the *poiesis* of a nature for which "to be is to create," such that the whole universe, for Claudel, is "nothing but a time-marking machine" of which human clocks are "unwitting copies" (43/27, 34/20).

These insights from Claudel are significant in two respects. First, they demonstrate the "passage between past and present" that joins the "ever new" with the "always the same," as Merleau-Ponty seeks in his working notes. In other words, they demonstrate a positive and creative sense for nature being always "at the first day."

Second, they do so not by tracing time to the subject but rather by recognizing a fundamental resonance between natural time within and without: "What time is it within and outside me, according to my closing or opening myself? I hear my heart within me, and the clock in the very middle of the house. I am. I feel, I listen, within myself, to the beating of this machine, confined between my bones, a machine through which I continue to be" (PA 46/28). The marking-time of the heart resonates with the marking-time of the universe such that time is neither reducible to my subjectivity nor independent of it, situating me within an infinite fabric of differences by which my being is generated. I emerge as part of the same wave of the past as all other things that I encounter, so that "there is no cause but a total one" and "each effect is the varying evaluation of the whole moment" (55–56/35). The entire passage of the universe continues to exert its efficacy with each following moment such that the present is never a point but a growing fabric that is at each instant wholly different and wholly demanded as the complement to the entirety of what has preceded it. In this case, there is no truly cyclical time of the body any more than of nature writ large, save through the isolating effects of our understanding.

The Memory of the World

It is from Whitehead that Merleau-Ponty draws the completion of this line of thinking, which is to recognize a "passage of nature" that is neither an empty repetition nor simply correlated with the embodied subject. Merleau-Ponty's survey of historical conceptions of nature in his 1956–57 course reaches its culmination with Whitehead, and while the latter's work receives no direct discussion in the text or notes published in *The Visible and the Invisible,* we do have another clue to Whitehead's significance. Sartre recounts a conversation from 1959 in which Merleau-Ponty suggested that he may write about Nature. "And then, to lead me on," Sartre writes, "he added, 'I read a sentence in Whitehead which struck me: "Nature is in tatters" *["la Nature est en haillons"]'*" (Sartre 1990, 204; 1965, 309). Sartre admits his puzzlement about the meaning of this phrase, which undoubtedly refers to Whitehead's (2004, 50) remark, in *The Concept of Nature,* that "nature as perceived always has a ragged edge."[3] As Merleau-Ponty recognizes, this phrase expresses Whitehead's rejection of punctual spatiotemporal existences (N 153–54/113). In contrast with the "flashpoint" of classical physics that reduces time to the punctual moment, Whitehead proposes an overlapping relation of events as the foundation of space-time. On Merleau-Ponty's reading, Whitehead's critique of unique emplacement makes salient the ontological value of perception: "What I perceive is both for me and in the things. Perception is made starting from the interior of Nature" (N 159/117). In other words, the perceiving body is itself one event within the overlapping series of events that constitutes space-time, and the mind equally participates in this "passage of nature." Consequently, Whitehead's descriptions suggest a reversal of the role played by nature and subjectivity in the unfurling of time. Ironically, in a passage that we cited at the opening of this chapter, it is with reference to Sartre that Merleau-Ponty makes this contrast explicit:

> With Sartre, Being is without exigency, without activities, without potentialities. Sartre, like the whole of the philosophical tradition from Saint Augustine to Bergson, defines matter by instantaneity, the instantaneous present, and conceives memory and the past only by mind; in the things there is only the present, and correlatively, the "presence" of the past or of the future requires mind or the For-itself. (N 161/118–19)

By contrast, for Whitehead, nature need not be leavened with subjectivity to effect its own spatiotemporal unfurling. Whereas measured or serial time is relative and subjective, "there is a time inherent to Nature":

> This time, in Whitehead, is inherent in the things, it embraces us, to the extent that we participate in the things, or that we take part in the process of Nature. It is essential for us, but insofar as we are Nature. Subjectivity is caught up in the system of a cosmic time, in a subjectivity of Nature. (N 161/119)

Rather than nature requiring subjectivity for its passage, the passage of subjectivity is an event of nature.[4]

Followed through to its conclusion, this suggests a further complication of the structure of radical reflection. We have shown that reflection incorporates the natural time of the body as its own immemorial past and that radical reflection—what Merleau-Ponty will, in *The Visible and the Invisible,* refer to as hyperreflection *(surré-flexion)* (61/38, 70/46)—aims to take this liability to the unreflective into account. In the wake of Claudel and Whitehead, this structure of radical reflection requires two revisions. First, the immemorial moment that it enfolds cannot be a cyclical time of empty repetition. Insofar as the body is an event within ragged-edged nature, it cannot be isolated from this nature's generative unfurling. Even the time of the anonymous body, such as the rhythmic beating of the heart, must be understood as a poetic event called to respond to the generative differences laid out by the entire history of nature. The creative passage of nature therefore provides the best interpretation of how it is that nature is always "at the first day." On this understanding of Herr's phrase, the perennial novelty of nature is related to its Latin etymology: *nascor,* "to be born" (N 19/3). And, as Claudel notes, "we are not born alone. To be born *[Naître],* for everything, is to be born together *[co-naître].* Every birth is a knowledge *[connaissance]*" (PA 62/40). Natural time *is* the continual cobirth of all in generative difference.

This points toward the second revision of radical reflection, which is the synchrony of the immemorial time at the heart of reflection with the spatiotemporal unfurling of the perceived world. The pyramid of time on which every reflective moment balances is the entire memory of the world, its pure past. Consequently, reflection must also be understood as an event of nature that eventuates its passage. This means that every reflection, and every experience more generally, perches atop this pyramid of time that precedes and exceeds the duration of our embodied lives. For every lived moment to be haunted by the world's memory suggests that every such moment is essentially bound up with vast durations, including those of the deep past and far future. Extending Merleau-Ponty's radical reflection as we have proposed would therefore entail an encounter with the elemental past: what will the "Memory of the World" mean when considered from the perspective of deep, geological time?

2

The Elemental Past

In a lecture to the Collège philosophique on January 12, 1951, Georges Bataille recounts a barroom debate held the night before with British philosopher A. J. Ayer, who was then stationed at the British Embassy in Paris and had presented a lecture to the group on the previous day. The topic of the debate, in which Maurice Merleau-Ponty and atomic physicist Georges Ambrosino also participated, is described by Bataille in the following terms:

> We finally fell to discussing the following very strange question. Ayer had uttered the very simple proposition: There was a sun before men existed. And he saw no reason to doubt it. Merleau-Ponty, Ambrosino, and I disagreed with this proposition, and Ambrosino said that the sun had certainly not existed before the world. I, for my part, do not see how one can say so. (CN 190/80/111)

Although Bataille suggests that a compromise was finally reached at around three in the morning, he says nothing about its terms. Instead, his lecture takes up Ayer's proposition as an example of "nonknowledge," *non-savoir,* because, even though it is "logically unassailable," it is nevertheless "mentally disturbing, unbalancing." This disturbing character is a consequence of the proposition's violation of the requirement for both a subject and an object, because what we find in this case is "an object independent of any subject"— and, consequently, "perfect non-sense" (CN 191/81/112, 190/80/111).

This may seem little more than an interesting anecdote, but Bataille's account of his debate with Ayer has been identified by Andreas Vrahimis (2012, 11) as "the first explicit announcement, in the twentieth century, of the division between Anglophone and Continental philosophy" (see also Critchley 2001, 36). As Bataille puts it, the conversation with Ayer "produced an effect of shock. There exists between French and English philosophers a sort of abyss which we do not find between French and German philosophers" (CN 191/80/111–12). I suggest that this remark concerning the parting of ways of philosophical traditions is of more than merely historical interest. The debate over the sun's existence prior to human beings anticipates and even enacts the split between analytic and Continental philosophy because it already sketches out what is at stake philosophically in this split, namely, the fate of naturalism. To any naturalist, and especially to the inner naturalist of common sense, the position taken by the Continental thinkers in this debate is so absurd as to function as a *reductio* of their position. Even for those whose sensibilities align with the Continental side, or at least for many of them, it will be Bataille's position that seems shocking, rather than Ayer's.[1] How, today, could anyone— Continental thinkers included—deny the anteriority of the sun to human existence? Indeed, it is precisely by criticizing such absurdities that Quentin Meillassoux's speculative realism has attracted attention. Nevertheless, it is my intention here to reanimate this old debate and to argue on behalf of the Continental position: the sun exists only within a world, and a world emerges only at the confluence of a perceiver and the perceived. But this does not deny the insistence of a time before the world, a primordial prehistory that haunts the world from within, which is the truth of the naturalist's conviction about a time prior to humanity. Only the resources of phenomenology can clarify this encounter with an elemental past that has never been for anyone a present.

Close readers of Merleau-Ponty will immediately recognize that the debate over the sun's existence echoes an infamous passage at the end of the "Temporality" chapter of *Phenomenology of Perception,* where Merleau-Ponty considers the objection that the world existed "prior to man" (495/456). In response to Merleau-Ponty's claim that "there is no world without an Existence that bears its structure," his imagined critic counters that "the world preceded man," because "the earth emerged from a primitive nebula where the conditions for life had not been brought together." Merleau-Ponty nevertheless insists that "nothing will ever lead me to understand what a nebula that could not be seen by anyone might be. Laplace's nebula is not behind us, at our origin, but rather out in front of us in the cultural world" (495/456).

Now, for reasons that we suggested earlier, this remark has been controversial in recent Merleau-Ponty scholarship. Some, like Thomas Baldwin (2004, 20), see in it merely a confused theory of linguistic meaning that has long since been debunked. Others might take this remark as an unfortunate vestige of Merleau-Ponty's early commitment to Husserlian transcendental phenomenology, which, they will say, prevents his account of time in *Phenomenology of Perception* from truly escaping a "philosophy of consciousness." Going further still, Graham Harman (2005, 52–53), in his *Guerrilla Metaphysics*, cites the nebula passage as evidence that Merleau-Ponty "retains all of the antimetaphysical bias that typifies phenomenology as a whole." By denying that there can be any genuine interactions between things in their own right, unmediated by humans, Merleau-Ponty "artificially limits the scope of the cosmos to that of human awareness." In short, Harman's assessment is that Merleau-Ponty's ontology remains fundamentally anthropocentric and incapable of thinking the world of things on their own terms. Harmon's own "object-oriented ontology" is quite close to the "speculative realism" of Meillassoux, who argues in *After Finitude* that the post-Kantian "correlationism" of phenomenology, by which thinking and being may be understood only in their relation and never independently, makes it impossible for phenomenology to speak meaningfully about "ancestrality," that is, about a time anterior to the emergence of thought or life in the cosmos. For the correlationist, according to Meillassoux, statements about such an ancestral time—a time prior to all manifestation—are strictly meaningless. It follows that phenomenology is incapable of providing a meaningful foundation for the sciences, which should motivate us to revise its fundamental commitment to the correlation of thought and being.

Starting from these three critiques, we can specify more precisely what is at stake in the question of whether the sun existed before human beings. At stake, first of all, is phenomenology's rejection of realism or metaphysical naturalism, and therefore its fundamental incompatibility with the dominant strands of analytic philosophy. If any détente or compromise is possible between phenomenology and naturalism, it will turn on the treatment of time.[2]

Second, then, at stake is the phenomenological account of the time of nature—of the cosmos, of the elements, and of the evolutionary history of life—and the relationship of this time to that of cultural and personal history. To investigate this, we will return to Merleau-Ponty's remarks in *Phenomenology of Perception* about the absolute past of nature as a past that has never been present as well as to the references in his later writings to nature as the "Memory of the World." As we will see, Merleau-Ponty's rejection of a sun before human beings rests on his commitment to the ontological primacy of the perceived world. We might say, then, that just as the earth does not move, the sun does not endure; it does not age. As the lived basis for time, it remains outside of time, at its beginning or at its end. But our embodied immersion in the memory of the world tears us apart, scattering us across an incommensurable multiplicity of temporal flows and eddies. We encounter, then, an asubjective time, a time without a world, at the heart of lived time. This world-less prehistorical time, independent of any subject, is precisely the time of the elements, of ashes and dust. The experience of such a mythical "time before time," as Merleau-Ponty tells us, is one that "remembers an impossible past" and "anticipates an impossible future" (VI 296/243, 163/123). This impossible future is surely a return to the elements, of dust to dust; in other words, it is the apocalypse to come.

Let us begin with the three critiques of Merleau-Ponty, starting with Baldwin, who exemplifies the perspective of the naturalistic philosopher intent on appropriating Merleau-Ponty's descriptions outside the context of transcendental phenomenology. Baldwin (2004, 20) argues that Merleau-Ponty's position "can no longer command serious assent," thanks to its

> commitment to a foundationalist theory of meaning which ties the meaning of our words, even "nebula," back to some "pre-scientific experience" in such a way that the "valid meaning" of sentences about nebulas includes a reference to the pre-scientific life-world. . . . The meaning, or reference (there is no significant distinction in this case), of "nebula" is a type of stellar system, and in coming to understand what nebulas are one also learns that the existence of nebulas is wholly independent of that of human beings, and indeed of any intelligent

consciousness. So the realist, having noted Merleau-Ponty's dependence upon this untenable theory of meaning, can pass on unmoved.

Here Baldwin plays the part of a present-day Ayer, interpreting the argument as about linguistic meaning while failing entirely to recognize that his naturalistic interpretation is incompatible with Merleau-Ponty's ontology. As Bataille admits, Ayer's proposition is "logically unassailable" (CN 191/81/112). Merleau-Ponty makes the same point by describing Laplace's nebula as "out in front of us in the cultural world," the world within which linguistic formulations are learned and deployed. The issue is not, then, whether the signification of the statement is valid, which Merleau-Ponty admits, but rather the tacit framing of all language and concepts by the structures of human perceptual experience. The issue, once again, is not one of understanding the word *nebula* but of understanding what a nebula *not seen by anyone* might be. And here it is significant that the lineage of thinkers that Baldwin cites in his favor—the Vienna Circle, Quine, Putnam, Kripke—does not include Husserl, whose account of the technicization of the objective sciences in the *Crisis* is intended to demonstrate their ongoing tacit dependence on the structures of lifeworldly experience, even as they presume to downgrade such experience to the merely "subjective-relative" (Husserl [1962] 1970, sec. 34). This is why Husserl (1940, 2002) can unabashedly pronounce that, despite Copernicus, the earth of our perceptual lives does not move, precisely because it is the very foundation for the movement or rest of objects. Such a "transcendental earth" can neither be the object of scientific investigation nor refuted by it, because scientific inquiry necessarily presupposes this same earthground in defining its proper scope and methods.[3]

In emphasizing Merleau-Ponty's proximity and debt to Husserl, however, we have perhaps played into the second critique, namely, that Merleau-Ponty's remarks concerning the world prior to human beings, coming as they do at the end of the "Temporality" chapter of *Phenomenology of Perception,* are symptomatic of this text's failure to escape a philosophy of consciousness. It is in this chapter, after all, that Merleau-Ponty equates time with the subject, both understood in terms of autoaffection (487/449), thereby reproducing the classic formulation of phenomenological presence as, in Derrida's

(1967b, 83; 2011b, 64) words, "proximity to oneself in interiority" (see also Lawlor 2003, 28). We might hope, then, that in Merleau-Ponty's later work, which, as we saw in chapter 1, complicates the subjectivist tendencies of this earlier text, and especially its treatment of time, his remarks concerning the world before humans would not stand without at least some qualification. But in fact, we know that Merleau-Ponty takes up again the theme of the nebula a decade later, in his 1954–55 course on passivity, where he unambiguously reaffirms his earlier conclusion: "If there is emergence, this means that humans will never be able to think a nature without humans, and ultimately that the pure in-itself is a myth. Every cosmogeny [is thought] in perceptual terms" (IP 172/129).

Nevertheless, if truth is not prior to us, neither is it through us alone—a position that Merleau-Ponty here attributes to the "philosophy of consciousness" of his teacher Léon Brunschvicg (1964, 2), whose thesis, *La modalité du jugement,* opened with the assessment that "knowledge constitutes a world that is for us *the* world. Beyond this, there is nothing: a thing that would be beyond knowledge would be by definition inaccessible, indeterminable, that is to say equivalent for us to nothing." Now, Merleau-Ponty is clearly distancing himself from Brunschvicg's position, precisely because the world for Brunschvicg is constricted to what knowledge discloses, whereas for Merleau-Ponty, it is the perceptual exchange, the exchange "between a world ready to be perceived and a perception that relies upon it," that is the starting point for ontology. Significantly, Merleau-Ponty elucidates his position here with explicit reference to Husserl's claim that the earth does not move. "Objectivist ontology cannot be maintained," he writes, because "there is no objectivity without a point of view, in itself; i.e., an observer is necessary, with his 'levels,' his 'soil,' his 'homeland,' his perceptual 'norms,' in short, his 'earth'" (IP 173/129). And the lived correlate of such an earth, as John Sallis's (2000, 2012) investigations demonstrate, is the elemental sky. Sallis (2000, 195) refers us back to Heidegger's remark in *Being and Time* that "'time' first shows itself in the sky, that is, precisely there where one comes across it in directing oneself naturally *according to it,* so that time even becomes identified with the sky" (Heidegger 1963, 419; 1962, 471–72). "This time of the heavens," as Sallis (2000, 194) notes, "is measured out by the course of the sun and, first of all, as the alternation between day and night." In parallel with the claim that the earth of our primordial experience does not move, then, we might similarly insist that the sun does not endure; it is not an object within time but fundamentally the primordial measure of time. We find a similar insight in Claudel's *Poetic Art*—a text whose significance for Merleau-Ponty we explored in chapter 1—where Claudel describes "the whole universe" as "nothing but a time-marking machine," with the sun as its weight and movement as its flywheel (34–35/20–21).

Nevertheless, Merleau-Ponty's continued insistence on our inability to think a world prior to humans seems to play directly into the third criticism of his position, namely, Meillassoux's critique of correlationism. For the correlationist—and Meillassoux believes that "every philosophy which disavows naive realism has become a variant of correlationism" (AF 18/5)—thinking and being can be considered only in their correlation, never separately. The relation itself is primary, whether we call this relation intentionality, *Ereignis*, language, or flesh. But this leaves us, Meillassoux argues, with a "strange feeling of imprisonment or enclosure" (AF 21/7), insofar as the only exteriority that we can encounter remains relative to thought. And so, what correlationism has lost, and what speculative realists and object-oriented ontologists claim to recover, is "the *great outdoors*, the *absolute* outside [*le* Grand Dehors, *le* Dehors *absolu*] of pre-critical thinkers: that outside which was not relative to us, and which was given as indifferent to its own givenness to be what it is, existing in itself regardless of whether we are thinking of it or not" (AF 21–22/7). Now, if we want to give the lie to this exclusion of the great outside, Meillassoux argues, we need only demand an account of a time prior to all thinking, prior to all manifestation— and, we might add, prior to all perception. For surely we encounter the traces of such a prior time in the radioactive decay of isotopes or the emissions of a distant star. And what such "arche-fossils" confront us with is "ancestrality," the time prior to the emergence of human—or any—life in the cosmos. While Meillassoux's own examples do not include the sun or Laplace's nebula, and he never mentions Bataille or Merleau-Ponty by name, his argument seems intended precisely to intervene on Ayer's side of the debate, and at a more profound level than does Baldwin.

Let us consider, then, whether Meillassoux's approach to arche-fossils offers insight into the geological past by turning to a famous scene in its scientific discovery. In a posthumous 1805 biographical sketch of James Hutton, often referred to as the founder of modern geology, his friend John Playfair (1822) recounts their 1788 trip to Siccar Point, on the east coast of Scotland, to view a geological formation that has since become known as Hutton's Unconformity. At this site, erosion had made clearly visible the juxtaposition of horizontal strata of red limestone with underlying nearly vertical columns of greywacke. The scientists' interest with this formation was due to what it implied about the incredible expanse of time required for its generation, the patiently slow and sequential accumulation of each layer of rock compounded by the folding over of older millennia of deposited strata into their own perpendicular layer below. For Hutton, this scene provided incontrovertible evidence of his theory of uniformitarianism, according to which the geological past must be explained by the same gradual processes of sedimentation and erosion operating today, leading him to propose a concept of geological time with "no vestige of a beginning,—no prospect of an end" (Hutton 1788, 304). Nowadays, geologists studying Hutton's Unconformity date the lower layer of Silurian greywacke at around 435 million years old and the upper layer of Devonian sandstone at 370 million years, with the seam of the unconformity marking a 65-million-year hiatus of "missing" time. Certainly these numbers astound none of us today in the way that they did Hutton's contemporaries; we are all perfectly familiar with the general concept, if not the particulars, of the geological timescale and with linear representations of the age of the earth that indicate the emergence of *Homo sapiens* at the fractional tail end of a long temporal comet. But can we truly say, even today, and with our extensive theoretical knowledge of geological time, that we *comprehend* the scales of time involved?

Hutton's Unconformity is to geologists what the Galápagos Islands are to biologists, and references to it rarely miss the opportunity to mention Playfair's (1822, 80–81) famous retrospective account of his trip with Hutton, with its invocation of the temporal sublime:

> We felt ourselves necessarily carried back to the time when the schistus on which we stood was yet at the bottom of the sea, and when the sandstone before us was only beginning to be deposited, in the shape of sand or mud, from the waters of a super-

incumbent ocean. An epocha still more remote presented itself, when even the most ancient of these rocks, instead of standing upright in vertical beds, lay in horizontal planes at the bottom of the sea, and was not yet disturbed by that immeasurable force which has burst asunder the solid pavement of the globe. Revolutions still more remote appeared in the distance of this extraordinary perspective. The mind seemed to grow giddy by looking so far into the abyss of time; and while we listened with earnestness and admiration to the philosopher who was now unfolding to us the order and series of these wonderful events, we became sensible how much farther reason may sometimes go than imagination can venture to follow.

Although geological theories since Hutton's time have undergone the same tumultuous upheavals that he ascribed to this ancient seabed, the abyssal and vertiginous experience of geological time remains contemporary. The ground beneath our feet is scarcely reassuring as we try to wrap our minds around the breakup and reassembly of the earth's continents, the cornucopia of long-vanished species that flourished in worlds we can scarcely reconstruct, or the billions of years that light has traveled from distant galaxies to reach our eyes. This is not just meganumerophobia, a fear of very large numbers; we encounter the abyssal unfathomability of time affectively and viscerally, in our heart of hearts, like a wedge driven through our lived experience of daily rhythms, our personal memories and anticipations, and the historical fabric of cultural events. Indeed, the very "depth" of geological time is the bottomless free fall into which it throws all markers and touchstones by which we orient ourselves within the temporal horizons of our world.

For Hutton, there was no prospect of a beginning to geological processes, but today we rely on radiometric dating, based on the constant rate of decay of trace radioactive elements, to estimate the earth's age at around 4.5 billion years. The samples used for such dating are paradigmatic of what Meillassoux has termed "arche-fossils," material traces of an "ancestral" reality or event "anterior to the emergence of the human species—or even anterior to every recognized form of life on earth" (AF 25–26/10). According to Meillassoux, as we have noted, the literal truth of empirical claims about such an ancestral reality cannot be admitted by post-Kantian

52   *The Elemental Past*

correlationism, including that of phenomenology. As an absolute Outside, ancestral time would no longer be the correlate of any subject; in its absolute indifference to subjectivity, it would no longer reflect back to us our own involvement and inherence in the world.[4]

Now, although Meillassoux does not present his view in these terms, he is clearly concerned with the end of the world, at least of the world as we know it. This is why he begins his argument with the "ancestral," with reality "anterior to every recognized form of life on earth" (AF 25–26/10), and later pairs this with "possible events that are *ulterior* to the extinction of the human species" (AF 155/112), such as would be entailed, he says, by "hypotheses about the climatic and geological consequences of a meteor impact extinguishing all life on earth" (AF 155–6/112). The Outside, for Meillassoux, always has the air of apocalypse. This is the case despite the fact that the absolute Outside is not only anterior or ulterior to our world but also absolutely exterior to us in the present, as a kind of mathematical doppelgänger of our world defined by its radical indifference to human existence (AF 160/116). Beyond the horizons of our world, as its Great Outside, this "world without us" presumably does not touch on our lived world in any practical or perceptible fashion.

Just as Meillassoux trades on our everyday notion of world, so he fails, like Baldwin, to thematize the problem of time, which for him seems to be reducible to a formula for designating the properties of an event, much as it would be, in his example, for a scientist using thermoluminescence to date the light emitted by stars. What requires explanation, on his account, is the truth of such scientific conclusions about the "date" of prehuman events, or the "age" of the universe, and such dates are designated by numbers on a line (AF 24/9). Furthermore, the problem of how to understand these numbers and this line first confronts us only in the era of modern science, because for him, the ancestral past is a past that we come to know primarily or exclusively through scientific investigation (AF 39/28). In fact, although Meillassoux does not mention this, it was not until the early twentieth century, in 1913, that Arthur Holmes published his famous book *The Age of the Earth,* which proposed the first absolute dates for the geological timescale based on radiometric methods. But clearly such scientific research makes no claim to explain what is meant by "past," nor can it do so, because it takes for granted our lived, prescientific experience of time (IP 171–72/128). If the geological scale of time means anything more to us than numbers on a line, this is because our experience—our levels, our perceptual norms, our earth—opens us to a past, and even to an incomprehensibly ancient prehistory. It does so because, as Merleau-Ponty emphasizes in his reading of Whitehead, we are ourselves embedded, mind and body, within the temporal passage of nature; its pulsation runs across us (N 159–62/117–19). And this pulsation transcends the past–present distinction in such a way that past and present are enveloping–enveloped, *Ineinander*, each moment entering into relations of exchange and identification, interference and confusion, with all the others (VI 321/267–68; IP 36/7). This is why Merleau-Ponty identifies time as the very model of institution and of chiasm (IP 36/7; VI 321/267) and calls nature the "Memory of the World" (VI 247/194; N 163/120; Merleau-Ponty 1996a, 114–15; 2022, 56–57). On one hand, this is the truth of Merleau-Ponty's rejection of a time "in itself" that would be entirely purified of any point of view, because we cannot think time apart from our own emergence within it and our subsequent reconstruction of it. On the other hand, this entails no reduction of time to a correlate of thought, because institution here is nearly the opposite of constitution: whereas "the constituted makes sense only for me," "the instituted makes sense without me" (IP 37/8). Simply put, just as institution is nearly the opposite of constitution, chiasm is nearly the opposite of correlation.[5]

Meillassoux's critique of the correlationist position relies on the understanding of geological scales of time first opened by scientists like Hutton. But, interestingly, Hutton's Unconformity does not precisely qualify as an arche-fossil in Meillassoux's sense: the Silurian seas were teeming with life, and forests were already spreading across the continent of Laurasia by the late Devonian period. A true arche-fossil must point back more than 3.7 billion years to precede the earliest fossil evidence of life on earth (which, of course, does not rule out life's existence elsewhere in the cosmos). Meillassoux takes no account, then, of deep time's distinctive stratigraphic rhythms—cosmic, geological, evolutionary, prehistoric— nor the differential ways that these affectively involve us. In fact, Meillassoux's invocation of ancestrality, despite its reliance on a scientific understanding of deep time, never recognizes the intensely

54   *The Elemental Past*

interruptive and disorienting character of abyssal and immemorial time. He cannot do so, because his view sunders reality into two worlds and two times, one correlated with subjectivity, the other describable only in mathematical terms. What Meillassoux misses is precisely the chiasm between lived time and natural time that makes any genuine encounter with the immemorial possible, and this is linked to his failure, throughout *After Finitude,* to thematize the problems of world and materiality on which his view depends. More generally, in his single-minded effort to avoid the *co-* of correlationism, Meillassoux fails to grasp the chi, the chiastic intertwining that is constitutive of materiality, world, and time.

Yet this ontological response, even if it meets Meillassoux's challenge, remains abstract; it guarantees only the *possibility* of a phenomenology of the prehistoric, the geological, and the cosmic past. For what characterizes the experience of the deep past is precisely its unsettling, vertiginous character, the loss of all common markers and measures. It is our ability to open onto a past that was never our own possibility, never our own memory—an impossible and immemorial past—that makes any scientific investigation or mathematical representation of such a past possible. It is only through phenomenology that we can investigate this impossible immemoriality, this memory that belongs to the world rather than to us; and, to my knowledge, this phenomenology remains to be carried through. We cannot find it elaborated in Merleau-Ponty's writings, although I think we can take our start from several hints there.

Let us begin, though, not with the cosmic time of the sun or of Laplace's nebula, but rather with something that is literally dug from the earth, that is, with a fossil. Phenomenology has generally avoided the fossil. You may recall that Husserl uses the example of "fossil vertebrae," in the first of the *Logical Investigations,* as illustrative of an indication, because such fossils are signs "of the existence of prediluvian animals" (Husserl 1928, 24; 2001, 184). This means that, for a thinking being, belief in the reality of the fossil motivates belief in another reality, namely, the past that it indicates. But here we are still at the level of the cognitive content of the fossil, whereas what makes it phenomenologically interesting is, rather, the way that it explodes our efforts to fill out its content. A nondescript, grapefruit-sized lump of brown sandstone found on the beach at Fossil Point, near Coos Bay on the Oregon coast, breaks neatly in half to reveal the shell of a scallop. Based on the surrounding geology, paleontologists date this sandstone formation from the Pliocene, roughly three million to five million years before the present. But does our wonder at this strange object arise only from this ungraspably large number, affixed like a price tag to what is otherwise one object among many? Or is it rather that the fossil, in our very perceptual encounter with it, already possesses the hint of paradox and the beginnings of vertigo? The stone itself, Heidegger would say, is worldless. Yet, inhabiting it as a part of its very substance is the trace of a life and the intimation of a world always already closed to us. There is an invitation in this very refusal, an invitation to which only our imagination, ill equipped for the task, can respond. Furthermore, this invitation and this refusal are intensified by the paradoxical intersection of two different pulses of time, that of the evolutionary past of life, on one hand, and that of the rock, of the elements themselves, on the other. The fossil therefore embodies the very paradox of our encounter with the immemorial past, and it does so before our scientific explanations gain traction. If this were not so, how could Xenophanes and Aristotle each have recognized fossils as the remains of ancient life?

Now, my point is not that our scientific account is somehow already contained within the sensible encounter with the fossil, nor that we can, today, purify how we perceive this object of all that we have been taught about it and about how to perceive it. My claim is, rather, that we are first motivated to provide an account of the fossil—as have been many other people, in different ways, throughout history—precisely because it confronts us perceptually, viscerally, with an immemorial past that both invites and refuses us. If I am right that this confrontation is embodied in the fossil itself, then the question becomes, what makes it possible for me to resonate with this ancient past, to catch a marginal and brief glimpse of its abyssal expanse? How is such an incomprehensible time already sketched out within my own being such that it prepares me for this encounter?

Before we investigate this question directly, let us take a moment to retrace the steps that have brought us to this point. Our guiding question, posed to phenomenology, concerns whether there is a nature that precedes and conditions the emergence of the experienced world while remaining inaccessible to it. Merleau-Ponty's response to this question is both counterintuitive and enigmatic, because he apparently denies that we can speak meaningfully about such an objective ancestral past, and this denial marks a singular point in the subsequent divergence of philosophical traditions. To clarify what is at stake in this question, we considered three critical responses to Merleau-Ponty's position: the naturalist critique, the rejection of phenomenology as a philosophy of consciousness, and the speculative realist charge against correlationism. In response to the naturalist, we reaffirmed the primacy of the lifeworld as the unacknowledged ground for scientific objectivity. In response to the second charge, that Merleau-Ponty's position is the unfortunate vestige of a philosophy of consciousness, we noted that his denial of any pure in-itself rests on an understanding of the world as emerging through perceptual exchange rather than as derivative from consciousness. Every ontology therefore presupposes a transcendental earth that does not move and a transcendental sun that does not age; every ontology, in other words, presupposes elementals. Finally, we considered the most challenging objection, namely, that phenomenology's correlationism rules out any encounter with ancestral time. This objection truly brings us to the heart of the matter, that is, to whether phenomenology can genuinely claim to open an encounter with nature that is distinct from and more fundamental than naturalism.

Our response to this objection has two moments. The first is that the ancestral past is indeed meaningful within our lived, prescientific experience of time—and, furthermore, that the deep evolutionary, geological, and cosmic dimensions of the past gain their true sense *only* in relation to experience. Speculative realism effectively flattens time while claiming to deepen it, which is a strategy that it shares with garden-variety naturalism. The consequence of this first point is that phenomenology, far from ruling out an encounter with the ancestral path, is the only fruitful method for investigating it. This anticipates the second point in response to the charge of correlationism, which is that phenomenology has never been content with correlationism in Meillassoux's sense. According to Meillassoux, the "paradox of the arche-fossil" is expressed by the question "how can a being manifest being's anteriority to manifestation?" (AF 37/26). On his view, correlationism cannot take such a question seriously, because it is inherently contradictory: "being *is not* anterior to givenness, it *gives itself* as anterior to givenness" (AF 32/14). And yet, far from dismissing the anteriority of the world as self-contradictory or as a mere illusion, phenomenology has doggedly pursued it precisely by embracing the contradiction as constitutive of our experience of the world. As Merleau-Ponty puts it, there is a significant distinction between "the sterile non-contradiction of formal logic" (Merleau-Ponty 1947, 126) and "the justified contradictions of transcendental logic" (Merleau-Ponty 2007, 95), that is, the contradictions that are constitutive of the perceived world. Our task as phenomenologists is precisely not to resolve or dismiss such contradictions but to recognize in them an encounter with what strains the very limits of conceptual elucidation, with what can be encountered only through experience even as it outstrips that very experience. Such encounters with what is constitutive of experience while haunting it from the margins of sense have in fact been phenomenology's perennial concern, and the past that we encounter embodied in the fossil is just such a transcendental contradiction, the paradoxical character of which is what marks it precisely *as* the elemental past.

We return, then, to the question of how this elemental past, as a past prior to all manifestation, is sketched out in our very being and in the being of the world. Even though Merleau-Ponty never thematizes this question in our terms, several of his analyses nevertheless provide us with crucial hints. The first can be drawn from the gestalt ontology of his first book, *The Structure of Behavior*, where matter, life, and mind are described as a nested hierarchy of gestalts that compose reality. Life is emergent from matter, and mind from life, in an ontologically continuous manner, each new level reorganizing its antecedents and yet carrying them along like the residue of its own crystallized history. Human consciousness takes up and reconfigures organic life on its own terms, just as organic life animates the matter of which it is composed. But this hierarchical emergence is never complete and never without remainder, so that consciousness always finds trailing in its wake the inertia of those subordinated gestalts that lend it substance. Our bodies continue to lead lives of their own that reflection can never equal, and at moments even our materiality can exercise its own resistance to our projects as an index of its autonomy. The clue here concerns the interpretation of the relationship between these gestalts in terms of time, because organic life is the forgotten past of consciousness, a past that we never cease to carry within our own substance, while our materiality is our liability to the forgotten past of the elements themselves. As Merleau-Ponty puts it, for the gestalts of life and mind, "there is no past which is absolutely past. . . . Higher behavior retains the subordinated dialectics in the present depths of its existence, from that of the physical system and its topographical conditions to that of the organism and its 'milieu'" (224/207–8). In other words, there is truly no moment of cosmic or geological history, however remote, that is not still borne by our own material bodies and by consciousness itself. Furthermore, to be embodied is precisely to remain indebted to this prehistory, because our own materiality is never merely an object for us but instead "a presence to consciousness of its proper history and of the dialectical stages which it has traversed" (225/208; see Toadvine 2009, chap. 1).

Through this lens, we can see that the many analyses of the "anonymity" of the body that Merleau-Ponty develops in his sequel, *Phenomenology of Perception,* continue this concern with our liability to a forgotten past, now more precisely at the level of organic life. As we saw in chapter 1, the "someone" within me who is the agent of my sensing body, and who is distinct from the personal self of my reflective consciousness, lives in a "prehistory," the "past of all pasts," which is the time of our organic rhythms (287/250, 302/265, 114/87). Merleau-Ponty refers to this cyclical time as "the time of nature with which we coexist," an "absolute past of nature" incommensurate with the narrative, linear time of the personal self (517/479, 171/139). If we understand the phrase "elemental past" to refer broadly to this "absolute past of nature," then one of its dimensions is our own biological life, our animality, insofar as this is lived as an anonymous and immemorial past in relation to the narrative history of our personal lives.[6] Because this past is anterior to the distinction between subject and object, or between human and nonhuman, anonymous sensibility cannot be a conscious experience; it cannot occur within personal time, the time of reflection, insofar as it makes such time possible. Sensibility as an organic inheritance is therefore the generative ground of experience, even as it remains for each of us, in our reflective lives, a past that has never been present.[7] As Gary Madison (1981, 158–59) has already noted,

Merleau-Ponty's descriptions here locate a "prehistory" at the heart of personal and reflective existence. The sensibility, sedimented habits, and organic rhythms of our bodies offer the most proximal and constant encounter with the immemorial past—by which I mean an anonymous and asubjective prehistory that haunts and conditions my present, without this past ever having been present for me. And yet this organic time of the body does not exhaust the dimensions of the immemorial past. In sensibility, I not only reenact my own animality but I also, through my participation in the elementality of things, take up at the heart of my existence the entire history of the universe. The phenomenological encounter with the vertigo of deep time, of which I catch a glimpse in the fossil, is the echo within my body of an asubjective time of matter, of an unfathomably ancient passage that haunts the heart of the present. Beyond organic time, we encounter that dimension of our existence that resonates with the pulsation of the geological and the cosmic, that is, with elemental time in its broadest registers. Recall Bataille's insight that talk of the sun prior to human beings is "mentally disturbing, unbalancing—an object independent of any subject." It is not the violation of logic that makes this claim unbalancing but indeed the dissolution of subjectivity into the worldlessness of the elemental.

Our best guide for such an encounter with the elemental remains Levinas's *Existence and Existents,* in which he describes how "the anonymous current of being invades, submerges every subject, person or thing" (94/52). What is left after the world has come to an end, after the dissolution of the world into the elemental *there is . . . ,* is not pure nothingness but also no longer this or that, no longer something. As Levinas writes,

> this universal absence is in its turn presence, an absolutely unavoidable presence. It is not the dialectical counterpart of absence, and we do not grasp it through a thought. It is immediately there. There is no discourse. Nothing responds to us but this silence; the voice of this silence is understood and frightens like the silence of those infinite spaces Pascal speaks of. *There is,* in general, without it mattering what there is, without our being able to fix a substantive to this term. *There is* is an impersonal form, like in it rains, or it is warm. . . . The mind does not find

itself faced with an apprehended exterior. The exterior—if one insists on this term—remains uncorrelated with an interior. It is no longer given. It is no longer a world. (94–95/52–53)

The vertigo of deep time has its source in the disruption of any correlation between self and world, in the impersonal worldlessness of the elements. And here the anonymity of the elemental bends around time; it is both the prehistoric, ancestral past and the eternity of an unimaginable future. The "eternal silence" of "infinite spaces" invoked by Pascal concerns the "eternity that lies before and after" the short duration of our lives, that "infinite immensity" of time that engulfs us while we remain ignorant of it—and it of us (Pascal 2004, 64, 22). This mirroring of a past and a future without us is also recognized, as we have mentioned, by Meillassoux, for whom the *ulteriority* of human extinction poses the same problems as the *anteriority* of the ancestral past, requiring us to consider the meaningfulness, on his example, of "hypotheses about the climatic and geological consequences of a meteor impact extinguishing all life on earth" (AF 155–56/112). In short, the time before the world is inseparable from, perhaps indistinguishable from, the time after the world's dissolution. If, along one dimension, we are beings-toward-death, then along another—anonymous and asubjective—dimension, we are beings-toward-the-end-of-the-world, already hearkening to the eternity of silence that waits to swallow all that we are and know and can imagine. "World-withdrawal and world-decay can never be undone," Heidegger (1977, 26; 1993, 166) reminds us; and, we might add, neither can they be deferred. The apocalyptic imagination that obsesses contemporary culture is not a *consequence* of our technological domination of the planet and ourselves, therefore, but is made possible only by the revelation within our hearts of an impossible future that outstrips every imagination.[8] To truly encounter the very materiality of our own minds and bodies is to fall into the abyss of such elemental time, which means to rediscover it as the kernel of organic and personal time. We do not need science to first encounter such a time, as it constantly haunts us; it is one of the ways that our subjectivity is caught up in the cosmic pulse of nature. Furthermore, to be caught up in the confluence of the immemorial past and future—in its cosmic, geological, evolutionary, and organic trajectories, each with its own rhythm and duration—is to endure the incommensurability of these durations and so to find oneself never simply self-present but always untimely. In this respect, we are like the fossil, caught up in the fault line between temporal flows, unable to hold our world open or to let it close.

Perhaps this is why the fascination with fossils is not limited to our particular epoch, as has become apparent to paleoanthropologists just over the last few decades. Several specimens of Lower Paleolithic Acheulian hand axes produced some four hundred thousand years ago by *H. heidelbergensis* feature fossilized bivalves or sea urchins. These hand axes were the first bilaterally symmetrical human tools, and in each case, the implement was painstakingly crafted so that the fossil would be symmetrically centered. *H. heidelbergensis* is currently thought to be the last common ancestor of *H. neanderthalensus* and *H. sapiens,* and our Neanderthal cousins alongside our own ancient forebears collected fossils in abundance—scallops, brachiopods, ammonites, trilobites, crinoids, and corals—which they carved into tools, perforated for threading onto necklaces, or engraved with human faces. One of the few artifacts discovered at Lascaux was a fossilized gastropod shell with a carefully sawed slit for threading. Yet it is the petrified sea urchin, circle shaped and with a distinctive five-pointed star, that has received the greatest interest over these hundreds of thousands of years and across much of the world. Kenneth McNamara goes so far as to suggest that the ubiquity of the stylized five-pointed star in current culture may be a consequence of our long coevolution with these fossils, which were its original template and came to be associated with the stars of the heavens only through our ancestors' imaginations.[9] Earth and sky, elementals bound together in the figure of the fossil. Furthermore, from the time of the Cro-Magnons until just a few thousand years ago, these fossil sea urchins were commonly buried with the dead, sometimes singly, sometimes in quantities that number in the hundreds or even the thousands. In a world that both invites us and remains closed to us, our ancestors contemplated a world that both invited and refused them, linking in their own imaginations the incomprehensible past with the impossible future.

The sea where this fossilized creature once lived its life, the world where our ancestors once lined the graves of their dead with fossils, the future of those generations to come after we have long since passed into dust, all these we can greet only in the eternal silence of Pascal's infinite spaces. In a famous working note in *The Visible and the Invisible* from February 1959, Merleau-Ponty makes allusion to "Sigē the abyss" (233/179). Sigē was the Gnostic goddess of silence—the silence that precedes the world and that welcomes it at its end. Merleau-Ponty borrows this reference again from Claudel, who concludes his investigation of time in *Poetic Art* with these words:

> Time is the means offered to all that which will be to be, in order to be no more. It is the *Invitation to Death* extended to each sentence, to decay in the explanatory and total harmony, to consummate the word of adoration, whispered in the ear of Sigē, the Abyss. (7/35)

3

Recursive Reflection and the Music of Nature

In chapter 1, drawing on Claudel and Whitehead, we described the *poiesis* of natural time as the generative difference by which each moment calls for its harmonic complement as sketched out by the world's total memory. But when we considered, in chapter 2, the implications of our entanglement in multiple and incompossible durations at incomprehensible scales, we discovered that this figure of total harmony effaces the resistance and silence of the elemental past, precisely what makes the deep past abyssal. Our investigation into asubjective time has thus rekindled two of the oldest and most profound insights into nature. The first insight, following the famous aphorism of Heraclitus, is that "nature loves to hide." Pierre Hadot (2006) has shown how a series of interpretations (and, in his view, misinterpretations) of this aphorism has been decisive for Western philosophy's approach to nature. Phenomenology has disclosed nature's self-concealment precisely through its attention to our everyday encounters with its autonomous resistance. We should recall in this context Heidegger's (1977, 33, 9; 1993, 172, 150) descriptions, in "The Origin of the Work of Art," of the "essentially undisclosable" withdrawal of the earth, which grants to natural things their "independent and self-contained" character, or again, Merleau-Ponty's descriptions, in *Phenomenology of Perception,* of the "non-human" aspect that lies hidden in things and gives them a "hostile and foreign" otherness that our everyday perceptions cover over (378/336). Simon James (2009) draws on such descriptions to respond to the charge that phenomenology is incapable of encountering nature on its own terms, *real* nature, because phenomenology necessarily takes its departure from nature *as experienced.* One of phenomenology's "great virtues," according to James (2009, 128), is its potential, in contrast with environmental realism, to show "what it means to perceive, in an immediate and visceral way, the independent reality of the natural world." In other words, nature announces its autonomy precisely through its self-concealment, and phenomenology is in a privileged position to disclose this very *resistance to* disclosure.

The second ancient insight into nature that our descriptions have rejuvenated would seem to be in tension with this experience of nature's resistant autonomy. This second insight is that nature, as a temporal *poiesis*, is fundamentally musical, or even that it *is* music. If this idea seems quaint today, this is perhaps because we are quick to equate music with patterned waves of air pressure. Yet the link between nature and music has a complex history that is just as subject to reinterpretation in the light of changing conceptions of its terms. From the Pythagoreans—who, Aristotle reports, held "the whole heaven to be a musical scale and a number" (*Metaphysics* I.5)—to Boethius and Kepler, the most influential versions of this thesis have been variants of *musica universalis,* the positing of harmonious proportions in the movements of celestial bodies. Because these proportions paralleled musical intervals, celestial movements were considered musical in a more fundamental sense than mere audible sounds. As the seventh-century encyclopedist St. Isidore of Seville summarized it, "without Music, there could be no perfect knowledge, for there is nothing without it. For even the universe is said to have been put together with a certain harmony of sounds, and the very heavens revolve under the guidance of harmony" (cited in Crosby 1997, 140). This characterization of the cosmos as musical goes beyond mere metaphor, because worldly, audible music is here taken as a derivative imitation of the cosmic harmony. Claudel's references to the total harmony of the poetic unfurling of natural time echo this traditional notion of universal music. Structural parallels between music and nature need not be understood in terms of cosmic harmony, however, even if they are relationally and temporally isomorphic. For instance, Jeremy Leach and John Fitch (1995), scholars of algorithmic composition, posit a common event structure of music and nature based on the fractal distributions of their temporal changes.

Just as phenomenology has rediscovered, on its own terms, a sense of the withdrawal of nature, so it has also given new meaning to the notion of *musica universalis*, now inspired by ecological relationships, the "melodies" of organic behaviors in "counterpoint" with their environments, rather than the harmonies of celestial motions. Phenomenologists first uncovered the link between life and music through the contribution of gestalt theorists like Kurt Koffka and Wolfgang Köhler, for whom melody serves as a privileged example of a temporal gestalt.[1] Inspired by Köhler's descriptions of chimpanzee behavior as "melodic," for example, Merleau-Ponty relies on the figure of melody to describe the unity and form of organic life in *The Structure of Behavior*, often referring to the organism's dialectical relation with its environment as a "melodic development" or a "kinetic melody."[2] The description of organic behavior as melodic is also a regular theme in the writings of Estonian ethologist Jakob von Uexküll, whose work has been influential on phenomenology and inspired the development of biosemiotics and posthumanism.[3] For Uexküll, nature is fundamentally composed of meanings that emerge in the exchange between organisms and their *Umwelten*, their environments, and this process can be literally described as a kind of music making in which contrapuntal meanings replace sonic harmonies (FW 144–45/188–89). Uexküll's version of *musica universalis* is therefore the intricately composed score of meanings constituting the interlocking environments of all living things—amounting, in Giorgio Agamben's estimation, to a "radical dehumanization of the image of nature." As Agamben writes,

> where classical science saw a single world that comprised within it all living species hierarchically ordered from the most elementary forms up to the higher organisms, Uexküll instead supposes an infinite variety of perceptual worlds that, though they are uncommunicating and reciprocally exclusive, are all equally perfect and linked together as if in a gigantic musical score. (O 45/40)

Although Uexküll himself was not a phenomenologist—he describes his own philosophical approach, not unproblematically, in Kantian terms—his influence on key figures in the phenomenological tradition is well known. Heidegger, in his 1929–30 lectures *The Fundamental Concepts of Metaphysics*, had already singled out Uexküll's studies as "the most fruitful thing that philosophy can adopt from the biology dominant today" (383/263; cited at O 54/51).

And Merleau-Ponty, again in *The Structure of Behavior,* already quotes Uexküll's famous line that "every organism is a melody which sings itself" (172/159).[4]

Yet I have already suggested that a tension exists between these two ancient ideas about nature—first, that nature loves to hide, as manifest in its resistance to and withdrawal from reflection, and second, that nature is a kind of all-encompassing symphony of ecological niches, perpetually singing itself into existence through the meaning-making activity of organic life. If both of these claims concern one and the same nature, and if both have a genuine foundation in experience as phenomenologically described, then what is their relation? More precisely, how can the music of nature, if this is more than a mere metaphor, be the event both of nature's disclosure and of its withdrawal? As suggested by our investigation thus far, our guiding clue will be the temporality of nature understood through the figure of the memory of the world, approached here through the perspective of organic, evolutionary time. To pursue these questions, I first trace the development of the role of musical structures in Merleau-Ponty's ontology, in conversation with Uexküll, to examine critically the resources that they offer for thinking nature's musicality together with its withdrawal. Here we see that, while his first work, *The Structure of Behavior,* relies on musical structures to propose an architectonic of gestalts as ontologically fundamental, it only tacitly accounts for nature's propensity to hide. Merleau-Ponty's sequel, *Phenomenology of Perception,* deepens his investigation of the immemorial past that haunts reflection from within. Each of Merleau-Ponty's first two books, then, foregrounds only one of nature's dual aspects, its musicality or its secrecy, yet without illuminating the relation between these faces of nature or the principle of its dehiscence. We will see that such a principle begins to emerge from Merleau-Ponty's late ontology of nature. There he once again privileges such musical structures as Uexküll's "animal melody" and Vinteuil's "little phrase," while also emphasizing the *écart* of the world's flesh, as the moment of absence that forms reflection's hinge. These later hints toward a new *musica universalis* are challenged, however, by Merleau-Ponty's own apparent denial, in *Eye and Mind,* of the ontological import of music (14/353). Taking up Lévi-Strauss's critique of Merleau-Ponty on this point, we find a moment of alteraffection in Merleau-Ponty's account of the reflexivity of voice and hearing, revealing a debt of the sonorous to a fundamental silence. We propose that this fundamental silence marks the time of the world's withdrawal while also opening the horizon of cultural expression and philosophical reflection.

Gestalt Ontology as *Musica Universalis*

The ontology that Merleau-Ponty develops in his first book, *The Structure of Behavior,* is fundamentally a form of *musica universalis* insofar as its fundamental components—perceived gestalts—and the culminating integration of these gestalts in human consciousness are characterized in musical terms. Yet the limitation of this musical ontology, to which Merleau-Ponty himself alludes in his conclusion, is that it grants too little to the secrecy of memory, that is, to the historical remainder at the heart of every gestalt, a remainder that makes their integration fragile and incomplete. The integration of gestalts, as the enfolding of this irrecuperable memory, already guarantees a secret dimension of withdrawal or suspension that remains inaccessible to the "outside spectator" from whose perspective these descriptions are carried out. It is precisely in disclosing this inaccessible dimension that Merleau-Ponty's first work clears the way for the analysis of *Phenomenology of Perception,* where nature's secrecy may be approached from within, that is, from the event of originary perception. To trace the moment of nature's secrecy within the ontology of gestalts, let us first consider how this ontology develops as a *musica universalis* that is comparable to yet distinct from that of Uexküll.

The Structure of Behavior is unique among Merleau-Ponty's writings for its attempt to construct an ontology within which the fundamental components are gestalts—meaningful wholes at the physical, vital, and mental levels, each of which incorporates and transcends the levels that precede and condition it. The sensible unity of these gestalts is repeatedly described as melodic, even at the physical level (148/137), although more often at the level of life. In a phrase that sounds remarkably Uexküllian, Merleau-Ponty writes that "the world, in those of its sectors which realize a structure, is comparable to a symphony" (142/132). Although Merleau-Ponty extends this symphony further than Uexküll by locating melodic anticipations already at the purely physical level, it is once again at the level of life that this figure takes center stage, particularly in the organism's melodic exchange with its environment, and here we can measure the distinctiveness of Merleau-Ponty's position vis-à-vis that of Uexküll.

First, for Merleau-Ponty, a melody, like a life, consists of a unified flow of discontinuous events, structured by its "distribution of intensities and intervals, the choice of notes and the determination of their order of succession" (SB 94/85). It is from this discontinuous distribution of rhythms and intensities that one moment stands out from the next, that developments and denouements are composed, and that meaning or significance emerges. In an important sense, then, both nature and melody depend on constitutive gaps or silences.

Second, the temporality of melody, as of organic behavior, has a hologrammatic character, insofar as the first note already anticipates and contains the last. A note is heard as the note that it is, in a particular key, only within the context of an entire musical phrase, so that changing any single note also reorders the remaining notes within the phrase as a whole. The time of the melody or of a lived moment is not serial, then, but consists of mutually enfolded durations that occupy their place only by internalizing their interwoven relationships.[5]

Third, organic behavior parallels melody in that both are oriented toward a norm, toward a significance or value that emerges in counterpoint with the environment. Uexküll shows that each organism extracts, through its capacities for perception and action, those signs that it will find meaningful and that will constitute its specific environment. Although Merleau-Ponty takes a similar approach, his innovation rests in recognizing that the organism does not mechanically follow a plan laid out by Nature, Uexküll's master composer. Instead, he argues that the organism is oriented toward its individual goals, toward what it finds attractive and away from what it finds repulsive, and its pursuit of these aims may be consummated or thwarted. Therefore the organism does not simply occupy a specific environmental niche but is polarized toward what its species-specific norms make salient. So, Merleau-Ponty says, we can speak of a "species a priori," a melody that, however individually interpreted, constrains what can have value for a particular form of life (see, e.g., SB 110/100, 134/123, 139/129). And just as a musician following a score may play well or badly, the organism's behavior may accord better or worse with the theme it finds itself constrained to play.

Fourth, like a melody, the style of an organic behavior is transposable; it can shift to a different key or a different register, play itself out in different actions or on different organs, and be taken up by a different organism or a different species altogether. Uexküll recognizes one level of this transposition when he describes the counterpoint between the spider's web and the fly, influential on Deleuze and Guattari's account of nonfilial becomings and involutions (FW 21/63, 120–22/158–60; ATP 386/314). Yet, for Uexküll, the perception-marks and effect-marks of a species are tied to a functional cycle that rules out repetition of the same meaningful melody on variant registers. Merleau-Ponty draws on the experimental work of Köhler and others to show that the same meaningful behavior can be played out differently by the same animal at different times, or by different animals of the same species, as well as across species. Styles of behavior can be shared, imitated, appropriated, or reinterpreted in different keys. This possibility, as we will see, holds special significance for Merleau-Ponty's understanding of the relation between human and nonhuman behavior.

More generally, what distinguishes Merleau-Ponty's appropriation of the figure of melody from that of Uexküll is that Merleau-Ponty understands the organism's dialectic with its *Umwelt* as a gestalt. While Uexküll appreciates that the functional cycle between perception and effect is a relation of meaning rather than of causality, he continues to think of the stimulus and the response as correlated in a one-to-one fashion, so that we can imagine the world of, say, the tick as an additive assemblage of perception-marks and effect-marks. But for Merleau-Ponty, neither "stimulus" nor "response" can be extracted from their contextual configurations, because the melodic line of behavior, encompassing organism and environment, is a nondecomposable whole. Furthermore, whereas reality, for Uexküll, is the all-encompassing musical score, the assemblage of all the songs sung by each kind of organic behavior, this reality does not form a unified whole, a gestalt—at least, not for us or for any other living thing. This is because, according to Uexküll's well-known expression, each organism is trapped within its *Umwelt* as in a soap bubble, a monad that has no possibility for direct communication with any other. What unites these monads is the unfathomable "plan" of Nature, who, as the master composer, is "inaccessible to all environments forever" (FW 102/135).

Let us note, in passing, that this is how Uexküll reconciles nature's propensity to hide with its musical disclosure, precisely by juxtaposing the many worlds of melodic appearance with a noumenal nature-in-itself: "forever unknowable behind all of the worlds it produces, the subject—Nature—conceals itself" (FW 102/135). So, when Uexküll describes the environment of each organism by contrasting this with the organism's objective "surroundings" *(Umgebung)*, in fact this turns out to be a contrast between its soap bubble and our own human bubble, the latter being inescapably structured according to our own species-specific spatial and temporal distributions and our own categories in a quasi-Kantian sense. In short, we are just as trapped in the bubble of our own *Umwelt* as are all other living things, even if we conflate our human perspective with "objective" reality. Of course, this suggests any number of methodological difficulties for Uexküll's own efforts to interpret or reconstruct the environments of nonhuman organisms, insofar as these efforts themselves are reliant on purportedly objective empirical data.

Turning back to Merleau-Ponty, we can see his gestalt-interpretation of organic behavior as an effort to avoid these difficulties. For Merleau-Ponty, the *Umwelten* of organisms do not exhaust the gestalt structures of reality. Living behavior integrates within itself the lower-order gestalts of physical reality, and it may, in turn, be integrated into the more complex gestalts of symbolic behavior that define the specifically human openness to the virtual. In other words, Merleau-Ponty's position is that, while gestalts are ontologically basic, they are not limited to the "soap bubbles" of the many diverse *Umwelten.* Instead, the many melodies of life integrate themselves by a process of iteration or self-referentiality. This opens the possibility, Merleau-Ponty argues, for encountering the one, common universe beyond the self-enclosed bubble of any species-specific environment.

As Merleau-Ponty describes it, this shift from many environments to one universe is made possible by the integration of organic behavior into the more complex structure of symbolic thought. The transition from the organic to the symbolic is effected by a shift of focus toward the structure of structures as such. Merleau-Ponty explains this transition in musical terms and, more specifically, as a transposition of musical structure. As we have noted, a certain level of transposition is possible already at the organic level, as when two distinct behaviors have the same vital meaning. But this only transposes a melody from one behavioral embodiment to another. When the structure of a structure, the essence of a melody, is extracted so that it can be transposed into entirely different expressive mediums, a virtual level of behavior becomes possible. Merleau-Ponty's own example is the ability to play a musical instrument, which involves transposing a single melody from its written form on the score to a series of kinaesthetic movements to a pattern on the keyboard to an audible distribution of notes (SB 131–32/120–21). Through these transpositions, the very structure, the musical essence, of the melody animates entirely different bodies.

It is this capacity to extract such essences, the structures of structures, and to transpose them into different expressive forms that defines symbolic behavior for Merleau-Ponty (SB 133/122). Symbolic behavior is a kind of melody in its own right that sings the distilled essence of other melodies in a recursively nested structure. This recursive melody opens us onto the virtual because it allows us to transpose structures in unlimited ways: to locate ourselves on a map or to create tools with open-ended uses or to spontaneously improvise on a musical instrument. In short, while the melody of the nonhuman organism is constrained by the norms of its species, the human is defined by its capacity "of going beyond created structures in order to create others" (SB 189/175). It is this ability to break with the constraints of our organic norms that allows us to treat our own bodies as one thing among many, to adopt a disinterested perspective, and therefore to describe the universe in objective terms.

This shift into the symbolic is presented by Merleau-Ponty as a further stage in the integration of the forms that constitute reality. Just as life introduces a level of structural complexity that incorporates physical matter while going beyond it, so does symbolic thought integrate within itself both matter and life. Nature, therefore, consists of a hierarchy of nested gestalts of ever-increasing complexity, and we can conceive of this complex structure as a symphony of nested melodies. Symbolic thought, as a recursive melody of melodies, is the perspective from which this symphony is comprehended.

Despite the elegance of this musical ontology, it leaves us with two difficulties. First, part of what attracts Merleau-Ponty to the figure of melody is that it is irreducible to physical explanation. A melody is not a thing but rather a meaning, that is, a perceived reality. This is true of gestalts more generally (SB 97/88, 156–57/144–45, 207–8/192–93), so that Merleau-Ponty's account of nature as a hierarchy of nested gestalts has an ambiguous ontological status. On one hand, that gestalts are essentially perceptual is exactly the point that Merleau-Ponty wishes to press against naturalism, including the naturalistic biases of the gestalt theorists themselves, who in the end always try to translate the higher levels of structure into physicalist terms (SB 142–47/132–37; cf. PP 73–4/48). But, on the other hand, what does it mean to describe the fundamental elements of reality as "perceptual"? Does it mean that they are ultimately correlates of subjectivity, so that nature is in the end to be reinterpreted as "consciousness of" nature? Certain of Merleau-Ponty's formulations in *The Structure of Behavior* seem to point in this direction.[6] As Renaud Barbaras (2001, 37) compellingly argues, it is only in Merleau-Ponty's later work that he is willing to embrace the possibility that being is fundamentally perceptual without reference to a subject that would perceive it. To the extent that our symphony of melodies is ultimately the noema of some subjective intending, melody would not provide nature's ultimate ontological foundation. But if we embrace the perceptual quality of being without a subject, then subjectivity can be an emergent property of the symphony itself, just as Merleau-Ponty's account of symbolic thought as recursive melody suggests.

A second and related difficulty concerns the integration of matter and life into spirit or mind, which would suggest that mind—albeit an emergent and immanent mind—is the telos of nature's musical development. Merleau-Ponty does recognize that the hierarchical integration of gestalts is a historical, contingent, and never fully realized process. When physical matter takes on the new structure that transforms it into a living body, the physical matter, even though integrated into a more complex whole, retains its historical density and inertia—that is, its *memory*. This means that every integration is partial and fragile, obtaining only in degrees and constantly subject to fragmentation. As Merleau-Ponty admits, "there is always a duality which reappears at one level or another," because "integration is never absolute and it always fails" (SB 226/210). In other words, while Merleau-Ponty will claim that the human being integrates its own biological life into a higher and more complex unity, so that, in his words, "'life' does not have the same meaning in animality and humanity" (SB 188/174) and, furthermore, that "Man can never be an animal: his life is always more or less integrated than that of an animal" (SB 196/181), it remains the case that our biological life can and does assert its own autonomous rights (SB 224–26/208–10). Because integration proceeds historically, our more or less composed human selves carry with them, in kernel, the sedimented stages through which we have passed, so that, even to the extent that we do sublimate our animal natures, we remain perennially liable to them.[7]

We can illustrate this by returning to the figure of melody. If the melody of life integrates the melody of matter, and mind consists of a recursive expression of such melodies, then at every stage of integration, there is a condensation of the entire history of lines of song into denser phrasings. This follows from Merleau-Ponty's recognition that physical gestalts bear within themselves a reference to the entire history of the universe as their emergent condition (SB 150–55/139–43), while, at the vital level, the contrapuntal melody of every organism folds into itself, as an organic memory, its entire evolutionary history. Every phrase and every note of each organic melody is therefore rich with the micromelodies of this accumulated history, an immemorial past that could never be entirely unfolded.

Think of the phrase of a melody as having a structure like Mandelbrot's fractal coastline such that, as you approach it more closely, you find the same degree of intricately enfolded structure at every scale. Furthermore, because each integration and transposition is only partial, the synthesis by which the past is folded into the present will always be selective and creative, that is, expressive: it will simplify along one dimension, creatively improvise along another, and leave remainders throughout. So the fact that integration always fails at one point or another is just the obverse of the fact that this symphony of gestalts is incessantly re-creating its past as well as itself, carrying along its immemorial history while constantly recomposing it. And it is precisely within this ongoing folding of the entire history of nature's symphony into the very next line of every behavioral melody—and the iterative turn by which one melody symbolically expresses this process of becoming as such—that we can locate the moment of nature's self-concealment. Nature's secret withdrawal is precisely the immemorial past enfolded within the phrases and intervals of its interwoven melodic lines.

Immemorial Nature as Chiasmic Remainder

By characterizing nature's withdrawal in terms of the immemorial past carried within the heart of every gestalt, we have certainly gone beyond Merleau-Ponty's own position in *The Structure of Behavior*, even if we have done so following his own clues, especially his admission that lower-order gestalts persist as a kind of internalized history that demands its due, a memory of matter that haunts life and a memory of life that haunts spirit. In his concluding remarks in *Structure*, as he sketches out the "problem of perception" that will occupy his sequel, Merleau-Ponty admits that the standpoint of his investigation thus far has not itself been situated within the matter investigated. In other words, the ontology of gestalts has been described "objectively," from the third-person perspective of an "outside spectator," rather than from the only theoretically consistent point of view—according to which the one who thinks is situated within the matter thought about and is consequently constrained by this situatedness.[8] By describing reflection as itself a recursive gestalt, so that we are, ultimately, gestalts thinking gestalts, Merleau-Ponty takes us a long way toward reinstating reflection within the nature from which it emerges. But in so doing, he also calls attention to reflection's liability to its own emergence, that is, to the challenge in principle of thinking nature from within it.

When Merleau-Ponty returns to this problem in *Phenomenology of Perception*, as we have already seen, it is posed in terms of reflection's relationship with the unreflective (see, e.g., 88–91/62–65, 258/221, 264/227, 341/302, 402/360, 417/376, 512/474). On one hand, reflection does not fail to make contact with the prereflective moment from which it opens, as our very ability to indicate and describe that prereflective moment attests. Yet, on the other hand, reflection never coincides with the prereflective or presents it transparently, because it necessarily transforms the structure of the prereflective in opening it to reflection. To define reflection properly, Merleau-Ponty argues, we must take this entire structure into account; as he puts it, we must "reflect upon this reflection" and thereby "understand the natural situation it is aware of replacing and that thereby belongs to its definition" (89/63). We have seen that what Merleau-Ponty calls "second-order" or "radical" reflection in *Phenomenology of Perception* is this effort of reflection to account for its own foundation in a nature from which it emerges but that remains for it an unthematizeable past, a past that "has never been present" (289/252). This immemorial past appears within our experience as the resistance that our prereflective lives and experiences offer to reflection, as the remainder that resists thematization even as it conditions reflection and makes it possible. It is our very inherence within nature, the fact that we can only open onto it from a situation within it, and consequently that we can never fully thematize our own emergence from it, that necessitates this immemorial remainder. In other words, nature in its primordial autonomy appears precisely as the resistance that the unreflective offers to reflection.[9] And thus we find ourselves back at the first ancient truth concerning nature, that it loves to hide, but now in such a way that the hidden depths of its withdrawal constitute the very act of philosophical reflection from within.

This brings us level with the difficulty posed at the outset of this chapter, that of the relation between Nature's musical structure and its hidden secrets. And now we can see that both accounts intersect at reflection's relationship with its own past, with the residue of nature that constitutes reflection from within. In *The Structure of Behavior,* reflection was posed as the recursive "structure of structures"; in *Phenomenology of Perception,* it becomes a second-order "reflection on reflection," and, in each version, the effort of thought to acknowledge its debt to its own unthinkable origins is at stake. Nature's resistance and autonomy is the very withdrawal that conditions reflection and first opens its possibility. As Merleau-Ponty increasingly appreciates nature's resistance to reflection, the language of reflection as a "structure of structures" vanishes. As we have seen, this is first replaced by another iterative structure, that of second-order reflection. But the structure of reflection, and particularly its interruption by an unreflected that exceeds it, undergoes a further transformation in Merleau-Ponty's later work, where reflection takes the autoaffection of the body as its exemplar.

Although Merleau-Ponty will still occasionally speak of gestalts in his later writings, there his favored figure for our fundamental relation of entanglement is "chiasm." In English, the term *chiasm* is a shortened form of two words with apparently distinct meanings, one biological (*chiasma* in both English and French) and one rhetorical (*chiasmus* in English, *chiasme* in French). Within physiology, a *chiasma* is the point where anatomical structures, such as nerves or ligaments, cross—where they form an X, a *chi*. In rhetoric, on the other hand, a *chiasmus* is a figure of speech formed by a repetition of structure in reverse order: "Beauty is truth, truth beauty" (Keats). Merleau-Ponty's use of the concept intentionally borrows from both of these meanings, joining together the reversal and circularity of the chiasmus ("there is a body of the mind and a mind of the body and a chiasm *[chiasme]* between them"; VI 313/259) and the unity-in-difference of the chiasma ("like the chiasm *[chiasma]* of the eyes, this one is also what makes us belong to the same world"; VI 268/215). Such chiastic structures come to replace gestalt wholes for Merleau-Ponty as the fundamental ontological reality so that now, rather than a hierarchy of nested gestalts, as we saw in *The Structure of Behavior,* Merleau-Ponty's last writings propose to us that the world is fundamentally a nested structure of chiasms. In the words of Renaud Barbaras (2004, 307), "it is necessary ... to picture the universe as intuited by Merleau-Ponty as a proliferation of chiasms that integrate themselves according to different levels of generality."

A paradigmatic example of chiasm, for Merleau-Ponty, is the sensible–sentient structure of the body as revealed through the experience of one hand touching another. Merleau-Ponty initially borrows this example from Husserl's *Ideas II*, according to which our tactile experience of touching an object reveals two distinct sensations. If my hand is lying on a table, for example, I experience sensations that present to me the qualities of the table (as cool, smooth, firm, and so on). By shifting my attention, I can instead experience these same sensations as the effect of the table upon my hand (as cooling, applying pressure, and so on). When I touch one hand with another, the experience becomes more complicated, because now I have two sensations, each of which is "apprehendable or experienceable in a double way" (147/154). This follows from the fact that, for the hand that is actively touching, the hand that is being touched is never presented merely as an object. If I touch my left hand with my right, for example, my right hand experiences sensations that are objectified as features of the thing "left hand." But, as Husserl continues,

> when I touch the left hand I also find in it, too, series of touch-sensations, which are *"localized"* in it, though these are not constitutive of properties (such as roughness or smoothness of the hand, of this physical thing). If I speak of the *physical* thing, "left hand," then I am abstracting from these sensations. . . . If I do include them, then it is not that the physical thing is now richer, but instead *it becomes Body, it senses.* (145/152)

When Merleau-Ponty takes up the body's relation of self-sensing or autoaffection in *The Visible and the Invisible,* he emphasizes three characteristics that are, for him, essential to chiasmic structure. First, the ability of the hand to touch requires that it have a place among those things that are touchable. More generally, to be sentient, the body must be sensible. The body's autoaffection therefore discloses an ontological continuity or kinship between the sentient and the sensible, a kinship that is disclosed by the moment where the touch crosses over from organ to object and back again. What is most significant about the example of the touch touching itself, for Merleau-Ponty, is not its autoaffection but this essential link between sentience and sensibility, which first opens the body to the world. Second, the relationship between the two hands touching is reversible, in the sense that the hands may exchange roles: when one is agent of the touch, the other slips into the role of object touched. But with a change of attention, the roles reverse. The chiasm is the crossover point of this reversal. As Husserl's description demonstrates, this reversibility between activity and passivity may already be experienced in the sensing of an inanimate thing, but the reversibility is intensified or doubled in the experiencing of one's own body. On Merleau-Ponty's interpretation, then, a kind of reversibility obtains between the sensing body and the world such that the things touch me as I touch them. Last, although the touching–touched relationship demonstrates an ontological kinship and reversibility, it is nevertheless also characterized by a gap or divergence *(écart)*. When one hand touches the other, and the role of toucher and touched reverses, the hand that is touching never quite manages to touch the touching that was happening, only a moment before, in the other hand. Consequently, the touch can never quite touch itself as touching but only as touched. The moment when the touch crosses over into the touched is the site of this divergence.

Now, it is significant for our thesis concerning nature's secrecy that Merleau-Ponty's account of the sensible–sentient chiasm of the body, which serves as the paradigmatic example of reflection, always leaves a remainder. The coincidence of one hand touching the other is "always immanent and never realized in fact" (VI 194/147). Here the moment of nature's withdrawal and secrecy is precisely the *écart* between the touching and the touched. In the ontology of the flesh, the hierarchy of gestalts falls over on its side; rather than vertical ascendance toward higher levels of integration, lateral resonances and transgressions multiply differences as well as convergences, and every moment of unity is possible only as the span of an absence that ultimately cannot be effaced. We can still speak of material, vital, and symbolic dimensions of flesh, although these are not levels of an orderly ascension so much as entanglements of varying complexity and depth along a profusion of axes and at multiple registers. I am suggesting that the *écart* of the touching–touched, the resistance of the unreflective to reflection, and the slippage in the integration of gestalts are all variations on nature's withdrawal, its presentation of its own unpresentability. In each case, reflection comes up against what cannot appear to it directly, what it can only encounter as a resistance at the limits of its compass. Such resistance is precisely nature's indirect disclosure of its autonomy. Clearly the logic of chiasm carries us well beyond any straightforward "correlation" of subject and world. Our question now becomes whether this universe of interwoven chiasms, along with reflection as their iteration, can leave to nature not only its mystery but also its melody—and its memory.

Silence between Nature and Culture

The question of the proper role of music in Merleau-Ponty's last writings has already been raised by his close personal friend, the anthropologist Claude Lévi-Strauss (2006), in his 1971 memorial essay for Merleau-Ponty. There Lévi-Strauss proposes that Merleau-Ponty's treatment of music in his last works reveals a decisive ambiguity in his thought. In particular, Lévi-Strauss argues that Merleau-Ponty's depreciation of music in favor of painting in *Eye and Mind*, where music is described as providing no more than an "outline" of Being, is contested by the nearly contemporaneous treatment of music—and of the "outlines" of Being—in *The Visible and the Invisible*, where Vinteuil's "little phrase," a fictional piece of music in Proust's *In Search of Lost Time*, becomes a privileged example of the incarnate idea. For Lévi-Strauss, this ambiguous treatment of music is full of significance, because it demonstrates the gap between the phenomenological and the ontological in Merleau-Ponty's final writings. That Lévi-Strauss would focus his attention on Merleau-Ponty's treatment of music is unsurprising, because the anthropologist had, in that same year, completed his fourth volume of the *Mythologiques,* his monumental treatment of Indigenous "mythology" which was dedicated "To Music" and which argued for a fundamental parallel between musical structures and the structures of myths.[10] On Lévi-Strauss's view, music bridges nature and culture because it combines the temporal rhythms of the body with the musical scales and conventional forms laid down by culture. As he puts it, music operates according to two "grids":

> One is physiological—that is, natural: its existence arises from the fact that music exploits organic rhythms and thus gives relevance to phenomena of discontinuity that would otherwise remain latent and submerged, as it were, in time. The other grid is cultural: it consists of a scale of musical sounds, of which the number and the intervals vary from one culture to another. (Lévi-Strauss 1983, 16)

The significance of this bridging between nature and culture is ultimately temporal, because both music and myth are "instruments for the obliteration of time" (16). As Lévi-Strauss sees it, this is the obliteration of the "irredeemably diachronic" time of the body in favor of the "synchronic totality" of the artwork, which gives it an aura of "immortality" (16).

But Merleau-Ponty understands the time of the body, which is the time of nature, quite differently than Lévi-Strauss. As we saw in chapter 1, *Phenomenology of Perception* describes the body as living an anonymous and cyclical time, the time of the heartbeat or of daily bodily rhythms. This general and repetitive time of the body's unity with nature can never be fully thematized by our reflective consciousness, which lives in historical, diachronic time. Therefore, for the reflective self, the time of the body and of nature is always an immemorial time. Each perception "confirms and renews in us a 'prehistory,'" an "absolute past of nature," that has never been lived through as our present (PP 287/250, 171/139, 289/252). The "immortality" of music is therefore not an escape from time altogether but is instead the withdrawal into the anonymous time of the body, the time of its rhythms. Lévi-Strauss (1983, 16) admits this when he writes about the "physiological and even visceral time" of music, according to which "any piece of counterpoint includes a silent part for the rhythmic movements of heart and lungs."

Lévi-Strauss's remark about an interruption for breathing, a "silent part" internal to musical expression, raises the question of the silence on which music depends. The pause for breathing becomes incorporated into the structure of the music, as part of its phrasing. Similarly, the silences between the notes are the aural equivalent of the blink of the eye, the gaps that distinguish the sonemes and allow their combination into musical phrases. The indirect, diacritical relations that such gaps make possible are a silence internal to music as such. In "Indirect Language and the Voices of Silence," Merleau-Ponty makes a similar point concerning the indirect relations that constitute a language. The signification of language does not occur primarily through direct representation, Merleau-Ponty (1960, 53–54; 2007, 244–45) argues, but rather "at the intersection of and as it were in the interval between words," that is, through "things left unsaid." Therefore, he concludes, "all language is indirect or allusive. . . . It is, if you like, silence." Similarly, he will say of the musical idea behind Vinteuil's "little phrase" that it is "veiled with shadows" or appears "under a disguise" precisely because it is not heard directly in the notes themselves but somehow between or behind them: "We do not see, do not hear the ideas, and not even with the mind's eye or the third ear: and yet they are there, behind the sounds or between them" (VI 198/151). In other words, the musical idea haunts the audible notes without itself being localized within them, as Merleau-Ponty will describe the visible as haunted by invisible significations.

Merleau-Ponty often describes the task of philosophy in terms of the famous quotation from Husserl's *Cartesian Meditations*: "it is 'that pure and, so to speak, still-mute experience that must be brought to the pure expression of its own sense'" (PP 264/228; cf. PP 15/lxxix; VI 171/129).[11] All expression, as a means of "singing the world," undertakes the task of giving voice to what the world, in its muteness, wants to say. In this sense, the silence of nature parallels its immemorial past as a kernel of resistance that inhabits every present expression. This is the second and more profound sense, beyond the constitutive silences of its diacritical structure, in which music harbors silence. The paradoxical task of philosophy, for Merleau-Ponty, is to express this primordial silence, all the while respecting its withdrawal *as* silence, which is why he will later define philosophy as the "reconversion of silence and speech into one another" (VI 171/129).[12] Yet we might still wonder, as does Lévi-Strauss, what role music should play in this reconversion. In other words, what is the proper role of music as revelatory of Being?

Merleau-Ponty's famous remarks dismissing music's significance for ontological investigation occur in the opening section of "Eye and Mind," the last essay published during his lifetime, which concerns the ontology of painting. This is not the first essay that Merleau-Ponty devotes to painting, of course, but he never writes at length about music—not, that is, with the detail that Lévi-Strauss devotes to Ravel's *Bolero* or Rameau's *Castor et Pollux*.[13] This is perhaps explained by the odd position that music occupies, in "Eye and Mind," in relation to the writer and philosopher, who, because they work in the medium of words, are expected to "take a stand" and "cannot waive the responsibilities of man who speaks" (EM 14/353). Music, Merleau-Ponty tells us, is "at the other extreme"; it is "too far on the hither side of the world and of the designatable to depict anything but certain sketches of Being—its ebb and flow, its growth, its upheavals, its turbulence" (EM 14/353). Painting, then, occupies the middle ground, as the painter "is entitled to gaze upon everything without being obliged to appraise what he sees" (EM 14/353). It is striking that Merleau-Ponty describes this continuum in ethical terms—responsibility, obligation, appraisal—and then situates music at an extreme beyond any ethical purchase. Whereas painting is privileged because of its ability to bracket the ethical, to describe without appraising, music's presentation of the world fails even to reach an ethical register. In light of this treatment of music, recall Merleau-Ponty's (2007, 290) famous promise, made a decade earlier, to formulate an ethics simultaneously with a metaphysics:

> There is a "good ambiguity" in the phenomenon of expression, a spontaneity . . . which gathers together the plurality of monads, the past and the present, nature and culture, into a single whole. To establish this wonder would be metaphysics itself and would at the same time give us the principle of an ethics.

Although music would seem to effect this bridging of nature and culture, bringing the immemorial past and the prereflective silence of nature to expression, it is apparently excluded from both the ontological and the ethical dimensions.

Yet Merleau-Ponty's description of the reflexivity of voice and hearing suggests a privilege for the sonorous chiasm in revealing the turning point between nature and culture: "like crystal, like metal and many other substances, I am a sonorous being, but I hear my own vibration from within; as Malraux said, I hear myself with my throat" (VI 190/144). The reflexivity of hearing one's own voice parallels the touching–touched or the seeing–seen. Likewise, there is an *écart*, an eclipse of coincidence, in the case of hearing as well as touching or seeing. Because I am always on this side of my body, my own voice is for me always heard primarily from within, never quite the same as it would be heard by others or theirs by me.[14] Yet there is a significant difference between the *écart* in the case of hearing and in those of touch or vision. In the latter cases, the experience of reflexivity is always immanent and never realized in fact: as long as one hand remains in the sensing role, the other cannot quite be caught as sensing, and the eyes never manage to catch their own seeing glance in the mirror. Thus, for touch or vision, the positions of sensing and sensed may reverse, but they never quite coincide (VI 194/147–48). When "I hear myself both from within and from without," it would seem that a genuine coincidence is achieved, because the subject of the voice and the object of the hearing are the same and simultaneously experienced as a sonorous whole (VI 194/148). Yet the very moment of such coincidence is a doubling that, more overtly than one hand palpating the other, includes a circuit through the world: I hear myself from within through the vibrations of my body, but I hear myself from without through the medium of the world. Thus my voice returns to me mingled with the voices of the world, undecidably both mine and other, in a kind of alter-affection. This anticipates an insight from Leonard Lawlor (2009a, 18) that "just as my present moment is always already old, my interior monologue is never my own."

Merleau-Ponty's description of the reflexivity of hearing focuses on language, but Lévi-Strauss already recognizes the privileged position of music in this regard: "when *I hear* music, *I listen to myself* through it. And, . . . by a reversal of the relationship between soul and body, music *lives itself* in me" (Lévi-Strauss 1976, 39). And for Merleau-Ponty, because speech is fundamentally a sonorous exchange between the body and world, "to understand a phrase is nothing else than to fully welcome it in its sonorous being, or, as we put it so well, to *hear what it says [l'entendre]*" (VI 203/155). Consequently, speech remains ultimately derivative from the sonorous, the musical, and carries meaning in the same fashion as the musical idea. As Merleau-Ponty (2001, 18) writes in a working note on music, "music [is] the model of signification—of this silence from which language is made. . . . Interpret every perception, all its *eloquence* in this silence."

Part II
ANIMALITY

4

Beyond Biologism
EVOLUTION AS ALTERAFFECTION

Our account of the memory of the world holds important implications for how we relate to the time of life: the organic rhythms of our bodies, our entangled temporal relations with other lives, and our implication in evolutionary durations both past and future. In chapter 2, we discussed the temporality of the fossil as a paradoxical crossing of the time of life with the endurance of rock. We find ourselves at the confluence of incommensurate durations that span cosmic, geological, organic, and evolutionary scales. Our own organic rhythms are the corporeal trace of the history of life, which is itself a pulse of the world's enduring memory. What does this memory teach us about the relationship between human beings and other forms of life? Does our shared evolutionary past establish a continuity or kinship with nonhuman life? In chapter 3, we considered the role of life within Merleau-Ponty's gestalt ontology, where it reconfigures physical form while preparing the iterative structure of the symbolic. There we emphasized the moment of silence and withdrawal that interrupts the traditional understanding of life. Rather than understanding life as *auto*affection, as self-contact or self-presence, we must instead think life as radical *alter*affection, as exposure to otherness. How might the memory of world clarify the role that this fundamental alteraffection plays in our relationship with nonhuman life, and with what implications for our entanglements in the unfolding evolution of life?

The evolutionary continuity of humans and nonhuman animals has gained the status of a shibboleth within recent research aimed at undermining our historically anthropocentric mind-set. "In recent years," as Matthew Calarco (2008, 3) notes, "traditional human–animal distinctions, which posit a radical discontinuity between animals and human beings, have been relentlessly attacked from multiple theoretical, political, and disciplinary perspectives." Darwinism in particular has "had the effect of undermining human–animal dichotomies in the name of gradualist continuism." After Darwin, we are told, it is undeniable that human beings, whatever our peculiar characteristics, are simply animals, one species among those many with which and from which we have evolved. This narrative, ubiquitous in popular culture as well as the academy, traces our domination of and alienation from nonhuman life to anthropocentrism, our tendency to treat ourselves as exceptional and different in kind from other living things. Aided by the capacities that this very process of evolution has bequeathed us—language, consciousness, technology, religion, culture, and so on—we now find ourselves out of joint in the natural world, alienated from our fellows, and struggling to reconcile ourselves with our proper place on earth. It is precisely this anthropocentrism, as a vestige of Platonism or Cartesianism, that environmental consciousness seeks to root out and expose to return us to our rightful place as, in the oft-quoted words of Aldo Leopold (1968, 204), "plain member and citizen" of the biotic community.

As a typical statement of this view, consider the remarks of environmental philosopher and Leopold commentator J. Baird Callicott (1998, 350), offered in critique of the "man–nature dichotomy" enshrined in the 1964 Wilderness Act:

> Since Darwin's *Origin of Species* and *Descent of Man* . . . we have known that man is a part of nature. We are only a species among species, one among twenty or thirty million natural kinds. . . .
> If man is a natural, a wild, an evolving species, not essentially different in this respect from all the others, as Gary Snyder reminds us, then the works of man, however precocious, are as natural as those of beavers, or termites, or any of the other species that dramatically modify their habitats.[1]

In this view, humans are simply one animal species among many, and the qualities and capacities that distinguish us from other living creatures are no more the basis for an elevated status than the equally distinctive capacities of beavers, flamingoes, or paramecia.[2] At any rate, our differences from other animals would be no more than a matter of degrees along a continuum, thanks to our shared evolutionary heritage. It is this argument that Calarco (2008, 63) endorses when he describes the "commitment to biological continuism we find in such thinkers as Darwin, Dawkins, and de Waal" as "an essential path for thought."

It is against the grain of such arguments that Jacques Derrida, in his posthumously published *The Animal That Therefore I Am*, provocatively affirms an "abyss" between the human and the animal:

> To suppose that I, or anyone else for that matter, could ignore that rupture, indeed that abyss, would mean first of all blinding oneself to so much contrary evidence. . . . I have thus never believed in some homogenous continuity between what calls *itself* man and what *he* calls the animal. I am not about to do so now. That would be worse than sleepwalking, it would simply be too asinine *[bête]*. (A 52/30)

The play on words at the end of this citation, *trop bête*—"too stupid," but literally "too beastly"—at first suggests that Derrida is mocking his own claim to deny any continuity. As he later clarifies, beastliness can truly be said only of the human being: "One can always speak of the *bêtise* of men, sometimes of their bestiality; there is no sense in speaking of the *bêtise* or bestiality of an animal *[bête]*, no right to do so" (A 93/64). In other words, if the proposal of continuity between humans and animals is *trop bête*, it thereby marks the very difference that it purports to deny.

This affirmation of an abyss and denial of continuity between humans and animals has been a key stumbling block in the reception of Derrida's text. Calarco (2008, 145) calls this "one of the most dogmatic and puzzling moments in all of his writings." Indeed, Calarco goes on to reject what he sees as a "false dilemma" motivating Derrida's insistence on the human–animal distinction: "either we think of human beings and animals as separated by a single indivisible line (classical philosophical discourse) or we efface the distinction between human and animal altogether and risk lapsing into a kind of reductive homogeneity (biologistic continuism)" (149). Calarco is not alone in raising such criticisms (see, e.g., Cavalieri 2009, 98–99; Wolfe 2009, 126–27). Even as sympathetic a commentator as David Wood (2004, 134) hesitates to follow Derrida's affirmation of an abyssal rupture between the human and the animal.

Set alongside the received interpretation of our evolutionary kinship, Derrida's remarks seem unexpectedly brusque and dismissive. When he returns later in the text to the question of human continuity with animals—introducing the term *animot*, which forces us to hear the plural term *animals* in the singular—it is to cut off any further consideration of the continuity position:

> This does not, of course, mean ignoring or effacing everything that separates humankind from the other animals, creating a single large set, a single grand, fundamentally homogenous and continuous family tree going from the *animot* to the *homo* (*faber*, *sapiens*, or whatever else). That would be an asinanity [*bêtise*], even more so to suspect anyone here of doing just that. I won't therefore devote another second to the double asinanity of that suspicion, even if, alas, it is quite widespread. (A 73/47–48)

Derrida's reference to a "family tree" calls to mind the phylogenetic or evolutionary tree used to depict relationships of descent and popularized by Darwin, whose *Origin of the Species* included one of the first such illustrations.[3] In fact, Derrida associates the continuity thesis with a "geneticism" or a "biologistic continuism" (A 52/30), suggesting that the effort to establish human–animal continuity on the basis of a shared biological or evolutionary heritage is precisely the target of his dismissal.

Yet Derrida's position is more complex than commentators like Calarco have appreciated. It can be read neither as a simple appropriation of the Heideggerian abyss between Man and Animal, as we will show later, nor as further evidence of "postmodern" skepticism concerning the objectivity and validity of the scientific enterprise. Derrida's denial of continuity between Man and Animal concerns not only the terms of this relation but, just as important, how we are to understand life in relation to autoaffection, immanence in relation to transcendence, and naturalism in relation to phenomenology. In other words, at stake in the denial of continuity is a more profound response to Platonism than that proposed by scientific accounts of evolution, a response that can be made only by carrying forward the legacy of transcendental philosophy. Here I develop this response in three steps. First, to unfold Derrida's rejection of "homogenous continuity" between humans and (other) animals, I clarify his association of this homogenization with a "biologistic continuism, whose sinister connotations we are well aware of"

(A 52/30). At stake in Derrida's approach is the very logic of the limits between the human and the animal, which must be confronted obliquely to destabilize the biologism–humanism alternative. This points us toward an abyssal logic that thickens and multiplies differences, eliminating any hierarchy between humans and animals while leaving a space for what Merleau-Ponty has called a "lateral overcoming." But this lateral overcoming cannot be understood in traditionally naturalistic or evolutionary terms. To do so would merely overturn Platonism rather than twisting free from it.

Second, I consider whether there are nonnaturalistic ways to understand the intimacy between humans and other animals, such as the bodily comportment and "strange kinship" that Kelly Oliver (2009) draws from her reading of Merleau-Ponty. Starting from the communicability of corporeal behaviors, Merleau-Ponty describes a kinship based on the reversible flesh of the world, thereby steering a course between biologism and humanism. This kinship remains strange, nevertheless, thanks to the ineliminable *écart*, the divergence, of the autoaffection of flesh. Yet this divergence still returns us, for Merleau-Ponty, to a gathering, a coming-to-self of Being, that is incompatible with the abyssal destabilization of the logic of limits. We find, then, that the strangeness of our kinship must be intensified by a transition from autoaffection toward what Derrida calls "hetero-affection," the recognition of death within life. As heteroaffection—or, in our terminology, alteraffection—the folding of flesh is rent by a fault, so that we might trace life's intimacy to its powerlessness. This leaves us with two unanswered questions. First, is this fault necessarily a failure, a lack, or does it have a positive and transformative moment, precisely through the becoming-other that it effects? Second, how might such a conception of life be reconciled, if at all, with the biological account of life?

Finally, by taking these questions at their intersection, I consider the transformation of naturalism that would be required to seek its rapprochement with phenomenology. Our clue to this transformation is an interpretation of abyssal intimacy in terms of pleasure and desire, first as introduced in Merleau-Ponty's investigations of instinct, then developed more fully in Elizabeth Grosz's (2008) account of evolution as sexual selection. Rather than understanding evolution as adaptation for survival, these accounts locate nature's impetus toward creative differentiation in the pleasurable

92 *Beyond Biologism*

intensification of sensation, which itself involves the continual folding of abyssal differences into the body. This offers us, first, a positive account of the creativity of alteraffection according to which phenomenology and evolution may be reconciled and, second, a figure for thinking the thickening and multiplying of the differences between human and nonhuman, living and nonliving, the corporeal and the cosmic—and, perhaps, even the transcendental and the empirical.

The Blunt Instrument of Biologistic Continuism

Biologistic determinism, or simply biologism, is the view that human life can be understood and explained in strictly biological terms, that the human is reducible to the biological. In other words, human behavior and social life introduce no "emergent" or higher-order properties that remain recalcitrant to explanation in terms of biological causes. Although this view is widely shared today, especially in its sociobiological form popularized by Edward O. Wilson (1975), it is not a necessary presupposition of biology and has been contested by scientists as well as philosophers.[4] In fact, recent work in philosophy of science, inspired by complexity theory and current scientific practice, has rejuvenated the concept of "emergent" properties that are causally and explanatorily efficacious while remaining essentially irreducible to lower-level properties.[5] Such irreducible emergent properties can be admitted even within a strictly materialist perspective; in philosophical terms, they suggest one manner of thinking transcendence as within or right on immanence (see Lawlor 2007, 4). The reducibility of the human to the biological is not a conclusion reached through scientific investigation, then, but is rather an assumption or ideal of scientific research that pursues the traditional reductionist program. Consequently, biology does not entail biologism, and the rejection of biologism need not entail any denigration of evolutionary theory or of science more generally.

The "sinister connotations" of biologism to which Derrida alludes concern, of course, its historical association with social Darwinism and eugenics. As Derrida demonstrates in a series of texts, Heidegger's critiques of biologism are bound up with his efforts to distance himself from the racist ideology of Nazism (see

G 420/165–66; OS 85–88/54–56, 73–74; A 197/144). In his Nietzsche lectures, Heidegger (1961, 524–25; 1982, 45) characterizes biologism as follows:

> When certain predominant views in biology about living beings are transferred from the realm of plant and animal life to other realms of being, for example, that of history, one can speak of a biologism. The term designates the . . . extension—and perhaps exaggeration and transgression of boundaries—of biological thinking beyond its own realm.

But biologism is not merely the unfounded extension of concepts, according to Heidegger (1961, 525; 1982, 45), because this extension rests on biology's lack of power over its own essence: "biologism is not so much the mere boundless degeneration of biological thinking as it is total ignorance of the fact that biological thinking itself can only be grounded and decided in the metaphysical realm and can never justify itself scientifically." Biologism is neither simply a scientific mistake nor the mere confusion of different kinds of knowledge but forgetfulness concerning science's reliance on another, nonscientific manner of thinking, which Heidegger (1961, 522; 1982, 43) here calls "metaphysical reflection."[6] Precisely insofar as he thinks Being as "life" and defines man as "beast of prey," Nietzsche avoids biologism, Heidegger (1961, 526; 1982, 46) argues, because the grounding of Nietzsche's claims is metaphysical rather than biological.

As Derrida notes, Heidegger's interpretive strategy, which aims to "withdraw [Nietzsche] from any biologistic, zoologistic, or vitalistic reappropriation," is also "a politics." Even if Nietzsche's texts, insofar as they represent the last metaphysics, still concern absolute subjectivity, they do so not as Hegelian spirit but as spirit's doppelgänger, "the absolute subjectivity of the body, of impulsions and affects," that is, as a nonvital and nonbiological animality (OS 117–18/73). The politics that flow from this reading of Nietzsche are equivocal at best, as has been noted concerning Heidegger's treatment of race.[7] And this equivocation, as Derrida so patiently shows, extends to Heidegger's efforts to establish a difference of kind, an abyss, between the human and the animal, first with respect to the hand that cannot be subsumed into the organic body and second with respect to the poverty of the animal, by which it

94 *Beyond Biologism*

both has and does not have world.[8] In short, Heidegger's efforts to avoid both biologism and metaphysical humanism commit him to an unbridgeable difference in kind between humans and non-human animals that turns on the animals' "poverty" in world, that is, their incapacity to encounter beings "as such."[9]

Derrida also recognizes an essential connection between Heidegger's efforts to distance himself, by way of his reading of Nietzsche, from biologism and its unsavory political ramifications, on one hand, and the "anthropocentric or even humanist teleology" that his separation of human *Dasein* from the biological and the living risks reintroducing, on the other:

> on the one hand, if privative poverty indeed marks the caesura or the heterogeneity between non-living and living on the one hand, between the animal and human *Dasein* on the other, the fact remains that the very negativity, the residue of which can be read in this discourse on privation, cannot avoid a certain anthropocentric or even humanist teleology. (OS 86–87/55)

Despite the care with which Heidegger frames his use of *poverty,* the term implies hierarchization and evaluation, even if any evolutionary or biological account of such hierarchization is eschewed. Yet, according to Derrida, this "humanist teleology" remains, in our own time no less than in Heidegger's, the "price to be paid in the ethico-political denunciation of biologism, racism, naturalism, etc." At the time of the writing of *Of Spirit,* Derrida admits that the question remains open whether the logic that binds the rejection of biologism with a certain vestigial humanism can be avoided or even transformed (87–88/56).

Derrida takes up precisely this task, the transformation of the logic of the biologism–humanism alternative, in *The Animal That Therefore I Am,* and his critique of biologism must be understood in this context. Derrida's strategy for this transformation is already suggested in *Of Spirit,* where he notes that Heidegger's thesis on the animal maintains the "dogmatic hypothesis" that "there is one domain, one homogenous type of entity, which is called animality *in general,* for which any example would do the job" (OS 89–90/57). The rejection of this hypothesis opens an oblique line of attack on the logic of the humanism–biologism alternative, because the "blunt instrument" of homogenous continuity between "what calls *itself* man and what *he* calls the animal" relies on precisely this premise of an animality in general within which the human should be subsumed (A 52/30).[10] Once this assumption is rejected, the choice between continuity and discontinuity can be dismissed in favor of a more interesting problematic: "to think what a limit becomes once it is abyssal, once the frontier no longer forms a single indivisible line but more than one internally divided line; once, as a result, it can no longer be traced, objectified, or counted as single and indivisible" (A 52–53/30–31). In other words, Derrida's own rejection of biologism seeks to avoid a correlative humanism precisely by "thickening" and "multiplying" the differences, subjecting the logic of the abyss to an abyssal logic of limits.

The difference between Heidegger's and Derrida's rejections of biologism turns, then, on the different logic of limits at work in their respective accounts, between a logic of the abyss and an abyssal logic. It is this distinction that Calarco fails to appreciate when he attributes to Derrida the dilemma of continuity versus discontinuity, because Derrida's abyssal logic confounds these alternatives. The "abyssal rupture" as Derrida describes it does not have two edges, a unilinear division between Man and Animal in general; it has a "history," even if this history can be spoken of "only from one of the supposed edges of the said rupture," that of the so-called human; and, beyond the human, yet without opposing it, the rupture discloses a "multiplicity of organizations of relations" between the organic and the inorganic, the living and the dead. These relations cannot be classified as continuous or discontinuous, because they are "at once intimate and abyssal, and they can never be totally objectified. They do not leave room for any simple exteriority of one term with respect to another" (A 53/31). In Derrida's sense, then, it is impossible to speak of "an" abyss between the human and the animal in the sense in which one might posit *a* line or *a* division. We can find here neither the discontinuity that Heidegger wished to draw between the metaphysical and the biological nor the homogeneity of a gathering or a kinship. This abyssal logic leaves us, nevertheless, with the difficulty of understanding the relation as "intimate" without reifying it into the generality of a concept.

Tracing Derrida's oblique approach to the logic of this limit, Leonard Lawlor (2007) identifies the twin risks that frame this logic as "biological continuism," on one side, and "metaphysical separationism," on the other. Biological continuism, which Lawlor equates with biologism and naturalism, is the position reached by attempting to overturn the oppositional limit directly, frontally, which results in a homogenous continuity between humans and animals, but only by reducing the human to the biological, to "irrational instincts and forces." In other words, biological continuism erases any difference between a response and a reaction, between the living and the mechanical (25). References to "prewired" or "hard-wired" behavior in naturalized accounts of human (or other animal) behavior efface precisely this difference.[11] On the other hand, the rejection of this flattening to the biological tempts us to return to an oppositional interpretation of the limit, that is, to treat the terms as substances and reify their distinction metaphysically. From Derrida's perspective in *Of Spirit*, Heidegger fails to avoid either risk. As Lawlor explains,

> on the one hand, Derrida thinks that Heidegger's spiritualization of biological force implies that he does not demarcate himself from biologism. On the other, because he does not demarcate himself clearly from biologism, he then in turn opposes biologism only "by re-inscribing spirit in an oppositional determination, by once again making it a unilaterality of subjectivity, even if in its voluntarist form" (OS 65/39). Heidegger's strategy results in the worst; it capitalizes on both the risks or both the evils: by not demarcating itself off, it ends up sanctioning Nazism, or, more generally, racism, by spiritualizing it, and when it demarcates itself off, it ends up, through spirit, making a gesture that is still metaphysical. (26)

The extremes of biological continuism and metaphysical separationism therefore frame the logic of the relation that, in Lawlor's terms, commits us to the least possible violence. Note that these two extremes are very similar, even identical, with the terms of the "false dilemma" that Calarco imputes to Derrida, as cited earlier. By terming this a false dilemma, Calarco suggests that Derrida would have us choose between only these two options. But the point is rather to undermine the very terms of this oppositional logic. Doing so is not merely a matter of finding a third option or a golden mean; it is necessary instead to locate the difference that destabilizes the initial choice.

At stake in this logic is nothing less, as Lawlor shows, than the project of twisting free from Platonism. On this point, the new logic of the limit rejoins the efforts of the critics of anthropocentrism noted earlier. These critics, by adopting biologistic or naturalistic arguments for human continuity with animals, attempt a frontal attack on separationism. Consequently, they manage only a reversal of Platonism, an anti-Platonism that risks reducing immanence to "this world down here" and reason to calculation (Lawlor 2007, 36).[12] Rather than twisting free, this mere reversal remains bound up with the logic of the false dilemma. To truly break with Platonism requires something more than naturalism, as Lawlor argues; it requires that we be, quoting Derrida, "responsible guardians of the heritage of transcendental idealism" (Derrida 2003d, 188; 2005b, 134; cited by Lawlor 2007, 3).

The abyssal logic of the limit, to free itself from Platonism, must avoid both the homogenization of biologism and the discontinuity of a metaphysical opposition. This means that the relations between humans and animals, between different species and populations of animals, between animals and plants, between life and the inorganic—all must be understood abyssally, multiplying and thickening differences that defy objectification, that refuse to be parsed into either one or many, that remain intimate without congealing into a continuum. In this case, there is no single, dividing line between humans and animals save the one constituted historically through our own autobiographical narrative, by means of what Agamben has termed the "anthropological machine" (O 38–43/33–38).[13] It follows that we can no longer speak of "lowering" humans to the level of animals or of "raising" animals to the level of the human, because the abyssal differences cannot be arranged hierarchically or teleologically.[14] Rather than vertically, we must picture these multiplying differences horizontally. Indeed, we seem very close here to the nonhierarchical relation that Merleau-Ponty, in his lectures on nature, calls a "lateral" overcoming or an *Ineinander* (N 273/211, 339–41/271–73). Biologism has therefore taken on a new sense. It is not a matter of "reducing" the human to the animal but of collapsing the singular differences that are

98 *Beyond Biologism*

constitutive of the manifold organizations of life, and even of the self-differentiation that constitutes life itself. This brings us to the question of autoaffection, which is at the heart of the legacy of transcendental idealism.

Strange Kinship as Alteraffection

We have seen that the intimacy between animals and humans is not to be understood as a homogenous continuity; that is, it cannot be based on naturalism. But is there any nonnaturalistic, nonbiologistic way of understanding this abyssal intimacy? Oliver (2009, 8, 9, 208) claims to find in the work of Merleau-Ponty a "type of continuity that cannot be reduced to biological continuism," namely, the "thickness of the flesh." This "strange kinship," as Merleau-Ponty calls it in his *Nature* lectures, is based not on "evolutionary continuity," according to Oliver, but rather on "embodiment and the resulting styles of life." As Oliver points out, Merleau-Ponty's phrase "strange kinship" echoes a phrase from Heidegger's "Letter on Humanism" that Merleau-Ponty discusses at the very close of his 1958–59 course Philosophy Today. There Merleau-Ponty (1996a, 148; 2022, 78–79) summarizes Heidegger's remarks concerning the human–animal relation as an example of an essential "malaise" in the latter's thought:

> [Heidegger] looks for a direct expression of being whereas he also shows that it is not susceptible to direct expression. It would be necessary to attempt an indirect expression, i.e., show Being through the *Winke* of life, of science, etc. So philosophy is perhaps possible as *"das rechte Schweigen"* [the proper silence] of which the *Letter on Humanism* speaks.[15] For example, he says, one can already "think" about "the being of a stone or even life as the being of plants and animals."[16]
>
> *Denken* the living is the quasi-ontological problem of its relationship to us: it is our closest relative and yet separated from us by an abyss: "our scarcely conceivable, abysmal bodily kinship with the beast."[17]
>
> A kinship with us that is stranger than the distance of man to God, so immense is it—distant proximity—the living and its *Umgebung* [surroundings], which is not *Welt* [world], which is not *Being*.

Although Merleau-Ponty's later references to our "strange kinship" with other animals are intended to echo Heidegger's "abysmal bodily kinship,"[18] it is hardly the case that Merleau-Ponty adopts Heidegger's interpretation of this relationship. Instead, Merleau-Ponty takes Heidegger's remarks as the provocation for another thinking of this kinship in terms of our intertwining, our *Ineinander,* with the body and animality.

For Merleau-Ponty, on Oliver's (2009, 218) reading, "there is a fundamental kinship among all living beings through our shared embodiment." This kinship is not derived from Darwinian evolution but flows from the inherent communicability of corporeal behavior and style. In Oliver's words, it is "based on neither generation nor descent but on figuration" (224). Such behavioral figuration, manifest in the melodic relation between the organism and its *Umwelt* and the protosymbolic rituals of mating, is already an interrogation of Being, a certain manner of posing questions to the world and responding to its replies: "If behavior is a style of questioning, then asking and answering questions is no longer the privilege of man. . . . Rather, metaphysical interrogation begins in the body" (217). It follows that the disclosure of beings as such has its roots in corporeal exchange with the world and that no line can be drawn in this respect between the "environment" of the animal and the "world" of the human being. Rather than an abyss founded on the disclosure of being-as-such, or the hierarchy of an evolutionary teleology, shared corporeal style suggests a kinship that is lateral and differential (218, 220).

The corporeal interrogation of the world rests on the reversibility of flesh that Merleau-Ponty often illustrates paradigmatically with the experience of tactile reversibility, the double sensation of the two hands touching. If all corporeal behavior opens onto metaphysical interrogation of the world, then the reversibility of touch obviously cannot be restricted to the human hand. Insofar as they are bodily gestures, lending a hand, the handshake, and even the folding of hands in prayer express a style that is open in principle to communication with nonhuman animals. But furthermore, the reversibility of touch introduces a divergence that prevents this kinship from lapsing into homogeneity, that keeps it "strange." In the experience of one hand touching another, the active and passive moments never merge or coincide; as we have discussed previously, there is always a slippage or gap, an *écart,* between the touching hand and the one that is touched. Even as their roles are exchanged, this gap remains as a kind of hinge that joins while separating the two moments of the experience. It is well known that Merleau-Ponty extends the *écart* within the experience of reversibility to the embodied encounter with others, as through the handshake. Consequently, the divergence inherent within flesh figures a continuity without homogeneity, a unity-in-difference, among all embodied beings: "flesh engenders both the divergence *(écart)* and the connection of beings" (Oliver 2009, 223). It thereby offers a means of "thickening" the limit between human and animal, according to Oliver, steering a course between biological continuism and metaphysical separationism by giving us "a figure in between the two" (222–23).

But to the extent that the reflexivity of flesh provides a kind of continuism, even one that avoids naturalism, can it fully incorporate the abyssal logic that we are pursuing? Is the gap between one hand touching another an abyssal gap? As Lawlor (2007, 4, 60–61) notes, the immanence of autoaffection has always defined life, and the examples of mimicry and mating rituals that Merleau-Ponty and Oliver offer to illustrate the protosymbolism of animal life emphasize its autoaffective character. Because Merleau-Ponty aims to show that the self-givenness of human consciousness is founded on the reflexivity of the body, and that this reflexivity is in turn a moment of Being's "coming-to-self" (N 335/268), we can say that he has shifted the locus of autoaffection from the subjective to the ontological register. But does this amount to an "ontologistic" continuism in place of a biologistic one, and thereby not a thickening of the differences between forms of life and the nonliving but rather another metaphysics of life that tacitly privileges sentience and human consciousness as the moments of Being's self-recognition? Our answer turns on how seriously we take the element of dehiscence or differentiation represented by the *écart* of the two hands touching. Does this hiatus, as a "coinciding from afar" (VI 166/125), represent merely an incipient continuity, or does it represent a destabilization of the logic of continuity/discontinuity?

For Lawlor, following Derrida, the granting of autoaffection to animals is insufficient to destabilize the original axiom of human exceptionalism. Instead, autoaffection, including the reversibility that Merleau-Ponty attributes to flesh, must give way to alteraffection. As Derrida writes,

> if the autoposition, the automonstrative autotely of the "I," even in the human, implies the "I" to be an other that must welcome within itself some irreducible hetero-affection (as I have tried to demonstrate elsewhere), then this autonomy of the "I" can be neither pure nor rigorous; it would not be able to form the basis for a simple and linear differentiation of the human from the animal. (A 133/95; cf. Lawlor 2007, 60ff.)

As Derrida argues in "*Geschlecht* II (Heidegger's Hand)," Heidegger identifies the hand with the possibility of giving, and ultimately of giving itself, whereas a prehensile organ, such as a paw, would be limited merely to taking. In taking, the paw "has no access to the essence of the being *as such*" (G 432/175; cf. Lawlor 2007, 49). The giving of the hand, as the gift of itself, opens access to the "as such" of beings, to their gathering—as the two hands fold into one. It is precisely this folding of hands together, their autoaffection, that Heidegger would deny to animals (see Heidegger 1971, 51; 1968, 16).[19]

But Derrida argues that the separation of giving from taking cannot be rigorously carried out, with the consequence that even human access to the as-such—and this will ultimately extend all the way to the as-such of one's own death—is never assured.[20] Whereas Merleau-Ponty can speak of the "coming-to-self" of Being, an ontological autoaffection that would ostensibly extend access to the essence of beings-as-such to all living bodies—in Oliver's (2009, 221) words, "the ontic and ontological are two sides of the same body"—Derrida's strategy is to destabilize the very opposition between the world-openness of the human and the world-poverty of the animal, as this turns on access to the phenomenological as-such.

Following this strategy, autoaffection must be reconceived as alteraffection, illustrated by Lawlor (2007) with the example of seeing one's reflection in a mirror. To see oneself in the mirror requires a distance, temporally as well as spatially, that itself remains invisible: "Remaining invisible, the space gouges out the eye, blinds it. I see myself over there in the mirror, and yet that self over there

102   *Beyond Biologism*

is other than I, so I am not able to see myself as such" (62). This blind spacing, necessary for all forms of autoaffection, is of course what Merleau-Ponty describes as the *écart* between the two hands touching. But Lawlor argues that the touching–touched must be understood as a variant of the seeing–seen, prioritizing the spacing of vision: "it is as if in the gathering of the fingers, there is a gouged-out eye that forbids the gathering of being into any 'as such'" (63).[21] For Merleau-Ponty, the image in the mirror is "something of me in the things" so that vision's break with the immediacy of touch "reestablishes the unity by the mirror, in the world" (N 345/278; cf. VI 309/255–56). For Merleau-Ponty, then, the mirror allows a new gathering beyond what is possible for the folded hands.[22] Yet for Derrida and Lawlor, the blindness inserted into autoaffection becomes abyssal to the point where it introduces death into life: "The mirror is there right between the hands that touch one another, even in the hands that are folded together for prayer. Yet the mirror, with its spacing, with its nonsimultaneity or anachronism, is an experience of blindness; it is even the experience of death" (Lawlor 2007, 74). The access to the self is necessarily always an access to another, to one who arrives either too early or too late for its rendezvous with itself. And one cannot say for certain who or what this other is, or even whether it is human or nonhuman. Rather than a mere "gap" between the touching and the touched, here we must speak of a fault line, an abyss. It is this essential death within life that leads Lawlor to speak of a "mortalism" to replace biologism and naturalism.[23]

What follows from thinking the reversibility of flesh as alter-affection, as a thinking of death within life? A first consequence is that the fault or defect by which "man" has hitherto distinguished himself from "the animal," justifying the logic of sacrifice along with metaphysical separationism, must now be granted to life in all of its differentiated forms, and even to the inorganic. The fault would be the moment of nature that loves to hide.[24] And taking seriously Merleau-Ponty's efforts to displace human subjectivity as the "flaw" within the "great diamond," we must even locate the fault within Being as such, as the engine of its self-interrogation.[25] For Lawlor, this "fault without a fall" provides us with a point of comparison, albeit an abyssal one, between all living things, namely, their powerlessness. According to this "staggered analogy," our fault—our failure to know ourselves as such, our mortality in the face of a death that we also cannot know as such—resembles the fault of other animals, their poverty of world (Lawlor 2007, 69–70). Although Oliver (2009, 220) worries that this staggered analogy risks reinstating hierarchy, the resemblance of the staggered analogy is between two faults that have no common measure; it is a comparison "without comparison or gathering" that leaves both terms "fundamentally indeterminate" (Lawlor 2007, 78–79).

Yet if we can speak of the reversibility of flesh as alteraffection, it is still necessary to account for its "affection," that is, the moment of desire. Rather than a gouged-out eye, the fault of flesh is an eye turned elsewhere; the blind spot of my vision is the point that another can see, that even the other who is myself can see before or after me. This is why, for Merleau-Ponty, the dehiscence of beings is creative and expressive and why the moment of *écart* is to be associated not only with the moment of nature's withdrawal but also with the moment of its productivity. Nature in this sense could not be conceived as a pure origin; it would be nature "always already technologized," already subjected, at the least, to the repetitions of temporalization, as Merleau-Ponty's descriptions of life as "melodic" underscore.[26] If life is melodic, the fault is the essential spacing, the silences between the notes, and even the silence that provides the background against which the melody can be heard. The creativity of life is therefore inseparable from the opening of the abyss within Being, the failure of Being to know itself as such.

But where does this leave us in relation to the sciences of life? Can such a nonnaturalistic interpretation of the creativity of life be reconciled with biology, with evolution? On Lawlor's (2009b) interpretation, what biologism and naturalism miss is precisely the moment of death within life, with all of the consequences that this entails. But as we have noted, the scientific discipline of biology is not essentially tied to biologism as a philosophical commitment. Does the phenomenological opposition to naturalism entail an opposition to the research of the sciences? More precisely, must our rejection of biologism imply a rejection of evolution? In particular, how are we to understand our implication in the temporality of evolution, and what consequences does this hold for thickening our abyssal relations with life?

Evolutionary Desire

As we have noted, Calarco (2008, 63) considers the lessons of biological continuism, such as they are developed by Darwin, Richard Dawkins, and Frans de Waal, to be an "essential path" for thought. To this end, he differentiates such *biological* continuism from the *biologistic* continuism rejected by Derrida and cautions against abandoning a "naturalistic framework" for understanding the relations and differences between humans and animals (148). It is worth noting that Merleau-Ponty, in *The Structure of Behavior*, also presents naturalism as an essential path for thought, as harboring a certain truth, but one ultimately to be transformed by its confrontation with the transcendental perspective. Both perspectives, he concluded, must be redefined to "integrate with [transcendental philosophy] the very phenomenon of the real" (SB 241/224).[27] David Wood (2003) has also argued for a "rapprochement" between phenomenology and naturalism, though neither by embracing the naturalistic framework on its own terms nor by integrating phenomenology into this framework (the project of "naturalizing" phenomenology); rather, he maintains the "nonreductive orientation to phenomena" as the central tenet of phenomenology (226).[28] Wood identifies regions in which the relations of causality and intentionality become inextricably entangled, such as the plexity of time and the boundaries of thinghood, with twofold consequences: first, that intentionality is "firmly lodged within my bodily existence, within the natural world," and second, that a "certain naturalization of consciousness would require, at the same time, an expansion of our sense of the natural," because natural phenomena "spill over into what we normally think of as distinct questions of meaning, identity, and value" (222, 224). This opens the prospect of taking up in a tentative way phenomenology's traditional claim to legislate the sciences, or at least of offering a perspective on nature that complements while remaining independent of naturalism (231). While Heidegger is undoubtedly correct to insist that the biological and zoological sciences presuppose, without being able to found, an ontological access to and interpretation of the entities that they study, it is no less the case that ontology always tacitly relies on a conception of the sciences and of empirical reality more generally.[29] Therefore, when Derrida takes both Heidegger and Lacan to task for offering no "zoological" or "ethological" evidence in support of what turn out to be metaphysical claims of human exceptionalism, we may take this as a further encouragement to rethink the relation between biological evidence and philosophical insight (G 428–29/173–74; A 182–83/133, 196–97/143).

Merleau-Ponty's nature lectures are, of course, precisely an attempt to draw out the philosophical assumptions and implications of research in the biological sciences, and Oliver (2009, 241) has seen in this research a productive "reanimation and reinterpretation of science" that stages a reciprocal exchange with philosophy, enlivening both. In these lectures, Merleau-Ponty distances himself from interpretations of evolution that point in a sociobiological direction by critiquing the utilitarian dogma of adaptation. Discussing the example of mimicry, Merleau-Ponty writes that "adaptation is not the canon of life, but a particular realization in the tide of natural production" (N 241/184). Because some forms of mimicry contribute nothing to the animal's survival, and may even complicate its existence, it is necessary to consider some elements of the differentiation of living forms in terms of their *expressive* value:

Life is not only an organization for survival; there is in life a prodigious flourishing of forms, the utility of which is only rarely attested to and that sometimes even constitutes a danger for the animal. We would thus have to allow an intrinsic relation between the substratum and the animal, a possibility of indivision between the surrounding and the animal. (N 243/186)

Therefore, alongside the "economy of life," it is necessary to recognize a "frenzied freedom of life," which is precisely its expressive creativity; as a "power to invent the visible," life is a manifestation of nature's "autoproduction of meaning" (N 243/186, 248/190, 19/3).

Nevertheless, Merleau-Ponty still interprets this excessive production of sense in terms of a gathering, because it is founded on an "intrinsic relation" and even an identification between seer and seen: "The identity of that which sees and that which it sees appears to be an ingredient of animality" (N 248/190). The course notes repeatedly emphasize this identification between the individual organism, other organisms, and their milieu, finding in this interrelation a "global" phenomenon that the scientific descriptions of evolution presuppose.[30] Life is described as "a lack in the things as such," but only by relation to and in divergence from a whole that provides its overall orientation and meaning (N 206–9/155–58).

Merleau-Ponty does offer, however, a more fruitful suggestion as an alternative to utilitarian adaptation, namely, desire. Oliver (2009, 213) notes that, whereas for Heidegger instincts are aimed toward self-preservation, for Merleau-Ponty instincts are "themes or styles of behavior oriented to pleasure." Adaptation presumes a "punctual correspondence" between the present environment and the actions of the organism, but instinct anticipates the possible and orients itself toward the irreal. Thus instincts are oriented toward no goals but are pursued merely for their own pleasure; they are pure desire (N 250–52/192–93). This desire is at the root of ceremony and ritualization in animal behavior, the very behavior that we noted earlier as evidence of their autoaffection. But if the lack, the fault, that makes animal narcissism possible is at the same time an orientation toward an irrealized possible, toward the desired, this suggests an alternative figure for alteraffection: not the gouged-out eye but rather the eye that looks elsewhere, beyond its own reflection, and that falls in love with what it sees.

To develop this alternative, we borrow an insight from Elizabeth Grosz (2008), who treats the excessive productivity of nature, including the evolution of natural diversity, in terms of sexual selection. Like Merleau-Ponty, Grosz rejects the explanation of evolutionary creativity as merely adaptation for survival. It is true that all life must survive to propagate itself, which involves the capacity for selectivity, for extracting the materials and processes on which it depends from the surrounding profusion of forces and structures— what Grosz, following Deleuze, terms "chaos" (5, 26–27). The evolving attunement of this extraction, Bergson's "organic memory," already introduces into life a capacity for innovative and unpredictable response, breaking its behavior loose from causal determinacy.

Life's "most momentous invention," according to Grosz (2008, 6, 29), is sexual difference, which provides a new expressive dimension for the fundamental instability of the organism–milieu relation, opening it to dynamic self-transformations that exceed, and sometimes even complicate, the requirements of survival. Sexual attraction is a process of transformative becoming, a "fundamentally dynamic, awkward, mal-adaptation that enables the production of the frivolous, the unnecessary, the pleasing, the sensory for their own sake" (7). Whereas Merleau-Ponty's descriptions of instinct had focused on the captivated response to pleasure, Grosz turns her lens toward the process of creative differentiation that aims at the production of the pleasurable. And because sexual selection depends on the elaboration of differences that allure and seduce, it introduces experimentation and indeterminacy into the evolutionary process in ways that fundamentally disrupt the causally closed models of geneticism and sociobiology (6–7n6).

Locating the impetus for nature's dehiscence in sexual attraction loosens naturalism's hold on evolution, because this is no longer a causal process between reified beings but is rather the explosion of difference through an abyssal process of transformation and exchange. Furthermore, attraction offers a figure for alteraffection that, without returning into a gathering, submits life to the fault of death, of interruption by the nonliving. While Lawlor's "staggered analogy" concerns the resemblance between sufferings that have nothing in common, here we might speak of a "passion" of bodily becoming that is univocal only insofar as it is characterized by continual and mutual becoming-other. The locus of this alteraffection is the intensification of sensation, the extraction of qualities that act directly on the bodily senses, which Grosz (2008, 9–10) describes in the structure of "excessive and useless production" common to both art and nature:

> Art takes what it needs—the excess of colors, forms, materials—
> from the earth to produce its own excesses, sensations with
> a life of their own, sensation as "nonorganic life." Art, like
> nature itself, is always a strange coupling, the coming together
> of two orders, one chaotic, the other ordered, one folding and
> the other unfolding, one contraction and the other dilation, and
> it is because art is the inversion and transformation of nature's
> profusion that it too must participate in, and precipitate, further
> couplings.

Grosz's aim here is to demonstrate the roots of artistic creativity in the evolutionary processes of sexual selection, and their ongoing parallel, while endorsing neither the reductive enterprise of scientific naturalism nor any metaphysical anthropocentrism. In contrast with Merleau-Ponty's descriptions of an immersion of seer and seen within a common flesh, the intensification of sensation that Grosz finds at work in nature and art transforms "the lived body into an unlivable power, an unleashed force that transforms the body along with the world" (22). The body becomes an "unlivable," "nonorganic" power by the insertion between its very hands and eyes, at the moment of its self-folding, of the imperceptible chaos of nature. This insertion spurs on "material becomings" such that "imponderable universal forces touch and become enveloped in life, in which life folds over itself to embrace its contact with materiality, in which each exchanges some elements or particles with the other to become more and other" (23). Sensation cannot, then, be incorporated into the self-reflexivity of the body as phenomenologically described, insofar as it rends the body open toward "cosmological forces, forces of the outside, that the body itself can never experience directly" (3n2). Rather than Being that returns to itself by way of the autoaffection of the body, here the body's alteraffection with the nonliving is constitutive of life's ongoing process of expressive transformation. It does not do so, however, by leaving the invisible to its invisibility, by gouging out the eye. Instead, the invisible invades and catalyzes the body such that a new power of visibility, a new form of life, is produced. Sensation as alteraffection therefore rejoins, while transforming, Merleau-Ponty's definition of life as the "power to invent the visible" (N 248/190).

This figuration of alteraffection, founded on the intensification of sensation rather than self-reflection, is not foreign to phenomenology, even if it implicates the lived body as phenomenologically described in a dimension of affectivity that founds and exceeds experience while remaining radically imperceptible. The demarcation between causality and intentionality turns abyssal at the confluence of the lived and the unlivable, allowing them an intimacy that is nevertheless incommensurable. Just as the relations between humans and animals, life and nonlife, must be thickened and multiplied, then, so must the relations between the transcendental and the empirical, because a single line can no longer demarcate their domains. To embrace this thickening would open the path for a kind of nonhuman evolutionary becoming of the human. As Deleuze and Guattari (1991, 173; 1994, 183) write in *What Is Philosophy?*, "the being of sensation is not the flesh but the compound of nonhuman forces of the cosmos, of man's nonhuman becomings, and of the ambiguous house that exchanges and adjusts them, makes them whirl around like winds."

This swirl of becomings-other, call it chaos or nature, is not simple disorder but precisely the consolidation, transcoding, and weathering away of the assemblages of vibratory relations of which humans, other animals, plants, the inorganic, and cosmic forces are constituted. Philosophy, science, and art emerge, in their own turn, as modes of nonorganic life that organize chaos by extracting their own characteristic melody from its cacophony. Understood in these terms, phenomenology and the sciences of nature are incommensurable, and perhaps untranslatable, modes of sense making that nevertheless cross into and transform one another in unpredictable and creative ways. The difference between the ontic and the ontological may be, as Oliver (2009, 221) holds, a "difference of configuration," but this will not be the two sides of a single leaf, a simple "fold in nature." The reflective movement of every living body opens onto an interrogation of being, just as every extraction of order from chaos is doubled by the natural light. Let us return, then, to what this thickening and multiplying of differences means concretely for the relationship between humans and nonhuman animals. Taking seriously Derrida's insistence that there is no "the" animal suggests the need to focus on specific forms of life. Does a nonhuman life—a bee, for example—have a world of its own? Is there any meaningful sense in which phenomenological description can open onto such a world?

5

The World of the Bee

Insects have long fascinated philosophers, whose pages swarm with metaphors and examples drawn from the diminutive lives of flies and beetles, locusts and moths. The figure of the insect continues to exert a chthonic influence on conceptions of ontology and subjectivity, offering, from Darwin to Kafka, Lacan to E. O. Wilson, a complex and often morbid analogue of human sensibility and society. Within this philosophical *Kunstkammer,* a special place has always been reserved for the social *Hymenoptera*—ants, bees, and wasps—who serve as potent emblems of the human capacity for intersubjectivity and ontological disclosure. Our fascination with social insects is no doubt inspired by the long and widespread human association with *Apis mellifera,* the western honey bee, in particular. Epipaleolithic paintings in the Araña Caves, near Valencia, Spain, depict gathering of honey from wild hives, and systematic apiculture has been practiced in Egypt and Greece since antiquity. Yet, beyond this cultural association, honey bees have attracted philosophical interest because of the apparent perfection of their communal life, including their complex social structure and division of labor, the mathematically ideal engineering of their hives, and their inscrutable methods of communication. Since at least the time of Plato, the hive has explicitly been imagined as a miniature monarchy, and the devotion of the bee to the hive and its queen exemplifies, from our human perspective, a kind of moral duty, privileging the good of the whole over the freedom of the individual and elevating preparation for the morrow above gratification today.[1] Bees have attracted so much attention from philosophers precisely because of the unmistakable ideal they offer as a contrast with our own individual morality and political arrangements, an ideal that challenges us to defend our apparent faults and to guard zealously for ourselves the definition of genuine intelligence and intersubjectivity. Our defense against this unflattering comparison has generally followed the line of reasoning that Derrida identifies concerning the human–animal relation more generally: it is the very perfection of bees that is simultaneously the evidence of their limitation, of their merely instinctive nature, while the fatal flaw of the human being, its "original sin," opens it to genuine freedom, consciousness, language, and community.[2]

At stake in this appropriation of the hive as an ambivalent double of human society is less the nature of insects than the contestation of our own nature, and especially our relation with nature writ large. This tradition is already apparent in classical authors such as Aristotle and Vergil and finds its contemporary continuation in the writings of Maurice Maeterlinck, Henri Bergson, Jakob von Uexküll, Max Scheler, and Martin Heidegger. Whereas Aristotle inserts the bee into a serial hierarchy of relations, all of which are incorporated into the being of the human, Vergil emphasizes the incompossibility of the farmer's perspective with that of the bees themselves. Vergil's efforts to reconcile these perspectives frames the legacy of philosophical interpretations of the human–bee relation into the twentieth century. In Bergson's *Creative Evolution,* for example, *Hymenoptera* represent the culmination of instinct, manifest in unreflective sympathy and tracing an evolutionary trajectory parallel with human intelligence. The instinct guiding a wasp to paralyze without killing its victim demonstrates an intuition directed toward life, while intelligence focuses on inert matter. The "double form of consciousness," instinct and intelligence, are therefore made necessary by the "double form of the real," the dehiscence of being into matter and life, and philosophical intuition becomes the task of taking up the insect's sympathy for life as a conscious human intention. Bergson's contemporary Maurice Maeterlinck, in *The Life of the Bee,* shares the former's views on the limits of the intellect and its common source with instinct, yet he resists the temptation to bring the "hive mind" to self-consciousness as a moment of human intuition, insisting rather on our inescapably alien remove from the intelligence of the bee. We cannot dissolve again into the ocean of life or subsume its tendencies into a becoming-bee of philosophical thinking, and consequently, the ambivalent juxtaposition of our world with the bee's own remains insurmountable, abyssal.

Accounting for this ambivalence, the contiguity of perspectives that touch only across a distance, invites us to consider in what sense it is meaningful to attribute a "world" or "perspective" to the bee at all. Uexküll's rich descriptions of the bee's *Umwelt* initially appear to confirm this attribution, yet the subjectivism and functionalism of his method require strict agnosticism about the bee's own experiences or inner life. Heidegger, whose account of the animal's "world-poverty" develops in dialogue with Uexküll, has famously denied that the animal relates to its environment "as such," remaining instead "captivated" by the stimuli that disinhibit its drives, as experiments with bees putatively demonstrate.

The bee has no *Umwelt,* no world, and nothing that might be called a "perspective" in the subjective sense, for Heidegger. Yet Heidegger's account of the animal's *resistance* to our efforts to transpose ourselves into its world and his failure to consider the implications of symbolic communication among bees undermine his conclusions. A phenomenology of this resistance returns us to the Janus-faced character of our openness to the bee, to the complex valences of invitation and refusal that constitute our interanimality. We suggest, therefore, an apian phenomenology that gathers scientific and poetic resources for a becoming-bee and celebrates the heterogeneous multiplicity of the real, yet without nostalgia for either mutual recognition or a translation of their "unintelligible syllables" into the language of reflection.

Intuitions of the Hive Mind

To trace the bee's rich tradition in Western thought, even among the ancient Greeks alone, would require at least a volume in its own right. But two moments of the classical tradition deserve particular attention here, as they frame the ongoing appropriation of the figure of the bee. The first is the ambivalence of our identification with the bee and the hive. Whereas Socrates (*Phaedo,* in Plato 1961, 71 [91c]) can compare his own philosophical interrogations, in their dogged pursuit of truth, with the sting of a bee, Aristotle (1998) emphasizes the sharp contrast between human and animal precisely on the point of orientation toward the good, taking the bee as his example.[3] As he writes in the first book of *Politics,* "it is clear why a human being is more of a political animal than a bee or any other gregarious animal. Nature makes nothing pointlessly, as we say, and no animal has speech except a human being." While a voice is sufficient to convey pleasure or pain, speech is peculiar to human beings, because "they alone have perception of what is good or bad, just or unjust, and the rest. And it is community in these that makes a household and a city-state" (Aristotle 1998, 4 [1253a7–18]). The beehive, lacking the specifically human dimension of community, is therefore not a *polis*, precisely because the bee lacks genuine language and the orientation toward the good that makes language necessary. Aristotle holds to this distinction despite his own careful description of the habits of the hive in *History of Animals*, which offer much to suggest collective judgment and orchestrated action (Aristotle 1984, 97–76 [book IX, 623b5–627b22]).[4] On one hand, in denying any genuine comparison between the hive and the *polis*, Aristotle cannot avoid reinscribing this analogy; it is precisely the seductions of the analogy that call for thought. But, on the other hand, the degree to which a comparison is possible will be based, for Aristotle, on our shared animality and relative placement within the hierarchy of living things.

The second moment, rather than resolving the ambivalence in the direction of hierarchized similarity, respects the inexorable difference and juxtaposition of perspectives, as we find in the fourth book of Vergil's *Georgics*. Vergil borrows the apian analogy as a commentary on the human relationship with nature by juxtaposing the farmer's perspective on the hive with the distinct point of view of the bees themselves. The prospects for our unity with nature are figured by the tensions between these two perspectives. Each perspective culminates in a putative vision of harmony, the first centered on our shared mortality:

> In the midst of the ranks the chiefs themselves, with resplendent wings, have mighty souls beating in tiny breasts, ever steadfast not to yield, until the victor's heavy hand has driven these or those to turn their backs in flight. These storms of passion, these conflicts so fierce, by the tossing of a little dust are quelled and laid to rest. (Virgil 1916, 203 [4.82–87])

The handful of dust ties the beekeeper's dissolution of the battle with the mortal interruption of human life, suggesting a parallel between our intervention in the world of the bees and the hand of fate operative within our own. With this image, as Stephanie Nelson (1998, 147) notes, Vergil "unites all mortal nature in an exquisite balance of humor, sorrow, and acceptance," sketching a vision of "the deepest unity of human beings and nature."

Similarly, shifting from the farmer's perspective to that of the bees, we find what Nelson (1998, 147) describes as the "purest vision of unity that the *Georgics* achieves," namely, the overcoming of death in nature's manifestation of the divine soul:

> Led by such tokens and such instances, some have taught that the bees have received a share of the divine intelligence, and a draught of heavenly ether; for God, they say, pervades all things, earth and sea's expanse and heaven's depth; from Him the flocks and herds, men and beasts of every sort draw, each at birth, the slender stream of life; yea, unto Him all beings thereafter return, and, when unmade, are restored; no place is there for death, but, still quick, they fly unto the ranks of the stars, and mount to the heavens aloft. (Virgil 1916, 211, 213 [4.219–27])

Yet this vision of unity is rent by a resistance located in the incompatibility of the two perspectives. While the farmer recognizes himself in the bees, which are farmers after their own manner, the bees cannot recognize any benevolence in his care; from their point of view, they neither have nor have need of any keeper, so that his removal of their stores of honey is met with violent rage. As Nelson (1998, 149) notes, "it is nature, in the person of the bees, that refuses the harmony."

There is, nevertheless, a moment of final reconciliation in bee–human interests, made possible precisely by the incongruity of their perspectives. Should the beekeeper, after removing the stores of honey, "fear a rigorous winter" and wish to "be lenient with their future, and have pity for their crushed spirits and broken fortunes," he is advised to fumigate with thyme to discourage pests and remove empty cells (Virgil 1916, 213 [4.239–42]). Although the bees cannot appreciate this action, the loss of their stores serves to stimulate their vitality. Because their glory is in the making of honey (211 [4.205]), the actions of the beekeeper, in driving them onward, encourage their own self-fulfillment. Nelson (1998, 150) aptly summarizes the lesson:

> Vergil has found the point of view from which the bees' sufferings are only apparent. To the bees, whose vision is inevitably limited, the farmer's efforts seem to destroy their own. In fact, they further them. The farmer, whom the bees see as their enemy, is in fact their ally. The two are joined in a single goal. There is a vision of the whole which the beekeeper understands but which cannot be shared by the bees. So also there may be a vision of the cosmos, apparent to God, but not to us.

As we are to the bees, so the divine knowledge of nature may be to us, suggesting neither omnipotence nor justification for mastery on our part but instead emphasizing a unity-in-difference, the shared finitude and limited perspective on the whole.

The tension between these two accounts, between unilinear series and complementary juxtaposition, echoes into the twentieth century, as we see in Bergson's description of the relation between instinct and intuition in *Creative Evolution*. For Bergson, instinct and intellect represent the two major, divergent courses of life's development, reaching their apogee in the *Hymenoptera* and humanity, respectively. The evolutionary aim of the intellect, Bergson argues, is not speculative knowledge but practical action and fabrication, hence its orientation toward discontinuous and inert matter. Consequently, intellect in its pure form cannot think genuine duration, movement, or evolution. Confronted with the effort to think life, the intellect "does what it can, it resolves the organized into the unorganized, for it cannot, without reversing its natural direction and twisting about on itself, think true continuity, real mobility, reciprocal penetration—in a word, that creative evolution which is life" (CE 632/162). Life necessarily retreats before science, as the latter takes its orientation from the intellect. Instinct, on the other hand, as an extension of the organization of vital processes, knows the unity of life from within through a kind of sympathy. This is a knowledge lived rather than represented. Bergson's examples include the unity of the beehive, which "is really, and not metaphorically, a single organism" (CE 636/166), and the paralyzing stings of various wasps, which know the precise means of immobilizing without killing their insect victims (CE 641/172). In its efforts to account for such instinctual sympathy, science can only claim to resolve it into habituated intellectual actions or pure mechanism. But this is where the role of science ends and that of philosophy begins (CE 643/174).

Bergson's account of instinct and intelligence as distinct yet complementary tendencies of life may be read as a radicalization of Vergil's position in contrast with that of Aristotle. This interpretation is encouraged by two points. First, Bergson himself contrasts his approach with the unilinear serialism of Aristotle:

> The cardinal error which, from Aristotle onwards, has vitiated most of the philosophies of nature, is to see in vegetative, instinctive and rational life, three successive degrees of the development of one and the same tendency, whereas they are three divergent directions of an activity that has split up as it grew. The difference between them is not a difference of intensity, nor, more generally, of degree, but of kind. (CE 609/135; cf. 643/174–75)

As Bergson emphasizes, intellect does not develop from instinct and cannot be hierarchically ordered with respect to it, because the two orders of knowledge are entirely distinct and opposed. Nevertheless, the two are complementary thanks to their common origin as divergent tendencies of the *élan vital,* and consequently, neither exists in a pure state but is always accompanied by the "vague fringe" of the other. As we will see, it is only due to the vague fringe of instinct accompanying our intellect that we can claim any access to the insect's sympathetic unity, the reflective recovery of which becomes the goal of philosophical intuition.

Bergson's account of the divergence of human and insect perspectives is anticipated in Maurice Maeterlinck's (1905, 2006) classic *The Life of the Bee,* which provides a second motivation for interpreting Bergson's project as a radicalization of Vergil.[5] Although *Creative Evolution* includes no reference to Maeterlinck, who would win the Nobel Prize for Literature in 1911, the similarity of their arguments suggests that Bergson was familiar with and inspired by the playwright's popular essay. Maeterlinck's literary reconstruction of the habits and life history of the hive tends toward anthropomorphism, but not unreflectively so. While he claims not to embellish the facts, he also repeatedly marks the limits of human comprehension, which can only reconstruct the bee's world from an alien and external perspective. Although Maeterlinck makes a case for bee intelligence, communication, and judgment throughout, rejecting explanations that reduce the hive's activities to instinctual mechanisms, our limited perspective finally cautions agnosticism, not only with regard to the intelligence of the bee but more generally concerning any apparent purpose of nature's evolutionary path.

The life of the bee, for Maeterlinck, is guided by *l'esprit de la ruche,* the "spirit of the hive"—or, in more contemporary translation, the "hive mind"—which, while following a path distinct from our own, demonstrates the "highest degree of intellect after that of man" (LB 27/15, 23/12; cf. 86/46). Yet nature can achieve the perfection of the collective life of the hive, with its singular orientation toward posterity, only through the sacrifice of the freedom of the individual. In the "almost perfect but pitiless" society of the honeybee, "the individual is entirely merged in the republic, and the republic in its turn invariably sacrificed to the abstract and immortal city of the future" (22/12, cf. 83/44). Indeed, "the god of the bees is the future" (46/25). The single-mindedness of the hive, rather than evidence of any mechanical impulse, is precisely a kind of sympathetic knowledge of the whole, as demonstrated by the communal judgments concerning the rearing of new queens, the appropriate times to swarm, and so on. Furthermore, Maeterlinck's descriptions of the juxtaposed limits of different forms of intelligence anticipate Bergson's own account of the opposed but complementary character of instinct and intelligence. "What we call our intellect," he notes, "has the same origin and mission as what in animals we choose to term instinct," and the sharp distinction drawn between the two is ultimately arbitrary (65/35, 103/55). Yet each form of intelligence is limited, concealing as much as it reveals:

> Are we to believe that each form of intellect possesses its own strange limitation, and that the tiny flame which with so much difficulty at last burns its way through inert matter and issues forth from the brain, is still so uncertain that if it illumine one point more strongly the others are forced into blacker darkness? Here we find that the bees (or nature acting through them) have organized work in common, the love and cult of the future, in a manner more perfect than can elsewhere be discovered. Is it for this reason that they have lost sight of all the rest? (111/59)

It is possible, Maeterlinck notes, that nature restricts us from understanding or following all of its desires, which must therefore be distributed into different modes of life. Our own unconscious desires, like that fringe of instinct described by Bergson, are perhaps the clue to precisely such buried alternatives: "We too are aware of unconscious forces within us, that would appear to demand the reverse of what our intellect urges. And this intellect of ours, that, as a rule, its own boundary reached, knows not whither to go—can it be well that it should join itself to these forces, and add to them its unexpected weight?" (LB 199/106). Even Bergson's metaphor of the whole of life as a single wave moving through matter (CE 720/266, 723/269) is anticipated by Maeterlinck's description of the "extraordinary fluid we call life" that, consciously or unconsciously, "animates us equally with all the rest" and "produces the very thoughts that judge it, and the feeble voice that attempts to tell its story" (LB 209/111).[6] Although Maeterlinck repeatedly grapples with the question of whether this "will" of nature can be attributed a purpose, he does, in the end, suggest the solution that Bergson's own alternative to mechanism and finalism will develop, namely, that the unity of life lies in its origin rather than its end: the progress of evolution, he writes, "has perhaps no aim beyond its initial impetus, and knows not whither it goes" (LB 300/156).

The difference between Bergson and Maeterlinck can nevertheless be traced from the conclusions that they draw concerning the disclosure of the bee's perspective in its own right. For Bergson, our access to the perspective of the bee is made possible precisely by that fringe of instinct that always surrounds the bright nucleus of our intellect, to which our capacity for aesthetic perception and sympathetic identification attests. The philosophical task is to bring this fringe of instinct to reflective awareness and thereby to think life from within, that is, to effect the passage from instinct to intuition: "it is to the very inwardness of life that *intuition* leads us—by intuition I mean instinct that has become disinterested, self-conscious, capable of reflecting upon its object and of enlarging it indefinitely" (CE 645/176). Philosophy, as intuition, is the effort to dissolve once again into the whole "ocean of life" (657–58/191).[7] Whereas the scientific entomologist knows the insect only "as he knows everything else—from the outside, and without having on

120   *The World of the Bee*

his part a special or vital interest" (642/173), the philosopher can discern its life from within. We may conclude, then, that the aim of philosophy is precisely a becoming-bee, a taking up of the bee's own perspective at the level of reflective self-awareness, which is a path reserved exclusively for human consciousness. While this becoming-bee involves a reciprocal enlargement of instinct and intellect, it remains unilinear with respect to bees and humans; the perspective of the bee is subsumed into human consciousness, while the limits of the bees' own perspective remain determinately circumscribed.

Maeterlinck, however, remains true to the Georgic narrative by refusing to recognize a subsumption of the bee's perspective into that of the human, and he does so by continually emphasizing our inability to exit the point of view of the outside spectator. We can do no more than "vaguely survey" the hive "from the height of another world," just as "an inhabitant of Venus or Mars" might observe us from a mountaintop (LB 43/23).[8] The outside perspective of divine fate that inscribed the limits of human knowledge in *Georgics* has here become the view from a radically alien intelligence, and ultimately that of Nature itself. Not only can we never claim to have absorbed the inner meanings of the bee's world but we also can never claim to coincide with the perspective of "the circular ocean, the tideless water, whereon our boldest and most independent thoughts will never be more than mere abject bubbles. We call it Nature today; tomorrow, perhaps, we shall give it another name, softer or more alarming" (207–8/110). While Bergson's philosopher dissolves again into the ocean of life, justifying his unique capacity to channel its emerging consciousness, Maeterlinck leaves us stranded as "waifs shipwrecked on the ocean of nature" (161/85). Here the ocean metaphor suggests the unity of our common origin in the ultimately mysterious workings of nature, but it makes no suggestion that the incompossibility of perspectives may be united as facets of a single vision. While we recognize an alien intelligence in the life of the hive, we can never coincide with it, never breach the externality of our perspective; we both are and are not of the same world. By extension, the centrality of our own perspective on the world is displaced, its limits perpetually opening it to an alien and incommensurable gaze.

The ambivalence of our relationship with the bee is thus reinforced: on one hand, we are inexorably invited to see ourselves reflected in its apparent intelligence and social life, while, on the other, its incomparable difference forbids our entry into its world. What is the basis for this ambivalence, this refused kinship, and on what grounds can we claim even this degree of access to a non-human life?

Umwelt and Resistance

Yet perhaps we have not formulated our problem correctly in imagining that the bee has a perspective of its own, a "world," to which we could, in principle, gain access. Does the bee have a world of its own? Uexküll imagines just such a world as follows:

> We begin such a stroll on a sunny day before a flowering meadow in which insects buzz and butterflies flutter, and we make a bubble around each of the animals living in the meadow. The bubble represents each animal's environment *[Umwelt]* and contains all of the features accessible to the subject. As soon as we enter into one such bubble, the previous surroundings *[Umgebung]* of the subject are completely reconfigured. Many qualities of the colorful meadow vanish completely, others lose their coherence with one another, and new connections are created. A new world arises in each bubble. (FW viii–ix/43)

Beyond this general description of the animal's "bubble" world, Uexküll proceeds to fill out the description of the bee's own particular perceptions, borrowing on Karl von Frisch's research on the bee's perception of form:

> We see the bees in their surroundings, a meadow in bloom, in which blossoming flowers alternate with closed buds. If one places the bees in their environment and transforms the blooms according to their shape into stars or crosses, the buds will take the form of circles. From this, the biological meaning of this newly discovered characteristic of the bees is effortlessly apparent. Only the blooms, not the buds, have meaning for the bees. (FW 45/84)[9]

For Uexküll, an animal's behavior cannot be explained mechanistically because every *Umwelt* is "subjective," composed of signs or meanings rather than objective causal relations. The bee's reactions can only be understood relative to the "perception signs" *(Merkzeichen)* and "effect signs" *(Wirkzeichen)* that are meaningful for it, because these sketch out in advance what it can perceive and what it can do. Consequently, the features that we assign to the "objective" world—space, time, the form and color of external objects, and so on—cannot be assumed to have the same structure or significance for the bee. Indeed, the "objective" world of the human being is simply our own soap bubble, our own phenomenal world of subjective appearances (see FW 10–11/53–54, 30/70, 102/135).

Understanding the structure of the bee's world does not require that we merge these bubbles, projecting ourselves sympathetically into its interiority, nor entertain any notions of "what it's like" to be a bee. As Uexküll admits, the biologist's perspective is always that of the external spectator, and the events that he observes cannot be transferred outside the frame of his own subjectivity: "he is always dealing with events that take place in *his* space and in *his* time and with *his* qualities" (Uexküll 1926, 136). Yet the identification of function-rules, as natural factors linking perception and effect signs, requires no projection into the psyche of the animal, nor any claims as to what the animal's own perceptions might be like. Whereas the latter may be of interest to psychology, it is not an issue for biology, on Uexküll's understanding.[10] The "subjective" world of the bee described so poetically by Uexküll turns out to be the scientist's functional reconstruction of the bee's world from elements of the scientist's own fund of meanings.

It is against the backdrop of Uexküll's descriptions of the animal's *Umwelt* that Heidegger, in his 1929–30 lecture course *The Fundamental Concepts of Metaphysics*, proposes his own famous theses on world: the stone is worldless *(weltlos)*, the animal is poor in world *(weltarm)*, and "man" is world-forming *(weltbildend)* (272ff./184ff.). Although their accounts of animal worlds are apparently at odds, Heidegger draws several examples from Uexküll, and he shares Uexküll's rejection of mechanistic and vitalist accounts of life as well as his refusal to locate the human and animal worlds as degrees along the same scale. In fact, for his preliminary description of the world-poverty of the animal, Heidegger depicts the *Umwelt* of the bee in terms that closely echo Uexküll's own:

The bee, for example, has its hive, its cells, the blossoms it seeks out, and the other bees of the swarm. The bee's world is limited to a specific domain and is strictly circumscribed. And this is also true of the world of the frog, the world of the chaffinch, and so on. But it is not merely the world of each particular animal that is limited in range—the extent and manner in which an animal is able to penetrate whatever is accessible is also limited. The worker bee is familiar with the blossoms it frequents, along with their color and scent, but it does not know the stamens of these blossoms *as* stamens, it knows nothing about the roots of the plant and it cannot know anything about the number of stamens or leaves, for example. (285/193)

Heidegger presents this description of the bee's world in a preliminary way and qualifies it immediately, because it may suggest that the bee's "poverty" is to be understood in terms of its limited extent or range by human standards, making poverty a matter of degree. As we know, the crux of the issue for Heidegger will turn on the bee's failure to encounter the blossoms and stamens *as such,* that is, as beings.

But even this preliminary description demonstrates a salient departure of Heidegger's approach from that pursued by Uexküll. Uexküll avoids describing the *Umwelt* of the animal as derivative from or subsumed within the *Umwelt* of the human being, which is why we cannot assume any common measure of space, time, or perceptual qualities. To this extent, Uexküll and Heidegger are in agreement that the differences between *Umwelten* are not a matter of degree. But Uexküll's functional method restricts him from drawing conclusions about the character or quality of the bee's experiences, and certainly Heidegger's claim concerning the "as such" oversteps the biological evidence. In one sense, Heidegger's willingness to carry Uexküll's description beyond its biological threshold follows from the "inner unity of science and metaphysics," insofar as any effort to think the essential nature of life or animality requires the mutual understanding and collaboration of both modes of inquiry (FCM 279/189). Because Heidegger's aim is to disclose the essence of the animal, he must necessarily transgress the limits that circumscribe the subject matter of biology alone.

But there is a deeper issue at stake concerning the very terms by which Uexküll has presented the animal's world, namely, his reliance on a Kantian metaphysics of subjectivity. Uexküll professes agnosticism about the apperceptions of the bee in its own right; what things are like for the bee may be a matter for psychological speculation, but we will never be able to grant such speculations scientific status. This agnosticism, however, reinforces the very sense of a mysterious "what it's like" that resists our grasp, remaining forever closed to our inquiries. Furthermore, Uexküll's willingness to relativize the human position, describing our world as one soap bubble alongside the others, suggests that the "subjectivity" of the *Umwelt* is a matter of its phenomenal representation, whereas noumenal Nature remains an inaccessible *Ding an sich*. According to the penultimate sentence of *A Foray into the Worlds of Animals and Men*, "and yet, all these different environments *[Umwelten]* are fostered and borne along by the One that is inaccessible to all environments forever" (FW 102/135).

Uexküll's perspective lends credence to the objection, therefore, that we can never know the true experiences of the bee and that any reconstruction will simply reduce its alterity to a variation of our own subjective phenomena. As William McNeill (1999, 213) notes, such objections are "themselves historically conditioned by the epoch of subjectivity":

> What is striking about such objections is that they presuppose that our perspective is at once subjective and purely human. They presuppose as unquestioned that human beings, through the subjectivity of their thinking, are undeniably at the center of the world, and that the "world," here conceived as the sum-total of beings (objects) in their being, is merely a result and "function" of human representation. The said objections presuppose both that we know what the human being is and that this conception of the world as our "representation" is unquestionable.

In his critique of the concept of empathy and rejection of the "philosophical dogma that man is initially to be understood as subject and as consciousness," Heidegger distances himself from this representationalist view (FCM 304–5/208; cf. 298/203, 302/206).[11] The problem of how we understand others is ontological rather than epistemic, whether such others are human or not.

The ontological problem of our access to animals does not concern whether we have understood an animal correctly in a particular factical situation. The issue is rather in what sense, if any, we may be said to "transpose" ourselves into an animal, to go along with it, and thereby to disclose its essential nature (FCM 296–97/202). Any effort to understand an animal in a particular situation will presuppose the possibility of such transposition, which is a matter neither of actually transferring ourselves into the animal's point of view nor of merely imagining ourselves to be in its place. As the various texts that we have considered concerning the world of the bee demonstrate, by their very entertainment of the question of the relationship between the bee's perspective and our own, the possibility of this transposition seems at least open to us: "we tacitly assume that this possibility of self-transposition and a certain going-along-with [the animal] exists in principle, that the very idea makes sense as we say" (301/205). Yet precisely insofar as transposition into the animal presents itself as a mere *possibility*, such going-along-with differentiates itself from our relation to other human beings, on Heidegger's understanding. This is because our transposition into our fellow human beings "already and originally belongs to man's own essence" and cannot therefore be raised as a genuine question (301/205). All of our mutual understandings and misunderstandings attest that our very manner of being is one of primordially going-along-with each other. What, then, of the self-evidentness with which we immediately embrace the possibility of going-along-with other living things as well?

Heidegger decisively rejects the Bergsonian answer to this question, namely, that we relate to the animal through a kind of sympathetic and instinctual attunement, as his criticisms of Max Scheler demonstrate. Scheler (1954, 28ff.), in *The Nature of Sympathy*, takes up Bergson's descriptions of the instinctive knowledge of the wasp paralyzing its prey as an example of "identification," which provides the primitive basis for all givenness of "the other." According to Scheler, "to be aware of any organism *as* alive, to distinguish even the simplest animate movement from an inanimate one, a minimum of undifferentiated identification is necessary" (31). The capacity for such identification, he argues, has atrophied in the modern, "civilized," adult male as a consequence of overdevelopment of the intellect, but a complete realization of human potential requires an integration of our instinctual and intellectual dimensions, of life and spirit. Although Heidegger declares Scheler's manner of posing the question of the relation between the vital and the spiritual to be "an essential one in many respects and superior to anything yet attempted," he nevertheless considers Scheler's effort to understand the human being as an integration of these levels of being to be a "fundamental error" that "must inevitably deny him any access to metaphysics" (FCM 283/192; cf. 106/70). While Heidegger's descriptions of the poverty of the animal's world and of the human as world-forming draw on Scheler's characterizations of life and spirit,[12] what Heidegger rejects in Scheler is precisely the effort to integrate these ontological orders, as the notion of "identification"—or Bergsonian intuition—would do.

The possibility of our going-along-with the animal is not consummated in any genuine identification or sympathy, according to Heidegger, precisely because this going-along-with, while apparently invited, is nevertheless refused. This refusal or failure, *Versagen*, is the key to the animal's poverty:

> The possibility of not having, of refusing, is only present when in a certain sense a having and a potentiality for having and for granting is possible. . . . And not-having *in* being able to have is precisely *deprivation*, is *poverty*. . . . The animal displays a sphere of transposability or, more precisely, the animal itself is this sphere, one which necessarily refuses any going along with. The animal has a sphere of potential transposability and yet it does not necessarily have what we call world. (FCM 308–9/210–11)

Heidegger's description is undoubtedly correct to draw attention both to the invitation to transposition with the animal and to the refusal of this transposition. Our everyday engagement with animals is characterized by precisely these two moments: on one hand, our conviction that nonhuman animals present a distinct and alien perspective on the world that we should, in principle, be able to take up, and, on the other, the resistance we encounter when trying to do so. As we have seen, the descriptions of this incompossibility of perspectives in the case of the bee may be traced from the *Georgics* to the present.

But the decisive question for evaluating Heidegger's account concerns whether he has described this moment of refusal adequately. Consider, first, that the refusal is not a structure of *Dasein* but is rather effected *on the part of* the animal, as an essential aspect of its being. The *animal* both invites and refuses *us*. To the extent that poverty is to be understood as a not-having in being able to have, is it not *we* who remain in poverty precisely with respect to the sphere of the animal? Does not the animal refuse our access to this sphere, and thereby hold us in this deprived suspense? Second, if it is the case, as Heidegger will suggest further on, that captivation is "quite different in the case of each animal species" (FCM 359/247), is this not just as true for the refusal? Are there not, in fact, many registers and variations on this melody of refusal? It is here that Derrida's critique of the very notion of the "animal in general" offers leverage (A 53–58/31–35). Heidegger's own decision to illustrate our invitation to transposition with the example of the household pet but the captivation of "the animal" with the bee illustrates the differential quality of refusal at work. Neither of these objections would carry weight for Heidegger, of course, because the animal's refusal merely reveals that there is nothing to be refused, that the animal lacks a world into which one may be transposed, that there is nowhere to which we may go-along together. The animal's refusal, for Heidegger, covers the shame of its poverty. But insofar as refusal *is* refusal, insofar as animals, in their disparate manners of being, resist our efforts to lay them bare, must not this refusal be given its own ontological due? What is the proper lesson to be drawn from the fact that here, as in the *Georgics,* it is the bees that refuse *us*?

For Heidegger, as is well known, the animal's poverty is given a positive description in terms of captivation, a relating or an opening toward that is nevertheless not an opening toward as such. Heidegger chooses bees, once again, as the privileged examples of captivation, both because their behavior is "more remote" than that of "higher" animals and because "insects have an exemplary function within the problematic of biology" (although he provides no further clarification of either point) (FCM 350/240–41).[13] Two experiments performed on bees play a key role in Heidegger's discussion. The first, drawn from Uexküll's (1926) *Theoretical Biology,* concerns a bee that continues to drink honey after its abdomen has been severed.[14] The second, discussed by Emanuel Rádl (1903), concerns the bee's ability to orient itself toward the hive when returning home from a long flight. Because the bee orients toward the hive

128   *The World of the Bee*

according to the angle of the sun, it will fly in the wrong direction for home if it is transported to another place in a dark box. In each case, Heidegger intends the example to demonstrate that, although the bee relates to the honey or the hive, it does not encounter anything in its surrounding *as such,* that is, as the being that it is.

According to Heidegger, the first experiment demonstrates that the bee has no relationship to the presence of the honey or to its own abdomen, because it is "taken by" its food. The bee continues to drink honey because it cannot register any "sense of satisfaction" that would inhibit its drive (FCM 352–53/242). Heidegger's interpretation of satiation as an "inhibition" of the bee's drive parallels Uexküll's own interpretation of this experiment as an example of the "subjective annihilation *[subjektive Vernichtung]*" of indications *(Merkmale)* (Uexküll 1926, 169–70). For Uexküll, the experiment is intended to distinguish between the "objective" annihilation of the indication, as in a case where the bee has consumed all of the honey, and its "subjective" annihilation in the case of satiation. The other example Uexküll offers of such subjective annihilation, the female insect's consumption of the male as prey after copulation, appears later in Heidegger's text to illustrate the "eliminative character" of behavior (FCM 363–64/250).

For Heidegger, these examples do not illustrate the annihilation of an indication but instead the inhibition of one drive to be replaced by another. This concept of "drive" is found in Scheler, for whom drives underlie all sensation in humans as well as animals: "What an animal can see and hear is only what is of importance to its instincts. . . . Even in the human being the drive to see underlies factual seeing" (HPC 22–23/14). Whereas animals remain circumscribed by the limits of their drives, which prevents them from escaping ecstatic immersion in their environments, humans are capable of a "free inhibition" *(Hemmung)* or a "de-inhibition" *(Enthemmung)* of their drives, which is one aspect of their "world-openness" (HPC 41/28). This world-openness is made possible by participation in spirit, which inhibits the drives to sublimate their power toward freely chosen aims. Scheler's description of the world-openness of humans obviously anticipates Heidegger's account of humans as "world-forming," and their descriptions of the limitations of animals share obvious similarities. But, as we noted earlier, Heidegger rejects Scheler's efforts to treat the human being as the cumulative integration of levels of being, including the drive-bound behavior of the animal. This is why, for Heidegger, the bee's eye is determined by the bee's specific capacity for seeing, but this has no corollary in our own potentiality for sight. Whereas animal behavior is founded on drives, human comportment is not (FCM 336/230, 345–46/237).

Heidegger's reliance on these examples to demonstrate the captivation of the animal in general has already received criticism from several angles. In addition to questions of evidence, the examples raise the issue of Heidegger's mode of access to the being of the animal. As we have noted, Uexküll's functional approach, by restricting itself to the animal's manifest behavior, risks reliance on a subjectivist interpretation of the animal's world. Yet Heidegger's alternative, to transpose oneself into the animal through a going-along-with that would reveal the animal's genuine essence, has already been foreclosed by the animal's resistance. Whereas Scheler could rely on the dimension of life shared commonly with non-human animals as the basis for our identification with them, Heidegger has rejected this option. From what standpoint, therefore, does Heidegger describe the animal's manner of being? And to the extent that his descriptions rely on scientific experiments that presume a subjective account, how does this compromise his approach? If Heidegger is reduced to approaching the behavior of the bee from a functional standpoint, it must be possible to specify the behaviors that are indicative of captivation, or at least to identify what behaviors are absent. But it is impossible to specify in Heidegger's account what behavior would count as evidence against captivation, despite the suggestion that his conclusions have the support of scientific experimentation.

Furthermore, Heidegger's claim that these experiments can serve as paradigmatic of the behavior of bees is unconvincing, to say nothing of his claims that they may stand in for animal behavior in general. As David Morris (2005) has noted, Heidegger approaches the bee in each case as an isolated individual, whereas we have seen that the intelligence of the bee has typically been attributed to its communal relationship with the hive, and especially its powers of communication. Yet, from the perspective that Heidegger has presented, no genuine community or communication among bees is possible, because bees can never relate to one another as such.

130 *The World of the Bee*

Self-absorbed and enclosed in its encircling ring, the bee "has" its hive and fellow bees, but it cannot relate to them other than as what activates its drives. Any genuine going-along-with, ontologically and factically, is thereby reserved for *Dasein*. This encircling ring, as the philosophical reinterpretation of Uexküll's *Umwelt*, also clarifies the Darwinian notion of self-preservation. The struggle for survival is actually the animal's struggle with its encircling ring (FCM 383/263, 377/259).[15] We cannot add, for Heidegger, that it "struggles alone," which would suggest a privative of being-with ascribable only to *Dasein*. The solitude of the animal is beyond any possibility of factically being alone. However, this description can hardly account for the readiness with which individual worker bees, which do not reproduce, sacrifice themselves for the perpetuation of the hive. It is precisely the fact that the "struggle for survival" takes place at the level of the hive, rather than the individual, that has led evolutionary biologists to formulate a theory of "kin selection" for bees and other social insects (see Hamilton 1964).[16] Would some evidence, then, of bee communication and cooperation count against Heidegger's interpretation of their captivation?

Transpositional Dances

Heidegger himself is already aware of such behaviors, as we know from a side remark much earlier in *Fundamental Concepts,* where Heidegger is distinguishing between zoology and philosophy: "our thesis is a proposition like that which states that the worker bees in the bee community communicate information about newly discovered feeding places by performing a sort of dance in the hive" (FCM 274/186).[17] Heidegger was aware, therefore, of von Frisch's early research on bee dances, although he elected not to discuss the implications of such behavior for his notion of captivation.

Von Frisch's early studies from the 1920s documented the so-called round dance by which bees indicate that food is to be found in the near vicinity of the hive.[18] Only subsequently, in the 1940s, did he recognize the symbolic complexity of what have come to be called *Schwanzeltanzen,* "waggle dances," by which bees communicate the direction, distance, and quality of distant food sources, thereby recruiting other foragers to join them in its collection (von Frisch 1950, 69ff.). Donald Griffin (2001, 190) has called this dance language "the most significant example of versatile communication known in any animals other than our own species." Subsequent research has confirmed and expanded our knowledge of these dances, which occur only when something needed by the colony (e.g., nectar, pollen, water, or wax) is in short supply and difficult to locate. When a forager returns from a rich source of this substance, she seeks out an audience of other foragers, then engages in a dance consisting of walking rapidly in a straight line while moving her abdomen back and forth, then circling back (alternating between clockwise and counterclockwise circles) to the starting point to repeat this walk. As von Frisch discovered, the orientation of this walk relative to vertical conveys the relation between the angle of the sun and the direction of the source. For example, a dance that is oriented straight up indicates that the source is directly in the direction of the sun, while eighty degrees to the right of vertical indicates that the source is eighty degrees to the right of the sun. The duration of the wagging run, and perhaps also its length, indicates the distance to the source, while the duration and enthusiasm of the dance communicate the desirability of the substance to be gathered.

From the perspective of symbolic communication, waggle dances are distinctive in several respects. First, the dances serve to communicate a complex message to other bees within the completely dark hive, where the other bees follow the dancing bee's movement by touch, scent, and perhaps also sound. Within this setting, the relation between the angle of the dance relative to vertical and the flight direction of the source has no "natural" basis; as Griffin (2001, 196) notes, this relationship "is more truly symbolic than any other known communication by nonhuman animals. The direction of the dance stands for the directions of flight out in the open air." Second, the waggle dances demonstrate "displacement" in that they communicate about a situation that is displaced in space and time from the context of the communication, sometimes with a lag of several hours (Griffin 2001, 196–97). Third, the dances are not "fixed" in the sense of being invariably produced or closed to spontaneous symbolic innovation. As noted, the performance of a dance is dependent on conditions within the hive, such as which materials are in short supply, and on the quality of the source discovered. A forager that returns to the hive to find that the material collected is no longer in need may instead perform a "tremble dance" that interrupts other waggle dances, discouraging the pursuit of further supplies of a given resource (Nieh 1993). Furthermore, von Frisch demonstrated in early experiments that bees may spontaneously alter their symbolic system to adapt to new constraints. If the comb within the hive is laid horizontally, so that the vertical direction of dances is no longer possible, foragers are no longer able to communicate food sources to others within a dark hive. If, however, any area of the hive is open to the sky, so that the polarization of light can provide an orientation relative to the sun, dancing resumes in such a way that the straight portion of the dance points in the actual flight direction of the source (von Frisch 1950, 86–96). This flexibility in the symbolic structure of the dance ill accords with our usual conceptions of the rigidity of instinctive behaviors.

Finally, recent research has focused on the communicative aspects of waggle dances employed when a swarm seeks a suitable location for a new hive, a phenomenon first documented by Martin Lindauer in the 1950s. When scouts return from potential hive locations, the enthusiasm of their dances takes into consideration variables like the size, dryness, and darkness of the site as well as its distance from the old colony. These scouts recruit other dancers to join them in communicating about the potential site, some of whom may then visit the site themselves, but many of whom will not. This demonstrates that messages can be passed along "secondhand," that is, disseminated by those who have not themselves undertaken the flight or inspected the site. Individual bees that do visit the sites described by others have been observed to revise their initial choices accordingly. This process continues for several days until a kind of "consensus" is reached, during which nearly all of the dancing bees are indicating the same potential hive location as the best option, after which the swarm travels en masse to the new location (see Lindauer 1971).[19]

Such documentation of the complexities of symbolic communication among bees does not alone resolve the question of their "captivation" by drives or their potential for an "inner world" distinct from our own, however. Adopting an explicitly behavioral approach, Griffin (2001, 210) argues that such studies provide evidence for conscious thought comparable to what we rely on in interactions with other humans:

The principal basis for our inferences about subjective, conscious thoughts and feelings in humans is the communicative behavior of our companions. And here we find that certain insects also communicate simple but symbolic information about matters that are of crucial importance in their lives, and they even reach major group decisions on the basis of such communicative behavior. . . . It seems both logical and reasonable to apply the same procedure that we use with our human companions and infer that . . . honeybees are consciously thinking and feeling something approximating the information they are communicating. Only by assuming an absolute human–animal dichotomy does it make scientific sense to reject this type of inference.[20]

Whatever we may think of Griffin's conclusions, his argument rests on assumptions that the phenomenological tradition has consistently rejected as flawed, namely, that the existence of consciousness in others is arrived at by a process of logical reasoning rather than being phenomenologically or ontologically basic. But then we must return precisely to the ambivalence that the bee presents to us in its phenomenological disclosure, insofar as it promises us a measure of transposition while, in its own differential manner, resisting precisely the kind of going-along-with that would yield an essential insight into its nature. Such studies of bee communication can provide the guiding thread for a phenomenological investigation of this ambivalent character of the insect's givenness.

One promising path for the development of apian phenomenology is already suggested by Heidegger himself in his consideration of our inability to transpose ourselves into a stone. As Heidegger notes, although we usually deny the possibility of such transposition, it nevertheless remains a possibility of our comportment to "animate" the stone:

There are two fundamental ways in which this can happen: first when human Dasein is determined in its existence by *myth,* and second in the case of *art.* But it would be a fundamental mistake to try and dismiss such animation as an exception or even as a purely metaphorical procedure which does not really correspond to the facts, as something phantastical based upon the imagination, or as mere illusion. What is at issue here is not the opposition between actual reality and illusory appearance, but the distinction between quite different kinds of possible truth. But for the moment, in accordance with the subject under consideration, we shall remain within that dimension of truth pertaining to scientific and metaphysical knowledge, which have together long since determined the way in which we conceive of truth in our everyday reflection and judgement, in our "natural" way of knowing. (FCM 299–300/204)

The significance of this remark is that it reveals the theoretical frame surrounding Heidegger's analyses of the animal's poverty just as much as it does the stone's lack of world. Because, in William McNeill's (1999, 230–31) words, Heidegger's course "problematizes the foundational primacy attributed to theoretical contemplation as our originary mode of access to the world," it simultaneously recuperates alternative openings onto the truth of animal being, even if we hesitate to accept Heidegger's own characterizations of those alternative modes and their limits. Consequently, a phenomenology of the ambivalent invitation of the insect, if it aims at a broader truth than that circumscribed by Western theoretical contemplation, must also consider the disclosure of the insect's mode of being through myth, art, and non-Western modes of knowing alongside the experiments and observations of Western science.

Within this broader context, the insect's resistance to our transposition is neither total, homogenous, nor static, and the many manners and degrees of going-along-with insects are themselves open to cultivation. This recognition encourages what David Wood (2006, 41–42) has called "biomorphizing," which, like Scheler's notion of identification, founds our transpositional encounters on shared and embodied modes of life. Furthermore, this concrete engagement with insects already implies the possibility of a transformative relation, a "becoming-bee," that, unlike Bergsonian intuition, would be operative in both directions. Deleuze and Guattari's reliance on another figure of *Hymenoptera* to illustrate their notion of dual becoming, namely, the wasp in its pollinating pseudocopulation with the orchid, is suggestive here (ATP 17/10, 291-92/238, 360/293–94). As Deleuze and Guattari note, the orchid has appropriated the wasp into its own reproductive cycle by borrowing a fragment of its "code," in some cases going so far as to produce pheromones of the female wasp. Such wasp–orchid nuptials are paradigmatic of what Deleuze and Guattari term "involutions," nonfilial blocks of becoming that span kingdoms and lead unlikely partners into creative mutual transformation. The account of "becoming-animal" that Deleuze and Guattari develop from this example, applied to the creative path of phenomenological investigation, returns us to Bergson's insight into the "double form of the real," only now differentiated into what Derrida calls "the heterogeneous multiplicity of the living" (A 53/31). As we have seen, philosophy is, for Bergson, a means of "becoming-wasp," taking up the insect's instinct for life in the self-reflective awareness of the intellect. Yet for Deleuze and Guattari, the becoming is a mutual resonance: as the entomological phenomenologist engages in a becoming-bee, the bee is equally caught up in a becoming-philosophical. The development of apian phenomenology must nevertheless negotiate the temptation to elevate our own poverty, our inability, finally, to disclose the as-such of the bee, into the principle of our superiority. In the end, it is just as impossible fully to claim the as-such for ourselves as it is to withhold it from the bee (see Derrida 2006, 2008a; Lawlor 2007).

Although the apparent unity of the honeybee hive had led to its use as a figure for obedient monarchism and harmonious democracy, any becoming-other is a far more fraught and complex event. Deleuze and Guattari's wasp–orchid block plays with the orchid's deceptions and the pollinator's desires to create a new possibility of relation. This frenetic energy animates Sylvia Plath's (1965) Bee sequence, a series of five poems in her collection *Ariel*. In "The Arrival of the Bee Box," the speaker of the poem finds herself afraid of the "box of maniacs" she has ordered, with its noise of "unintelligible syllables," and yet is unable to stay away from it. She imagines releasing the bees:

> I wonder how hungry they are.
> I wonder if they would forget me
> If I just undid the locks and stood back and turned into a tree. (60)

The poem conveys the speaker's ambivalent but hungry desire: even as she hopes the bees will ignore her, she imagines a petticoat of flowers that will make her their coevolutionary sexual partner and invite an intimate invasion by the swarm. An apian phenomenology, conjured out of the perilous relationship of bees and beekeepers, with its promise of honey and stings, suggests that in denying the rich world of the bee, we close ourselves off from the sweet possibilities of extending our loyalty beyond the reaches of humanity. Do we thereby also forget something of ourselves, of the evolutionary generation of differences by which our own worlds take on meaning? How might our organic memories open us to other forms of life?

6

Animal Memories

Phenomenology has played a key role over the past century in re-opening the question of the animal because it has continually endeavored to describe the animal dimension of our own humanity, that stratum of our nature that we putatively share with our nonhuman kin. This manner of posing the "question of the animal" is altogether distinct from a phenomenological description of the lives and experiences of nonhuman organisms on their own terms. Phenomenology has, of course, drawn on and sometimes inspired such descriptions, particularly in the works of Wolfgang Köhler, Jakob von Uexküll, and Frederik Buytendijk, among others. But such accounts are regularly appropriated for the more central debate over our own animality and its relationship with what makes us specifically human. The heart of the matter is not the animals outside but rather our own immanent animal nature, lived as both an origin and an ongoing inheritance, as our immemorial past as well as what we must transcend to be human in the present. This is why the phenomenological debates over animality must be read as an episode in the history of what Agamben calls the "anthropological machine," a set of mirrors by which we recognize a reflection of ourselves in the animal that we are not and thereby constitute ourselves as human through its exclusion (O 33–34/26–27).

Consider as a first example Husserl's extensive analyses in *Ideas II* of the constitution of "Animal Nature," which would later prove so influential on Merleau-Ponty. These studies concern what Husserl calls "animalia," human as well as nonhuman, and he is explicit that we should take the human subject here as one specimen of the more inclusive category of "animal subjects" (120–21/128). What Husserl investigates under this heading of "animal nature" is nothing zoological, and references to nonhuman animals in this text are rare.[1] This is because Husserl's primary concern is not with non-human animals but precisely with "man" as a "natural reality," that is, with the human considered abstractly in terms of its merely animal being (143/151). And so, when Husserl poses for himself the question "how does the animal Ego develop into the human Ego?" he is not asking a question addressed by evolutionary naturalism, because the animal in question here is precisely not a nonhuman organism but a stratum in the constitution of the full human person (339/350–51).

On one hand, it is possible to interpret Husserl's descriptions of our participation in a common animal nature as a reversal of the Cartesian legacy, thereby restoring the classical site for animal sensibility as an ontological stratum in its own right.[2] Insofar as it undermines what Frans de Waal terms "anthropodenial"—an unjustified refusal to recognize nonhuman cognition that has blinkered our scientific and philosophical encounters with animals for centuries—perhaps we can expect to find here the basis for a renewed sense of our continuity with animals, one motivated otherwise than by the usual Darwinian story of our common animal origins (de Waal, cited in Sober 2005, 85). According to David Wood, for example, Husserl's rediscovery of our common "animal sensibility" vindicates our capacity to empathize with our fellow sentient creatures, making this not an "anthropocentric" projection but a "biocentric" one, rooted as it is in our shared bodily natures.[3] For Wood, and he is hardly alone in this claim, our shared animal life bespeaks a common kinship with implications that are undeniably ethical.

On the other hand, it is precisely this common animal sensibility that is repeatedly contested in the development of phenomenology after Husserl, in different ways and with different stakes, by Scheler, Heidegger, Sartre, and Levinas. Arguably, it is only Merleau-Ponty, among the major phenomenologists of the twentieth century, who endorses something like an animal stratum of the human and finds in it the basis for what he will eventually call a "strange kinship" (N 339/271), as we discussed in chapter 4. This kinship is strange, for Merleau-Ponty, because the animal sensibility of the human being is not simply one given stratum to which another, "human" layer could be added, as we might think from Husserl's gesture of renewing the classical discourse of perceptual and rational souls. The animal level of human life is not simply identical or continuous with the lives of other creatures. We noted in chapter 3 that, for Merleau-Ponty in *The Structure of Behavior*, "life" does not have the same meaning for humans as for nonhuman animals, because "vital behavior" as such disappears with its integration into the higher-order human gestalt (188/174, 195/181). Consequently, Merleau-Ponty's early account of our vital behavior comes dangerously close to the "bare life" that, according to Agamben, is produced by the anthropological machine's logic of inclusive exclusion. Such life is neither an animal nor a human life but only a "state of exception, a zone of indeterminacy" at the turn of the hinge between our humanity and our animality (O 42–43/37–38). Is such a bare life all that remains of the animal nature integrated into our human selves, and if so, can we still speak of kinship in any meaningful sense?

To address this question, I first consider Merleau-Ponty's proximity with Max Scheler, whose remarks on the human–animal difference Merleau-Ponty cites frequently in *The Structure of Behavior*. It is Scheler, in *The Human Place in the Cosmos*, who first writes that "human beings can be *more* than animals and *less* than animals but they can never be an animal" (33/21). This is because, for Scheler, what defines the human essence is its participation in spirit, which is precisely a saying-no to life. Merleau-Ponty echoes Scheler's claim when he writes that "man can never be an animal; his life is always more or less integrated than that of an animal" (SB 196/181). Yet the reference to integration here marks a crucial difference: for Merleau-Ponty, the integration that defines the human being may wholly transform life, but it cannot do so without remainder. This remainder represents the contingency of death, what can never be fully integrated, and which is even necessary for the *staking* of one's life, in contrast with Scheler's sacrifice of life.

Second, the admission of the contingency of death into Merleau-Ponty's hierarchy of gestalts destabilizes it, toppling it over. This is why Merleau-Ponty's later work speaks of a lateral rather than a vertical transcendence and why that transcendence can be understood as intertwining or chiasm. In the chiasmic relation, the animal becomes me as I become it, bringing this exchange very close to what Deleuze and Guattari call "blocks of becoming" (ATP 290–92/237–39). But this moment of exchange, the intersection of

140 *Animal Memories*

the chiasm, is a moment that exceeds the exchange itself. To understand this moment, we need to consider its strange temporality as a generative passivity.[4] This generative moment is what Merleau-Ponty, in *Phenomenology of Perception,* names the anonymous "someone" who perceives within me without coinciding with my personal self. This anonymous someone is precisely my animal life, the life of my body as a natural self. But this means that my animal self lives a different temporality than my personal ego, a time of Aeon or of a past that has never been present.

Finally, I draw out the implications of this immemorial animality. First, my animal life, in its rhythmic generality, is neither singular nor plural. As the indefinite pronoun suggests, the "someone" who perceives within me is indefinite, a virtual multiplicity. Second, this animal someone, as the "logos of the sensible world" (N 219/166), is the generative ground for my personal self, and even for my ability to speak. We might say, then, that my speech is precisely the speaking through me of my own animal past. As Merleau-Ponty (1960, 27; 2007, 334) remarks in the preface to *Signs,* "all those we have loved, detested, known, or simply glimpsed speak through our voice." Last, if we are correct to identify the anonymous, natural self of the body with our own animal nature, then it is precisely this animal nature that perceives; the animals within us are the lives of "my eyes, hands, and ears, which are so many natural selves" (PP 261/224). And this means that, when I gaze into the eyes of another, nonhuman animal, it is the animals within me, the animals of my own generative past, that look back. This promises a deeper prospect for mutual encounter than any kinship in the present can offer.

Contingencies of Life and Death

The logic of the anthropological machine as described by Agamben concerns the relationship between animality and humanity *within* the human: to be human is precisely *not* to be animal, and *especially not* the animal that we already are. In other words, our "anthropogenesis," our constitution as human, requires the containment and policing of the animal within. What is at stake, in Agamben's terms, is our own internal negotiation of the relation between *zoē* and *bíos,* the biological and the biographical. The traditional logic of this relation is one of "exclusive inclusion" such that animal life is what is within us while not being us, while remaining unsynthesizable with our humanity and in need of its sovereign control. Agamben explicitly traces the operation of this logic through the thought of Heidegger, as "the philosopher of the twentieth century who more than any other strove to separate man from the living being" (O 44/39), but he otherwise makes no mention in this context of the phenomenological tradition. We can nevertheless trace the same anthropo-logic through the accounts of the human–animal relation in Scheler and early Merleau-Ponty. For example, Scheler defines "spirit," which for him essentially differentiates humans from animals, as *"opposite anything we call life, including life in the human being"* (HPC 39/26). This is why animals remain "ecstatically immersed" (39/27) in their environments, as the correlates of their drives, while humans can detach themselves from their biological lives sufficiently to achieve an objective perspective on the world and to choose values that run counter to biological needs. The key point here is that spirit, on Scheler's own description, opposes biological life in general, including human biological life, so that the essence of the human being is defined precisely by the "exclusive inclusion" of its own inner animality.

When Merleau-Ponty puts forward his own position on the essential distinction between humans and animals in *The Structure of Behavior,* he frequently cites Scheler, including the very passages to which we have just referred. What he adopts are Scheler's descriptions of the characteristics that are exclusively human, namely, the orientation toward truth and objectivity, the transformation of an environment into a world, the capacity for self-reflection, and so on. Yet Merleau-Ponty also distances himself from Scheler's account insofar as Merleau-Ponty treats spirit not as the negation of life but as its integration into a more complex gestalt. On this view, life and spirit are continuous, because both are simply different stages or degrees in the integration of form (143/133). Yet they are also discontinuous, because the emergence of a higher level of integration destroys the lower-order gestalt while incorporating it. Life as such, life in the animal sense of the term, disappears once it is integrated into the properly human dialectic. And so, for Merleau-Ponty, "one cannot speak of the body and of life in general, but only of the animal body and animal life, and of the human body and of human life" (195–96/181). Ultimately, human life and the human

142 *Animal Memories*

body do not exist as such in a fully integrated human being; their autonomous existence reappears only in cases of pathological disintegration (218–19/202–3). Consequently, for Merleau-Ponty, as for Scheler, what properly characterizes the human being will be the disappearance, we might say the "spiritualization," of *zoē* or biological life. Despite the differences between Scheler's negation of life by spirit and Merleau-Ponty's integration of life into spirit, then, we seem to arrive here at a very traditional hierarchical teleology according to which the human is precisely the inclusion of animal life through its exclusion.

There is more to this story, however, and what truly differentiates Merleau-Ponty's account from Scheler's turns out to be less the focus on integration than the inevitability of *dis*-integration. This emphasis on disintegration is introduced in the very last section of *The Structure of Behavior,* where Merleau-Ponty addresses what he calls the "truth of naturalism," and it ultimately effects a reversal of his position up to that point. Here Merleau-Ponty is concerned with the relation between, on one hand, consciousness as a structure that emerges through the integration of the subordinate structures of matter and life and, on the other hand, consciousness as "universal milieu," that is, as the dative of manifestation for the disclosure of anything whatsoever. In other words, he is addressing the same paradox that emerges at the end of Husserl's *Ideas II,* the paradox that Paul Ricoeur (1967, 76) would later call the "most embarrassing question" of this text, namely, the relationship between spirit and the transcendental ego. When Merleau-Ponty wrote *The Structure of Behavior,* he had not yet read *Ideas II,* which makes his resolution of the problem here all the more interesting. His solution, in brief, is to privilege structure over signification, that is, to emphasize the contingency of the emergence of consciousness from matter and life, and to make this emergent consciousness—what he calls "perceptual consciousness"—the condition and limit of any putatively universal consciousness. It is because consciousness as "universal milieu" remains an ideal promise rather than an actual achievement that Merleau-Ponty will later say that the most important lesson of the transcendental reduction is the "impossibility of a complete reduction" (PP 14/lxxvii). As we discussed in chapter 3, the reduction can never be complete, and the transcendental ego remains an ideal promise, because a complete and final integration of matter and life into spirit is unattainable. In Merleau-Ponty's words,

> there is always a duality which reappears at one level or another . . . ; integration is never absolute and it always fails—at a higher level in the writer, at a lower level in the aphasic. . . . This duality is not a simple fact; it is founded in principle—all integration presupposing the normal functioning of subordinated formations, which always demand their own due. (SB 226–27/210)

The subordinated gestalts demand their due because they have never truly disappeared; our animal past is never truly liquidated or spiritualized but continues to constitute our present lives from within.

To clarify the limits of this integration of the past of matter and life into the present of spirit, we might return to Merleau-Ponty's own comparison of ontological structure with musical form. As we saw in chapter 3, Merleau-Ponty relies on the figure of melody to illustrate the unity of gestalts throughout *The Structure of Behavior*, culminating in his claim that "the world, in those of its sectors which realize a structure, is comparable to a symphony" (142/132). In other words, the hierarchical integration of forms into the meaningful whole of nature is like the arrangement of musical phrases and counterpoints into a larger composition, a view that finds parallels in Uexküll's (1956, 2010) "composition theory of nature" and in the gestalt ontology of deep ecologist Arne Naess (see Naess 1989, esp. chap. 2). We saw that the integration of such musical forms occurs by recursion so that mind as a second-order melody transposes matter and life—which are its own past—into symbolic structures. Consequently, while every organism folds into itself its entire evolutionary history and even the memory of the universe itself, consciousness takes up this history as its own forgotten liability to what precedes it. I emphasized previously the contingency and partiality of such integration, as a consequence of the historical density and inertia of the lower-order gestalts, which always demand their due. The folded past at the heart of the present is also, then, a generative moment, because the inevitable failures of integration are selective and improvisatory. In short, our more or less composed human selves embody the sedimented stages through which we have passed so that, even to the extent that we do sublimate our animal natures, we remain perennially liable to them. We are never finished expressing our animality in and through the very heart of our humanity.

What truly distinguishes Merleau-Ponty's account from that of Husserl or Scheler is precisely this ongoing resistance of matter and life within spirit, because, for Merleau-Ponty, the pure spirit of Scheler or the transcendental ego of Husserl would eliminate all meaning for death. The truth of naturalism, of mind–body dualism, and of death is that every integration is liable to the "contingency of the lived" and is consequently temporary and fragile at best (SB 240/223). Nor is this a merely external limitation on what would otherwise remain an ideal possibility, because the contingency of the lived, as a point of passage in spirit's historical development, introduces that contingency into the very structure of spirit. As Merleau-Ponty writes, "consciousness experiences its inherence in an organism at each moment," and this inherence is nothing other than the "presence to consciousness of its proper history and of the dialectical stages which it has traversed" (SB 224–25/208). We are human, then, only as *having been* animal and only as *being still* animal in ways that exceed our efforts to take them into account. Because our animality can never finally be exhausted or excluded, Merleau-Ponty concludes that saying no to life is never an option; rather, it is only ever a question of "staking" one's life as a deeper way of living (SB 240/224). If phenomenology can contribute to the *désoeuvrement* of the anthropological machine, it may be precisely through such a putting into play of our own animality.

Lateral Overcoming and the Animal Past

The gestalt ontology that Merleau-Ponty proposes in *The Structure of Behavior* admits, in the end, the historical and contingent character of spirit, but it nevertheless says little in positive terms about the autonomy of life, that is, about the animal that continues to haunt our humanity from within. The procession from matter through life to spirit is presented here as teleologically oriented toward the achievement of genuine individuality so that the contingency of life is always presented under a negative aspect, for instance, as the "perpetual menace" that affords death its meaning (SB 240/223). But to take the contingency and autonomy of life seriously destabilizes the hierarchical arrangement of gestalts, which is why the vertical transcendence of Merleau-Ponty's first book gives way to the lateral transgressions of his later work, where he speaks no longer of the integration of gestalts but rather of the intertwining of chiasms. In his lecture courses on nature, Merleau-Ponty continues to say that the human being has "another manner of being a body" than the animal, but this relation is to be understood as *Ineinander,* as a being in-one-another, rather than as a simple hierarchy (N 276–77/214). "The relation of the human and animality," he writes, "is not a hierarchical relation, but lateral, an overcoming that does not abolish kinship" (N 335/268; cf. 338–39/271).

Here Merleau-Ponty's interpretation of the human–animal relation comes very close to that of Deleuze and Guattari in *A Thousand Plateaus,* where they describe the bidirectional transformations and exchanges between humans and animals as forming "blocks of becoming." For Deleuze and Guattari, becomings-animal are perfectly real—neither fictional nor mere imitations—even if "it is clear that the human being does not 'really' become an animal any more than the animal 'really' becomes something else." The reality of the becoming does not hinge on some product that would result, because "becoming produces nothing other than itself." "What is real," they write, "is the becoming itself, the block of becoming, not the supposedly fixed terms through which that which becomes passes" (291/238). If a veritable becoming-animal has no subject and no term apart from the becoming itself, if it is the very event of mutual transformation, then such becoming has the structure of a chiasmus: a becoming-animal of the human that is a becoming-human of the animal.

Now, despite this parallel, Deleuze and Guattari's account leaves unexplained the sense in which this chiasmic event should be understood, for Merleau-Ponty, as an "overcoming," even if this is lateral rather than hierarchical. We know that the figure for this "overcoming" is the reflexivity of the body itself, according to Merleau-Ponty's famous descriptions—inspired, once again, by Husserl's *Ideas II*—of one hand touching another (N 340/273). Although Merleau-Ponty's descriptions of the touching–touched relation are familiar from *The Visible and the Invisible* and other texts, they receive a slightly different inflection in the courses on Nature,

146 *Animal Memories*

where he is specifically concerned with accounting for the "animal of perceptions." Here Merleau-Ponty describes the *écart*, the gap, between the touching hand and the one it touches, noting that "their reciprocity breaks up at the moment that it is going to be born." But this failure, he continues,

> is precisely the very apprehension of my body in its duplicity, as thing and vehicle of my relation to things. There are two "sides" of an experience, conjugated and incompossible, but complementary. Their unity is irrecusable; it is simply like the invisible hinge on which two experiences are articulated—a self torn apart. (N 285/223)

We can see from this figure of the touching–touched, which Merleau-Ponty calls "reflection in figural form" and takes to be exemplary of the lateral relation of *Ineinander* (N 340/273), that "overcoming" here no longer means integration or dialectical synthesis. It is rather a kind of internal tearing apart or dehiscence, a bidirectional mediation that converts each term into its other while maintaining their noncoincident identity. And so when Merleau-Ponty speaks of the "man-animality *intertwining*," this expresses a parallel reversibility and duplicity that is resolvable neither into identity nor into difference (VI 328/274). We are human, then, only insofar as our humanity enters into kaleidoscopic exchange with our animality and insofar as our animality within enters into exchange with the animality without.

In the case of the two hands touching, their unity amounts to no more than the "invisible hinge" at the jointure of their exchange. It is worth noting that this unity, the invisible hinge, is not itself anything that can be touched; the unity is a kind of residue or remainder that conditions touch while remaining absent from it. This absent remainder has a temporal meaning, insofar as it is always in the past; even while it is generative of the present, it is encountered only in the mode of having slipped away. To put this another way, when one hand touches another, the hand that is actively touching—the subject hand—is always too late to touch the agency of the object hand, which has submerged itself into the things of the world. The object hand becomes for it an unpresentable past. This poses the problem of the temporality of our own animality.

As we remember from *The Structure of Behavior*, our animal life was there understood as the constitutive history of spirit, the traces of its process of integration, which was experienced as its present inherence in an organism. When integration is replaced by intertwining, this animal past becomes the prereflective moment of our immersion into the perceptual world, the time of our "perceptual consciousness," that is, our originary and never lived-through past. Our animal lives inhabit our present precisely as such an immemorial past, a past that is generative of this present while unfolding a distinct temporality of its own.

Voices of the Animal Past

To understand my association of our animal lives with the immemorial past, let us return to Merleau-Ponty's distinction between the "biological" and "personal" selves in *Phenomenology of Perception.* We saw in chapter 1 that Merleau-Ponty describes our biological existence as an "innate complex": "my organism—as a pre-personal adhesion to the general form of the world, as an anonymous and general existence—plays the role of an *innate complex* beneath the level of my personal life" (113/86). Although there may be times when my human life fully integrates my biological organism, as *The Structure of Behavior* had suggested, now Merleau-Ponty recognizes that such situations are relatively rare. Instead, as he writes, "most of the time personal existence represses the organism without being able to transcend it or to renounce it, and without being able to reduce the organism to itself or itself to the organism" (PP 113/86).

The language here of "complex" and "repression" recalls Merleau-Ponty's descriptions of the pathological failures of full human integration in *The Structure of Behavior* (192/177). But in *Phenomenology of Perception,* the autonomous structure of our biological organism has its own integrity, because this anonymous and general existence is precisely the subject of perception, the "someone" who perceives within me (260/223). This someone is not the personal, reflective self but instead that assemblage of "natural selves" that has already sided with and synchronized with the world (261/224). And this "someone," as I have repeatedly noted, lives in a "prehistory," the "past of all pasts," which is the time of our organic rhythms, a time incommensurate with the narrative and linear time of our conscious experience (287/250, 302/265, 114/87, 517/479, 171/139).

This allows us to clarify further the famous lines with which Merleau-Ponty concludes his chapter on sensing, to the effect that reflection fully grasps itself only when it takes into account its own prereflective history, a history that constitutes for it "an original past, a past that has never been present" (PP 289/252). This prereflective history is the immemorial past of nature, a nature with which we coexist at the level of sensation but which can never be fully recuperated by the reflective operations of the personal self. It is, in short, the absolute past of our own biological life, of our inner animality. As Alia Al-Saji (2008) has argued, it is necessary to distinguish here between sensibility and perception proper. "Sensory life," Al-Saji writes, "would be that 'primitive complicit[y] with the world'" which is the "condition of possibility of perceptual experience" but remains distinct from perception proper insofar as it is "anterior to the distinctions of subject and object and to the divisions between the senses" (47, 48). As the generative ground of experience, sensibility so understood cannot be a conscious experience; it cannot occur within personal time, the time of reflection, precisely because it makes such time possible. It therefore represents, for reflection, an im-possible and irrecuperable past, a past that can never be made present. This impossible and immemorial past is that of our own animality, the subject of our perceptions that inevitably escapes and exceeds our reflective gaze.

Several interesting implications follow from this immemorial temporality of our animal lives. First, as is already implied by Merleau-Ponty's use of the impersonal pronoun and his description of the natural *selves* of our senses, our biological lives exceed the distinction between the singular and the plural. This brings us close to Deleuze and Guattari's claim that "becoming-animal always involves a pack, a band, a population, a peopling, in short, a multiplicity." As they explain, "We do not become animal without a fascination for the pack, for multiplicity. A fascination for the Outside? Or is the multiplicity that fascinates us already related to a multiplicity dwelling within us?" (ATP 292–93/239–40). Our fascination with the pack would therefore be the resonance that it forms with our own anonymous multiplicity. And this introduction of an immemorial past into the very folding of the melody of life transforms what Deleuze and Guattari have called the "refrain." The refrain is a periodic repetition, a manner of oscillating or vibrating, that introduces and dissolves relations and becomings. Refrains come together to form milieus, or environments, as spatiotemporal blocks for ordering chaos, and living things are the intersections of just such milieus. When Deleuze and Guattari speak of "becoming-animal," they have in mind an appropriation or an exchange of refrains so that, while the human being takes on the style of an animal—the speed and slowness, or the relation between movement and rest, of the animal's elements—the animal is equally transformed into something else. In their favorite case of the composer Olivier Messiaen, for instance, the territorial breeding call of a song thrush—its refrain—is deterritorialized or extracted from its environment to be reterritorialized as notes in a musical composition.

According to our account of our own animality as an immemorial past, what Deleuze and Guattari say about the refrain must be supplemented by Deleuze's (1968, 1994) account, in *Difference and Repetition,* of involuntary memory. More precisely, becoming-animal involves a kind of Proustian reminiscence of our own animal past as a past that was never present, a past that could never present itself to our human awareness. This involuntary memory points toward a pure past that would be the past of life as such, the memory of its evolutionary unfolding. On Elizabeth Grosz's (2008) reading, as we saw in chapter 4, this means that we should see in the refrain a production and intensification of desire, precisely the desire that drives sexual selection. This desire cannot be separated, we are suggesting, from a slippage between the personal self, namely, the I that occupies its narrative position in the present, and the multiple we that takes up an immeasurable and infinite past—a past stretching all the way back to the very elements and to the geological dimensions of time.

Second, it is this anonymous multiplicity that expresses itself through the voice that I superficially take to be "mine." The self-coincidence of the voice has, of course, long represented the pure autoaffection of consciousness, because, when I speak to myself silently, I hear myself speaking with an apparent immediacy, as if my voice required no passage through the world. In chapter 3, I proposed that hearing oneself speak nevertheless involves a doubling, because I hear myself from within through the vibrations of my body while simultaneously hearing myself from without through the medium of the world. Even the putative self-coincidence of the voice therefore involves an alteraffection that mingles my voice with the world. Furthermore, as Leonard Lawlor (2009a, 18) has argued, the supposed purity of hearing myself speak is interrupted from the first by the voices of others:

> It is an irreducible or essential necessity that the silent words I form contain repeatable traits. This irreducible necessity means that, when I speak to myself, I speak with the sounds of others. In other words, it means that I find in myself other voices, which come from the past. . . . The problem therefore with the belief that interior monologue is my own is that others' voices contaminate the hearing of myself speaking. Just as my present moment is always already old, my interior monologue is never my own.

Now, we have already noted a very similar remark from Merleau-Ponty (1960, 27; 2007, 334) himself, when he writes that "all those we have loved, detested, known, or simply glimpsed speak through our voice." But now we must recognize that these voices from our past are not limited to the human voices of our narrative, personal history. They include the anonymous voices of an immemorial prehistory, the voices of the animals that we will have been.

Last, if we are correct to identify the "someone" who perceives within us with the animal dimension of our being, it follows that—in the same way that animals speak through our voices—they also look out through our eyes. The "someone" or the "we" that perceives within me, that is connatural with the world, is the multiplicity of my own animal becoming. But this means that, when I look at an animal and it looks back at me, what looks out through my eyes, from an impossible past, is my own animal organism. "And yet, sometimes a silent animal looks up at us and silently looks through us," Rilke (1989, 67) writes in the eighth of the *Duino Elegies.* Yet perhaps when this animal sees through our personal self, it precisely sees into our animal self. And what it sees there is not a kinship but instead a withdrawal. John Sallis (2012, 141) describes the moment of exceeding the look that emerges at the crossing of two glances: "A living being that not only has a look but also looks back at the viewer . . . may, through this compounded look, show itself as exceeding its look. In the eyes of the other, one sees that the other, no less than oneself, exceeds the look offered to one's vision. In such cases there are traces of a withdrawn depth that escapes the look." This withdrawn depth in the look of the other is essentially invisible, just as the *écart* of the two touches is intangible, and for the same reason: that rather than a presence to ourselves, we are essentially a self torn apart, torn between the human and the animal.

7

Extinction and Memory
FROM BIODIVERSITY TO BIODIACRITICS

When we imagine the end of the world, it is first the collapse of the human world, or more specifically a particular colonial–industrial civilization, that we have in mind. But once "we humans" are removed from the scene, other forms of life might certainly thrive; the end of a certain human world might well open the world for nonhuman others. Even climate collapse, which is expected to be as bad for the majority of familiar species as for the human poor and vulnerable, will create conditions under which certain other species may flourish, as they have in past periods of higher global temperatures. In J. G. Ballard's 1962 speculative fiction novel *The Drowned World,* often identified as a prescient work of climate fiction, devolution or recovery of the imprinted memories of the evolutionary past, for humans and nonhumans alike, quickly populates the planet with frenetic and unfamiliar life (Ballard [1962] 2014). The submergence of the remains of civilization and the anticipated extinction of the human species are not the end of the world writ large, although Ballard's new world hesitates between the recovery of a lost past, in a mode that can hardly be called nostalgic, and the opening toward a novel or even hybrid future. On the other hand, Margaret Atwood's (2003, 2009, 2013) dystopian MaddAddam Trilogy resolutely embraces precisely the hybridity of a future in which genetically modified organisms go rogue and challenge the supremacy and the separatism of those humans who remain.

The appeal of such counternarratives is due, at least in part, to their departure from the glaring possibility that the end of "our" world, "our" civilization, or "our" species could very well take all other life down along with it, as is already intimated in Rachel Carson's *Silent Spring* and the popular imagination of total nuclear destruction.[1] In our cultural imaginary and much scientific prediction, the eco-eschatological narrative is inseparable from species extinction. And what is extinction—which Holmes Rolston (1988, 143–46) terms "superkilling" insofar as it kills an entire kind rather than one or many individuals—if not the end of a distinctive way of life, a way that stretches back through immemorial evolutionary history and, in this sense, the definitive end of a world that predates all human worlds? For Rolston, each species is an "intergenerational narrative," so that "to kill a species is to shut down a unique story" (145).

Thom van Dooren (2014, 4) continues in a similar vein by asking, "What is lost when a species, an evolutionary lineage, a way of life, passes from the world?" Like Rolston, van Dooren's answer invokes narrative and storytelling, a narrative complicated by its temporal entanglements and complexity. Species, for van Dooren, are "incredible achievements: intergenerational lineages stretched across millions of years of evolutionary history," and appreciating what is lost in extinction demands of us the "difficult task of taking seriously . . . vastly different temporal horizons and their overlaps and intersections" (16). In van Dooren's example of the albatross, this includes not only the "historical lineage" that spans evolutionary time from speciation to extinction but also the lives of those individuals presently tasked with achieving the continuation of this lineage: "in some sense, millions of years of evolution are 'in' each of these albatross bodies: inheritances, histories, relationships, carried in the flesh" (34). The threat of extinction, of course, tightens the temporal knot, because these diachronic and synchronic perspectives intersect as well with the evolutionary emergence of human beings and the strange temporality of our technological by-products, especially "the life spans of seemingly immortal plastics, the half-lives of persistent organic pollutants" (22). Because each living species is an entanglement of incommensurate and intersecting durations that span evolutionary and human history, appreciating what is lost with the extinction of any species involves rethinking our own liability to organic memory and our evolutionary past.

As political leaders in the United States continue to renegotiate the terms and status of the Endangered Species Act, we can see the threat of species extinction as one example among many of the contestation over the line between life and death, perhaps the defining struggle of today's politics no less than of contemporary philosophy. From the plight of endangered species to military drones to climate change, we confront negotiations over what counts as life as well as over the right, or the authority, to end it, if not also the responsibility to preserve it. The stakes are real in these efforts to mark off a singular line between life and death, the living and the nonliving, what will live and what will die, what is living within us and what is not. Yet as Derrida has already reminded us, with particular attention to a privileged site of this contestation, the putative limit between Man and Animal, there is always a "heterogeneous multiplicity" of the living, a "multiplicity of the organizations of relations between living and dead, relations of organization or lack of organization among realms that are more and more difficult to dissociate by means of the figures of the organic and inorganic, of life and/or death." No singular line divides the living from the dead because these very terms are simultaneously "intimate and abyssal," nonobjectifiable, irreducible to simple exteriority (A 53/31). In previous chapters, I have put Derrida's insight that the relations between life and death are never a simple exteriority of terms into conversation with Agamben's claim that our humanity is itself a production of these negotiations between life and death, that *Homo sapiens* is in fact a machine for producing the human through a set of mirrors by which we recognize a reflection of ourselves in the animal that we are not and thereby constitute ourselves as human through its exclusion (O 33–34/26–27). This is why, as we saw in chapter 6, the phenomenology of animality, from Husserl through Heidegger to Merleau-Ponty, has always focused on and delimited the animal dimension *of the human being,* attending to *our own* share of "bare life" rather than to an investigation of the lives of nonhuman others on their own terms.

This complication of the problem of life destabilizes phenomenology itself, because phenomenology has always relied on an essential difference between intentionality and causality or between experience and objective events. As Derrida again has shown us, phenomenology always begins from and assumes a certain auto-affection, a certain self-presence, to the exclusion of whatever exceeds or refuses such presencing. Yet I have also been suggesting that phenomenology does not preclude alteraffection, an encounter with what can only be presented excessively and in its very refusal of our terms (A 95/133; Lawlor 2007, 60–63). If this is so, a phenomenology that can express the heterogeneous relations between life and death in their carnal manifestation may provide a distinctive opportunity, and bear a singular responsibility, in the effort to renegotiate our sense of animality, humanity, and life.

This question of how to think life without thereby setting it up as the opposite of nonlife, of recognizing its autoaffection without refusing alteraffection, is at stake in the ubiquitous charge to preserve "biodiversity." Since its introduction in the mid-1980s, this concept has become a leading buzzword of environmentalism, dominating public perceptions and conservation research and policy on an international scale (Maier 2012). Indeed, the term was first introduced to the public conversation in the hope of galvanizing support for conservation causes (Takacs 1996, 3, 37). The success of their efforts is reflected in the immense investment of resources into the biological study and management application of biodiversity in the intervening decades, so much so that ecological research since the late 1980s may well be described, in David Tilman's (2012, 109) words, as the "biodiversity revolution." Yet despite its resonance with the public, it is far from obvious that "biodiversity" can live up to its reputation. In the scientific context, biodiversity encompasses the diversity or variability of life at all levels, in a broadly inclusive sense (Koricheva and Siipi 2004, 29–30). But there is a growing consensus among scientists and environmental philosophers that biodiversity in this broad sense is not empirically tractable in a way that could be applied in specific management contexts (see, e.g., Koricheva and Siipi 2004, 35; Maclaurin and Sterelny 2008, 7; Norton 2008, 373). Furthermore, the long-standing assumptions about the relationship between biodiversity and different kinds of ecosystem functioning, such as the diversity-stability hypothesis— that greater diversity leads to greater ecosystem stability—have not been borne out by the scientific research, leading biological ecologists Diane Srivastava and Mark Vellend (2005, 285) to conclude that studies of the relationship between biodiversity and ecosystem function have "little to offer in the way of practical advice for conservation managers."[2]

The popular justifications for attributing ethical value to biodiversity, moreover, have been shown to suffer serious flaws. In *What's So Good about Biodiversity?*, Donald Maier (2012, 3) examines what he takes to be the most promising of these arguments and finds them "mostly so fragile that they crumble before modest scrutiny." In fact, he reports being stunned that he could not find "a single argument that does not have serious logical flaws, crippling qualifications, or indefensible assumptions" (2). The self-described aim of his book, then, is to "declare the Emperor naked" (3) in the hope of saving what is truly valuable in nature from the harms to which it is increasingly subjected through the application of this misguided concept.

Such critiques of the received concept of biodiversity raise the question of whether we do, in fact, value life for its diversity per se. This is a distinct question from whether we value particular species, however rare, or particular ecosystems, whatever their characteristics. The question is rather whether we value—for its own sake—the *differences between* the countless manifestations of life on all scales. There are numerous well-known arguments for the normative force of biodiversity that have tried to make the case that we do or should value life's differences, and it is just such arguments that Maier (2012) has cataloged and critiqued. Under his descriptions, the biodiversity project begins to look suspiciously like the reduction of nature to a "catalog of biota and biota-related entities" (423) that have been "sliced and diced in strategic and tractable ways" (416) for the purposes of scientific investigation and, perhaps ultimately, for economic evaluation. But in rejecting this biotic inventory approach, Maier also sets aside anything like a value for the difference or variability of life as such. So, the question remains: why do the *differences* within and between forms of life matter? An answer to this question depends, first of all, on how we understand these differences—that is, on whether there is an alternative conception of the variability of life to the slice-and-dice model assumed by biodiversity proponents.

I propose such an alternative here under the rubric of "biodiacritics," inspired in part by the "diacritical hermeneutics" advanced by Richard Kearney. Hermeneutics, for Kearney (2011, 1), concerns the "practice of discerning indirect, tacit or allusive meanings, of sensing another sense beyond or beneath apparent sense" (cf. Kearney 2015). And Kearney already notes that hermeneutics in this sense involves "interpreting plural meaning in response to the polysemy of language *and life*" (1, my emphasis). There are many senses of *diacritical* at play here for Kearney, but a significant one hearkens back to the medical practice of diagnosing bodily symptoms, that is, of *dia-krinein* as "reading the body," reading its differences as they negotiate the lines between life and death. For Kearney, such diacritical reading culminates in a "carnal hermeneutics" that definitively carries us beyond the human, extending, he claims, to "diacritical readings of different kinds of Others—human, animal or divine. All with skins on" (3).

My aim is to explore here in more detail what form such a diacritical hermeneutics of life, a biodiacritics, might take. To do so, I turn to a source that I share with Kearney, namely, the diacritical account of language, perception, and ontology that Merleau-Ponty developed, starting in the 1950s, on the basis of his readings of Saussure and Valéry. For Merleau-Ponty, the key insight of diacritical difference is that it describes a system consisting only of differences without positive terms. He presents this notion of the diacritical with respect to language in the opening lines of his 1952 essay "Indirect Language and the Voices of Silence":

> What we have learned from Saussure is that, taken singly, signs do not signify anything, and that each one of them does not so much express a meaning as mark a divergence of meaning between itself and other signs. Since the same can be said for all other signs, we may conclude that language is made of differences without terms; or more exactly, that the terms of language are engendered only by the differences which appear among them. (S 49/39)

Language is a system of differences without terms, but it hangs together as a system nonetheless, embodying what Merleau-Ponty calls a "unity of coexistence, like that of the sections of an arch which shoulder one another" (S 50/39). Merleau-Ponty increasingly comes to recognize that this notion of diacritical difference as a unity without positive terms applies not only to language but equally to perception and ultimately to ontology as such. As Emmanuel Alloa (2009, 2013) has argued, the famous ontology of flesh that Merleau-Ponty proposes in his final works can be understood as the culmination of this extension of the concept of the diacritical.

Starting from some hints in Merleau-Ponty's own remarks about life, I suggest that the diacritical perspective captures a certain phenomenological insight into the experience of life as difference—not only, that is, as variability between a ready-made catalog of tractable units but difference all the way down. Far from eliminating any sense of life's unity, though, a diacritical notion of life articulates our sense that life hangs together, that it has a "unity of coexistence"—like the sections of an arch—without this unity requiring anything like the harmony or balance of nature that underwrote early forms of scientific ecology and ecologically inspired environmental ethics. From here, we can also then explore the specifically hermeneutical task of biodiacritics, that is, its attention to the other sense "beyond or beneath apparent sense." Most important, such a hermeneutics reveals the immemorial temporal dimension of our relationship to diacritical life. It is precisely insofar as life, in its diacritical structure, institutes an evolving history or even a figured memory—a memory that embraces us as living creatures—that it commands our respect and hospitality.

Diacritical Difference from Language to Flesh

To understand what is at stake in "biodiacritics," we begin with the diacritical account of language, perception, and ontology advanced by Merleau-Ponty, who introduces the phrase "diacritical difference" to name the Saussurian insight that language consists only of differences without positive terms. Already at the level of language, this has interesting implications. First, it implies a reversal in our usual way of thinking about the relation between identity and difference, which is that we begin by identifying relevant subsisting units—sentences, words, phonemes—and on this basis determine their differential relations.[3] Merleau-Ponty's reversal suggests that differences do not presuppose identities; rather, difference precedes and constitutes identity (see Kearney 2011, 2). As he admits, "this is a difficult idea," even a paradox comparable to those of Zeno, because it seems that we would already need to know a language to learn it (S 49/39). But it is this paradoxical circle that properly defines language as an instance of diacritical difference, because language, "in the presence of those who are learning it, precedes itself, teaches itself, and suggests its own deciphering" (S 49/39). It can do so only through its internal distribution of differences, which is what the child enters into through the process of babbling, or what the reader encounters when learning the experimental grammar and vocabulary of a modernist novel, for instance. Language is "far less a table of statements which satisfy well-formed thoughts than a swarm of gestures all occupied with differentiating themselves from one another and blending again" (PM 161/115). This means that we can learn a language only by immersing ourselves in it and allowing its self-differentiation to play through us, through our bodily gestures, including the gestures of the vocal cords. It is through our corporeal mimicry of a language's style, its manner of segregation and precipitation, that a new register is opened for expression. One cannot learn a language piecemeal, then, but only by a total immersion into the play of differences that constitutes its expressive capacity.

Second, even though language is a swarm of differences, it maintains an effective unity precisely because it functions to express, to say something. And it is because language succeeds in expressing, that is, because we do speak and understand one another, that we know that its paradoxical circularity is only a theoretical problem. This unity of coexistence is possible because language is not a collection of preexisting units but a whole that differentiates itself, such that each node within this web consists fundamentally of its references to the rest. "It is the whole that possesses meaning, not each part" (PM 41/28), as Merleau-Ponty says, and yet there is an "immanence of the whole in the parts" (S 51/41) defined by each moment's reflection of its divergence in relation to all others. Furthermore, this system is in a constant ferment that incorporates semantic slippages and contingencies of all sorts, putting them into play to enrich its own expressive possibilities and thereby converting the accidental into the meaningful and the rational (PM 50/35). Merleau-Ponty calls this creative ferment "originary" or "primary" differentiation, an "inexhaustible power of differentiating" that leaves in its trail the sedimentations that we call words, syllables, and letters (PM 47/33).

We must nevertheless resist the temptation to think of this system as a thing, or as an assemblage of things, which is a temptation born of language's own tendency to cover its tracks as it leads us toward what it expresses. The meaning is in the whole, but it is not localizable, and certainly not in the sounds we hear or in the words on the page, which are only the traces that the process of differentiation has left in its wake. The meaning of an expression is not contained in the words but rather at their intersections and in the intervals between them, in their absences and folds (S 53–54/42; see also Kearney 2011, 2). Meaning requires these interruptions and intervals, just as the words on the page require space between them, or as the phrases that we utter require the punctuations of silence. We typically overlook the intervals, as well as the words, in favor of what we are speaking about, just as we see without ever giving notice to our eyes or to vision's regular interruption by their blinking.

The third interesting consequence of the diacritical perspective, then, is that language is essentially indirect and allusive, precisely because its meaning rests in the intervals of difference. As we noted in chapter 3, Merleau-Ponty goes so far as to say that all language is fundamentally silence (S 54/43). He is speaking here not of the sedimented words that populate dictionaries, which have perhaps become sufficiently reified to be affixed with a label, but rather of the event of expression as originary differentiation, where a "lateral or oblique" meaning begins to form among and between the jostling edges of words (S 58/46). It is when language is at its most expressive that it most keeps silent. And this returns us to Kearney's definition of hermeneutics as the practice of "discerning indirect, tacit or allusive meanings, of sensing another sense beyond or beneath apparent sense." Rather than reading or listening past the silences, such a hermeneutics cultivates a listening-between; it gives an ear to the silent call between the words.

Thus far, we have considered only the diacritics of language, but for Merleau-Ponty, this account will also apply, in its own fashion, to the sensible world and the sensing body. In a note titled "Perception and Language" from October 1959, he writes:

> I describe perception as a diacritical, relative, oppositional system—the primordial space as topological (that is, cut out in a total voluminosity which surrounds me, in which I am, which is behind me as well as before me . . .). . . . But there is all the same this difference between perception and language, that I *see* the perceived things and that the significations on the contrary are invisible. . . . The only thing finally that is seen in

162 *Extinction and Memory*

the full sense is the totality wherein the sensibles are cut out. (VI 267/213–14)

As this note already intimates, the sensible and language, or the visible and the invisible, turn out to be the primary axes of Merleau-Ponty's later ontology, the ontology of flesh. And Merleau-Ponty arrives at this ontology by following through the implications of diacritical difference that he first describes in the linguistic field.

This development is already at work in the lectures from Merleau-Ponty's 1953 course *The Sensible World and the World of Expression,* where we find the following note: "Conceptualize even sensation, sensing, as action of a figure on a background, modulation. E.g., noise [as] modulation of silence. Color [as] modulation of an open space that it varies. Every sign is diacritical" (Merleau-Ponty 2011, 206; 2020, 161). The reference here to sensation as always involving a figure-on-a-ground should remind us of Merleau-Ponty's earlier descriptions of perception as always having a gestalt structure. What I see, hear, or smell must stand out against a background; it must differentiate itself from a level that is taken as the norm. And we should also notice that this figure–ground structure is essentially differential: the figure can only be determined in relation to a ground *that it is not,* and it becomes a figure only by differentiating itself from the ground. If a figure-on-a-ground is the simplest moment of perception, then perception can have no positive or self-identical terms. The ontology of gestalts that Merleau-Ponty had proposed in his very first book, *The Structure of Behavior,* is already, then, an ontology of difference. But, with diacritics, we move beyond a nested hierarchy of figure–ground structures to recognize that each node or each fold within the system echoes the modulations of all the others and that such foldings incessantly institute new levels and dissolve old ones in a pell-mell, entangled, and baroque fashion. And this is precisely the insight of the diacritical system to which Merleau-Ponty will, in the end, give the name "flesh." As he writes in a note from December 1959,

replace the notions of concept, idea, mind, representation with the notions of dimensions, articulation, level, hinges, pivots, configuration—The point of departure = the critique of the usual conception of the *thing* and its *properties* . . . critique of *positive* signification (differences between significations), signification as a gap . . . founded on this diacritical conception. (VI 277/224)

As we can begin to see here, diacritical difference institutes its own internality, its own immanence; it has a kind of "for itself," which would not be that of consciousness as it is classically understood in terms of autoaffection—that is, as pure presence to itself—but would instead be a "for itself" through autodivergence, though a kind of incessant differentiation and deferral.

One way to think about Merleau-Ponty's aim here, as David Morris has compellingly argued, is as the effort to avoid confusing being with determinate being. For Morris (2018, 205),

> the error of thinking that being is determinate is the recognizable target of Merleau-Ponty's critique of the ready-made world. This error, and his effort to avoid it, are behind his concepts of structure, expression, the invisible *of* the visible, and *écart*. These all seek to conceptualize being as *engendering* determinacy—yet not from any already determinate sense.

And Morris shows in detail that this releasing of being from determinacy will demand a new thinking of the biological, because so many current views reproduce the prejudice that "determinate organisms must have already determinate developmental causes or 'programs'" (207). The diacritical perspective avoids such determinacy precisely because it is differentiation and deferral all the way down, because it is primordially the emergence and dissolution of intervals and spacings. And this is arguably why Merleau-Ponty insists that fundamental ontology can proceed only indirectly or negatively. As his often-cited note from February 1959 puts it, *"one cannot make a direct ontology. My 'indirect' method (being in the beings) is alone conformed with being"* (VI 233/179; see also Kearney 2013, 183).

Diacritical Life

Let us return, then, to the specific question of what this means for a possible biodiacritics, that is, for a diacritical conception of life. For a start, recall Heidegger's lesson that life is not a discovery of biology but rather something that biology—to the extent that life is

164 *Extinction and Memory*

its subject matter—must always presuppose. Heidegger (1989, 520; 1991, 41) explains the matter as follows in the third volume of his lectures on Nietzsche:

> As a science, all biology already presupposes a more or less explicitly drawn essential delimitation of appearances that constitute its realm of objects. This realm . . . is that of living beings. Underlying the delimitation of this realm there is again a preconception of what distinguishes and sets apart living beings as such, namely, life. The essential realm in which biology moves can itself never be posited and grounded by biology as a science, but can always only be presupposed, adopted, confirmed.

Whether it remains true that the sciences of biology today in their varied interdisciplinary forms—for instance, molecular biology or biogeochemistry—presuppose any sense of "life" as their focal realm is open to debate. But Heidegger's point is that a pretheoretical experience of life, life as a phenomenon, precedes any biological investigation of living things and cannot be derived from it. And, whether or not contemporary biology addresses itself to "life," human beings certainly continue to do so, particularly insofar as life challenges us to respond to it with a proper hospitality.

My suggestion, then, is that this pretheoretical understanding of life is fundamentally diacritical, not unlike our pretheoretical immersion into the sensible and the linguistic fields. And although his remarks concerning the diacritics of life are brief and condensed, we can already locate a proposal along these lines in the notes for Merleau-Ponty's 1959–60 course on the concept of nature, where we find the following:

> Life is not a separable thing, but an investment, a singular point, a hollow in Being, an invariant ontological relief . . . the establishment of a level around which the divergences begin forming, a kind of being that functions like an arch. . . . But life is not negativity: it is a pattern of negations, a system of opposition that means that what is not this, is that. (N 302/238)

Recall that it is precisely this example of the arch, the stones that hold each other up without any external support, by which Merleau-Ponty first characterizes the diacritical difference of language years earlier. This figure of the arch suggests a kind of "hanging-together," a unity of interdependence, that Merleau-Ponty himself calls a "unity of coexistence." This might call to mind the kind of holistic interdependence that is popularly associated with the science of ecology. For instance, deep ecologist Arne Naess (1989, 36) writes that "the study of ecology indicates an approach, a methodology which can be suggested by the simple maxim 'all things hang together.'" This "hanging-together" recalls the organicist conception of ecology put forward at the beginning of the twentieth century by Henry Cowles and Frederic Clements, which would later inspire the popularized notion of ecology as a science of interdependence, balance, and harmony.

According to Clements, healthy species communities function as "superorganisms" that naturally tend toward a mature "climax" state in which all organisms cooperate in an interdependent way to maintain the stability and integrity of the community. This organicist understanding of species communities was gradually replaced by the notion of an "ecosystem," popularized by Eugene Odum in the 1940s, which reconceived the superorganism as a dynamic energy system that maximizes efficiency and distributes benefits through adaptive cooperation. Although Odum's ecosystem model swaps in mechanistic and economic metaphors, it nevertheless continues to describe natural systems as tending toward a "homeostasis" in which the mutualism and symbiosis between species maintain the energy and resources of the system.[4] It is this conception of harmony and balance in nature that inspires Aldo Leopold's (1968, 224–25) famous proposal of a "land ethic" that takes the "integrity, stability, and beauty of the biotic community" as its highest good. As many critics have noted, this reliance on what Ned Hettinger and Bill Throop (1999) call the "ecology of stability" is out of step with recent trends in ecology that emphasize disturbance and instability as typical features of many natural environments.

One virtue of biodiacritics is that it suggests a way to understand the "hanging-together" of life without endorsing any "ecology of stability" that purports to discover in nature a tendency toward stability, integrity, or cooperation. On the diacritical view, what joins the different nodes and folds of life is nothing more than the intervals or gaps that constitute them; each implies the whole and therefore hangs together with the whole insofar as its own identity is the determinate negation of every other moment within that

166 *Extinction and Memory*

whole. Just as a gestalt joins figure with ground precisely insofar as it differentiates them, so biodiacritics connects every level and aspect of life as moments of its own dehiscence. And there is nothing metaphysically mysterious about this sense of hanging-together through difference rather than identity, because it is what we rely on constantly in the case of language and perception. More generally, the superorganism and the ecosystem are both models for thinking life that start from determinate being, which makes them incapable of grasping the emergence of determinacy from the primordially indeterminate process of differentiation itself. What escapes them both, in other words, is that life's self-differentiation is a process of *expression,* that is, of the autoproduction of sense.[5] It is because this autoproduction of sense has no transcendent guide or invisible hand that it can incorporate into its movement, just as does language, all manner of accidents and historical contingencies.

Evolutionary biologist George Williams (1992) compellingly makes this case in relation to the eye, that favorite of intelligent design theorists from William Paley to the present. The vertebrate eye achieves its function quite marvelously, but rather than offering an example of intelligent design, Williams argues, it is actually rather stupidly designed, given the functionally arbitrary and even downright maladaptive features that it must overcome, such as the inversion of the retina, which requires light to pass through the nerves and blood cells before reaching the rods and cones, and the placement of the optic nerve on the wrong side of the sensing layer, so that it must pass through a hole in the retina to reach the brain. This hole in the retina is the cause for our so-called "blind spot" (72–73). Now, this "maladaptive historical legacy," as Williams terms it, is hardly unique, and every organism manifests features that are functionally arbitrary or maladaptive. But the point is that, just as language converts contingency into meaning by orienting itself toward the task of expressing, so evolution transmutes historical contingency into a functioning organism—into an eye that, despite its inherited blind spot, gives us sight.

Neo-Darwinists will, of course, emphasize natural selection as the primary mechanism for this transmutation, and certainly fitness operates as a negative constraint—it weeds out what is not sufficiently adapted to survive. But as Williams's own examples show, life involves a productivity in excess of mere utility. Here we rejoin our critique of utilitarian theories of adaptation and our alternative account of the productivity of life from chapter 4. There we noted Merleau-Ponty's claim that "life is not only an organization for survival; there is in life a prodigious flourishing of forms, the utility of which is only rarely attested to and that sometimes even constitutes a danger for the animal" (N 243/186). It is this "prodigious flourishing" of sense, as the autoproduction of meanings generated through difference, that biodiacritics brings into focus. Quoting Merleau-Ponty again, "life is not uniquely submitted to the principle of utility, and there is a morphogenesis that has expression as its purpose" (N 240/184). Expression is the key term here, and this is what finds no place in the neo-Darwinian account. On this point, biodiacritics converges with Elizabeth Grosz's (2008, 9) insight that "art and nature, art in nature, share a common structure: that of excessive and useless production—production for its own sake, production for the sake of profusion and differentiation." Life evolves, elaborating and articulating itself, only because, like language, it creates its own conditions for fermentation, only because it too is fundamentally a primordial principle of differentiation. As we saw in chapter 4, Grosz focuses in particular on the excessiveness introduced by sexual difference and the selections to which it gives rise, selections that precisely reward what can stand out and be noticed, what appeals and attracts, so that for her, sexual selection's production of the pleasurable cuts across the grain of natural selection's bias toward utility. Sexuality is not primarily about reproduction but is instead, as we quoted earlier, "a fundamentally dynamic, awkward, mal-adaptation that enables the production of the frivolous, the unnecessary, the pleasing, the sensory for their own sake" (7). While Grosz seems correct to emphasize the new dimensions of expression that sexual difference opens, we must also account for the expressive productivity that makes the institution of sexual difference itself possible. What I have termed biodiacritics is the primordial, expressive ferment that produces all such differences, sexual difference included.

Biodiacritics and Evolutionary Memory

Our description so far should help us to measure the distance between biodiacritics and the received concept of biodiversity. The word *biodiversity* typically inspires us to imagine a natural setting populated with visually obvious variation, the maximally diverse grouping of species that we can picture together. But this particular place, with these particular species, is not equivalent to their diversity. To arrive at their diversity, we must first determine our level of analysis—genetic, taxonomic, ecosystemic—and within that level the composition, structure, or function under consideration. In short, we need to identify units and then measure how many we have and how different they are from each other. But notice that, once we have shifted to a consideration of the differences as such—to the biodiversity as such—we are no longer concerned with these particular individuals, or even these particular genes, species, or ecosystems. Indeed, we could swap out one for another and maintain the same level of diversity; we might even increase the diversity if the one that we swap in is more different from the others in relevant respects than the one removed. So, the first point is that biodiversity, as the differences between the units under consideration, is not to be confused with the units themselves—and preserving a certain degree of biodiversity does not guarantee preserving any particular species, or gene, or ecosystem (see Maier 2012, 121). In fact, the loss of any one species in particular, from the perspective of biodiversity in general, across its many levels and categories, is relatively insignificant.

While biodiversity is a measure of difference, the difference at stake here is not comparable to what we have been calling diacritical difference, as the example of swapping out one unit for another makes clear. This is because biodiversity presupposes the self-identity of the units in question; it treats this identity as independent of the differences that these units have from each other or the whole. In other words, the measurement of diversity presupposes determinate being. But the point of diacritical difference is that difference precedes identity, that the play of indeterminate difference is generative of determinacy. On this understanding, each node in the web of difference—each gene, each species, each ecosystem—is what it is only in terms of its immanently articulated difference from all of the others. Its differing from each of them in specific and concrete ways is what makes it salient as the particular node or fold within the whole that it instantiates. Each moment emerges like a figure from the complex ground of life as a whole, and so its identity bears a nonsubstitutable reference to this whole and to its situation within it. Consequently, from a diacritical perspective, the substitution of a single unit is a transformation of the whole and of all the differential relations of which it is composed.

To put this another way, when biodiversity aims to measure difference, it inevitably obscures the intervals, the deferrals, the gaps by which biodiacritics is defined, because it takes determinate identities as its starting point. But as we have said, the expressive moment of differentiation is located precisely in such intervals. Life is located not in its units but in the productive and expressive self-generation of the whole. And if we have some hesitations about the substitutability of any particular life for another, this may be because our pretheoretical intuitions about life reveal to us this manner of its hanging-together. If we can adjust our sensibilities to consider the interval itself, to practice a hermeneutics of the "sense beyond or beneath apparent sense," we will see that the intervals are not merely spatial gaps, like blank spaces on a page, but also temporal; they are, in fact, a form of memory. From the perspective of biodiversity, it is easy to replace one species with another, because their differences are of a common coin. But, for biodiacritics, each configuration of life is singular and nonsubstitutable.

Let me clarify this point by returning, first, to George Williams's (1992) account of evolutionary maladaptations. For Williams, the example of the eye illustrates the historicity of the evolutionary process, the fact that a particular historical legacy is written into the bodies of all living things. He offers us an evocative description of our own sense of loss when such a historical legacy vanishes from the earth:

> The generation of diversity by cladogenesis [i.e., by the differentiation of the phylogenetic tree] furnishes every population with a unique set of historical legacies. In this sense, an organism is a living record of its own history. . . . The loss of the Stellar sea cow and the Adam-and-Eve orchid were the same kind of loss to historical scholarship as the burning of the library at Alexandria. The current wholesale extinction of organisms is especially tragic and ironic because we are only now learning to read history in molecular structure, where the writing may well prove clearer and more detailed than in morphology and other phenotypic end states. (76)

Williams's insight here is even more profound than he manages to articulate. Each organism is a record of its own history because it embodies this history as a kind of corporeal memory, as a folding accumulation within it of the diacritical differences through which its ancestors became what they were, and through which it becomes what it is. This rejoins a Bergsonian insight from Grosz (2008, 6), cited previously, that "life, even the simplest organic cell, carries its past with its present as no material object does." Certainly Williams is correct that the vanishing of such memory is a great loss to knowledge. But more than this, because we are ourselves nodes within the diacritical structure of life, every such loss diminishes us as well; it reconfigures our own differential identities. The memory of *all* of life figures into the identity of *every moment* of life. It is precisely this kind of memory and loss that biodiversity indexes cannot measure. And it is this sense of loss that guides our intuitions about the irreplaceability of each form of life that vanishes from the world.

If our account of biodiacritics is correct, then it is precisely in the folds of life, in its gaps and spacings, that the immemorial dimensions of its evolutionary and cosmic history are lodged. Rather than compare each species to a book, or even to a library, it would be more appropriate to compare it with a language, because each species carries within it a unique reservoir of expressive possibilities that, although they exist as nothing more than virtual differences, embody a unique memory that is the dynamic legacy of their becoming. We know that, when a language is lost to the world and its last speakers fall forever silent, an entire cultural memory vanishes along with it, a whole world forever closes, and this loss is a diminishment of us all. When a language vanishes, we lose not only something within the world but the world itself, the very opening up of the world. The same must be said about each living thing, which embodies in the folds of difference that constitute it an immemorial history that distinguishes its life from ours even as it completes us. Extinction is therefore the loss of our own past, the redrawing of the differences that compose our own identity, not only in the present or the future but in a prehistory to which our identities remain liable. What will we have become, what will life have become, when the prehistory that makes our very time possible is rewritten, when life's relationship with death is renegotiated immemorially? At stake in such renegotiation is not only the loss of a species but, as Derrida has intimated, the very end of the world. This is most explicit in his death penalty seminars, where he writes that

> the death that one makes or that one lets come, thus, is not the end of this or that, of this being or that being, of someone or something *in the world*. Every time it dies *[ça meurt]*, it's the end of the world. Not of a world but of the world, of the whole of the world, of the infinite opening of the world. And this is the case for every living being: from the tree to the protozoa, from the mosquito to the human, death is infinite; it is the end of the infinite *[la fin de l'infini]*. The finite of the infinite *[le fini de l'infini]*. (Derrida 2015, 118–19; 2017, 81)

Part III
ESCHATOLOGY

8

Apocalyptic Turns
THE CHIASM OF COSMIC IMAGINATION

The final chapter of Bachelard's (1960, 1969) *The Poetics of Reverie*, devoted to "Reverie and Cosmos," describes the experience that transforms the everyday dreamer into a "world dreamer," a dreamer of the cosmos as a whole. This imagination of the cosmos has certain characteristic elements for Bachelard. First, it suspends all time, so that "time no longer has any yesterday and no longer any tomorrow" (148; 173). In other words, this imagination inhabits an eternity that lies entirely outside of the passage of time; it is before or after time. Second, such cosmic imagination is tranquil and entirely at peace with itself. This follows from the fact that, outside of time, nothing takes place, so that the very being of both World and Dreamer, their essential bond, is tranquility itself. Furthermore, such cosmic imagination offers to us a vision that has nothing in common with our everyday, mundane perceptions, because it involves no distance like that opened between the perceiver and the perceived. According to Bachelard, perception entails "fragmentation"; it shatters the preperceptual bond of tranquility that only cosmic imagination can reveal (149–50; 174). What is revealed to us as world dreamers is therefore a cosmos prior to perception, prior in the strange sense of being outside of time altogether, where we find the peacefulness of the Whole mirrored by the tranquility of our own souls. Last, this cosmic imagination grants a unity to the Whole by opening onto it through a single image, allowing this image to "invade the whole universe" in an immediate and undivided fashion. In Bachelard's examples, these images tend toward the elemental—earth and air, fire and water—and what they reveal is our taking root in a world that no longer has any "against," a world of harmony and friendship, of total fusion with a cosmos that dreams and loves us as much as we do it. Cosmic imagination therefore opens onto a metaphysics of our "adherence to the world" (169; 196), but a world that is diffused with well-being to the point that it is not merely a world but also a welcoming environment that cradles us at its center.

Such a description of harmonious cosmic reverie sounds quaint today, at a moment when our cosmic imagination tends in the opposite direction, not toward harmony and well-being but precisely toward anxiety and, in a word, apocalypse. To imagine the environment that embraces us now, in its cosmic dimensions, is to feel ourselves gnawed by destabilized climatic cycles, waste dumps of geological proportions, acidified and chemically laced oceans, bio-accumulating toxins, and so on. We might say, to borrow Bachelard's expression, that the Cosmic Word of our age is toxicity.[1] The cosmos of our apocalyptic imagination is undergoing an imperceptibly gradual yet immanent unraveling. To say that this imagination is apocalyptic is not meant to suggest that the disaster it envisions must occur suddenly, in one stroke. On the contrary, it may be the slow creeping, the invisible slide toward the end of the world as we know it, that becomes our new metaphysics, taking as its unifying image one of any number of imperceptible disintegrations of the environment: the intensification of toxins, the steady rising of the oceans, the inconspicuous vanishing of honeybees and tadpoles, the patient and silent unworking of things at scales so small and so grand that we can only wait in expectation of the eventual realization that somewhere back we entered into the entirely unrecognizable. This imagination is not apocalyptic in the sense of Armageddon, then, but in the etymological sense of an uncovering, a revelation of what is assembling out of sight, in the earth and the air, in the water and our flesh. It turns out that, in its apocalyptic mode, cosmic imagination is still a revelation of and through the elements. And to the extent that toxicity invades our own bodies and tissues, it still speaks of our adherence to the world, although now this is inherence to a world on the verge of dissolution. This apocalyptic imagination again refers to an immemorial time, but this is not a pure outside of time so much as a past and a future that unravel the present from within.

As an example of the kind of cosmic imagination that I have in mind, consider the example of nuclear semiotics. In the early

1980s, the U.S. Department of Energy convened a panel of engineers, physicists, anthropologists, and linguists to form the Human Interference Task Force (1984; see also Benford 1999, 33–85; Peterson 2018).[2] Their charge was to devise a warning system to dissuade future generations from tampering with permanent geological repositories of highly toxic nuclear waste. The early target was to devise a communication system that would function effectively for the next ten thousand years, roughly twice the length of written human history, but revised estimates now suggest that the waste we are producing will remain toxic for as many as thirty thousand human generations—that is, for the next one million years (Environmental Protection Agency 2005). Obviously, the engineering task of producing a physical containment system that will withstand changes in geology, weather, erosion, water flow, and the like for such an extraordinary length of time is already staggering. But the semiotic problem poses a different sort of challenge. What sign or symbol, what image, what architectural structure, will manage to communicate a warning across the eons without descending into glossolalia and also without the warning itself being reinterpreted as enticement, as a temptation to unearth buried treasure? Proposals have ranged from the establishment of an atomic priesthood to the breeding of "radiation cats" that would change color in the presence of dangerous emissions to the more pedestrian warning signs with skulls or pictograms of Edvard Munch's *The Scream*.

What is relevant to us here is the cosmic imagination that this exercise sets into motion, the way that it extends our toxic legacy, by the accumulation of banal increments, into an unimaginable future—into a world that is no longer ours, no longer an environment for us, a world that is precisely the end of *our* world. Despite the sensationalism of this particular example, it is hardly unique. Greenhouse gas emissions to date have already irrevocably committed us to an altered global climate for at least the next millennium, which will lead to sea level rise, widespread famines and plagues, mass migrations, and catastrophic weather changes (Solomon et al. 2009; Gillette et al. 2011). We have already changed the prospects for who will be born and who will not, who will live and who will die. Climate ethicists struggle to find the images that can motivate us to care about the future generations who will bear the brunt of these changes ten or one hundred generations into the future. But can we take responsibility for a future that we can imagine only as the gradual metamorphosis of our world into something unrecognizable?

Phenomenology has a key role to play in thinking through this apocalyptic turn in our cosmic imagination. In fact, phenomenology as a method is born from a certain imagination of the end of the world. In Husserl's famous thought-experiment in section 49 of *Ideas I*, he argues that the annihilation of the world of physical objects would leave the being of consciousness untouched. This imagination of the annihilation of the world is intended to demonstrate that, though no real being is necessary for the being of consciousness itself, the world of transcendent things bears an essential reference to actual consciousness. Consequently, as Husserl (1976, 105; 1982, 111) puts it, "a veritable abyss yawns between consciousness and reality." For Husserl, this demonstration is essential to establishing the sphere of pure consciousness as the fundamental field of phenomenology, attained through the phenomenological reduction, and nature is therefore to be understood strictly as a correlate of intentional acts. But the consequence of this interpretation of consciousness as our "universal milieu," as Merleau-Ponty will argue later, is that death can have no meaning (SB 220/204). To this we might add that no imagination of the end of the world could be truly apocalyptic, because the end of the world would leave us wholly unmoved—not "us" as embodied human beings, that is, but "us" as the subjectivity for whom the world meaningfully appears. As we have seen in prior chapters, Merleau-Ponty's alternative is to grant a meaning to death by recognizing the dependence of consciousness on the contingent material and biological structures from which it emerges and that never cease to demand their due. Our perpetual experience of our inherence in a bodily organism, for Merleau-Ponty, is precisely the presence to our consciousness of its own constitutive history, of the material and vital structures that it has integrated into itself, albeit temporarily and incompletely. The inevitability of our own eventual dissolution is therefore written into our very self-experience, into what it means to be an embodied subject.

In contrast with Gaston Bachelard's descriptions of our dreamy fusion with the cosmos, then, our contemporary cosmic imagination is figured by toxicity, the world's slow decomposition from within. This transforms our adherence to the world, including our relationship with the elements and time. To trace these implications, we turn once more to Merleau-Ponty and Levinas, who accord a privileged role to art in disclosing the origin and the end of the world. For Merleau-Ponty, Cézanne's paintings figure the very coalescence of the world in its spontaneous self-organization, a birth that we can accompany only paradoxically by way of a creative appropriation of what essentially exceeds our powers. Cézanne therefore offers an aesthetic revision of the phenomenological reduction, one that discloses our inherence in and liability to the very world that we aim to bring to expression. In his efforts to "join the wandering hands of nature," Cézanne enacts a strange variant of the touching–touched relationship that would inspire Merleau-Ponty's late ontology of flesh, a variant that encounters anonymous sensation below the perceptual exchange with the world. This return to anonymous sensation finds its parallel in Levinas's analysis of modern art as unveiling the impersonality of the elements, that is, as the effort to "present reality as it is in itself, after the world has come to an end" (EE 90/50). These studies point us toward a radicalization of our adherence in nature understood as a form of autoaffection, that is, as a cosmic chiasm. Taking seriously Derrida's criticisms of Merleau-Ponty's late analysis of the touching–touched relationship, we conclude that a phenomenology of the end of the world must break with any autoaffective telos. This involves taking more seriously than does Merleau-Ponty the disruptive implications of the immemorial past as well as rethinking the ontological figure of the chiasm as a radical alteraffection.

Nature's Wandering Hands

The first of Joachim Gasquet's three dialogues with Cézanne, titled "Le Motif," is set on a hill overlooking the Vallée de l'Arc near Aix, on a late summer morning in the 1890s, with Mont Sainte-Victoire dominating the horizon. The painting on which the master has been working for the past two months is going well, and he is in a good mood.

> To Gasquet, Cézanne remarks: "I have my motif . . . (He clasps his hands together.) A motif, you see, it is this . . ."
> "What?" Gasquet asks.
> "Oh, yes!" Cézanne replies. (He repeats his gesture, separates

his hands, spreading his fingers apart, and brings them slowly, very slowly together again, then joins them, clenches them, intertwining his fingers.) "That's what you have to attain. . . . Try to understand, I guide my entire painting together all the time. . . . Nature is always the same, but nothing about her that we see endures. Our art must convey a glimmer of her endurance with the elements, the appearance of all her changes. It must give us the sense of her eternity. What is beneath her? Perhaps nothing. Perhaps everything. Everything, you understand? So, I join her wandering hands." (CC 130/110)[5]

Merleau-Ponty knew these conversations with Gasquet very well. Not only are they cited frequently in "Cézanne's Doubt" and *Phenomenology of Perception* but Merleau-Ponty returns to this text years later to provide the epigraph for *Eye and Mind* (1/351). In fact, both in "Cézanne's Doubt" and in *Phenomenology of Perception,* Merleau-Ponty repeats the final line that I have just quoted concerning Cézanne's effort to "join the wandering hands of nature *[les mains errantes de la nature],*" which Merleau-Ponty interprets in terms of the synergy of our senses toward "the landscape in its totality and its absolute fullness," toward that "imperious unity" that is achievable only as the expressive confluence of body and world (CD 21–23/75–77; PP 311/274). Whereas Cézanne repeatedly describes his own method as a return to nature by way of "sensation," and even as a kind of "realism" (CC 155/127), Merleau-Ponty rigorously distinguishes this return to sensation from any empiricist obsession with sense-data; in his words, "nothing could be farther from naturalism than this intuitive science" (CD 23/77). By contrast, what Merleau-Ponty finds inspiring in Cézanne's notion of a motif that joins nature's wandering hands is, on one hand, that the motif is nature's own spontaneous self-organization. He speaks of the "spontaneous order of perceived things," "the birth of order through spontaneous organization," and "an emerging order, an object in the act of appearing, organizing itself before our eyes" (CD 18/73, 18/73, 20/74). This spontaneous self-organization of nature is what Cézanne refers to as the "logic of the eyes" in contrast with the "logic of the brain" (CC 144/120). On the other hand, even if this natural logic bypasses the brain, it does not eschew art, technique, or tradition. On the contrary—and this is precisely how Cézanne's motif joins hands with nature, how it avoids the dichotomy of "nature versus composition" (CD 18/73)—the artist discovers this logic of sensation only *through* the history of art and the refinement of technique, so that this is not a "return" at all but a coming forward to greet nature, an expressive cocreation, a collaborative event by which nature gives itself the means to express what it wants, through us, to say.[4]

This is why Cézanne's motif can serve, for Merleau-Ponty, as an aesthetic enactment of the phenomenological reduction, of that effort, in Husserl's words, to bring "still-mute experience" to the "pure expression of its own sense."[5] In fact, as Merleau-Ponty presents it, the paradox of expression that Cézanne embraces is the paradox confronted by any philosophical reflection radical enough to admit its own debt to a prereflective moment that precedes and exceeds reflection but that can be expressed only through its creative appropriation.

What Cézanne calls "nature" is precisely philosophy's prereflective source, that from which philosophy emerges and which conditions its very possibility—yet, for this very reason, can never be purely thematized by it. In other words, the metaphysical sense of Cézanne's doubt is the inherent contradiction of trying to unearth that moment when nature encompasses us and on which we continue to remain fully dependent even as it escapes us, even as we find ourselves always too late to confront it face-to-face. With Cézanne, Merleau-Ponty embraces this contradiction when he describes reflection as "a creative operation that itself participates in the facticity of the unreflected" (PP 88/62), thereby charging philosophy with the task of recursively accounting for its own conditioning by a nature that reflection can disclose only indirectly, only in its withdrawal. The key, for both Merleau-Ponty and Cézanne, is that this contradiction must be embraced: it is not a flaw to be overcome, in either artistic expression or philosophical reflection, but rather the very means to disclose our liability to a nature that naturalism has forgotten.

In his discussions of Gasquet's conversations with Cézanne, Merleau-Ponty does not explicitly draw attention to the artist's figural enactment of the motif with the gesture of the intertwined hands, even though this gesture clearly anticipates Merleau-Ponty's own fascination with the touching–touched relation. We know that Merleau-Ponty's primary inspiration for the analysis of double sensation was Husserl, particularly *Ideas II*, and that Merleau-Ponty had already called attention to double sensation as a distinguishing feature of the body in *Phenomenology of Perception* (121–22/94–95). But perhaps Cézanne's touching–touched is not so far from Husserl's. First, note that Merleau-Ponty brings Cézanne's "motif" together with Husserl's "motif," that is, with the phenomenological concept of motivation also developed in *Ideas II* (sec. 56). This is explicit in "Cézanne's Doubt," which elaborates the account of motivation as a foundation for freedom that had appeared earlier that same year in the final chapter of *Phenomenology of Perception*, and it does so precisely by reading the Husserlian and Cézannian motifs together.

It is interesting, therefore, to see that when Merleau-Ponty returns to *Ideas II* fifteen years later, in "The Philosopher and His Shadow"—a text that is key for understanding his appropriation of the touching–touched relationship—he attributes to Husserl the same chiasmatic relationship between nature and spirit that he had found earlier in Cézanne.[6] Note also that the unnamed interlocutor of "Cézanne's Doubt," especially the essay's motivational theory of freedom, is Jean-Paul Sartre. Sartre's own brief consideration of double sensation in *Being and Nothingess* dismisses it both as strictly impossible and as irrelevant for the development of a philosophy of corporeality (Sartre 1943, 351, 363–64, 408; 1994, 304, 316, 358). We should not be surprised, then, that when Merleau-Ponty returns to the touching–touched relation as the figure for corporeal reflection in his later work, it is at the same moment that he speaks of a "figured philosophy" expressed through painting (see Johnson 2010, 46–47). All of this suggests that the figural moment of Cézanne's motif, his enactment of a touching–touched relation with nature, if we can use this language, is an intimation of the ontology of flesh.

And yet the strangeness of this variation of the touching–touched is striking: it is neither the touch of two hands belonging to the same living body nor the handshake or caress of another body but somehow the joining of the artist's hand with nature's own "hand," the latter described by Cézanne as the eternal recurrence of dispersed becoming. Let us see what this strange figure for the human–nature chiasmus can tell us about our liability to a nature that naturalism has forgotten, and in particular about the role that art plays in its disclosure. I pursue this question here in two stages. First, we will see that, for Cézanne, joining hands with nature is a matter of silence as a return to sensation, where sensation is understood as the prereflective condition for perception, its anonymous and immemorial precursor. This brings Cézanne's notion of sensation very close to that of Francis Bacon, who, according to Deleuze (2003, xxxi), "reassumed the entire problem of painting after Cézanne." It is through this notion of sensation that we can understand what Merleau-Ponty means by claiming that the "frozen objects" of Cézanne's paintings hesitate "as at the beginning of the world [à l'origine de la terre]" (CD 22/76). These paintings mark the beginning of the world because they capture the transition from sensation to perception, from anonymous life to the personal self, from Aion to Chronos, from immersion in the elements to the institution of a world. The other side of the beginning of the world is therefore its anonymous and immemorial precursor, the rustling of the elements. This is the second moment of our analysis, the return to sensation as an encounter with the elements, and this brings us close to Levinas's early descriptions of art in *Existence and Existents* but also to the recovery of the elemental framing of the look of things in the work of John Sallis. We return here to what Levinas calls the "very strangeness of the earth," a silence that precedes the world and that is perhaps best disclosed through the world-poverty of elemental art, an art of the immemorial moment of nature's withdrawal and resistance (TI 116/142; cf. Sallis 1998, 158). This will lead us to reconsider Bachelard's claims concerning our cosmic imagination as figured through the elements and especially the role played by elemental time.

The Silence of Sensation

To appreciate what Cézanne's paintings tell us about the end of the world, in parallel with its beginning, we should first notice Cézanne's remarks about the necessity of the artist's return to sensation by turning away from representation. Merleau-Ponty had already noticed in his commentary on Cézanne that the artist must return "to the source of silent and solitary experience" (CD 25/78), and Cézanne is explicit that the artist's submission to nature requires silence: "His entire will must be silent. He must silence all prejudice within himself. He must forget, forget, be quiet, be a perfect echo" (CC 131/111). To be this perfect echo, an artist must suspend reflection and become a photographic plate or a recording device, a "receptacle for sensations," in Cézanne's words (CC 131/111). The artist's silence, as receptivity to sensation, is neither passivity nor primitivism; it is not a romantic recovery of a prelapsarian unity. It is too late for us to be primitive or innocent, Cézanne tells us; we are already civilized. And we are already born with a certain facility, with a craft—but precisely a poor one that requires education and training (CC 137–38/115–16). This is why the artist must "go to the Louvre via nature and return to nature via the Louvre" (CC 140/117). Nonetheless, a silence is required, and this is precisely a silencing of reflection in favor of sensation: Cézanne says that "the artist must never have an idea, a thought, a word in mind when he needs a sensation" (CC 138/116). It is a parallel privileging of sensation over representation that, according to Deleuze, places Francis Bacon in the same lineage as Cézanne; what Cézanne calls *sensation* and Bacon calls *the Figure* is a shared method of avoiding figuration. In Deleuze's (2002, 39; 2003, 31) words, sensation acts "immediately upon the nervous system, which is of the flesh, whereas abstract form is addressed to the head and acts through the intermediary of the brain, which is closer to the bone."

Interestingly, when Deleuze introduces this convergence of Cézanne and Bacon on the privilege of sensation, he refers approvingly to Merleau-Ponty's chapter on sensing in *Phenomenology of Perception* (Deleuze 2002, 39n27; 2003, 156n1). Several themes that we have already addressed from this text have a bearing on how we understand Cézanne and, through him, how we will understand the hinge between the beginning and the ending of the world. In particular, it is in this chapter that Merleau-Ponty explains the anonymity of sensation and its relation to an immemorial past. We have returned repeatedly to Merleau-Ponty's descriptions of how it is not "I" who perceives but rather an anonymous "someone" who senses in and through me (PP 260–61/223–24). This "someone" is not singular but an animal pack of natural selves that already sides with the world and that synchronizes with its cyclical and immemorial duration, its never-present past. This immemorial past is precisely the "eternity" of nature that Cézanne strives to unearth by immersing himself in sensory life. And insofar as he aims to capture the very "beginning of the world," the germination of experience and the emergence of objects by spontaneous organization, this is because he aims to paint the precise moment when perception emerges from sensibility, when eternity gives way to lived time, when the impossible generates the actual.

Merleau-Ponty himself underestimates the disruptive implications of this immemorial past for our lived experience of the present. This is apparent in Merleau-Ponty's frequent later references to Lucien Herr's remark, in his commentary on Hegel, that nature is "there from the first day," as we discussed in chapter 1. Commenting on this passage in the summary of his 1956–57 course on the concept of nature, Merleau-Ponty writes that nature "presents itself always as already there before us, and yet as new before our gaze. Reflexive thought is disoriented by this implication of the immemorial in the present, the appeal from the past to the most recent present" (N 94/133). For Merleau-Ponty here, the immemorial moment within each present is nature at the first day, always re-creating itself anew. But we can now see that this vision of nature remains very close to that of the cosmic imagination described by Bachelard. Apocalyptic imagination, by contrast, concerns nature not at the *first* day but at the *last* day, not as always undergoing a re-creating but as undergoing its own unraveling. This is also an immemorial aspect of the present, but precisely as the other face of re-creation, as its hidden side.

Merleau-Ponty's tendency to emphasize the effusive fecundity of the birth of the world also guides his reading of Cézanne, which privileges the emergence of balance, order, and wholeness. We have noted how Merleau-Ponty's attention is drawn to the ways that Cézanne's paintings express "the birth of order through spontaneous organization" by hesitating "at the beginning of the world" (CD 18/73, 22/76). But to emphasize here the beginning of the world is to repress the other face of this beginning, the way that Cézanne's paintings also reveal a prehuman world that is itself a kind of encounter with death. Yet we can find glimpses here of what remains disruptive beneath this emerging order, such as Merleau-Ponty's description of our vertiginous brush with uncanniness:

> We live in the midst of man-made objects, among tools, in houses, streets, cities, and most of the time we see them only through the human actions which put them to use. . . . Cézanne's painting suspends these habits and reveals the base of inhuman

nature upon which man has installed himself. This is why Cézanne's people are strange, as if viewed by a creature of another species. Nature itself is stripped of the attributes which make it ready for animistic communions. . . . The frozen objects hesitate as at the beginning of the earth [à l'origine de la terre]. It is an unfamiliar world [un monde sans familiarité] in which one is uncomfortable and which forbids all human effusiveness. (CD 22/76)[7]

That this nature is "stripped of the attributes which make it ready for animistic communions" distinguishes it from that world of sensuous reciprocity so eloquently described by David Abram (1996). This is instead an "unfamiliar" world the experience of which gives us a discomfort comparable, Merleau-Ponty tells us, to a "period of mourning" (CD 22/76). Cézanne's "beginning of the world" therefore operates at the hinge between the emerging order of perception and its dark precursor, which haunts it from within like a death within life. It is precisely this moment of immemorial death within life that is distilled within our apocalyptic imagination of the cosmos.

These insights from "Cézanne's Doubt" echo a similar analysis in the chapter on the thing and the natural world from *Phenomenology of Perception*. As I discussed in chapter 1, Merleau-Ponty writes that, in the context of our everyday dealings with things, our perception "bears upon the things just enough to find in them their familiar presence, and not enough to rediscover what of the non-human is hidden within them." Once we suspend our everyday familiarity, then the thing reveals itself as "hostile and foreign, . . . no longer our interlocutor, but rather a resolutely silent Other" (PP 378/336). As illustration, Merleau-Ponty refers to Fritz Novotny's description of Cézanne's landscapes as "those of a pre-world where there were still no men" (PP 379/337). This hostile and alien "pre-world" is the immemorial nature that precedes and conditions all experience and reflection, and which elsewhere Merleau-Ponty associates with a kind of elementality.[8] For instance, in his discussion of the "natural and non-human space" that underlies our human environment, Merleau-Ponty writes of focusing his eyes on the stone of a garden wall until he loses his gaze "within this coarse and yellowish surface, and then there is no longer even a stone, and all that remains is a play of light upon an indefinite matter" (PP 346/307).

This "indefinite matter" approaches the elemental character of sensations before the emergence of a world. Recall that, in the passage we cited earlier from Cézanne's conversation with Gasquet (CC 130/110), he noted that "our art must convey a glimmer of [Nature's] endurance with the elements." Cézanne's return to the silence of sensation is therefore not merely the effort to capture the emergence of the perceived world but equally to stage an encounter with the elements in their immemorial withdrawal.

Unworldly Elements

We have seen that Merleau-Ponty's approach to Cézanne's paintings emphasizes the beginning of the world, the moment when sensations converge to give rise to a perceptual harmony, the kind of harmony that inspires Bachelard's tranquil imagination of the cosmos. But we are suggesting that this moment of emergence, as it is disclosed through Cézanne's paintings, has another, hidden side and that, by reversing our perspective, we can also encounter a prehuman level of sensation that continues to haunt the present as its immemorial precursor. This level of sensation prefigures our apocalyptic imagination insofar as it introduces a moment of death into life. And when we turn our phenomenological descriptions to this encounter with the other side of the world, we find there the rustling of the elements.

This returns us to Levinas's analyses in *Existence and Existents,* which we introduced in chapter 2 and which are intended precisely to open the world to its outside—to what precedes it and survives it—by way of a shift from perception within a world to sensation of the elements beyond the world. The starting point, for Levinas, is the correlation between self and world: "the I in the world has an inside and an outside," and the adjustment of inside to outside is precisely the event of meaning or intentionality (EE 73–74/39–40). For an object to arise in the world is already for it to exist in relation to a subject, for it to be "destined for someone" (75/40). Consequently, as Levinas writes, "the very idea of a totality or of a whole is only intelligible where there is a being that can embrace it" (76/41). Remember Merleau-Ponty's language about the emergence of the world in Cézanne as an "indivisible Whole" or an "imperious unity" (CD 21/75). The point is that, as soon as there is

188   *Apocalyptic Turns*

an I—what Merleau-Ponty calls a "personal self" in *Phenomenology of Perception*—that I finds itself engaged with the objects that compose its world, that have sense for it. And so, as Levinas remarks, "existence in the world always has a center; it is never anonymous" (EE 58/29).

It is possible, nevertheless, for existence to withdraw from the world, and a privileged site for such withdrawal is art, the movement of which, Levinas tell us, consists in "leaving the level of perception so as to reinstate sensation" (EE 85/47). The aesthetic effect of art is produced by its "wandering about in sensation," which is described as a return to the "impersonality of the elements" (85–86/47). This is, of course, precisely the movement that we have retraced in Cézanne, and to the extent that we find Levinas's descriptions here to be reliable, they can deepen our understanding of what this encounter with the elements involves. First, we should note that the elements are what appear at the very end of the world, at its dissolution, which means that they are beyond the distinction of inside from outside, subject from object (cf. 87/48, 94/52). The elements are what remain after the destruction of representation (what Deleuze called figuration), when things are released from their destiny of being for someone and can stand forward in their nakedness. The common intention of modern art, as Levinas sees it, is precisely the effort to "present reality as it is in itself, after the world has come to an end" (90/50). This involves stripping away the form that clothes an object destined for our use to encounter its brute, impassive materiality. Such art makes possible a "paroxysm of materiality," in Levinas's phrase, which anticipates Deleuze's remarks about sensation's direct impact on the nervous system and which suggests a concept of matter having nothing in common with that of classical materialism (EE 91/51).

Second, Levinas's description of this breakup of the world extends Merleau-Ponty's insight into the "inhuman" character of the elements and of their irrecuperability by reflection. As Levinas puts it, "the disappearance of all things and of the I leaves what cannot disappear, the sheer fact of being in which *one* participates, whether one wants to or not, without having taken the initiative, anonymously" (EE 95/53). This "sheer fact of being" in which one is anonymously immersed is what Levinas terms the *il y a*, the *there is*.

It is well known that Merleau-Ponty also adopts this expression, especially in *The Visible and the Invisible*, but his usage tends to follow that of Sartre, who, in *Being and Nothingness*, deploys the expression *there is* simply for generalized existence, the being of "something." For Levinas, by contrast, *there is* names the anonymous existence of the elements when there is no longer a world, no longer an I, but only the palpable presence of a kind of silence (EE 94–95/52–53). And it is this silence that makes us uneasy in the genuine encounter with nature's aloof autonomy. Our insecurity, Levinas suggests, is "due just to the fact that nothing approaches, nothing comes, nothing threatens; this silence, this tranquility, this void of sensations constitutes a mute, absolutely indeterminate menace" (96/54). The "rustling" of the *there is*, its "murmur of silence," is therefore a kind of horror, which Levinas associates with the complete dissolution of all terms into an undifferentiated background, leaving only a "swarming of points," a "field of forces," or an "atmosphere" (98/55, 104/59, 96/53, 104/59). As Levinas points out explicitly, we can no longer speak here of correlation: "The mind does not find itself faced with an apprehended exterior. The exterior—if one insists on this term—remains uncorrelated with an interior. It is no longer given. It is no longer a world" (95/53). Nevertheless, this beyond of the world haunts the world as an indeterminate menace, like the anonymous vigilance of insomnia, and to this menace we find ourselves "exposed" (96/54).

Interestingly, Levinas notes that the extraction of elements from the world can have a temporal dimension, which is why "everything that belongs to past worlds, the archaic, and the ancient, produces an aesthetic impression" (EE 85/46). While he goes no further in explicating this link between the deep past and the elements, his descriptions suggest that what precedes and exceeds us on the scale of deep time is precisely a kind of asubjective materiality, of geological and cosmic elements: stones and stardust. The vertigo of our encounter with deep time would therefore be akin with this reflection on the dissolution of the world into elements, as if certain works of art opened a window onto the birth or death of the earth itself. The dizziness that befalls us when we try to imagine the world before or after us would not simply be caused by our struggle to conceptualize vast numerical scales; it would instead be the affective dimension of the bursting of our horizons of time. We encounter the deep past only as an impossible or originary past, as a past that has never been, for anyone, a present.

Levinas's description of the elements suggests an encounter with the unraveling of the world by which we have characterized the apocalyptic imagination, an encounter that leaves to this dissolving nature its essentially inhuman strangeness. Commenting on Levinas's description, John Sallis (1998, 152) notes that such an encounter with nature under the guise of the *there is* "will forsake its immediacy and familiarity":

> As it returns it will appear strange, as if belonging to a region distant from and alien to the human world. In a sense it will have cast off its disguise: it will no longer be the nature that is shaped and formed within the human world and in accord with the measures of that world but rather a nature capable, in its excess, of evoking feelings both of sublimity and terror.

In his reading of Levinas, Sallis holds open the possibility that the absolute strangeness of this elemental nature could provoke a responsiveness that Levinas himself denies, "a comportment that, rather than leading to self-reversion, would be drawn along in the withdrawal, responsive rather than reactive to the very strangeness of the earth" (159). And later, in his extended development of the phenomenology of elementals in *Force of the Imagination,* Sallis suggests that a "turn back to the sensible opens the way for a turn back to the elements" in such a way that would "redetermine nature itself in and as the holding sway of the elements" (154). Yet Sallis is led in this later text to distance himself from Levinas's assimilation of the elements to the *there is,* because for Sallis, this merely identifies the elements with the "obscurity of matter" and thereby risks "reinscribing the entire analysis of the elemental within the most classical philosophical conceptuality" (159n17). For this reason, Sallis focuses on the role of elementals—day and night, earth and sky, sun and storm—as "bound[ing] and articulat[ing] the expanse of the self-showing of things themselves" (154–55), rather than as the strange paroxysm by which our senses open themselves to an unbounded. This maintains an ontological difference between elementals and the things that show up in the world, because these elementals structure the very appearing of things, but it closes off any insight into the anonymous murmuring of the elements before the world and their immemorial interruptions of our world-making. Levinas's descriptions of the "materiality" of the elements, as we have emphasized, is anything but that of classical materialism; as Levinas himself remarks, this is a materiality that "no longer has anything in common with matter as opposed to thought and mind," a materiality that, insofar as it is unnamable, "can only appear in poetry" (EE 91/51).

Nevertheless, neither Levinas nor Sallis sufficiently accounts for the immemorial character of our encounter with the elements, as the prereflective moment that reflection must take into account as its own condition. For Levinas, the elements beyond the world are associated with the incessant rustling of the *there is,* being in general stripped of all its determinations, which manifests its unsettling presence, in the account put forward in *Existence and Existents,* through such phenomena as insomnia, the darkness of night, modern art, and mystical participation. Here the emergence of the world, as well as of time, awaits the "hypostasis" of an existent from within this anonymous rustling, which will require the encounter with the other. World and time are in a sense, then, the repression of the threat of the *there is,* which, as the "dark background of existence," always underlies the world that emerges from it. The world is therefore like a fortress installed against invading elemental forces. Later, in *Totality and Infinity,* Levinas will describe the establishment of the "dwelling" in a parallel fashion as holding the insecurity of the elements at bay while providing a safe haven for possessions and the fruits of labor (125–49/152–74). But to understand the world as the repression and exclusion of its elemental ground leaves unexplored the ambivalent role that the elements play within or on the margins of the world, as well as their evocation of an immemorial past that constitutively haunts our lived experience of time.

The Cosmic Chiasm

In *Phenomenology of Perception,* Merleau-Ponty had insisted that reflection must become recursive, that it must reflect on reflection and thereby "understand the natural situation that it is aware of replacing and that thereby belongs to its definition" (89/63). We have seen that what Merleau-Ponty calls "radical reflection" in *Phenomenology of Perception* and "hyper-reflection" in *The Visible and the Invisible* is this effort of reflection to account for its own foundation in a nature from which it emerges but that remains for it an immemorial past. This irrecuperable past appears within our experience as the resistance that the unreflective offers to reflection, as the remainder that resists thematization even as it conditions reflection and makes it possible. It is our very inherence within nature, the fact that we can only open onto it from a situation within it, and that we can never fully thematize our own emergence from it, that necessitates this immemorial remainder. This clearly complicates the straightforward relation of "adherence to the world" as described by Bachelard, because we can never coincide with our own immersion within nature; this immersion is given to us at the outset as a past that is beyond memory but also, in our apocalyptic imagination, as a future that is beyond our representation.

This returns us to Cézanne's own figuration of art as joining the hands of nature. We have discussed how the structure of reflection, and particularly its interruption by an unreflected that exceeds it, undergoes a transformation in Merleau-Ponty's later work, where reflection takes the self-touching or autoaffection of the body as its exemplar. In *The Visible and the Invisible,* Merleau-Ponty famously described the experience of one hand touching another as the primordial event of reflection. Yet, as we emphasized in chapter 3, he also recognizes there that the coincidence of one hand with another is "always immanent and never realized in fact" (VI 194/147). The *écart* between the touching and the touched is the moment of nature's immemorial withdrawal, leaving behind, in Jacob Rogozinski's (2008, 238) words, an archifactical "remainder." As Rogozinski points out, this remainder is "untouchable for my touch, but also invisible for my vision, inaudible for my hearing; we will never meet up with it in the world, as one element among others in our daily experience" (238). The remainder that the effort to touch ourselves touching always misses conditions the very possibility of touch itself, even while remaining absent from the world of touch.

Whereas Rogozinski is concerned only with the remainder of corporeal autoaffection, we know from Merleau-Ponty that the body's self-touching is only one salient example of an ontologically ubiquitous chiasm, that of the body with the world or of humanity and nature. This means that when my hand touches an object, there is a "kind of reflection," a subtle form of autoaffection, that eventuates in the touch. The thing touches me as I touch it; it becomes me as I become it. Yet in the moment that this chiasmus crosses over, where self switches into other, there is always a slippage. In the case of the body's self-touching, this slippage gives rise to a remainder or a precipitate, as Rogozinski describes. But in the exchange of the body with the world, the slippage is a consequence of the body's situatedness within the world that it touches, that is, the fact that it is of the world. Although we inhere in the world and are of its same stuff, this inherence always splits apart from within. When the world touches me as I touch it, the two touches can never be reciprocal. My incapacity to see myself seeing or touch myself touching, what Rogozinski calls the remainder, is precisely a consequence of the situatedness of my efforts to reflect on the nature that encompasses me. But, as Cézanne's paintings demonstrate, the fact that the elemental nature that precedes the world is, strictly speaking, unpresentable does not mean that it has no register in the world of sense. First of all, this impossible past, as a generative passivity, continues to haunt every present from within. It conditions all that can appear even in its own withdrawal from appearing. And furthermore, the archifactical, even while remaining absent from the world that it conditions, may nevertheless show up indirectly at the margins of experience or along its fault lines, in experiences that are not my own possibilities but, strictly speaking, im-possible. The inauguration of such im-possible experience, I am suggesting, is precisely the paradox that Cézanne embraces through the work of painting, taking the murmuring silence of the elements that haunt perception from within as his theme.

Now, this suggests that art may play a privileged role in disclosing nature's withdrawal and making its resistance salient. This insight converges with Amanda Boetzkes's (2010) characterization of recent earth art as revealing nature's "resistance to being subsumed into representation." "Since it cannot be contained within, or reproduced as, an artwork," Boetzkes writes, "the earth appears as a temporal or sensorial excess at the limit of representational form" (12). In particular, the elemental art of James Turrell or Roni Horn operates precisely by a kind of world-poverty that, rather than tracing the emergence of perception from sensation, allows us a glimpse of the end of the world, of its dissolution into elemental forces that outstrip the compass of reflection.

This investigation of sensation at the limits of perception, elements at the limit of the world, and art at the limits of representation allows us to reconfigure Bachelard's cosmic imagination in the wake of the apocalyptic turn. Returning to the four characteristics of the cosmic imagination for Bachelard, we can see, first of all, that the elements that precede and succeed the world are not simply outside of time, like the imagined cosmos for Bachelard, but inhabit a time of Aion irreducible to the Chronos of the world. This immemoriality haunts every present while itself remaining beyond presentation. We are not transported outside of time into a world of tranquility but precisely torn between multiple times whose incommensurable rhythms prefigure our own homelessness, our being out of joint between a welcoming environment that embraces us and an aloof nature that refuses us. We have seen that, as in Bachelard, this apocalyptic imagination returns us to the image of the elements, but no longer as the friendly and welcoming face of the fire in the hearth or the reflective waters of the pool. Now these elements rustle beyond the organization of the world, autonomous and wild, imparting their impact directly by way of sensation on the anonymous life of one's body. It is through the work of art that such elemental forces can expose themselves in the experience of a paroxysm of materiality. Finally, this exposure to the elements entails a complete transformation of Bachelard's sense of our "adhesion" to the world, which will no longer be a matter of fusion without gap but instead of an internal splitting, a dehiscence, on the part of both self and world. The apocalyptic imagination, then, is not merely a contemporary response to our technological and environmental context, to our enframing and destruction of the earth, but rather an intensification of nature's own fundamental dehiscence. This elemental dehiscence is a kind of horror, certainly. But perhaps it is also a kind of poetry, a kind of art. For example, Levinas speaks of a "musicality of sensation" once it breaks free from the bonds of perception, comparable to the musicality of a word once it has been emptied of its sense (EE 86/47). Perhaps the silence of the elements is therefore a kind of music in its own right, albeit one that sings to us at the very edge of sense, at the beginning of the end of the world. This silence of the elements would therefore be constitutive of the symphony of nature that we discussed in chapter 3.

This leaves us with the question of how far to embrace a model of our relation to nature figured on autoaffection, on the proximity of two hands that touch. As we have seen, Merleau-Ponty offers two important complications to this relationship. The first is the structure of "radical reflection" proposed in *Phenomenology of Perception,* according to which reflection—within the world and narrative time—recognizes its conditioning by what precedes and exceeds it, the past of nature that remains for it an immemorial and absolute past. To the extent that reflection thereby finds itself folded around what essentially withdraws from its grasp, the world that it discloses will bear the constitutive traces of its own immemorial outside.

The figure of the touching–touched is further transformed in *The Visible and the Invisible* by the logic of chiasmic reversibility. Extending the phenomenological account of the sensible–sentient relation of one hand touching another, the logic of the chiasm traces a dual becoming by which inside becomes outside and outside becomes inside through a mediation that does not efface the difference between its terms. Merleau-Ponty recognizes the logic of the chiasm across numerous relations: between mind and body, self and world, self and other, fact and idea, past and present, Being and beings, philosophy and nonphilosophy.

Yet the chiasm, as Merleau-Ponty describes it, insofar as it remains oriented by a telos of unity, self-givenness, and self-presence, does not avoid the risk of reabsorbing alterity. Derrida puts this point forcefully in his commentary on Merleau-Ponty's application of chiasmic logic to Husserl's account of intersubjective relations: "one runs the risk of reconstituting an intuitionism of immediate access to the other, as originary as my own access to my own most properly proper . . . [and] one also runs the risk of *reappropriating* the alterity of the other more surely, more blindly, or even more violently than ever" (OT 218/191). We have emphasized, of course, the significance of the *écart,* the gap or slippage, that Merleau-Ponty recognizes within chiasmic mediation: the touching hand never quite manages to coincide with the touch that is on the verge of emerging in the touched hand, and a parallel gap would mark all chiasmic relationships. Arguably, the later Merleau-Ponty is increasingly attentive to such moments of noncoincidence.[9] Yet even here, as Derrida compellingly shows, Merleau-Ponty's presentation reveals a preference for immanent coincidence and reciprocity, even as it recognizes the inevitability of noncoincidence (OT 238–43/211–15). But if coincidence is, in fact, always interrupted or deferred, then—as Derrida asks rhetorically—"shouldn't one have started with this impossibility?" (OT 230n1/355n27). In the end, Derrida withholds judgment concerning the hesitations between these alternative tendencies in Merleau-Ponty's later work.[10] Derrida's question therefore remains pertinent for our investigation: What would it mean to think the world's relation to its outside starting not from autoaffection, albeit immanent or deferred, but rather from a radical alteraffection? How might the world's relation to its own outside be understood as constitutive of the very world itself? For a preliminary account of the world's radical materiality that eschews autoaffective return, we consider Jean-Luc Nancy's descriptions of the world as, in the words of Marie-Eve Morin (2012, 43), "formed of limits or edges between singularities, of their articulations, of the play of their junctures."

Postdeconstructive Realism: The World Outside-In

As Nancy writes in *The Sense of the World,* "we know, indeed, that it is *the end of the world,* and there is nothing . . . illusory about this knowledge" (14/4). For Nancy, this means that "there is no longer the 'down here' of a world one could pass through toward a beyond or outside of this world," or in other words, "there is no longer any sense of the world" (13/4). It is just this "exposure to the abandonment of sense that makes up our lives" (11/2). Even so, this end of the world cannot be understood in cataclysmic or apocalyptic terms, on Nancy's interpretation, which would simply leave us caught up in "the regime of a signifying sense" (14/4). Rather, the world no longer "has" a sense, because sense has always been understood in relation to the beyond of the world, to another world or to God; the end of the world is, first of all, the realization that there is no outside or beyond of the world that might gift it with such a sense. The alternative to this granting of sense from beyond might seem to be the collapse into an utter lack of sense, into nihilism. But there is a third option, namely, the recognition that even if the world no longer *has* a sense, nevertheless it *is* sense. The world "is" sense not as a present fact or a collection of things but rather as being-toward *(être-à)*, which Nancy glosses as "rapport, relation, address, sending, donation, presentation *to*—if only of entities or existents *to* each other" (18/8). The sense remaining to the world would be precisely "this gift of sense the world itself is" (19/9) as the mutual exposure of each singular body to every other body that touches it. This means understanding "the sense of the world" chiasmically, as the bidirectional and dual becoming of both world and sense, without reference to any beyond of the world or even to any transcendence in immanence, but also without any closure or unification (achieved or merely immanent) into a coincidence or overarching signification. "The co-existence of the world (not 'in' the world, since the world isn't a container but the extension of co-existence itself), devoid of any given composition, system, synthesis, or final assumption, is what has to be traced" (AFT 306). At the end of the world as a unified signification, then, we rediscover the world as the co-implication and coexistence of singular bodies that are mutually exposed, and we rediscover sense as what happens between and at the limits of these singular bodies. Rather than relating the "inside" of the world to a beyond, here the inside of the world is already exposed, outside of itself, in the extension and spacing of material bodies. We may say then that, for Nancy, the outside of the world constitutes it from within: "The outside is inside; it is the spacing of the dis-position of the world" (BSP 31/13).

Because the world is, from the first, outside itself in the spacing and co-implication of bodies, its constitutive elementality lies precisely in the material differences of bodies as they actually exist. On Nancy's account, all matter is singularized into the discreteness of quanta, just as every singularity is material (SW 97/58, 103/62). Matter is therefore "first the very difference through which *something* is possible, as *thing* and as *some*"; or again, "matter means here: the reality of the difference—and différance—that is necessary in order *for there to be something and some things* and not merely the identity of a pure inherence" (SW 95/57). Rather than seeking a more originary materiality before or after the world, then, Nancy draws our attention to material difference as constitutive of the reality of things. Contra Heidegger, the stone is not worldless simply on account of its lack of "access" to the world; insofar as it also exists as *being-toward,* as extension and exposure, the stone is itself world, even as the human being also necessarily participates in a certain geomateriality (SW 99–104/59–63; cf. BSP 36–37/18).

This outside-in world also gives us pause to rethink the notion of the present and its relation to deep time. If the spanning and stretching of time can be realized only in its passage, then the eternity of time is not to be found in an infinite chronological succession but rather in the eternity of the present: "There is only eternity as the spacing out of every present of time. The very gesture of the present, the gesture of presenting, the place of the diffraction of the present. Much more remote, much more open than a big-bang, to which it alone can give rise." Thus we must seek the "untimeliness of time" precisely in an enriched notion of the present (SW 108/66). This affirmation of the present is of a piece with the end of any overarching sense of the world. If any possible vision of a "true humanity," a "goal of the world," or a "harmony with nature" has now dissipated—and this is the very meaning of the end of the world, for Nancy—then there is no longer a place for thinking in terms of crises or long-term plans, which always fall back on visions of remaking the world or remaking humanity (AF 54–58/33–35). Chronological and linear time of the sort assumed by projects of global sustainability—and no less by Meillassoux's speculative realism—project a future based on the "general equivalence" that converts all times to one homogenous measure.[11] By contrast, Nancy recommends that we work with other futures, incommensurable futures, precisely through a renewed attention to the present.

This insistence on the present might seem to entail a rejection of the significance of the deep temporal perspective and therefore a confirmation of Meillassoux's charges that we remain here within an anthropocentric view of the world. Nancy himself rejects the view that the world is a correlate of the human being, that it has meaning only for or through us, as well as the view that one's "access" to the world can decide its determinations: "the world beyond humanity—animals, plants, and stones, oceans, atmospheres, sidereal spaces and bodies—is quite a bit more than the phenomenal correlative of a human taking-in-hand, taking-into-account, or taking-care-of" (SW 92/55; cf. 100/59). Furthermore, this beyond of humanity is not to be understood mathematically but precisely materially. And perhaps thinking the *Spanne* of time in terms of this materiality offers us a glimpse of the depth of time within the present, spaced not chronologically but in the very extension and exposure of the elements at the heart of things:

> The heart of the stone consists in exposing the stone to the elements: pebble on the road, in a torrent, underground, in the fusion of magma. "Pure essence"—or "simple existence"—involves a minerology and a meteorology of being. . . . The event itself, the coming into presence of the thing, participates in this elementary essence. . . . The event is the taking-place of the being-there of the heart of things. . . . *There* is a measure of space, of spacing, that gives time its origin, *before* time. Movements, histories, processes, all times of succession, of loss, of discovery, of return, of recovery, of anticipation—all this time essentially depends on the space opened up at the heart of things, on this spacing that *is* the heart of things. (Nancy 1990, 202–3; 1993a, 171–72)

This returns us to the relationship between the world, its formation or destruction, and the elements. Just as every stone is outside the relation of life and death, stone remains liminal to the world that it nevertheless makes possible in quasi-transcendental fashion. This discloses the world's ongoing liability to elemental materiality and memory. Through its geological memory, stone therefore offers us a glimpse of how to understand our relationship with the future outside of the regime of general equivalence, outside of a sustainable management of the future that subjects it to totalizing foreclosure. To unfold the workings of the apocalyptic imagination, therefore, we must undertake a more direct investigation of the elements after the end of the world.

9

The Elements at the End of the World

Speculations about the end of the world are ubiquitous today. The popularity of apocalyptic fiction and film reveals the deep pleasure we take in imagining the world's destruction repeatedly and in every possible variation, a pleasure entangled with genuine anxieties about what the future holds. Apocalyptic narratives are not new, of course; they may be as old as civilization itself and probably exist in some form in every culture. But secular eschatological fiction is more recent, with Mary Shelley's 1826 novel *The Last Man* usually considered the first major example.[1] Shelley's novel was dismissed by critics at the time and soon forgotten, but the genre gained a wide popularity in the 1890s that has continued to the present. At the turn of the twentieth century, as W. Warren Wagar reports, most doomsday scenarios imagined that humankind would be wiped out by natural causes: plagues, earthquakes, floods, giant storms, and so on. But after World War I, most have imagined us destroying ourselves, usually in wars with technologically advanced weapons (Wagar 1982, 24). Since the 1960s, in the wake of Rachel Carson's *Silent Spring*, end-of-the-world fiction has increasingly drawn inspiration from what Wagar calls "fashionable prophesies of ecological disaster" (30). Indeed, since the end of the Cold War, and in certain respects as its legacy or continuation, ecological destruction has become our favored vision of the end, with the currently popular genre of climate fiction or "cli-fi" as its latest flavor.

We have been considering apocalyptic fiction, but actual predictions of ecological disaster also share in the appeal of the apocalyptic narrative: the accumulating biotoxins of *Silent Spring*, the population "bomb," the hole in the ozone layer, biodiversity collapse, genetic engineering gone awry, and so on. In fact, this narrative underwrites environmentalism's efforts to "save the world," and the religious overtones here are not irrelevant. Whether expressed openly as fear of the future or disguised as nostalgia for the past, an eschatological vision of the world is essential to environmentalism.[2] This is readily apparent in the public discourse and cultural imaginary surrounding global climate collapse, so that when journalist and activist Bill McKibben proclaims that stripping the remaining bitumen from Alberta's tar sands will mean "game over for the planet," he is appropriating an intimately familiar narrative.[3] Indeed, the "fashionable prophesies" of environmentalism and the cultural imaginary expressed through speculative fiction share a common eco-eschatological vision with roots in shared cultural sources, and they have fed and borrowed from each other to the point where they can no longer rigorously be distinguished.

Whether presented as empirical prediction or speculative fiction, the eco-eschatological narrative is always a phantasm or fable, a tale that we tell ourselves about the future that reflects our investments and anxieties in the present and that consequently constructs our current identities and institutions. Derrida makes a parallel point in "No Apocalypse, Not Now," presented at a colloquium on nuclear criticism five years before the opening of the Berlin Wall, in which he characterizes the prospect of total nuclear war as a "phantasm of remainderless destruction," destruction that might extend to humanity in its entirety or even to the earth as a whole (P 372/396, 369–70/393). By naming nuclear war a phantasm, Derrida was not at all denying the reality of stockpiled weaponry or the plausibility that this weaponry might be deployed with catastrophic consequences. His point was rather that such a war is "fabulously textual"—not only because the weapons themselves rely on codes and texts of all sorts, and because the strategies of deterrence were themselves textual games, but most importantly because total nuclear war has never yet taken place, so that it "has existence only by means of what is said of it and only where it is talked about" (370/393). In other words, nuclear catastrophe is a fabulous tale, and nevertheless—or precisely for this reason—it effects a positive construction of present reality, so that the "whole of the human *socius* today" would be marked by it directly or indirectly, the whole of what Derrida, in 1984, could call the "general institution of the nuclear age" (369/394). As a terrifying fable about the future, the prospect of total destruction therefore confronts us—humanists, in particular, insofar as we are "specialists in discourse and in texts" (368/391) and insofar as the imagined destruction threatens uniquely and in particular the juridico-literary archive (376–77/400)—with a contemporary task: "The terrifying 'reality' of nuclear conflict can only be the signified referent, never the real referent (present or past) of a discourse or a text. At least today. And that gives us to think the *today*, the presence of this present in and through this fabulous textuality" (369/393). Ecological disaster, including climate collapse, is fabulously textual in just this sense. Turning our attention, as humanists, to the eco-eschatological narrative as a phantasm implies no skepticism about the very real dangers that we face but may instead be the only responsible way to think the present insofar as it is constructed through our fables about the future.

In calling attention to the eschatological dimensions of environmental rhetoric, my intention is neither to challenge the credibility of scientific predictions nor to debate their effectiveness for influencing public opinion. There is every reason to believe that climate collapse will result in catastrophic changes for life on our planet, human and nonhuman, and that we have a responsibility to act immediately and collectively to the best of our abilities to curb its effects.[4] But the eschatological framing of this narrative, as obvious or unavoidable as it may seem—and precisely for this reason—goes beyond a simple presentation of the facts or a call to action. Closer attention to our eschatological imaginary reveals tacit presuppositions that frame our understanding of the world, time, and responsibility, and these are not without significance for how we think about what it means to act ethically in the present.

One interesting aspect of the eco-eschatological narrative is its construction of the present as suspended between the geologically deep past and an indefinitely distant future. As I have mentioned, Mary Shelley, whose *Frankenstein* is often credited with inaugurating modern science fiction, also authored the first major work of secular eschatology, *The Last Man*, published in 1826. Set in the late twenty-first century and putatively based on ancient prophetic writings, the novel tells the tale of the destruction of the human race by a global plague, leaving the last survivor, based autobiographically on Shelley herself, to wander the world alone. It is hardly coincidental that Shelley's novel appeared just as biologists were coming to accept Georges Cuvier's evidence, based on reconstruction of fossilized skeletons, including those of mammoths and mastodons, that the world was once populated with creatures that had subsequently gone extinct. Cuvier (1812, 3, 70) intended these findings to "burst the limits of time" just as scientific genius had "burst the limits of space," thereby providing a window into the "former world," a world prior to all human history, that he believed had been catastrophically destroyed.[5] Surely if a natural catastrophe could drive so many other species to extinction and bring their entire world to an abrupt end, then the same could be imagined for our species; our world must be equally precarious and finite and our days on earth similarly numbered. This construction of our present as suspended between prehistorical catastrophe and anticipated extinction continues to shape contemporary discussions of climate collapse, as we see, for example, in astrophysicist Neil deGrasse Tyson's remarks (quoted in Mooney 2014) on the National Geographic television series *Cosmos*:

> We're dumping carbon dioxide into the atmosphere at a rate the Earth hasn't seen since the great climate catastrophes of the past, the ones that led to mass extinctions. We just can't seem to break our addiction to the kinds of fuel that will bring back a climate last seen by the dinosaurs, a climate that will drown our coastal cities and wreak havoc on the environment and our ability to feed ourselves. . . . The dinosaurs never saw that asteroid coming. What's our excuse?

For more concrete examples of what I am calling the "temporal suspension" of the present, consider current efforts toward global sustainability that extrapolate from deep-past trends to predict and manage far-future scenarios, thereby tacitly assuming that our responsibility toward future generations is to sustain the world in a state that as much as possible resembles our present. One example would be ongoing efforts to establish permanent repositories for radioactive waste, which must avoid human intrusion and environmental degradation on the scale of tens of thousands or even millions of years. As I mentioned in chapter 8, the field of nuclear semiotics emerged from the efforts of the Human Interference Task Force, convened by the U.S. Department of Energy in the 1980s with

the charge of devising a warning system to dissuade future generations from tampering with repositories of toxic waste for at least
the next ten thousand years, roughly twice the length of written
human history (see Human Interference Task Force 1984; Ialenti
2014; Peterson 2018; Skrimshire 2018). These efforts were continued by research teams for the Waste Isolation Pilot Plant in New
Mexico, which included speculative fiction authors among the ex-
perts consulted.[6] Similarly, the Greenland Analogue Project studies the deep history of ice sheets on Greenland's western coast to
design the first operational geological repository for high-level radioactive waste, scheduled to open in Olkiluoto, Finland, within the
next decade.[7]

A second example would be the economic practice of "discounting the future" to assess how much we should spend today to limit
the future effects of climate change. Recent studies hold that greenhouse gas emissions to date already commit us to an altered global
climate for at least the next one thousand years (Solomon et al.
2009; Gillette et al. 2011). But if we calculate the future growth of
the world's economy on the basis of past trends, then the people of
the future will be increasingly richer than we are today. How much
should we ask the (relatively) poorer people of today to sacrifice for
the (relatively) richer people of tomorrow? The answer will vary
depending on the "discount rate" that economists choose to apply,
similar to money market interest rates that track what investors are
willing to pay today for a certain level of future benefits.[8] My point
is that policy decisions and resource allocations being made today
on an international scale rely on what I am calling the temporal
suspension of the present between the deep past and the far future.

To briefly review, first I have suggested that our obsession with
the end of the world, in the form of the eco-eschatological narrative
that frames speculative fiction as well as environmental prediction,
is a phantasm that reflects our desires and anxieties in the present and that leaves its mark, directly or indirectly, on our individual
and collective identities, institutions, and sense of the world here
and now. Second, I have proposed that this phantasm has a history,
that it develops in parallel with the emerging conception of deep
time: our awareness of an ancient geological past that precedes us
opens our imaginations to an indefinitely distant future after us.
And third, I have offered some contemporary examples of efforts

to calculate and manage the distant future on the basis of the deep past. These examples tacitly embody an approach to time that is inseparable from the eco-eschatological narrative. That is, this conception of time lends our end-of-the-world fantasies their seductive force and ubiquity, even as, in return, these fantasies serve to perpetuate and reify this historically specific conception of time. The deep past and far future are not merely chronological bookends for the bubble of human time but rather anachronistic ruptures in the heart of the present. The invasion of the present by deep time is one of the many ways that our encounter with time has, in the words of David Wood (2007, 9), "become fractured, dispersed, irregular . . . plural." The consequences of this fracturing of time rebound onto our conceptions of human identity, our relation with other living things and the material elements, and our responsibility toward the future, which is why our historical moment is caught up in pondering the end of the world.

To open these questions, I first clarify the distinctive phenomenological approach to the world and consider what it means for "the" world to end, bringing together Donn Welton's example of the destruction of the Twin Towers of the World Trade Center with Levinas's critical reflections on Husserl's thought-experiment of world annihilation in *Ideas I*. As we shall see, our eco-eschatological imagination projects a dissolution of the world, not as an objective fact, but as the meaningful horizon of our lives. Yet this destruction is not without remainder, even in our imaginations, because it leaves in its wake the ashes and dust of the geomaterial elements from which the world is composed.

We next turn to Jean-Luc Nancy's notion of the "equivalence of catastrophes," which helps to unpack what is at stake in our doomsday obsession by illuminating the relationship between our eco-eschatological narrative and the suspension of the present. The interdependence that characterizes globalization evacuates the present of its singularity, its nonequivalence, in its calculative efforts to manage the future. The generalized equivalence of time presupposed by these projections of the future is a consequence of the ecotechnical proliferation of ends and means without final end, a vacuum that can only be filled by phantasms of apocalypse. As an alternative to this general equivalence of time, I suggest an ecophenomenology of the singular present, but one that takes seriously the lessons of deconstruction. This reveals an ambivalence or equivocation, best expressed by Nancy, in how we understand the end of the world: either as the end of the sense of the world as a total horizon of intelligibility or as the rediscovery of this world here *as* sense, without reference to any purpose or meaning beyond itself.

Derrida suggests an alternative to Nancy's account in his description of the death of any singular living thing as the end of the world, which he presents as a radicalization of Husserl's thought-experiment. Derrida insists that the death of any living thing is the absolute end of *the* world, rather than the end of *a* world, and confronts us with an (im)possible responsibility for mourning. This leads Derrida to suggest, in the final session of his last seminar, *The Beast and the Sovereign*, that there is no one world, no common world, even if we must carry on *as if* such a world obtains. The phantasm of the world's destruction, I argue, serves precisely to bolster this pretense of a common and shared world: imagining the world as under threat reinforces our projection that the world exists.

Central to our investigation is the relationship between the world, its formation or destruction, and the elements. Just as every stone is outside the relation of life and death, stone remains liminal to the world that it nevertheless makes possible in quasi-transcendental fashion. This discloses the world's ongoing liability to elemental materiality and memory, especially the memory of earth and stone. Derrida's investigations of the problem of world in *The Beast and the Sovereign* take us part of the way toward understanding world's liability to the elements. But it is to Nancy that we must turn for an account of our own elemental liability and of the exposure of stone that, beyond life-death, may not *have* a world but nevertheless *is* a world. Through its geological memory, stone therefore offers us a glimpse of how to understand our relationship with the future outside of the regime of general equivalence, outside of a "sustainable" management of the future that subjects it to totalizing foreclosure.

This returns us, finally, to our apocalyptic vision of the world, which approaches everything within the world against a background of absolute contingency or nothingness. By threatening things with the specter of their own destruction, we force their presentation into self-identity. As Nancy notes, "destruction takes place in the world and not vice versa" (I 245/85), which is why he enjoins us to "learn to stop dreaming of the end, to stop justifying it.... We need to take our leave of the romantic-historical mode of thinking that promises an apotheosis or an apocalypse—or both, one in the other"—and rediscover the resistance of existence itself as spacing and permanent revolution (I 247/87). This requires not a better architecture of the future but a deepening of our exposure to and within the present. Ecodeconstruction thereby becomes an ethos of the rediscovery of the world right at the very end or limit of the sense of the world.

Has the World Already Ended?

Unsurprisingly, the world that is under threat in our eco-eschatologies is typically presented in a naturalistic way, for instance, as nature or planet Earth. What is genuinely at stake, however, is not the planet as a collection of physical entities but rather the world *as we know it,* the total horizon of meaning, value, and possibility within which our lives unfold. In other words, what is at stake is world in the phenomenological sense. Phenomenology's thematization of the world as a philosophical problem is perhaps its most significant legacy, teaching us to understand the world not merely as a given totality of entities or events—our planet, for example, or the universe more broadly—but rather as the nonthematic referential or horizonal structure that the appearance of anything whatsoever presupposes.[9] Phenomenology therefore opens a path for describing the world that is distinct from either the Kantian treatment of it as an a priori form correlated with consciousness or the speculative metaphysical effort to account for the world in terms of another being or another world—both of which fall back on an explanation of the world in worldly terms, by way of what the world alone makes possible. This is why Eugen Fink (1933, 338; 1970, 95), in his famous *Kant-Studien* article, describes phenomenology's task as the effort to uncover "the origin of the world," an origin that could not be anything within the world, outside of the world, or in another world. According to Fink, this strange logic of the origin is the key to phenomenology's distinctive understanding of the transcendental, although it also leads to a series of well-known paradoxes that concern how this logic can be communicated or understood in relation to that of worldly beings. Jacques Derrida's early work takes its inspiration from these paradoxes, as Leonard Lawlor (2002) has shown, so that deconstruction may also be understood as a radicalization of the problem of world and its genesis.[10]

We will return to the question of the origin of the world, but first let us consider instead the end of the world and, more precisely, what comes after it. In an essay on "World as Horizon," drafted a few months after the horrific events of September 11, 2001, Donn Welton (2003, 223, 224) explains the phenomenological sense of world—which he describes as a "nexus of significance" distinct from "something like a natural environment or a socio-historical reality or the totality or whole of all such worlds"—with reference to the collapse of the Twin Towers of the World Trade Center. He describes the initial shock caused by the news of the first plane hitting the tower as an example of "dissonance"—a recalcitrant and inexplicable event, though one still occurring against the background of a stable and familiar world, still teleologically oriented toward unity and integration. With images of the second plane being crashed intentionally, dissonance gradually gives way to disintegration, so that, in his words, "with the collapse of the second tower the world itself literally flies apart" (225). As his essay concludes, "it was not a particular fact or a string of facts within the world, but the world itself, the very context and background of our everyday life, that came unraveled on September 11" (231).

Welton illustrates the horizonal character of the world as a stable and pregiven nexus teleologically oriented toward unity and harmony by calling attention to its fragility, its vulnerability to collapse. The world is not guaranteed; it can and does end. Now, we can distinguish, at least formally, between the disintegration of world as a nexus of significance and its material dissolution, that is, the factual destruction of concrete, plaster, glass, paper, furniture, electronics, and human bodies. The world as such does not consist of things and events, but it holds them together, gives them significance, unity, place, duration. When a tool breaks down within the world, Heidegger's famous hammer, the momentary dissonance remains bound within the web of the whole. But when the web itself unravels, does everything material simply vanish? Hardly. We then find ourselves instead awash in the detritus of world, in piles of rubble, decomposing bodies, clouds of dust. Welton does not mention the cloud of toxic dust that blacked out the sun, a cloud visible from the International Space Station, which gradually settled into a three-inch-deep layer of fine powder covering every surface for blocks. Despite the singular ecceity of this dust, it cannot but remind us of the miles of cinders that replaced Hiroshima in 1945 or the tons of mud that choked New Orleans in 2005. Dust, cinders, and mud are what remain of the very materiality of the world after the end of the world; they are world's body dissolved, disintegrated, no longer harmonious or unified, no longer forming a whole, a background, a context. After the world, we are confronted by the geomaterial elements, that from which the world is formed and to which it ultimately returns.

Welton's description of the events of 9/11 as the "end of the world" reminds us that, alongside phenomenology's interest in the *origin* of the world, it has also been invested from the beginning in a certain vision of the *end* of the world. We return here to Husserl's thought-experiment of world annihilation in section 49 of *Ideas I*. Husserl introduces this thought-experiment as the final and decisive step toward the phenomenological *epochē*, intended to purify consciousness of the general thesis of the world. Here he describes the "quite conceivable" possibility that our experiences might be so irresolvably conflictual that they "dissolve into illusion," and not "just for us but in themselves" (Husserl 1976, 103; 1982, 109). Rather than every illusion or conflict resolving itself by pointing toward a greater truth in a more inclusive whole, experience could imaginably reveal itself to be, in Husserl's words, "refractory to the demand that it carry on its positings of physical things harmoniously, that its context might lose its fixed regular organizations of adumbrations, apprehensions, and appearances—in short, that there might no longer be any world" (103; 109). In this imaginable—though, for Husserl, obviously counterfactual—scenario, the world would be reduced to more or less complete chaos. It might, nevertheless, as he points out, still be haunted by the specters of things, in the form of crude and transient "unity-formations" that lack the endurance and stability to cohere into genuine physical things in themselves (103–4; 110). This is the debris of the world, the dust of things, neither quite a physical object nor simply nothing at all.

At first glance, Welton's example—although he refers to it as the "end of *the* world"—is not comparable with the world annihilation described by Husserl. At best, this was the end of "a" world, a disintegration of world localized in space and time, not the end of "the" world. The dust that once blocked out the sun has been subjected to analysis by toxicologists, and whether it was the cause of higher cancer rates among first responders is an ongoing topic of legal debate. Even if we might grant that the world as a whole looks different to us now, that *the* world has been irreversibly transformed by this event, the one world as such retains its integrity. But things are not so simple, because we must also ask, *for whom?* If the world has been reconstituted, reintegrated, cleaned up and put back to work, this is so only for the survivors. And how to separate survivors from victims, those whose worlds recovered from those whose worlds remained in tatters, is not obvious if we consider the sufferers of posttraumatic stress, those who continue to mourn lost loved ones, or those who have subsequently perished from exposure to toxic dust. At a phenomenological level, this raises the question of how much irresolvable conflict, how much illusion, the world can tolerate and still be called "the" world, still hang together as a whole from which we can expect a teleological progression toward the truth. Is there, after all, only one decisive end of the world, or might it slowly unravel or even end repeatedly, perhaps even constitutively?

Writing in 1984, at the height of the second Cold War, Levinas (1990, 12) offers the following reflections on Husserl's thought-experiment: "doubtless, the seventy years which separate us from Husserl's text— two world wars, totalitarianisms of the right and left, massacres, genocides, and the Holocaust—have already signified (if one can still speak meaningfully) an experience torn to shreds, one impossible to put back together." For Levinas, "our epoch" is characterized by the fact that Husserl's "epistemic reflection"—carried out, as it was, before the outbreak of World War I, and therefore at a time when it might not have been possible concretely to imagine the world "invert[ing] itself into a non-world"—has subsequently taken on an "apocalyptic sense." He names here, in particular, "the nuclear menace which weighs upon our planet, the explosion or universal conflagration that humanity stands in fear of tomorrow," which would be, in his view, the literal enactment of what Husserl had imagined (Levinas 1990, 12–13). The world as an intelligible whole, as an object for our self-conscious contemplation and technological manipulation, has therefore long been unraveling and now teeters on the brink of its inversion into a nonworld populated by non-things. Furthermore, on Levinas's view, this apocalyptic situation is inseparable from modernity's drive toward mastery of the world, from its attempt to grasp all otherness as a unified whole under the "universal gaze of knowledge." The futile effort of the transcendental "I think" to "reassemble the fantastic images of the real into a world" is therefore less a philosophical failure than a "cosmic catastrophe." In short, apocalyptic destruction is the very culmination of the phenomenological conception of the world, insofar as this is bound up with the modernist technoscientific agenda through its privileging of transcendental subjectivity.

The end of the world does not, therefore, entail the total destruction of all that factually exists but rather the disintegration of our horizons of significance and possibility, of the context and background presupposed by any worldly thing or event. What our eco-eschatological imagination projects is such an unraveling without return, without recovery, a final and complete dissolution of meaningful horizons. This poses the phenomenological problem of the world in its most radical form, pushing it to its limit: because every question that can be posed, every future that can be pictured, presupposes the world as its horizon, from what perspective can the total destruction of the world even be imagined?

Ecophenomenology and the Ecotechnical

Deconstruction, in the work of both Derrida and Nancy, carries through this turn toward the end of the world. From his early reading of Husserl, which follows out the paradoxes inherent in phenomenology's account of the origin of the world, to his final seminar, which insistently repeats Heidegger's question—*Was ist Welt?* What is world?—Derrida demonstrates that the concept of the world already implies a relationship to its end, to death and to the nonliving at the heart of life. In fact, if we have learned anything from deconstruction, it is that nothing is less obvious or less certain than that we know what we mean by *world*, that we know who or what "has" world, or even that there *is* a world at all. The trajectory of deconstruction is toward the *end* of the world in the sense of both its goal and its limit, and the question of what, if anything, comes after it. In its claim that every autoaffection is fundamentally and

The Elements at the End of the World 213

inescapably alteraffection, that every experience involves a passage through the world and through the other, deconstruction can be understood from its very beginnings as the most radical form of ecophenomenology, one that stakes the sense of the world on its liability to interruption and dissolution. Coming to terms with our apocalyptic obsession, and in particular with its implications for the sense of the world here and now, requires an ecophenomenology of the end of the world, but one that, through its encounter with deconstruction, stretches both *eco-* and *phenomenology* toward a hyperbolic transformation.

Eco- here would no longer refer to ecology in either the informal or the strict sense—either as any form of organic community or as the scientific study of organism–environment interactions—but instead evokes what Nancy calls the "ecotechnical," in two senses. First, the ecotechnical refers here to the *technē* of bodies according to which all properness or self-relation is originarily interrupted by transplantation, prosthesis, or foreignness at the very heart of the self.[11] This already entails a transformation of phenomenology, which can no longer understand itself as a return to sense in the interiority of self-contact, even as the contact of one hand touching the other, but must instead suffer the suspension and interruption of sense as the extension and exposure of bodies. A phenomenological alteraffection, if such an expression is meaningful, must touch on the outside, be touched from the outside, and discover its inside as already outside itself in its vulnerability to being touched. Such a reappropriation of phenomenology and of touch is not without unavoidable and perhaps insurmountable risks, as Derrida compellingly demonstrates (see, e.g., OT 133–49/116–30). Yet, if ecophenomenology is possible in the wake of deconstruction, if it can assume such risks, then it might parallel Nancy's own path toward a "radical materialism" or, in Derrida's phrase, a "postdeconstructive realism," the touchstone of which would be touch itself (CW 55/51; OT 60/46; see also O'Byrne 2012; Gratton 2012).

Second, ecotechnics names the contemporary situation of worldwide technology, the "global structuration of the world as the reticulated space of an essentially capitalist, globalist, and monopolist organization that is monopolizing the world" (SW 159–60/101). This situates us beyond any demarcation of the "natural" from the "technological" that could prescribe principles, ends, or norms for

214   *The Elements at the End of the World*

environmentalism, and in this respect environmentalist critics are right to see in deconstruction—from Derrida's *Of Grammatology* to Nancy's *After Fukushima*[12]—the subversion of any hope for a foundationalist return to pure distinctions between nature and culture, wilderness and technology, materiality and signification.[13] The ecotechnical in this sense makes salient the global regime of economic, technological, and political interdependence that presumes a general equivalence or interchangeability between all means and ends while pursuing no greater end than its own totalizing expansion (see AFT 43–48/24–27; C 88–89; SW 65–67/40–41; Nancy 1994, 48–50; 1996b, 25–26; BSP 157–68/132–43; CW 140–43/94–95). Because existence is essentially technological, we have no recourse here to a more natural or authentic way of life. But the contemporary situation is nevertheless ambivalent or equivocal: on one hand, ecotechnics raises the specter of absolute closure into the immanence of global sustainability, by which the future is entirely programmed and managed to avoid the real threat of a final destruction, be it nuclear war or climate collapse. On the other hand, precisely in the unhinging of technology from production, in its unworking of the relation between means and ends (AFT 47–48/26; I 244/84), there may be an opening toward the sense of the world here and now—no longer as nature or ecology but rather as the exposition of singular bodies in the ever-renewed present (see C 36–37; AFEC 62–63/37). In this latter case, the world no longer *has* a sense—it makes no reference to any creator, to any other world, or to any gathering into a whole—but rather it *is* sense in all of the plural and fragmentary singularity of its material existence. Ecotechnics therefore hovers ambivalently between the end of the world as *mundus* or *cosmos* that would ground a meaning and orientation for our lives and its rediscovery as this world here, absent any purpose or meaning beyond its own existence. As Nancy recognizes, such a rediscovery of the world as sense demands a new philosophy of nature, albeit one that transforms both philosophy and nature (C 36–37; SW 64/40, 103/62, 237–38/157). Nature would henceforth be the "exposition of bodies," a "network of confines," or the *there is* of the sensible world that is "neither *for* us nor *because* of us" (C 36–37; SW 65/40; I 245/85).

The equivocal situation of the ecotechnical is illustrated by

Nancy's discussion of the 2011 Fukushima nuclear disaster, where he explains that there can no longer be any purely "natural" catastrophe, because the proliferating and uncontainable repercussions of every catastrophe are also inextricably cultural, economic, and political. Nancy terms this the "equivalence of catastrophes," not to suggest that all disasters are equivalent in terms of their consequences or destructiveness, but because all are marked by the paradigm of nuclear catastrophe, which "remains the one potentially irremediable catastrophe, whose effects spread through generations, through the layers of the earth; these effects have an impact on all living things and on the large-scale organization of energy production, hence on consumption as well" (AFEC 11–12/3). With nuclear catastrophe as their paradigm, all disasters today are equivalent with respect to the pervasive entanglement of their consequences, which is the obverse of the complex and ever-deepening interdependence and interconnection of systems worldwide: ecological, technoscientific, sociopolitical, logical, and so on. Globalization is precisely the process of this ever-deepening interdependence, which presupposes a common medium of conversion, translation, substitution, and exchange. Starting from Marx's insight that money serves as a "general equivalent," because every cost and benefit can be translated into economic terms, Nancy finds that contemporary capitalism and technological development have generalized this notion of equivalence even further, so that "the regime of general equivalence henceforth virtually absorbs, well beyond the monetary or financial sphere but thanks to it and with regard to it, all of the spheres of existence of humans, and along with them all things that exist" (16/5). This is characterized by a "limitless interchangeability of forces, products, agents or actors, meanings or values" (16/6). If this general equivalence makes greater interdependence of all of our systems possible, then it is the reason catastrophes cannot be circumscribed in their effects. But more than this, it is the general equivalence itself that is catastrophic, insofar as it inspires a proliferation of means and ends that are ultimately oriented toward no final end, no ultimate goal other than their own continued expansion and proliferation. What takes the place of any final end is instead our constant awareness of the possibility of our own self-destruction. As Günther Anders (quoted in AFEC 38/19–20) writes, "today, since the apocalypse is technically possible and even likely, it stands alone before us: no one believes anymore that a 'kingdom of God' will follow it. Not even the most Christian of Christians."

Nancy recognizes that the regime of general equivalence has implications for how we relate to time and to the future, and the examples that I proposed earlier—the planning of nuclear waste repositories and economic discounting of future climate costs—illustrate his point perfectly. The absence of any final end or ultimate goal for our ecotechnical interdependencies apart from their own self-perpetuation traps us in a cycle of planning and management of the future in general. Furthermore, the extrapolation of the past to calculate the future demonstrates the sway of general equivalence in our understanding of time, because each chronological present moment is substitutable for every other.[14] As Nancy puts it, "no culture has lived as our modern culture has in the endless accumulation of archives and expectations. No culture has made present the past and the future to the point of removing the present from its own passage" (AFEC 67/40). The alternative here is to recognize the *nonequivalence* of the absolutely unique and nonsubstitutable events and moments that compose our quotidian experience and thereby to deepen our respect for the present. In Nancy's words, "what would be decisive . . . would be to think in the present and to think the present. No longer the end of ends to come, or even a felicitous dispersion of ends, but the present as the element of the near-at-hand" (62–63/37). Because the aim here is to respect the nonequivalence of the present, this is a proposal for what we might call ontological or temporal justice. Such justice would be absolutely distinct from any respect for nature in the sense typically encountered within environmental philosophy, which, for Nancy, would remain within the economy of valuation and therefore of general equivalence (66/39).

This call for temporal justice does not imply a rejection of the ecotechnical but rather its extraction from the general equivalence of capitalism and therefore its return to the *technē* of finitude or the spacing of existence. As Nancy explains in *A Finite Thinking*, "technology 'as such' is nothing other than the 'technique' of compensating for the nonimmanence of existence in the given. Its operation is the existing of that which *is* not pure immanence. . . . Insofar as its being *is* not, but is the opening of its finitude, existing is technological through and through" (44/24). In other words, technology in its root sense is a compensation for the original absence of any self-sufficiency of nature, of any given natural order of means and ends, and is therefore the essence of finite existence. Nancy adds in *The Sense of the World* that the world of technology is precisely the world becoming *world*, because "a world is always a 'creation': a *teknē* with neither principle nor end nor material other than itself.... It is necessary to come to appreciate 'technology' as the infinite art that supplements a nature that never took place and will never take place. An ecology properly understood can be nothing other than a technology" (66/41). Because ecotechnics characterizes finite existence, as the in-finition or unfinishability of the finite, it undoes any return not only to a given nature but more broadly to any pure autoaffection or immanent closure, whether of life or of sovereignty; against the understanding of life as automaintaining and autoaffecting, the ecotechnical reveals "the infinitely problematic character of any 'auto' in general" (CW 140/94), and it "washes out or dissolves sovereignty" (BSP 162/137). The spacing or finitude of the world opened as ecotechnics "*is itself the empty place* of sovereignty. That is, it is the empty place of the end, the empty place of the common good, and the empty place of the common as good" (BSP 162/137).

Here we reach the heart of what Nancy calls the "terrible ambivalence" of the ecotechnical: "*the* world, *as such, has by definition the power to reduce itself to nothing just as it has the power to be infinitely its own sense, indecipherable outside of the* praxis *of its art*" (SW 67/41). Ecotechnics can spiral out of control as the infinite proliferation of means and ends without final end in a growing totalization—with nuclear catastrophe or environmental collapse as its ultimate consequence—or it can take on "the sense of the disruption of all closures of signification, a disruption that opens them up to the coming of (necessarily unprecedented) sense" (SW 161/102; cf. BSP 158–68/133–43). Because technology is the "incessant displacement of ends," it reveals the empty place of all former ends, of the world as having a linear history oriented toward completion; consequently, it has "made possible the modern apocalypse—the modern revelation—of destruction" (I 244/84). The hesitation or ambivalence of ecotechnics concerns whether this revelation slides toward infinite mastery or a rediscovery of the finitude of the world

218 *The Elements at the End of the World*

and the singularity of sense. In *Corpus,* Nancy expresses both the radicality of this understanding of the world and the revolutionary promise of its alternative:

> Our world is the world of the "technical," a world whose cosmos, nature, gods, entire system is, in its inner joints, exposed as "technical": the world of the *ecotechnical.* The ecotechnical functions with technical apparatuses, to which our every part is connected. But what it *makes* are our bodies, which it brings into the world and links to the system, thereby creating our bodies as more visible, more proliferating, more polymorphic, more compressed, more "amassed" and "zoned" than ever before. Through the creation of bodies the ecotechnical has the *sense* that we vainly seek in the remains of the sky or the spirit.
>
> Unless we ponder without reservation the ecotechnical creation of bodies as the truth of *our* world, and a truth *just as valid* as those that myths, religions, and humanisms were able to represent, we won't have begun to think *this* very world. . . . The ecotechnical deconstructs the system of ends, renders them unsystematizable, nonorganic, even stochastic (*except* through an imposition of the ends of political economy or capital, effectively imposed nowadays on the whole of the ecotechnical, thus re-linearizing time and homogenizing all ends, but capital also has to stop presenting a final end—Science or Humanity—and, moreover, the creating of bodies harbors revolutionary force). (88–89)

Nancy's account suggests that our fixation on the destruction of the world by technology expresses a genuine intuition into the ecotechnical unworking of any system of ends or ultimate ordering of the world. What ecotechnics reveals is that the world as *cosmos* or *mundus* has already ended, that the world no longer has a sense—a meaning or a direction (cf. SW 13–15/4–5). But our mistake is in interpreting this end of the world as "a cataclysm or as the apocalypse of an annihilation"; the end of the world cannot be given a determinate sense as annihilation or total destruction (SW 14–15/4–5). Indeed, to understand the end in these terms is precisely to remain within the regime of general equivalence that inspires our calculative management of the future at the expense of the ever-unfolding and inestimable present, a present "in which something or someone presents itself: the present of an arrival, an approach," rather than a chronologically ordered and countable present moment (AFEC 64/38). The promise of the ecotechnical is in its ever-renewed and in-finite creation of the finitude of sense, which offers an entirely distinct understanding of the world, no longer as the correlative of a sense but rather as sense itself: "for as long as the world was essentially in relation to some other (that is, another world or an author of the world), it could *have* a sense. But the end of the world is that there is no longer this essential relation, and that there is no longer essentially (that is, existentially) anything but the world 'itself.' Thus the world *no longer has* a sense, but it *is* sense" (SW 19/8). The world *as* sense is precisely the ever-renewed creation and differentiation of bodies in their exposure to and being-with all others, a world that has unity only as "a differential articulation of singularities that make sense in articulating themselves, along the edges of their articulation" (SW 126/78). The end of all ends of the world is therefore the rediscovery of this world here, with no sense or end beyond itself.

"In a World without World"

On the face of it, this ambivalent interpretation of the end of the world—the end of the world as *cosmos* that is the renewal of the world as sense—would seem remote from Derrida's own treatment of the end of the world. Although the theme of the end of the world appears in Derrida's earliest writings,[15] it becomes increasingly prominent in his later work, where it is most often associated with death: the death of a friend, for instance, as we see in many of the memorial essays collected in *The Work of Mourning* (the French title of which makes this theme explicit: *Chaque fois unique, la fin du monde*). As we mentioned at the close of chapter 7, Derrida extends this to the death of any living thing, including insects, protozoa, and plants (see Derrida 2015, 118–19; 2017, 81). Derrida repeatedly insists on the seemingly paradoxical formulation that each and every death of a unique living thing is *the* end of the world, absolutely and infinitely, and not merely the end of *a* world or of a living thing *within* the world. This insistence is intended to respect the incommensurability and inappropriability of the other as a singular origin of existence, with a unique and untranslatable exposure to experience and time.[16]

It is impossible, however, to assign any fixed sense to what is meant by "world" in Derrida's discussion, and for essential reasons. We should recall here Derrida's cautions about whether one should expect from "big bad words" like *world* anything like an exact sense (OT 17/7), as well as his commentary on the difficulties Heidegger raises concerning the question of world: "it's a bit like it is for the question of being, we do not know what it is, world, what being it is and therefore in view of what we are questioning. . . . A question about the world is about everything and nothing. About everything, therefore about nothing, it's an empty question that bites the tail of its own presupposition" (BS2 97/58). But the recoil of this question onto its own presupposed horizons becomes even more acute when we follow out the implications of Derrida's discussion of the death of the other, which paradoxically undermines any notion of a common or shared world and, consequently—insofar as any shared meaning presumes an horizon in common—of any meaning at all. This "end of the world" as the withdrawal or liquidation of any sense of a common world, of a *cosmos* or a lifeworld, is, as Derrida presents it, the very situation of ethics. Derrida confronts us with the possibility that the world itself is a fiction or a phantasm, even if one that is in certain respects necessary and perhaps even what our responsibility toward the other requires.

Derrida first suggests that death is each time the end of the world in a much-discussed passage from "Rams," where it introduces his reading of Celan's poem "Vast, Glowing Vault," especially its final line: "Die Welt ist fort, ich muß dich tragen" (The world is gone, I must carry you). As Derrida writes,

> for each time, and each time singularly, each time irreplaceably, each time infinitely, death is nothing less than an end of *the* world. Not *only one* end among others, the end of someone or of something *in the world*, the end of a life or of a living being. Death puts an end neither to someone in the world nor to *one* world among others. Death marks each time, each time in defiance of arithmetic, the absolute end of the one and only world, of that which each opens as a one and only world, the end of the unique world, the end of the totality of what is or can be presented as the origin of the world for any unique living being, be it human or not. (R 23/140)

As Derrida emphasizes here and elsewhere,[17] the death of any living thing marks not merely the end of *a* world or of a life *within* the world but rather the absolute end of *the one and only* world. This follows from the fact that the other's world is never a mere variation of my world, never analogous with or translatable into my world, but remains an absolute interruption of my world that can never be appropriated or made properly my own. World is therefore not a general type of which individual worlds would be specific tokens; in its very singularity, the end of "any" world can only be the end of the world tout court. Nor is the other's world simply alongside my world as one among others, because my "own" world is not properly mine, as I *am* only in the ethical response, the "I must," of carrying the other: "I only am, I can only be, I *must* only be starting from this strange, dislocated bearing of the infinitely other in me" (76/161). This means that I do not first "have" a world of "my" own, because what might be called my world is from the first only an exposure and bearing toward the infinite distance of the other.

Furthermore, as Derrida makes explicit in the closing pages of his essay, this way of understanding the end of the world is intended precisely as a way of pushing to its limit Husserl's own thought-experiment of world annihilation in paragraph 49 of *Ideas I*. "Isn't this retreat of the world," Derrida asks, "the most necessary, the most logical, but also the most insane experience of a transcendental phenomenology?" (R 74/160). As Derrida notes, Husserl's hypothesis "does not threaten, by right and in its meaning, the sphere of phenomenological and pure egological experience. On the contrary, it would open access to this sphere," and, on his reading, Celan's poem "repeats without weakening this phenomenological radicalization. It pushes to the limit this experience of the possible annihilation of the world and of what remains of the world or still survives it, to wit, its sense 'for me,' for a pure *ego*" (75/161). This is a first step, then: *the world is gone.* "No world can any longer support us, serve as mediation, as ground, as earth, as foundation or as alibi" (68/158).

This brings us, in a second step, to what Derrida calls the most "worrisome test" of Husserlian phenomenology, which is that, once the world is gone, once we find ourselves in the "absolute solitude of the pure *ego*," "the *alter ego* that is constituted in the *ego* is no longer accessible in an originary and purely phenomenological intuition" but is instead "constituted only *by analogy*, by *appresentation,* indirectly, inside of me" (R 75–76/161). *I must carry you,* but precisely in the most paradoxical sense, where "to carry" no longer means "to include, to comprehend in the self, but rather *to carry oneself or bear oneself toward* the infinite inappropriability of the other, toward the absolute transcendence in the very inside of me, that is to say, in me outside of me" (76/161). The infinite distance that the other's transcendence opens within my world announces my responsibility to carry the other's world within me, to mourn it, after the other's death—but also the melancholic impossibility of my doing so, precisely because I can never contain or encompass this unique and singular opening of the world. And this ethical moment, the paradoxical responsibility to carry the other, requires the withdrawal of the world, in the sense of any common ground or foundation that might serve to mediate between us. The survivor is left "in some fashion beyond or before the world itself . . . responsible without world *(weltlos),* without the ground of any world, thenceforth, in a world without world, as if without earth beyond the end of the world" (23/140).

Furthermore, the end of the world does not, strictly speaking, await the actual death of the other, because the melancholic certainty that one friend will survive the other's death interrupts every friendship from its first moment: "from this first encounter, interruption anticipates death, precedes death" (R 22/140; see also Derrida 2001, 107; Naas 2015, 53). More generally, it follows that each and every encounter with each and every living thing already announces the heart of absence interrupting and constituting my world, calling me to respond with mourning both ineluctable and insufficient. The end of the world therefore haunts every world from within, dissolving its pretense of being "one and only," "unique," the "totality of what is"; we find ourselves "there where the world is no longer between us or beneath our feet, no longer ensuring mediation or reinforcing a foundation for us" (76/161). And so, from the first moment when the ethical injunction "I must carry you" announces itself, the world as *cosmos* or *mundus* has already disappeared. "I am alone in the world right where there is no longer any world" (68/158). In other words, Derrida's claim that death is each time the absolute end of the one and only world concerns not only an event that comes to pass with each living thing's death but just as much the structural necessity of the dissolution of any common world—as referential horizon of possibilities—already entailed by our exposure to the other.[18] This is consistent with Derrida's insistence that death is each time the end of *the* world, and not only of *a* world, of one possible world among others. Our ethical responsibility goes beyond the exigency of carrying the other's world within our own, then, but rather situates us already beyond the recourse to any ground, earth, or foundation.

Several interesting consequences follow from Derrida's account, the first being that the end of the world is already implicated within and even constitutive of the world itself; the world is not a self-enclosed totality that maintains itself until interrupted from the outside but rather has its outside on the inside. If this is so, we must think the relation between the world and its coming-to-an-end with more nuance than eschatological thinking allows, as Derrida has so often shown concerning the relationship of life with death. Second, because death is each time the end of the world, there is no perspective from which to compare, evaluate, or hierarchize this end of the world in comparison with, say, total nuclear war or ecological collapse. As Derrida writes in "No Apocalypse, Not Now," "there is no common measure able to persuade me that a personal mourning is less grave than a nuclear war" (P 379/403). Even if there is no basis for comparison, Derrida nevertheless does distinguish, in the final lecture of *The Beast and the Sovereign,* between the death of an individual as the "absolute end of the world" and the stakes of world war as "the end of the world, the destruction of the world, of any possible world, or of what is supposed to make of the world a *cosmos,* an arrangement, an order, an order of ends, a juridical, moral, political order, an international order resistant to the non-world of death and barbarity" (BS2 359/260).[19] Last, Derrida's account makes clear that the end of the world is an ethical matter, and perhaps the very opening of ethics insofar as it first eliminates any recourse to a ground or foundation and confronts us with the monstrousness of the other that is also the monstrousness of the future.[20] Consequently, what our responsibility to the other requires is not holding on to the world, attempting to sustain it at any cost, but precisely letting it go.

Nevertheless, there is an ambiguity or ambivalence in Derrida's approach to the end of the world that becomes clearest in the second year of his final seminar, an ambivalence that may allow us to bring Derrida's position on the end of the world closer to that of Nancy. Responding to Heidegger's three theses on world from *Fundamental Concepts of Metaphysics*,[21] Derrida frames this year's seminar in the first lecture with three theses of his own, three theses that are apparently incompatible with each other, briefly summarized as follows: (1) animals and humans incontestably inhabit the same "objective" world, even if they do not have the same experience of "objectivity"; (2) animals and humans incontestably do not inhabit the same world, because the human world is not identical with that of nonhuman animals; and (3) no two individuals, whether human or animal, inhabit the same world, and the differences between their worlds are essentially unbridgeable. This third thesis follows from the fact that "the community of the world is always constructed, simulated by a set of stabilizing apparatuses, more or less stable, then, and never natural, language in the broad sense, codes of traces being designed, among all living beings, to construct a unity of the world that is always deconstructible, nowhere and never given in nature" (BS2 31/8–9). Between my world (which, for me, can only be the unique and only world, encompassing all others) and the world of any other, therefore, "there is first the space and the time of an infinite difference, an interruption that is incommensurable with all attempts to make a passage, a bridge, an isthmus, all attempts at communication, translation, trope, and transfer that the desire for a world or the want of a world, the being wanting a world will try to pose, impose, propose, stabilize. There is no world, there are only islands" (BS2 31/9).

Derrida returns to the first and third of these theses in the tenth and final session of the seminar, where he again emphasizes, developing the third claim, that the unity of the world is a merely presumptive construction, a means of reassuring ourselves in the face of the absence of the world. Here, the end of the world—again associated with the line from Celan, "Die Welt ist fort" (The world is gone)—does not await the death of the other but is instead "the ever unsewn and torn tissue of our most constant and quotidian experience," something that we know "with an undeniable and stubborn, i.e., permanently denied, knowledge" (BS2 367/266). The presumptive unity of the word *world*, then, is intended to mask our panic . . . , to protect us against the infantile but infinite anxiety of the fact that *there is not the world*, that nothing is less certain than the world itself, that there is perhaps no longer a world and no doubt there never was one as totality of anything at all . . . and that radical dissemination, i.e. the absence of a common world, the irremediable solitude without salvation of the living being, depends first on the absence without recourse of any world, i.e. of any common meaning of the word "world," in sum of any common meaning at all. (366/265–66)

Here, without mention of death, Derrida draws the full consequences of his view that the death of the other is the end of the world, which is that, from the outset, there is no world at all, no world in common, and consequently no common meaning. In other words, we have moved from treating the *end* of the world as a phantasm to recognizing that the phantasm is actually *the world itself*, that the phantasm of the world is intended to mask the *absence* of the world. Understood in this context, our anxieties about the end of the world, insofar as they present the world as fragile and vulnerable, precisely reinforce our belief in its reality. In this situation, according to Derrida, *ich muß dich tragen*, "I must carry you," can mean one of only two things: either that, with both of us sharing this knowledge that the world is no longer, I must carry you into the worldless void, or that what I must do, "with you and carrying you, is make it that there be precisely a world, just a world, if not a just world, or to do things so as to make *as if* there were just a world, and to make the world come to the world" (369/268). On Michael Naas's (2015, 60) reading, Derrida places his hope in the second option, which Naas describes as a poetic making or remaking of the world ex nihilo in full recognition that there is no world: "Aware of its own powerlessness, undone by its own ability, this *poiesis* would be a making *as if* that leaves within the world a trace of the end or loss of the world." Without a poetic making or remaking of the world, a making of the world with and for the other, we remain *weltlos*, worldless, like the stone.

Here Derrida seems quite close to Nancy's claim, in *The Sense of the World*, that "there is no longer any world: no longer a *mundus*, a *cosmos*, a composed and complete order (from) within which one might find a place, a dwelling, and the elements of an orientation"

(13/4). For Nancy, this calls not for a poetic remaking of the world in the mode of *as if* but instead for a recognition of the ex nihilo coming-to-presence of the world as sense. Ex nihilo in Nancy's sense implies no relationship to a creator, poetic or otherwise, but instead a growing from nothing, without roots, that would be the "genuine formula of a radical materialism" (CW 55/51; cf. BSP 35/16). This creation of the world from nothing implies, in the words of Marie-Eve Morin (2012, 43–44), "that it has no presupposition or precondition, no ground or reason, no origin or end." While Derrida and Nancy seem very close, then, in their account of the end of the world as shared horizon or common ground, Derrida does not seem to move in Nancy's direction concerning a rediscovery of the world as sense, as the exposure and intersection of the material singularity of bodies, as this world here. This is consistent with Derrida's remarks, in the French preface to *Chaque fois unique, la fin du monde*, distinguishing his view on death as "the end of the world in totality, the end of every possible world, and each time the end of the world as unique totality, thus irreplaceable and thus infinite" from Nancy's account of anastasis in *Noli me tangere*, which, according to Derrida, concerns only the end of *a* world, of one possible world among many, and therefore the chance—rejected by Derrida—for replacement, survival, resurrection (see Derrida 2003c, 9–11; Nancy 2003b, 33–36, 70, 74–75; 2008b, 18–19, 41, 45).[22]

Derrida's final seminar does suggest, however, another reconstructive path for understanding the world, namely, in the first of the three theses introduced in the first session: "animals and humans inhabit the same world, the same objective world" (BS2 31/8); as living beings, they share in common "the finitude of their life, and therefore, among other features of finitude, their mortality in the place they inhabit, whether one calls that place world or earth (earth including sky and sea) and these places that they inhabit in common" (33/10). When Derrida returns to this common sense of world in the final session, he again stresses that it is the same space of inhabitation or cohabitation, a common habitat, characterized precisely in terms of the elements: "water, earth, air, fire" (363/263). This returns us to the problem of the elements and their ambivalent relationship with world. We have seen how the elements are left behind with the world's dissolution, such that the disintegration of our buildings and tools into dust figures the world's absolute reference to its finitude, its liability to the arche-materiality that grants its endurance and holds its horizons open. If the world has its outside on the inside, if it bears an essential reference to its own dissolution as its fundamental condition and ultimate horizon, then this liability is figured in its paradoxical relation to the elements, as neither precisely things within the world nor wholly outside it. Derrida's remarks here suggest that the elements, while remaining liminal to world in the phenomenological sense, nevertheless open a space and time that traverses all worlds.

Memories of Stone

Derrida notes at several points that the departure of the world, *die Welt ist fort*, exceeds and disrupts Heidegger's three theses on world, that its irreducibility to the categories of worldless, world-poor, and world-forming requires us to rethink the very thought of the world (R 79/163; cf. BS2 159/104, 243/169). Nevertheless, even if our situation of carrying the other is irreducible to either of these categories, Derrida repeatedly describes it using Heidegger's category for the worldless stone, "We are *weltlos*" (BS2 31–32/9; cf. R 23/140; BS2 253/177; Derrida 2003d, 213; 2005b, 155). Of course, we are "clearly not" worldless in the same manner as Heidegger had attributed this to the stone, as Derrida says explicitly (BS2 32/9), but then how are we to think this strange lithic proximity? Recall that, for Heidegger, the stone, as present-at-hand, is "absolutely indifferent," insofar as it remains entirely outside or before the difference between being indifferent or not indifferent to its own being (OS 39–41/19–21); it is neither awake nor asleep (A 203/148); it cannot be deprived of world because it has absolutely no relationship with other entities, no experience of the sun that shines upon it or the lizard that rests atop it (OS 79–81/51–52; cf. A 212–13/155–56). Furthermore—and for Heidegger this is the *Prüfstein*, the touchstone (BS2 115/173)—the stone "does not die, because it does not live" (BS2 171/113; cf. AA 211/154). It is finite while lacking finitude (A 206/150) and therefore entirely outside of the relation between life and death, of mortality or life-death. What is the status of this "outside" of the world, which cannot be a simple exclusion? That the stone may be without world obviously does not entail that the world is without stone. For Derrida, the death of any *living thing* is each time the end of the world, but could there be a world without stone, without earth, without the elements? Could there be a shared habitat of the living?[23]

Derrida calls attention to the fact that, in Heidegger's theses on world, the stone stands in as the sole example of "material things," of the "lifeless" or the "inanimate": "Why does he take the example of an inanimate thing, why a stone and not a plank or a piece of iron, or water or fire?" (BS2 27–28/6; cf. A 209–10/153). By privileging "the" stone as exemplary of the material thing, Heidegger participates in what Jeffrey Cohen (2015, 4) calls "a long tradition of mining the philosophical from the lithic," which poses the question of what stone's ontological exemplariness reveals as well as what it conceals. For Derrida, the choice of the stone as exemplar serves to cover over the ambiguities of the concept of life, which becomes obvious when one considers where to locate plants, for example—or cadavers—in relation to the general categories of "life" or "material things" (BS2 28/6). But in attending here only to the complications of any pure distinction between what is inside or outside of life-death, Derrida never addresses—as he does so well with the general category of "the" animal—the fact that there can be no "the" stone, no "the" material thing, but only a plurality of material singularities—as, for Nancy, matter is "always singular or singularized" (SW 97/58), the very difference and *différance* "through which *something* is possible, as *thing* and as *some*" (SW 95/57).

The stone is, for Heidegger, *vorhanden,* present-at-hand, a mere part of the world in distinction from the human being as one who also *has* world. With this in mind, it is curious that Derrida begins the second year of *The Beast and the Sovereign* with his own example of a stone, a polished pebble found lying on the beach with the inscription "The beasts are not alone" (BS2 26–28/5–6). This stone is a "stumbling block *[pierre d'achoppement]*," an obstacle that "interrupts one's progress and obliges one to lift one's foot," but it is also—like death for Heidegger—a "touchstone" (28/6). It seems to serve these functions, however, not insofar as it is stone or a stone but only in terms of its cryptic inscription, an inscription that Derrida soon abandons for being "like this stone, isolated, insularized, forlorn, singularly solitary" (29/7). Yet the stone is, then, the very figure of an island, of the *Einsamkeit,* the loneliness or solitude, that Heidegger reserves for "man" as what first brings him into proximity to the world (59–60/30). Consequently, like the beasts of its inscription, the stone is not, can never be, alone. Can this absolute isolation, beyond any solitude, still constitute a manner of being-toward, of *l'être-à*, such that, as Nancy suggests, even if the stone does not "have" a world, it nevertheless *is* a world? "To be sure, the concrete stone does not 'have' a world . . . but it is nonetheless toward or in the world *[au monde]* in a mode of *toward* or *in* that is at least that of *areality*: extension of the area, spacing, distance, 'atomistic' constitution. Let us say not that it is 'toward' or 'in' the world, but that it is world" (SW 103/62; cf. 48/28).

Beyond the distinction between life and death, the stone is consigned to the edge or margin of the world, at or beyond the world's limits, like a pebble washed up on the shores of a deserted island. The pebble on the shore, lying in the sand, knows nothing of its position or its situation, knows nothing of the sand or the beach on which it lies. The pebble may change locations with the waves and tides, but it nevertheless remains unmoved. Of course, the sand, in its turn, consists primarily of smaller stones. And the island also consists of rock, just a stone at a larger scale, bathing in the ocean waters while projecting into the air, immersed in the elements and weathering their changes. Pebble, stone, rock. The English term *pebble*, referring to a small stone rounded by the actions of water and sand, has uncertain origins that may relate to the Latin *papula*, a swelling or pustule on the skin, or may echo onomatopoetically the sound of walking on pebbles or of the movement of waters with which they are associated. By comparison, the French equivalent, *galet*, is diminutive of the Old French *gal*, stone, which is cognate with Old Irish *gall*, stone pillar, and *gallán*, large upright stone. *Stone*, like the German *Stein*, descends from the Proto-Germanic *stainaz*, related to the Proto-Indo-European *steyh-*, "to stiffen," and cognate with the Greek στία, small stone or pebble, while the French *pierre* follows from the Latin *petra* and Greek πέτρα. *Rock*, meanwhile, derived from the Old English *stanrocc*, "stonerock," is cognate with the French *roche*, both from Old French *roke*, cognate with the postclassical Latin *rocca*. While *rock* names the solid mineral matter of the lithosphere that encircles the outer layer of our planet, *a* rock, stone, or pebble is a clast or fragment of this materiality. Pebbles are stones and made of stone; stones are rocks and made of rock. According to the scale for grain size introduced by geologist Chester Wentworth in 1922, pebbles are between four and sixty-four millimeters, larger than *granules* but smaller than *cobbles*. But our geological terms in English have generally not been characterized by precision or consistency. As Cohen (2015, 14) notes, "Middle English *ston* could designate any lithic chunk from the smallest pebble to a towering menhir."

What, then, of the world of the stone? *The* stone? Is there any "the" stone, any stone in general or as such—or rather pebbles, stones, and rock of unimaginably diverse sorts, sizes, and placements, each one singularly unique, each one a world of its own whose originary spacing is the effective exteriority of all else that exists? Nancy responds to Heidegger's three theses on world by stressing precisely what they exclude of our "effective exteriority": "These statements do not do justice, at least, to this: that the world beyond humanity—animals, plants, and stones, oceans, atmospheres, sidereal spaces and bodies—is quite a bit more than the phenomenal correlative of a human taking-in-hand, taking-into-account, or taking-care-of: it is the effective exteriority without which the very disposition of or to sense would not make . . . any sense" (SW 92/55–56).

The stone is both a part of the world and also, as its effective exteriority, constitutive of the *there,* the spacing and material singularity, of the world. As a clast of the lithosphere, of the stony planetary skeleton that undergirds any earthly lifeworld, the stone also recalls or remembers the elemental geomateriality that precedes and exceeds all worlds. Just as creation stories envision the emergence of the world from formless waters and earth, the raging elements are a recurring motif in our eco-eschatological imagination: rising waters, glaciation, parched sands and storms of dust, hurricanes and earthquakes. "Some say the world will end in fire, / Some say in ice," according to the famous lines from Robert Frost (1923). Whether by fire or ice, our vision of the end of the world is haunted by its dissolution into elemental materials and forces of sublime scope and scale. As Levinas notes, "the element comes to us from nowhere; the side it presents to us does not determine an object, remains entirely anonymous. It is wind, earth, sea, sky, air" (TI 139/132). The stone extracted from the elements to become part of the world remains nevertheless inhabited or haunted by this anonymous elementality to which the world must inevitably return. This is why our imaginations of the world's end run up against a limit that is, finally, indestructible: the fact that *there is* something, that existence as such continues, perhaps independently of all subjectivity or even all life, if only in elemental form: fire and ice, dust and gas, atomic radiation, the stars.

Many stones have proper names, among them the Rosetta Stone, the Blarney Stone, Plymouth Rock, the Stone of Scone, the Rock of Gibraltar—and their destruction would, in many cases and in some sense, be mourned. But stone as such, like the other elements, is not subject to death or even to destruction; it is a world that survives the absolute destruction of world, which reveals its peculiar relationship with deep time, both past and future. Stone holds a preeminent place among the elements precisely because of its peculiar temporality, its geological memory. We owe our conception of the deep past to this memory of stone, which Buffon in 1778 could call "the world's archives"; just as we reconstruct human history from ancient inscriptions and artifacts, so it is possible to "extract ancient monuments from the earth's entrails" to "place a certain number of milestones on the eternal road of time" (Buffon, cited in Rudwick 2014, 64). This archival memory of stone spans all times and worlds, outstripping and undergirding the juridico-literary archive. Christopher Tilley (2004) demonstrates how Neolithic menhirs embody the traces of prehistoric perceptual worlds, even as the accumulated geomaterial records of our own lives pass into the far future in the form of nuclear waste, the stratigraphic traces of radioactive elements from nuclear blasts, and fossilized plastiglomerates (Corcoran, Moore, and Jazvac 2014). This timeless memory of stone situates it both within the world and beyond it, seesawing at its edge, which makes it the ideal boundary marker, milestone, or tombstone. As John Sallis (1994, 26) writes,

> stone comes from a past that has never been present, a past unassimilable to the order of time in which things come and go in the human world; and that nonbelonging of stone is precisely what qualifies it to mark and hence memorialize such comings and goings, births and deaths. As if stone were a sensible image of timelessness, the ideal material on which to inscribe marks capable of visibly memorializing into an indefinite future.

232   *The Elements at the End of the World*

The stone is always somehow from another world even as it subsists in this one, like a meteor, a fossil, or a glacial erratic, haunted by its immemorial passage across worlds.

Alongside the phantasmic projection of a world in common, a world of shared meaning that would bridge our separate islands, then, we must take into account the persistent geomateriality that grants existence its areal spacing and its temporal span. This is less a matter of common habitat than of the essential and constitutive lithic materiality of every living being. As Nancy writes, "a stone is the exteriority of singularity in what would have to be called its mineral or mechanical actuality. But I would no longer be a 'human' if I did not have this exteriority 'in me,' in the form of the quasi-minerality of bone" (BSP 37/18; cf. SW 100–102/60–61).[24] Our liability to this minerality is figured in the skeleton as symbol of death, as the endurance of our own lithic elementality into the rhythm of a temporality other than or exceeding that of life-death, just as the fossil, as we saw in chapter 2, offers a glimpse of the intersection of the time of life with the immemorial past of stone. Can we love, can we mourn, a stone, even the stony skeleton that from within makes possible all our loving and mourning, that bears us toward the other even as it harbors the obscure memory of its birth among the elements before all worldly time and anticipates its passage through stone and dust to other times and other worlds? In parallel, John Llewelyn (2004, 89) asks:

> Do stones have to become human beings before they can become subject matter for phenomenology? Or, for *physis* to comprise stones, do we at least have to be able to ask sensibly what it would be like to be a pile of stones? And must it not be sensible for us to ask this if a pile of stones or something very like it—a handful of dust, ash, earth—is what all of us are destined by nature to become?

To rediscover the world's liability to the elements requires forgoing any eschatology that approaches everything within the world and the very sense of the world itself against a background of absolute contingency or nothingness, vulnerable to total destruction. Eco-eschatology not only deforms our relationship to time but also prevents us from encountering the materiality of the thing in its absolute singularity. By threatening things with the specter of their own annihilation, and therefore silhouetting them against the screen of nothingness, we force their presentation into self-identity, positivity, immanence; they either fully are or fully are not. But, as Merleau-Ponty already points out, taking a pebble as his example, this framing is a denaturing of the thing: "Is not thinking the thing against the background of nothingness a double error, with regard to the thing and with regard to nothingness, and, by silhouetting it against nothingness, do we not completely denature the thing? Are not the identity, the positivity, the plenitude of the thing—reduced to what they signify in the context in which experience reaches them—quite insufficient to define our openness upon 'something'?" (VI 213/162). Nancy develops this insight by adding that the "regulating fiction" of total destruction always leaves something behind, something indestructible: "the pure being of a world or of 'something' in general," the world or the something that no longer refers to us for its existence or its sense (I 245/85). The true last thing of eschatology would then be the *there is* of existence itself:

> The pure *there is* as the indestructible, the gift that cannot be refused (since it has no one to give it), of a space without a subject to arrange it, to distribute it, to give it sense. A *there is* that would be neither *for* us nor *because* of us. Either that or the "sensible" world outside the "sense" given to it by a sentient subject: the very thing that philosophy has never been able to think, still less to touch, even though it has doubtless always been obsessed with or haunted by it. (245/85)

There would be little comfort, as Nancy recognizes, in recognizing the indestructibility of being on the verge of our own destruction, but the point is that the end of the world as we know it is not the price for this knowledge, because "we already know this, here and now. 'Being' or the 'there is' or 'existence' is, in us, what happens before us and ahead of us, arising from the very step beyond us" (246/85). This neither prevents nor justifies our own self-destruction, which remains an ever-present possibility. But it does invite us to "stop dreaming of the end, to stop justifying it" and to attend to what, in the here and now, incommensurably resists our efforts to manage the world toward its own annihilation. "The indestructible measures each one of our destructions, their impotence. Existence resists" (246/86). To think this resistance, to encounter it as "permanent revolution" in the materiality of things and ourselves, is to move beyond apocalypse or apotheosis and thereby to rediscover the world after the end of the world.

10

Climate Change and the Temporal Sublime

It is commonplace today to hear climate change described in apocalyptic terms as the single most important challenge facing humanity. Consider the headlines from COP24, the United Nations (UN) Climate Change Conference held in Poland in December 2018. UN secretary-general António Guterres opened the proceedings by calling climate change "the most important issue we face" (PBS 2018). The secretary-general's remarks paraphrase the opening line of the UN's climate change web page, which announces that "Climate Change is the defining issue of our time and we are at a defining moment" (United Nations, n.d.). Such statements about the singular significance of climate change—*the* most important, the *defining* issue—are often followed by proclamations about what hangs in the balance, and this was the case at COP24. There the celebrated British naturalist Sir David Attenborough warned that "collapse of our civilizations and the extinction of much of the natural world is on the horizons," amounting to, in his words, "disaster of global scale, our greatest threat in thousands of years" (PBS 2018).

As common as this rhetoric is, and despite the important strategic role that it plays in the context of international climate negotiations, it leaves me profoundly uneasy. I say "uneasy," rather than "skeptical," because I am a skeptic neither about anthropogenic climate disruption nor about the scientific evidence and predictions of terrible times to come. What leaves me uneasy is how *the present* is interpreted when climate collapse is identified as *the* most important issue *we* face, threatening the collapse of civilization as such. This suggests, first, that civilization has been going along just fine and would continue to do so if not interrupted by something more or less external to it, something not essential to it or to its continuation. We are called to marshal all available resources as quickly as possible to address the single greatest challenge the world has ever faced, in the hope that we can preserve it in its present form, sustain it, into the future as far as possible. I am uneasy with this assessment of our present state of affairs and this emergency prioritization of its continuation as *the* decisive issue of our time.

Second, I am uneasy about the "we" who here claim to speak for humanity, for "our civilizations." How much of humanity does this "we" include? Would the 10 percent of the world's population living in extreme poverty today, or the nearly half of the world's population that struggles to meet basic needs, agree that climate collapse is the most important issue "we" face (World Bank 2018)? Those whose lives, livelihoods, and communities have been violated by extractive industries, settler colonialism, forced migration, environmental injustices, police violence, anti-Black racism, the intersections of violence and oppression that have made and continue to make "our" civilization possible—would they agree that climate change is "the defining issue of our time" or that every available resource should be mobilized to maintain the world in its present form? This is far from obvious to me.

To be clear, I do not believe that *anyone* will be *better off* as a consequence of climate disruption. It is well established that the most vulnerable—the poor, women, children, the elderly, communities of color, the displaced, the incarcerated—will suffer the most. And even the wealthiest and most privileged will be unable to avoid its effects entirely (see Collings 2014, esp. chapter 1). In this sense, it could be considered a common danger, a danger shared by everyone. Some see in this a reason for political optimism. Traditionally, communities of color have been "our" environmental sacrifice zones, the dumping grounds for extractive and polluting industries, incinerators, toxic waste, and so on, so that the costs of "civilization" could remain out of sight and out of mind for those who accrue its benefits. But climate change is happening to everyone, and the violence of the extractive industries that feed it is already impacting educated, wealthy, white communities, so that new coalitions have become possible.[1] Those with political and economic clout, or at least some of them, are now motivated to address the root causes of climate change because they can no longer avoid its effects. But this is precisely why the "we" rings hollow when it declares climate change the decisive issue for everyone, rather than for those who are most invested in the continuation of the world as it is. Commenting on today's postapocalyptic culture, Claire Colebrook (2017, 103) notes that our end-of-the-world scenarios are "accurate depictions of what life already is, and has necessarily been, outside the luxuries of first-world anxieties about the future of 'humanity.'"

We begin, then, by asking whether this prioritization of climate destabilization as *the* defining threat of recorded human history is justified. In his book *Stolen Future, Broken Present,* David Collings (2014) suggests that climate disruption deserves this status because it fundamentally alters our relationship to the future as such. As he describes in a chapter titled "The Ruins to Come," climate predictions portray our *present* culture and lives, the world of today, as *future* ruins. Looking around us right now, we should see this world shadowed by the ruin it is on the verge of becoming. Still, this is not enough to make climate collapse the definitive danger of human history: civilizations have ended before, and we have all admired the picturesque ruins that they have left behind. And certainly, at various points, those whose civilizations were in decline had premonitions of what was coming and could also picture their own worlds as future ruins. But there is more. The future ruins of climate change are not confined to a few buildings, or a city, or a landscape. This time, the future ruins encompass the earth as a whole (105). Before, we might have said that, while civilizations rise and fall, nature endures. This is no longer true. Before, those whose cultures were collapsing might still have had hope in a different future for themselves or their children, the possibility to rebuild elsewhere. But this time, survivors will witness the definitive eclipse of humanity's future, with no guarantees of any new beginning (107). As Collings concludes,

> our own mortality fades in comparison to something altogether more harrowing—the possible mortality of our societies, the natural systems we know, and to some extent the biosphere itself. In our world, the temporal coherence of a future into which our individual lives vanish—the coherence, in short, of mortality itself—is falling into decay. (112)

At stake in climate disruption, then, is not merely the ruin of *a* world, that of the civilizations of today, but the ruin of the very basis for *the* world and even for time itself as we know it.

Collings is not alone in seeing the ruins of the future in the figure of climate disruption. For Andrew Benjamin (2017), in an essay titled "The World in Ruins," it is the task of philosophy to think the end of the world starting from a double sense of catastrophe. A catastrophe in the first and transformative sense would decouple the existing link between climate change and injustice, thereby bringing about the creation of a new world (103). But such a transformative catastrophe may no longer be a possibility for us today. In that case, we are left only with the second sense of catastrophe, catastrophic climate change, without transformation or continuity. As Benjamin writes, "the end to be thought is the end of the world *as such,* that is, a world that is *now* present without always already bearing within it the inscription, image, or possibility of another beginning" (103). It is this "ending without a beginning" (104), an "ending that is not itself a preparation for a beginning" (109), whose insistence demands thought.

Framing Benjamin's inquiry is the conviction that philosophy can no longer remain apathetic to its own predicament, that it is no longer possible to refuse, on philosophical grounds, the relation between philosophy and the *now* in which it takes a stand (101–2). By "the *now,*" italicized to distinguish it from our simple sense of now, he intends "a thinking of the present as that which generates the philosophical task" (118n1). The insistent *now* of such a philosophical task would be entirely distinct from either the self-evident now of empiricism or the inevitable now of naturalism. With this redefinition of philosophy's task, Benjamin takes us a long way toward articulating an essential aim of critical phenomenology, which, in taking a stand, would "allow the question of its own stand in relation to the *now* to delimit a specific philosophical project" (102). Benjamin's own contention here is that "what determines or defines the *now* is the ineliminable presence of catastrophic climate change, a change that is leaving the world in ruins" (102). In short, where philosophy stands *now* can be thought only in relation to this predicament, so that, as he succinctly puts it, "what has to be thought is the end of the world" (101).

Here I take up this task of thinking the *now* in its relation to the future, or to the end of the future. But I do so by asking after the image of time that this orientation toward the end implies or unfolds. More precisely, my starting point will be popular narratives of climate change, and environmentalism more generally, with respect to their apocalyptic structure. Apocalyptic fantasies weave through contemporary culture and intertwine themselves with our scientific predictions and our efforts to manage the future. I propose that these apocalyptic fantasies enact a temporal narrative that first became possible with our discovery of deep geological timescales, scales of time so vast that they explode all efforts to integrate them with the time of human life. The emergence of secular apocalyptic narratives goes hand in hand with this expansion of the horizons of time, so that time encompasses pasts that precede us as well as futures that survive us. In short, a radical end of the world first becomes thinkable through a new image of time, a new temporal sublime, that underlies apocalypticism in its recent forms, including speculative fictions, nuclear fears, environmental disaster, and climate disruption.

On this basis, I explore a series of questions posed by such apocalyptic narratives: Does this image of time exhaust our possibilities for relating to the sublime dimensions of the deep past and far future? Does it skew our relation to the present, to the *now*? What investments or fears are expressed through this apocalyptic image, and what does it reveal about our responsiveness to and responsibility for the past, present, and future? Does justice demand of us a different image of time, and what form might this take?

I proceed first by briefly summarizing the transformation of temporal horizons opened by geological scales of time and past extinctions as a reconfiguration of the temporal sublime. I turn then to the role of apocalyptic narratives in climate change rhetoric and the image of time that frames these narratives. Here I am especially interested in the role that crisis plays as the passage from the corrupt present to a purified future, marked by the transfiguration of time in the crucible of Judgment Day. On this basis, I consider some of the investments and motivations underlying the tragic and comic modes of time that drive climate narratives. I argue that these instantiate what Jean-Luc Nancy has called "general equivalence," leveling time into homogenous and substitutable units to facilitate the predictability and manageability of the future. Rather than owning our temporal responsibilities, then, apocalyptic narratives in fact seek to liquidate our obligations to the past, obscure the singularity of the present, and exert absolute control over the future. A just image of time faces two demands: responsiveness to the singularity of the present and to the entanglement of this present in the plexities of past and future. I conclude with two explorations of this figure of temporal justice: Kyle Powys Whyte's proposal of "spiraling time" as a living dialogue with our ancestors and descendants and artist Roni Horn's installation *Library of Water* in Stykkishólmur, Iceland.

The Temporal Sublime

I begin with some historical context for our shifting horizons of time, which I read through the lens of the temporal sublime. The fact that long expanses of time confront the human mind with a sublime dimension was recognized by both Hume and Kant, although neither devotes much attention to this experience (Hume 2007, 274–80; Kant 2007).[2] Kant's ([1764] 2007, 26) entire treatment of this topic in his precritical *Observations on the Feeling of the Beautiful and the Sublime*, for instance, appears in the following few lines:

> A long duration is sublime. If it is of time past, it is noble; if it is projected forth into an unforeseeable future, then there is something terrifying in it. An edifice from the most distant antiquity is worthy of honor. Haller's description of the future eternity inspires a mild horror, and of the past, a transfixed admiration.

In the later terms of the *Critique of Judgment* (Kant [1790] 1987), this suggests that the past confronts us with an experience of the mathematical sublime, and indeed Kant refers there to past time as an infinite magnitude (111), although this later text offers no further mention of time's sublime character. The unforeseeable future, on the other hand, although never mentioned in the *Critique of Judgment*, would be a species of the dynamically sublime, arousing fear in us in a way that is somehow parallel to the elemental examples that Kant favors: threatening rocks, thunderclouds, volcanoes, hurricanes, and the like (120).[3] The reference here to Albrecht von Haller's (2002) "Uncompleted Poem on Eternity" suggests that, for Kant, the future is not to be thought as an infinite magnitude because it is progressing toward its end. And, indeed, he returns to Haller in his 1794 text "The End of All Things"—a rebuke of Prussian millenarian politics—where what is at stake is not a future proceeding to infinity but precisely eternity as the horrifying abyss that opens beyond the edge of time, beyond the Judgment Day that brings the sensible world to its conclusion. Eternity beyond time is unthinkable, and its "frighteningly sublime" character is due in part to its obscurity; yet according to Kant (1996, 221), "in the end it must also be woven in a wondrous way into universal human reason, because it is encountered among all reasoning peoples at all times, clothed in one way or another." The caution of Kant's tale is to remember that the religious and cultural imagery with which we clothe this notion of eternity must be understood according to the moral order and not in literal or physical terms.

For both Hume and Kant, the sublime past is revealed only through cultural antiquities, never through natural or elemental phenomena.[4] But in the thirty years that separate these sparse references to the temporal sublime in Kant, developments in what would come to be known as geological science were setting the stage for a dramatic reorientation in our relationship with long durations of time. As I discussed in chapter 2, James Hutton's (1788) *Theory of the Earth* famously proposed a concept of geological time with "no vestige of a beginning,—no prospect of an end" (304), and through the writings of his friend and popularizer John Playfair, this newly opened horizon of what would come to be known as "deep" time was characterized from the outset in sublime terms.[5] In chapter 9, we saw that this discovery of the deep past simultaneously opens the horizons of the far future and our contemporary cultural obsession with apocalypse. Georges Cuvier's evidence for prehistoric extinctions laid the groundwork for Mary Shelley's exploration of future human extinction in her 1826 novel *The Last Man*, generally recognized as the first secular apocalyptic novel. The genre of apocalyptic speculative fiction inaugurated by Shelley first gained popularity by imagining our demise from natural causes, but the First World War shifted our fantasies toward the prospect of self-annihilation by weapons of mass destruction. And Rachel Carson's *Silent Spring*, written during the lead-up to the Cuban Missile Crisis, played a key role in transferring our nuclear anxieties to the emerging threat of ecological collapse.

Contemporary climate apocalypticism is therefore simply the latest phase in our cultural efforts to manage the sublime dimensions of our uncertain future. Just as the threat of total nuclear war—what Derrida (2007, 396) in 1984 termed the "phantasm of a remainderless destruction"—framed human reality during the Cold War period, so the phantasm of future climate collapse constructs our present today. Ongoing debates over whether to name our contemporary geological period the "Anthropocene" are symptomatic of this transfigured temporal perspective, which offers a vantage from which humanity can hold itself responsible—for the first time—for our long-term ecological transformations of the globe, while raising—also for the first time—the question of our ethical obligations toward an unimaginably distant future. At stake, then, in environmentalism's adoption of apocalyptic narratives is an underlying image of time, one that becomes especially salient in climate change narratives. Let us consider, first, the reliance of climate discourse on apocalyptic narratives and then draw out the image of time by which these are framed.

Climate Collapse as Judgment Day

During the final week of the 2009 UN Climate Change Conference, four Greenpeace activists paraded on horseback through the streets of Copenhagen dressed in costumes representing Famine, Pestilence, War, and Death. Invoking the four horsemen of the apocalypse from the biblical book of Revelation, their intent was to dramatize the stakes of climate change negotiations. In a press release from Greenpeace International, Sini Harkki of Greenpeace Nordic explained that "the spectre of the four horseman [sic] is looming over these climate negotiations. . . . Yet world leaders are still failing to grasp the urgency of the crisis" (Greenpeace International 2009). This is but one dramatic example of the widespread use of apocalyptic rhetoric to describe climate change—by activists, the media, scientists, political actors, advertisers, and popular culture. Over the past decade, such rhetoric has been the subject of interdisciplinary scholarly debate, which has focused primarily on whether framing the narrative of climate change in apocalyptic terms helps or hinders efforts to mobilize individual and collective responses. This debate has generated a proliferation of ways of defining the key elements of apocalyptic narrative and a range of interpretations concerning how the climate change variation extends or remakes the earlier apocalyptic narratives that have framed U.S. environmental discourse since the 1960s (e.g., Rachel Carson's *Silent Spring,* Paul Ehrlich's *The Population Bomb*). It has also drawn new attention to environmentalism's relationship with the nuclear apocalypticism that preceded and informed it and to the long history of religious apocalypticism in Judaism and Christianity.[6] These debates tend to start from an understanding of "apocalypse" as straightforwardly synonymous with catastrophe, with the end of the world "as we know it," whether that means the end of "our" current standard of living, or the end of human civilization in any historically recognizable form, or the literal extinction of the human species, and so on. And when apocalypse is read as synonymous with catastrophe, the rhetorical deployment of the narrative is understood to be in the service of galvanizing individual action and political will through fear and horror at the likely consequences of inaction. This rhetorical strategy can then be criticized as ineffectual or counterproductive fearmongering along lines familiar from Nordhaus and Shellenberger (2007).

Representative of this approach is geographer Mike Hulme's (2010) frequently cited typology of four biblically named climate change "myths": Lamenting Eden, Constructing Babel, Celebrating Jubilee, and Presaging Apocalypse. Whereas *Lamenting Eden* voices our misplaced nostalgia for pristine nature's lost autonomy, *Constructing Babel* expresses our hubristic desire for increased technoscientific control, most implicit in geoengineering schemes. *Celebrating Jubilee* serves our "instinct" to do the right thing by taking the climate crisis as an opportunity to establish social and environmental justice. And finally, *Presaging Apocalypse* "lends a sense of danger, fear and urgency" to climate discourse by exhorting us to "save the planet" before it is too late (44). But the "counter-intuitive outcome" of this framing, Hulme argues, is "disempowerment, apathy and skepticism among its intended audience" (45). Now, as Hulme is aware, these four narratives rarely operate in isolation, because the apocalyptic mode is driven by a sense of nature's fragility borrowed from Lamenting Eden, and the crisis mentality that it engenders is precisely what motivates Constructing Babel and Celebrating Jubilee. So, going beyond Hulme, we might conclude that Presaging

Apocalypse is not merely one alongside the other myths but rather the heart of our cultural response to climate change. This would follow from the recognition that environmentalism, at least in the United States, has always defined itself by apocalyptic narratives and that climate change lends itself to appropriation as *the* paradigmatic apocalypse (see Killingsworth and Palmer 1996; Fiskio 2021).

We can note several interesting points about Hulme's treatment of the Presaging Apocalypse "myth." First, he intentionally limits his use of *apocalypse* to its "popular sense," which he understands as "impending large-scale disaster or destruction," in contrast with the concept's "original Greek—and Biblical—usage, meaning simply 'disclosure or revelation'" (Hulme 2010, 55n7). With this decision, Hulme participates in the trend noted by Stefan Skrimshire (2014) of stripping references to apocalypse of their "theological nuances" in favor of their "sensationalist elements" and particularly of treating such discourses as reducible to fear of the future. What is obscured here, Skrimshire reminds us, is precisely the "complex dramatic structure" of the religious apocalyptic narrative, which includes "the creation of tension between the corruption that is endured in the present age and the hope in the new age that is yet to come" (237). The temporal, eschatological element of apocalyptic thinking is precisely to be found in this productive tension, which revolves around an explicit or implicit "Judgment Day."

Furthermore, like others who evaluate the apocalyptic narrative in terms of its rhetorical efficacy, Hulme seems to suggest that such narrative framings are something that we can consciously pick and choose according to our political aims, rather than—at least in part—historical structures that frame our very experience. Obviously, there are those activists, reporters, politicians, and authors who seize on an apocalyptic description as a tactic; but their tactics resonate precisely because of the ways we have come to experience the world through an essentially apocalyptic mode. That this mode is more complex than simple fearmongering is already suggested by the deep cathartic pleasure that we take in imagining worldwide cataclysmic destruction, repeatedly and in endless variation, as demonstrated by our insatiable appetite for apocalyptic films and novels and the new genre of cli-fi. I do not believe that we can explain this away as disaster capitalism's effort to "transform apocalypse into exciting entertainment for the multitudes," as Frederick Buell (2010, 31) suggests. Our appetite for world-ending fiction long predates the disaster capitalism that Naomi Klein (2007) describes, which must itself be understood through our deep cultural identification with the apocalyptic mode.

Finally, it is notable that both Hulme and Buell point to the introduction of new scientific language, especially that of systems theory, as influencing the specific forms of apocalyptic discourse in the environmental movement and climate change in particular. Prophetic revelation is a key feature of the Judeo-Christian apocalyptic tradition, and today's augurs are the scientists who have introduced us to nonlinearity, tipping points, feedback loops, and other chaotic disruptions of our received models for change. That such models inform our cosmic, that is, spatial, understanding of the possibility of catastrophe is clear, but they also have eschatological, that is, temporal, implications.[7] If we now live the world in an apocalyptic mode informed by nonlinearity, has this not also complicated our experience of time?

Turning now explicitly to apocalyptic temporality, we find that one of its defining features is said to be its linear directionality, either guided by divine providence or driven by natural forces, toward a catastrophic end point, a "Judgment Day," beyond which all individual human judgment is irrelevant (Foust and Murphy 2009, 154). Alongside the spectacular destruction of the current world, this narrative structure "prophecies (directly or implicitly) a new world order," and Judgment Day marks the passage into this new age, which is therefore also a new time (Foust and Murphy 2009, 154, citing Brummett). Nevertheless, finer-grained distinctions are possible within this broad characterization, as Christina Foust and William Murphy have shown through their examination of climate press coverage. Foust and Murphy take up Stephen O'Leary's distinction between "tragic" and "comic" variations of the apocalyptic narrative and show that these correspond to distinct temporalities. The tragic narrative is fatalistic, marching unstoppably toward preordained or necessary destruction regardless of human actions. The tragic therefore "promotes a view of time and human action as closed" (quoted in Foust and Murphy 2009, 154). When this narrative is adopted, time is shortened or accelerated in its rush toward an unambiguous end point, and this unalterable plunge is often characterized in terms of feedback loops, tipping points, and the destabilization of phenological cycles. Such tragic narratives are often supported by analogies with examples from fiction or from the deep geological past, such as a volcanic extinction event 250 million years ago (Foust and Murphy 2009, 159). In other words, they are modeled on temporalities that are either counterfactual or incommensurable with our mundane, linear conceptions of time. The tragic narrative is reassuring in its own way precisely because there is nothing to be done, and we can resign ourselves to letting the course of things unfold—nothing to be done, that is, except to repent for our role in the corruption of the present (Foust and Murphy 2009, 161–62). The new world that succeeds final judgment will be purified of all corruption because it will continue on in its own pristine eternity, without us.

By contrast with this tragic narrative, although often mixed with it, the comic perspective is more optimistic about the prospects for human agency to influence the course of events. Things are headed badly due to our mistakes, and these can be righted. While we may not avoid disaster entirely, we might avoid the worst. The temporality of the comic, then, is open, and the point toward which it aims is less determinate. Rather than rushing toward a tipping point beyond which all human intervention is impossible, the comic mode slows things down long enough to give us time to think and to act. Within this narrative structure, then, we can hold on to the distinction between crisis and catastrophe (Foust and Murphy 2009, 160). Because Foust and Murphy approach the issue of apocalyptic rhetoric through the lens of its communicative and political efficacy, their proposal is for "communication scholars and climate scientists" to work together "on the difficult task of providing appropriate perspectives toward time," perspectives that will encourage audiences to see climate change as urgent but manageable (163). For them, this means promoting the "comic" perspective.

Nevertheless, this sorting into tragic and comic modes remains superficial until we contextualize it within the temporal structure of the full apocalyptic narrative. Whereas the tragic mode destabilizes and accelerates time toward the definite moment when duration gives way to eternity, the comic mode aims to maintain a regular pace, a continuity with lived time, long enough to prepare us for judgment. But judgment still comes, in the sense that we must pass through a crisis for which we are as yet unprepared, a crisis that maintains its full catastrophic potential depending on what we do next. On the comic mode, the world still passes into a new age and a new time, even if this is a new age in which we might still have a place. But this new age, this new time, and this new place are as yet unimaginable.

In insisting on the moment of crisis as a temporal hinge, as the turning point between "our" time and a time to come, I am borrowing an insight from political theorist Ben Jones (2017), who examines the appeal of Christian apocalyptic thinking for secular political theorists. Jones focuses on the strand of Christian thinking that he terms "cataclysmic apocalyptic thought," exemplified by the book of Revelation, among other texts, which "identifies crisis as the path to the ideal society" (2). On this view, crisis is not to be avoided but rather welcomed, because it is the only path that can wipe away the current state of corruption and replace it with lasting utopia (3). The truly apocalyptic crisis, then, is the final crisis, the one that installs us in a time beyond all crises. And this leavens our everyday struggles, here and now, with transcendent significance, insofar as they are moments of the larger progression toward final purification; we may be losing the local struggle, but we are still on the winning side of the cosmic battle.[8] My suggestion is that our cultural fascination with fictional apocalyptic narratives is a manifestation less of our desire for our own destruction than of our yearning for this transcendent significance; we are ready, in our heart of hearts, to wipe the world away and start again, even at the risk that we might be wiped away with it. In the Christian version of this narrative, of course, the crisis and its aftermath unfold under the guidance of divine providence, and we need only have faith in this. Secular versions proceed without this safety net or try, like Marxism, to replace it by other mechanisms. In any case, the way that we live the apocalyptic narrative today is through our deep pleasure at the prospect of leaping into an unimaginable world and a new age without any guarantees of survival—and, importantly, without any unpaid debts to the past.

The radicality of this image of time follows from the unique moment of judgment, which is precisely a singular break where time folds, dehiscing into the old that is washed away and the ideal future to come. This returns us to Kant's (1996) late essay "The End of All Things," in which he calls attention to the strange temporality of Judgment Day as the hinge between time and eternity, which both horrifies and attracts us with the full force of the sublime. For Kant this is a transition between the happening of events under the conditions of time, on one hand, and an eternity in which nothing can come to pass, on the other, a situation that cannot be rationally comprehended but is to be understood according to the moral order of ends. Judgment Day is always a selection, a differentiation of the corrupt from the pure, that represents an absolute break with the past—toward which no further debts are owed—and entrance into a finality beyond which no further beginning, no future as such, is possible. What contemporary apocalyptic thinking retains from this structure is the linear sorting of time into a corrupt present and an ideal beyond, with the moment of judgment as their transition. As with Kant, it is the eternal or the utopian moment that remains sublime, unthinkable—and transcendent.

Apocalyptic Equivalence and Temporal Liability

The suggestion I have been developing here is that our contemporary apocalypticism remains fundamentally eschatological, that it embraces crisis as a Judgment Day that marks the hinge between our corrupt present world and a new dawn, even or especially when this eschatological frame is not consciously or explicitly theological. It is this basic narrative that has underwritten environmentalism since at least *Silent Spring,* despite the modifications that it has undergone in the light of new technologies and shifting political contexts (see Killingsworth and Palmer 1996; Buell 2010). This narrative justifies itself in terms of our ethical obligations toward the future, and yet it assumes a figure of time that conceals our ethical obligations—not only toward the future but also toward the past and present.

To see why this is so, we must first recognize that the apocalyptic image of time participates in what Jean-Luc Nancy (2015) has termed the "equivalence of catastrophes." As we saw in chapter 9, Nancy describes our global ecotechnical situation as an ever-expanding entanglement of interdependencies between political, military, industrial, financial, logical, natural, and other systems. This interdependence depends on the translatability of units across all of these systems, which requires that the units have a common denominator, a common measure of equivalence. This is most obvious in the equivalence of bits and bytes, such as when a picture taken on a "smart" phone is stamped with GIS location data, sent by Wi-Fi to the cloud, distributed across social media platforms, viewed around the world, backed up on Google's hard drives, added to law enforcement facial recognition databases, and so on. The interdependence of all systems means that our catastrophes, such as the 2011 disaster at the Fukushima Daiichi Nuclear Power Plant discussed by Nancy, are uncontainable in their effects. But the deeper catastrophe, as Nancy argues, is the general equivalence that makes the interdependence of systems possible in the first place, namely, the leveling of all measures into a common denominator that facilitates translation across domains. This general equivalence inspires a proliferation of means and ends without orientation toward any final end or ultimate goal other than their own continued expansion and proliferation. It is this loss of any ultimate sense or direction that Nancy (1997, 4–5) has called the "end of the world." Our constant awareness of the possibility of our own self-destruction stands in place of any final end as the secret fulfillment of the leveling of time into a homogenous continuum (Nancy 2015, 17–20). The operations of this catastrophe of equivalence can be traced in those approaches to sustainability that extrapolate from deep-past trends to predict and manage far-future scenarios, thereby tacitly assuming that our obligation toward the future is to "sustain" the world in a state that resembles as closely as possible our present.

This catastrophic leveling of time is precisely a means of repressing the sublime dimensions of the future through calculative management. In other words, by leveling time into homogenous and exchangeable units, we defang the future of its unpredictability; we contain it as an infinitely repeatable present. Thus managed, the threat of our extinction or of the end of the world can be indefinitely deferred. On this approach, the threat of the end of the world (and the end of time) justifies absolute management of the world through the homogenization of time. Judgment Day, as the only decisive interruption of the linear and calculable equivalence of "nows," always looms on the horizon as the absolute danger demanding further ecotechnical interdependency, further integration of substitutable systems. This firm grip on managing the future inevitably seesaws into resignation, into the realization that Judgment Day cannot be indefinitely deferred. But this resignation satisfies another deep desire, namely, the complete liquidation of the past, a wiping clean of the slate of past debts and obligations. As a repression of the temporal sublime, Judgment Day is both the specter that drives the proliferation of catastrophic equivalence and its consequence.

To make this diagnosis more concrete, we can turn to Potawatomi scholar Kyle Powys Whyte's (2018) critique of settler environmental rhetoric surrounding the Anthropocene and apocalypticism more generally. Whyte notes that settler apocalyptic narratives, proposed as the effort of stopping "a dreaded future movement from stability to crisis" (227), erase the legacies of colonial violence that have been experienced by many Indigenous people as repeated and ongoing apocalypses. As Anishinaabe scholar Lawrence Gross writes, "Native Americans have seen the ends of their respective worlds. . . . Indians survived the apocalypse" (cited in Whyte 2018, 227). Drawing on the work of Tahltan scholar Candis Callison, Whyte notes that "the hardships many nonIndigenous people dread most of the climate crisis are ones that Indigenous people have endured already due to different forms of colonialism: ecosystem collapse, species loss, economic crash, drastic relocation, and cultural disintegration" (226). Furthermore, by seeking to liquidate the past and the present in a new beginning, the settler apocalyptic narrative imagines for itself an innocent future, one in which all obligations and debts for past and present colonial violence are assumed to be discharged. While Whyte's discussion here concerns the experience of Indigenous peoples specifically, his critique of settler colonialism can easily be extended to the historically linked legacy of enslavement.[9] Historian Gerald Horne (2018, 9) writes that "what is euphemistically referred to as 'modernity' is marked with the indelible stain of what might be termed the Three Horsemen of the Apocalypse: Slavery, White Supremacy, and Capitalism." Such considerations trouble the ubiquitous narratives that, from some quarters, announce climate change as *the* apocalypse *to come,* while turning a blind eye to the past and continuing violence that has made the present world a possibility. How might different narratives, guided by a different image of time, do justice to these experiences?

The Deep Temporal Sublime and the Singular Present

Breaking with the apocalyptic image of time requires, first, that we come to terms with the plexity of deep time and, second, that we rediscover the singularity of the unique and nonsubstitutable present. On the first point, the explosion of our temporal horizons far beyond the limits of human history considered by Hume or Kant and the parallel opening of a deep temporal future that continues beyond human extinction confront us with the fact that our personal and historical temporalities are entangled and shot through with anachronistic and incompossible durations—those of our evolutionary history, for example, and, further still, of our own elemental materiality. Michel Serres (2003, 24; 2018, 12), explaining what he calls the Grand Narrative, the topologically folded multiplex of temporal scales, writes the following: "The senses open the body on to the world, it is said; no, they make us descend into an immemorial duration, towards long lost environments." We have seen that the experience of the deep temporal sublime is characterized precisely by its incommensurability with the narrative structures of personal and cultural history, by the vertigo of losing all common markers and measures. This testifies to our entanglement in a past that was never our own possibility, never our own memory—an impossible and immemorial past. Indeed, the very "depth" of geological time we have described is the bottomless free fall into which it throws all markers and touchstones by which we orient ourselves within the temporal horizons of our world. The schema of general equivalence is our unsuccessful attempt to repress this abyssal vertigo.

If we give up the effort to regiment time within general equivalence, then we open ourselves to our ongoing involvement, both material and symbolic, in time's incommensurable vectors and scales: cosmic, geological, elemental, organic, evolutionary. As Serres (2003, 55; 2018, 32) writes, "insofar as I am a memory, I participate in things. Insofar as they are things, they have memory." The encounter with the vertigo of deep time is thus the echo within us of evolutionary memory and the asubjective time of matter, which anachronistically interrupt our lived experiences of time from within. A full accounting of the temporal sublime would therefore recognize the confluence of the immemorial past and future in its cosmic, geological, evolutionary, and organic trajectories as a tangle of rhythms, durations, and memories. This takes us well beyond an image of time as linear or metrical; it is instead multiple, folded, percolating. In Serres's words, time flows "according to an extraordinarily complex mixture, as though it reflected stopping points, ruptures, deep wells, chimneys of thunderous acceleration, rendings, gaps—all sown at random, at least in a visible disorder" (Serres and Latour 1995, 57). Because of this nonlinear plexity, what seems closest to us chronologically may in fact be distant, while often what we believe to be out of date is fully contemporary.

Doing justice to our entanglement in a chaotic multiplicity of durations and memories means breaking with the homogenous leveling of time into substitutable and homogenous units, what, following Nancy, we have called its catastrophic equivalence. To break with this leveling of time requires recognizing the *nonequivalence* of the unique and nonsubstitutable events and moments that compose our lives, moments that cannot be exchanged precisely because of their entanglement in the plexities of the past and future. To recognize this singularity of every moment deepens our respect for the present, understood not as an immediate or ephemeral "now" but rather as the time of manifestation in which someone or something, always singular and incommensurable, presents itself. The singularity of what appears in the nonsubstitutable present demands from us an attention and respect, an esteem for the inestimable (Nancy 2015, 39–40). Wendell Berry (2015, 174), the leading proponent of agrarian ideals in the United States, expresses what may be a parallel sentiment when he writes that "we are always ready to set aside our present life, even our present happiness, to peruse the menu of future exterminations. If the future is threatened by the present, which it undoubtedly is, then the present is more threatened, and often is annihilated, by the future."

Nancy (2017, 119, 121) sometimes speaks about the moment of presence as an interruption or suspension of continuity, a deferral of time's self-presentation, in favor of a relationship that demands a gesture or a response. Yet we see that what presents itself to us, what demands our esteem and our response here and now, may itself be of the past or of the future. A recovery of the present outside the calculable general equivalence of time also places us in an entirely different relationship to pasts that have created our present possibilities and to futures that we do not plan or project.[10] Responsibility to the present therefore already involves us in the demands of justice for the past and the future. How might we work with such an image of time responsibly in the era of climate change?

For one profound example of how such temporal justice might be enacted, we can turn again to the work of Whyte. In contrast with settler narratives of "finality and last-ness," Whyte (2018, 229) describes Indigenous experiences of "spiraling time" that maintain a continuous dialogue with one's ancestors and descendants. Whyte's account situates these experiences of time within specific Indigenous cultural contexts, yet he also invites non-Indigenous allies to engage in "counterfactual dialogue" and critical reflection on how the world that we inhabit today—that is, the world of colonial violence as well as climate change—is the dream and the gift of our settler ancestors, designed and constructed to "fulfill their fantasies of the future" and to "provide privileges to their descendants" (229, 237). Acknowledging that we are living the fantasy of our ancestors simultaneously opens a dialogue with our descendants, who pose to us the question of what kind of ancestors we ourselves will be and what kind of world we will leave to those who follow. Counterfactual or fictional dialogue operates here not as an escape from our responsibilities to past and future, as we have seen in apocalyptic narratives, but rather as active affirmation of a spiraling of time that binds the manifestive present to the past that conditions it and the futures that it makes possible or forecloses. In contrast with the calculative management of the future on the basis of the substitutability of homogenous times, and the linear finality of a Judgment Day that liquidates both past and future, such time spiraling interrupts and thickens the event of the present, in its inestimable singularity, with an antiapocalyptic and anticolonial figure of temporal justice.

I close with one final example of how we might think the *now* in an antiapocalyptic mode, in this case through the work of art. *Library of Water* is a long-term installation by New York–based artist Roni Horn that occupies a former municipal library in the small town of Stykkishólmur on the southwestern coast of Iceland. The building is situated on a high rock promontory overlooking Breiðafjörður Bay, where its expansive windows reflect the meeting point of earth, sky, and water. Horn has described this space, which hosts community activities as well as private contemplation, as "a lighthouse in which the viewer becomes the light" (Artangel 2007). The central installation, titled *Water, Selected,* consists of twenty-four floor-to-ceiling glass columns, each of which contains water collected from the ice of one of Iceland's major glaciers. Unsurprisingly, these glaciers are retreating at the fastest recorded rates, and one of those represented in the installation—Okjökull—is now classified as "dead" by glaciologists due to climate disruption. The glass columns reflect and refract light from the windows, from each other, and from visitors as they move through their irregular arrangement. The floor on which they stand is embedded with words in Icelandic and English representing the weather. Because each glacier has a distinctive chemical and mineral content, no two columns are identical, and each displays a unique footprint of sediments. With proper names representing the glaciers from which they were drawn, these columns face the visitor like clustering and dispersed figures, solitary yet interacting through plays of light mediated by water and glass. As Jay Fiskio has observed, the glass of each column echoes the ice of the glaciers without any pretense of representation or substitution.[11] These are not the glaciers themselves, in their varying states of precarity, but precisely their absence, the library and archive of their present and future memory. They are the future ruins of the Icelandic landscape and simultaneously a counter-Narcissus that involves the viewer in their predicament. The work thereby conveys, on one hand, the excess of the glaciers beyond any possible preservation or representation; their elemental duration cannot be encompassed by any human world. And, on the other hand, it reveals their entanglement in a history and culture that ultimately threaten their disappearance.

Like the spiraling time that Whyte describes, *Library of Water* binds our singular present to a nonsubstitutable past and future, now at a grander temporal scale. The glacial water remembers annual snowfalls over the course of millennia, gradually compressed into solid ice by the pressure of patient accumulation. The disappearance of a glacier is literally the liquidation of this past. The proper names of the glaciers reflect their role in the history and culture of Iceland; current rates of glacial retreat have been compared with their historical extent by tracing the journeys recorded in the tenth- and eleventh-century Icelandic Sagas. By naming the installation a library, Horn gestures to the indefinite future for which these memories are preserved. Furthermore, the multilingual terms for weather embedded in the floor also remind us of our temporality: Serres observes that "the French language in its wisdom uses the same word for weather and time, *le temps*. At a profound level they are the same thing" (Serres and Latour 1995, 58).

My aim here has been to consider what image of time might break with the apocalyptic narratives that structure our approach to climate change. This requires first coming to terms with the folded, nonlinear, incommensurable, and rich multiplicity of time. As Serres (2003, 22; 2018, 11) points out, none of the European tradition's great thinkers of time—Bergson, Husserl, Heidegger—ever completed a transatlantic flight. But does not the mundane experience of jetlag teach us something about our corporeal entanglement in the plexities of time that would be difficult to learn in any other way? Furthermore, we must break with the catastrophic equivalence that homogenizes the singular moments of our lives, the present in which something inestimable, incalculable, presents itself to us and demands our response. How are we to live in the heartbreaking present? One example is provided in Whyte's account of spiraling time. This is an example to be approached with care, because Whyte is not proposing a general or universal experience of time but rather describing an experience and practice specific to Indigenous communities. Yet, in urging non-Indigenous allies to take responsibility for their ancestral fantasies, Whyte suggests an obligation of spiraling temporal justice that extends to settlers, as well, at intergenerational scales. At the scale of elemental time, *Library of Water* expresses our predicament in the geological *now* by inviting us to register the links of memory that bind the glacial past to the far future and to work with other futures on the basis of the inestimable present.

11

Future Fossils
THE ANTHROPOCENE AND THE EARTH

Against the background of geological scales of time, our contemporary efforts to manage the future often seem guided by a temporal myopia fixated on sustaining the world that we find familiar. Yet we know that worlds entirely foreign to our own have occupied the planet for the majority of its history. For most of the three hundred thousand years since *Homo sapiens* appeared, we shared the planet with our now-vanished human cousins, the Neanderthals and Denisovans, among others (Longrich 2019). And even as we struggle to hold ourselves accountable for a sixth mass extinction, we also know that past mass extinctions have been followed by a resurgence of life through adaptive radiation (Krug and Jablonski 2012). Or consider Rachel Carson's (1962) *Silent Spring,* so influential on the birth of the modern environmental movement in the United States, which takes its title from the loss of birdsong that would result from continued use of synthetic pesticides. From a broader evolutionary perspective, birdsong is a relatively late development, and living things have lacked the capacity for auditory communication for most of the history of life. For billions of years, the earth was silent, apart from the elemental sounds of wind, waves, and weather. How should such a perspective inform what we value, what we seek to preserve, and how we aim to preserve it? As we weigh the consequences of anthropogenic climate collapse and imagine ourselves as future fossils, we must also reckon with the prospect that the world as we know it offers no yardstick for evaluating or managing the future.

The transformation of our sense of time goes hand in hand with a reconsideration of our relationship with the geomaterial elements, both solid and fluid, that are the literal and metaphorical foundation of our earthly existence. Rocks and their sediments provide the ground on which we walk, the soil in which we plant, materials for our tools and constructions, and places to bury our wastes. The air we breathe and water we drink rejoin larger cycles in the skies and oceans. The world as we know and inhabit it, with its places, biota, and weather patterns, is framed spatially and temporally by myriad geological and atmospheric processes of local, regional, and global scale. Geomateriality serves, then, as a basic ontological substratum for the natural and built environments of our daily lives, our lifeworlds, insofar as it furnishes the constitutive elements for every physical reality, our bodies included, and therefore conditions all life and thought. Advances in our scientific understanding of these geomaterial elements and processes increasingly inform our everyday lives and culture, inspiring, in the words of Elizabeth Ellsworth and Jamie Kruse (2012, 7), "a growing recognition that the geologic, both as a material dynamic and as a cultural preoccupation, shapes the 'now' in ever more direct and urgent ways." One important symptom of this urgency is our belated recognition of the human influence over processes of planetary scale and geological duration, succinctly expressed in the proposal to name our current geological epoch the "Anthropocene," which sharpens our appreciation of the ethical dimensions of our inescapable entanglements in elemental relationships.

What many have found attractive in the language of the Anthropocene, as we noted in the introduction, is the claim that human beings have become the dominant influence on Earth systems at a planetary scale. This is presented as a shift from the scale of our impact prior to the Anthropocene, with ongoing debate over the timeline and markers of this shift. Many critics of the "Anthropocene" label have emphasized that it obscures the historical, political, and economic contexts that have made the disruption of planetary systems possible. The controversy over the idea of the Anthropocene has therefore focused largely on the perceived political and ideological assumptions that frame it, especially who counts among the "we" of *anthropos*, with implications for understanding the root causes of global environmental problems, to whom responsibility should be assigned for these problems and their causes, and the role of technological and management approaches in addressing them.

Proponents of the Anthropocene declare that it heralds a unique historical transformation of the relation between "humans" and "nature," a transformation in which "we" displace nature, for better or worse, as drivers of the planet's future. Atmospheric chemist Paul Crutzen, one of the scientists credited with coining the term *Anthropocene,* writing with journalist Christian Schwägerl (2011), famously claims that "we humans are becoming the dominant force for change on Earth. A long-held religious and philosophical idea—humans as masters of planet Earth—has turned into a stark reality. . . . It's no longer us against 'Nature.' Instead, it's we who decide what nature is and what it will be. . . . In this new era, nature is us." As Jeremy Baskin (2015, 19) notes, this rhetoric plays a double game, alleging to reinsert humans into nature while elevating them as its masters. More importantly, such claims to our postnatural status raise central philosophical questions about the autonomy of nature, the relation between human and geological temporality, and on what basis humanity can be considered as a collective in the absence of any "nature" in common.

Embracing humanity's new role *as* nature, as Baskin (2015, 14) points out, can be pursued either in a "Promethean" mode that celebrates our capacity to remake the planet in ways that suit ourselves or with "Aidosian" humility that cautions us to repair the damage we have caused. Regardless of these "differences in tone," both accounts of the Anthropocene "remain points on a common spectrum: all are 'post-nature' in some sense, and are technophilic and planetary-managerialist in orientation" (14). This postnatural rhetoric of Anthropocene discourse follows directly from the conclusions of Bill McKibben's (2003) *The End of Nature,* the 1989 book that first introduced climate change to a popular audience. By changing the atmosphere, according to McKibben, "we make every spot on earth man-made and artificial. We have deprived nature of its independence, and that is fatal to its meaning. Nature's independence *is* its meaning; without it there is nothing but us" (60–61). In a retrospective introduction to the revised 2003 edition, he adds, "We are no longer able to think of ourselves as a species tossed about by larger forces—now we *are* those larger forces. . . . That is what I meant by the 'end of nature'" (xiv). The parallel with Crutzen and Schwägerl's description is obvious, with the exception that, for McKibben, it is this loss of independent nature that is climate change's most lamentable consequence. Proponents of the Anthropocene have set aside any nostalgia for a nature independent of humanity and are rolling up their sleeves to build nature anew.

The double logic of the Anthropocene intersects in unexpected ways with what initially appears to be an entirely distinct postnatural discourse, epitomized by Steven Vogel's *Thinking Like a Mall: Environmental Philosophy after the End of Nature.* Vogel counters the claims of McKibben and like-minded environmental theorists by arguing that no autonomous and independent nature has existed since the appearance of human beings on the planet. Although Vogel never mentions the Anthropocene debate, he agrees with its proponents that "nature" is socially constructed in a literal sense. Their disagreement concerns only the moment when nature disappeared, which for Vogel would be the moment when human beings first appeared on the scene, rather than any of the proposed golden spikes signaling the human footprint in geological strata.

The differences between Anthropocene and social constructionist rejections of nature dissolve, then, if we adjust the temporal scale: "nature," in both cases, applies to times that precede and succeed the human. As a consequence, we can say that both accounts treat nature as equivalent to what historian Dipesh Chakrabarty calls the "planetary," which operates on geological registers of time beyond all human experience. As we noted in the introduction, Chakrabarty (2021) emphasizes the incommensurability of the all-too-human "global" perspective of the historian and the inhuman "planetary" perspective of Earth system science. Chakrabarty fully endorses the need for climate justice, but he also argues that critiques of capitalism and globalization are limited to the perspective of human history, what he terms the "global" perspective, and consequently miss the larger picture (4). This global perspective must be distinguished from the "planetary" perspective adopted by Earth system scientists, which takes the long view of deep geological and evolutionary time. In this retelling of the Anthropocene debate through a temporal lens, the geological and planetary end up assuming the guise of autonomy and independence formerly attributed to nature, its "profound otherness," reframing the classic human–nature divide in temporal terms (89). As Chakrabarty poses it, the central challenge becomes how we are to "mix together the immiscible chronologies of capital and species history" (42).

We may gain valuable insights into the postnatural discourses of Vogel's social constructionism and Chakrabarty's planetary perspective by reading these together, with particular attention to their treatments of materiality and time. Vogel's efforts to replace discourses of nature with those of the built environment are challenged by his own descriptions of the essentially resistant, wild, and unbuilt processes that condition all building. What resists the conversion of nature into a purely artifactual environment are nonconstructed elemental processes that function as a quasi-transcendental geomateriality. Chakrabarty hopes to account for the resistance and alterity of the elements through his category of the planetary, yet he reinscribes a problematic simplification of our embodied relationship with multiple and incommensurate temporal scales. In short, in his rejection of the phenomenological category of the earth, Chakrabarty also misses the significance of the memory of the world.

After Nature: The Built Environment

It has often been noted that the term *nature* is one of the most ambiguous and multivalent in everyday use, perhaps paralleled only by the equally notorious term *being*. More than a century ago, John Stuart Mill (1874) distinguished two principal yet conflicting senses of nature that continue to dominate our usage today. For Mill, nature in the first sense connotes "the sum of all phenomena, together with the causes which produce them," which makes nature in this sense "a collective name for all facts, actual and possible" (5, 6). On this properly scientific sense of the term, nature includes humans and all of their activities. In conflict with this first sense, Mill identifies "the common form of speech by which Nature is opposed to Art, and natural to artificial" (7). This second and everyday sense of nature, then, names "what takes place without the agency, or without the voluntary and intentional agency, of man" (8). It is nature in Mill's second sense that is at stake in McKibben's (2003, xiii) claim that we have "ended nature as an independent force." In parallel, for proponents of the Anthropocene, it is this second sense of nature that human domination of the planet has definitively brought to an end. Vogel is also clear that he has no quarrel with nature in Mill's first sense as the totality of the physical world, including us along with everything else, which he calls "Nature" with a capital *N*.

What he forcefully rejects is nature in Mill's second sense as distinguished from the artificial and purified of any trace of the human, which he calls "nature" in the lowercase. Not only is there no such nature today, in Vogel's view, but there has not been any for as long as humans have been on this planet. To clarify the relation between the different senses of the "end of nature," we now focus our attention on Vogel's account.

For Vogel (2015, 26), the starting point for environmental theory should be the recognition that nature has never existed and "that the concept of 'nature' is itself so confusing and ambiguous and even intellectually dangerous that any coherent environmental theory would be well advised to eschew it in any case." In fact, for Vogel, the concept of nature is not only confused or a distraction but positively pernicious for environmental thought: "the view of nature as something that needs to be protected because of its independence from human beings may itself be a central part of the environmental problem we face today" (31). The independence of nature is incompatible with the presence of human beings, on Vogel's view, because humans, like all other organisms, construct their environments and are constructed by them in turn. Our environment is something that we build together, the product of our collective labor; it is quite literally socially constructed by human practices. Rather than chasing after, trying to restore, or taking as our moral guide a pristine or, truth be told, noumenal nature-in-itself—a nature that we can neither think nor speak about without sullying its purity—we would be better off focusing on the one real world, which is the built environment we live in day in and day out.

Vogel is undoubtedly correct to criticize any concept of nature defined in mutual exclusion from the artifactual or that purports to provide a normative yardstick for environmental goals, the sort of nature whose loss McKibben grieved. In this respect, Vogel's position has affinities with Nancy's notion of the ecotechnical discussed in chapter 9. But let us consider two further consequences of Vogel's argument. First, if we take Vogel's conclusions literally and reject any distinction between the natural and the built, then it becomes true by definition that everything in the world is built. There is no remaining point of contrast with "built" in this sense, and so we might speak here of Built with a capital B—which then turns out to be coextensive with Nature with a capital N. However, while we do sometimes use the word *Nature* to refer to the totality of the physical world, we do not in everyday language use the word *Built* to refer to the totality of our environment, nor to everything within it. We do not say that the ocean is built because someone has sailed on it or sneezed in its direction, nor that a tree is built (or artificial) because it is planted in a yard, nor that an arm is artificial because a doctor has put a cast on it to heal a fracture, and so on.[1] Consequently, *built* has here become a term of art that retains little in common with our everyday uses. This leaves Vogel without philosophical resources to understand our everyday, prephilosophical distinction between what is built and what is not, between what we call in prephilosophical terms the artificial and the natural, or to think meaningfully about any relation or interdependence between these. This distinction has a foundation in our experience and is not merely a construction of environmental theorists.[2]

Second, Vogel's argument draws all of its force from the initial mutually exclusive way that "natural" and "artificial" are defined, which Vogel (2015, 10, 34, 68, 139) reinforces throughout the text by referring to nature or the natural as "a world other than us," a world "beyond the human," and similar formulations. He entertains no serious alternative to this mutually exclusive definition, which he claims to find in the theorists whom he critiques. This is certainly correct in some cases: McKibben (2003, 48, 53) writes of nature as "the world apart from man," the world "outside human history." But on the very first page of Vogel's book, three of the four quotations about nature from environmental philosophers (Routley, Rolston, Callicott, and Taylor) speak not of separation but rather of "relations": environmental ethics is about the "relations" between people and nature, not about nature's independent existence (Vogel 2015, 1). Furthermore, given the logical structure of Vogel's argument, one could legitimately come to an opposite conclusion. First, X and Y are defined as mutually exclusive. Second, one argues that there is no X that fully excludes Y, and so everything is Y. But one could just as easily have argued that there is no Y that fully excludes X, and so everything is X. There is nothing natural that is not artificial, so everything is artificial. But it follows just as well that, if there is nothing artificial that is not natural, everything is natural. The conclusion follows from the logical structure of the argument and not from any fact about the world, which is why it cannot allow for the possibility that what is natural and what is artificial are in fact *not mutually exclusive* but rather *interdependent*.

After the opening chapters, in which Vogel (2015) repeatedly emphasizes the rejection of nature as such, he gradually shifts toward a more nuanced position, one that recognizes this interdependence. The point seems less to be one of replacing the natural with the built and more one of "debunking the dualism" itself, so that existing independently and being produced are not mutually exclusive (40–41). In later chapters, Vogel begins to speak of an "entanglement" of the built and the natural and even to say of our one-and-only environment that "it's always built and it's always natural, both at once" (119, 175, 64).

The Unbuilt and Wildness

Surely Vogel is correct that our environment, our lifeworld, is built through our material and social practices—which include thinking, speaking, and writing. But it is also true that every act of building depends on and incorporates things, forces, and processes that are not built. To avoid any terminological confusion over definitions of "nature," let us simply refer to this as the "unbuilt," an intentionally negative concept intended to pick out what we neither construct, nor control, nor necessarily understand, but on which our building constantly relies, such as pollination, fermentation, metabolism, sedimentation, erosion, sunshine, rain, gravity, air pressure, and friction. The environment is built, surely, but only as entangled with the unbuilt, with all of what we do not build but on which our building inevitably depends.[3]

There are two points to clarify with this distinction between built and unbuilt. First, our acts of building are often (though not always) about converting unbuilt processes into built ones. Rather than waiting for strawberries to turn up, we plant them. Rather than waiting for rain to fall on them, we irrigate. Rather than waiting for the air to get colder, we air-condition. Rather than waiting for bees to show up and pollinate our fruit trees, we transport them from orchard to orchard or invent pollination drones to take their place. These are cases where a built process replaces an unbuilt process to make it more manageable and reliable (and often, of course, more profitable). So, the intersections between built and unbuilt aspects of any environment can shift depending on the context and our aims. There is no need to air-condition where the ambient temperature is already comfortable. But if we want to walk on the moon, then we need to bring our own oxygen and air pressure with us, rather than relying on their unbuilt availability, as we typically do.

The second point to clarify is that this built–unbuilt distinction carries no normative implications. There is no principled reason to prefer nonirrigated berries to irrigated ones or to prefer open fires to woodstoves with catalytic converters. Whether to rely on an unbuilt process or build our own replacement seems like a contextual decision that might weigh likely risks, impacts, benefits and costs, and so on. It might also weigh our own preferences, in some contexts, for what is relatively less artificial, on one hand, or for what is more predictable and manageable, on the other. But the distinction is valuable because this decision—between whether to adapt ourselves to something unbuilt or to build our own replacement for it—is at the heart of many environmental challenges. Presumably this is because replacing what is unbuilt with something built can introduce new kinds of risks, like the risk of destabilizing an unbuilt process without being able to effectively replace it with one that we can genuinely manage. It can also multiply human and environmental costs while externalizing these costs in ways that are less apparent and less accountable (e.g., climate engineering, genetic modification, or nanobots that eat oil spills). Vogel is consistently dismissive of environmentalists who raise alarms about what our technology might do, because he wants to insist that the world is, in a sense, technological through and through. Here we arrive, then, at a justification for managing nature indistinguishable from those championed under the moniker of the Anthropocene. Perhaps the planet is a technological artifact, but because our technology is always interdependent with what is not our technology, what is not built, then different kinds of interventions can carry different kinds of risks. Our concerns over redrawing the line between what we have built and what we have not are legitimate and not simply nostalgia for some mythical "other world" of nature.

Vogel (2015) goes at least halfway toward what I have proposed in his account of the "nature of artifacts" as the reverse side of the artifactuality of nature. Our artifacts, from malls to restoration projects, are never reducible to what we intend; they also have an autonomy—Vogel will even say a "nature"—of their own (96–97). Consequently, there is always what Vogel calls "the gap" between what we intend and what we actually build, always an element of unpredictability and uncontrollability (113–15). Vogel's insight here is a compelling reply to those like Eric Katz (2000), who claim that every human intention converts its products, seamlessly and without remainder, into tools that serve human purposes. This gap, Vogel says, is a consequence of "wildness," and his examples are paradigmatic of what I have referred to as the unbuilt: metabolism, gravity, decay, oxidation, and so on (113–15). Furthermore, he is even willing to equate such wildness with nature in some carefully delimited sense and to recognize that this is what some people mean by "nature" (104–5). He writes that "these processes operate outside us and beyond us; we do not fully understand their workings, and we cannot predict their outcome with any precision" (112). Even though what Vogel calls "wildness" here is very close to what I have called the "unbuilt," he treats this wildness as more or less a given, not as something that is subject, in many cases, to our technological management and control, such as the cases that I mentioned earlier that involve a technological shifting of the relation between built and unbuilt. Obviously, all such efforts reintroduce their own gap between intentions and outcomes, and they always rely, at one level or another, on further wild or unbuilt processes. But this negotiation between built and unbuilt, between artifacts and their wildness, is precisely where our technological interventions pose the greatest risk and where we need a healthy respect for what exceeds our management. Maybe we cannot disturb gravity very easily, but we can certainly destabilize pollination, the weather, microbial and insect life, and many other unbuilts that are essential for human flourishing (Vogel 2015, 111).

Although Vogel (2015) never admits that wildness in his sense deserves serious consideration by environmental thinkers, others have in fact proposed that wildness, defined in comparable ways, is an environmental good that deserves our respect and preservation (see, e.g., Hettinger and Throop 1999; Thompson 2009). Furthermore, wildness is here equivalent to our everyday, pretheoretical understanding of nature in contrast with the artificial. On this point, it is helpful to return to Mill's original differentiation between the two senses of nature that Vogel borrows in framing his argument, that is, between the capitalized and the lowercase senses. When Vogel introduces the second, lowercase sense of nature as what contrasts with artifice, he immediately takes these terms in a mutually exclusive sense. He writes that nature in Mill's second sense is "exactly what McKibben suggests—the nonhuman world, the world from which human action and its products have been excluded" (12). He continues, on the following page, with the following: "As Mill pointed out, in the first sense of the word, where nature means everything in the physical world, everything we do and make is natural; in the second, where nature is the nonhuman, nothing is" (13). Here Vogel's insistence on a sharp metaphysical dualism between the natural and the artificial leads him to read this distinction back into Mill. But Mill's own descriptions point in a different direction. Yes, Nature in the first (capitalized) sense includes us and everything that we do. But Mill says nothing to hypostatize nature in the second sense into a "nonhuman world," a world absolutely independent from us. This second sense of nature is simply what takes place without voluntary and intentional human agency. And Mill's own examples of how we are included within Nature in the first sense already amply demonstrate that our agency is always entangled with and materially inseparable from nature in the second sense. That is, his examples beautifully illustrate what I have called the essential unbuilt element within the built, or what Vogel has called the wildness within every artifact. Here are Mill's (1874, 7–8) own words:

> Art has no independent powers of its own: Art is but the employment of the powers of Nature for an end. Phenomena produced by human agency, no less than those which as far as we are concerned are spontaneous, depend on the properties of the elementary forces, or of the elementary substances and their compounds. The united powers of the whole human race could not create a new property of matter in general, or of any one of its species. We can only take advantage for our purposes of the properties which we find. A ship floats by the same laws of specific gravity and equilibrium as a tree uprooted by the wind and blown into the water. The corn which men raise for food

grows and produces its grain by the same laws of vegetation by
which the wild rose and the mountain strawberry bring forth
their flowers and fruit. A house stands and holds together by
the natural properties, the weight and cohesion of the materials
which compose it: a steam engine works by the natural expansive force of steam. . . . In these and all other artificial operations
the office of man is, as has often been remarked, a very limited
one: it consists in moving things into certain places.

My point, then, is simple: Mill's effort to capture the essence of the
everyday distinction between the natural and the artificial presents
us with no two worlds, no mutually exclusive terms, but rather precisely the dynamic of built and unbuilt forces, of the artifactual and
the wild, that is at the heart of and the very condition for the one
world in which we live, our environment.

Wild Elements

This brief foray into the phenomenology of wildness suggests certain parallels with Merleau-Ponty, as well as a path for further developing his thinking. If we wish to avoid substantivizing nature
into an entity distinct from us, or noumenalizing it as a hidden
world behind the sensible world, then we must consider how to respect its "nonconstructed" and "noninstituted" character while allowing for its entanglement with the human, with history, custom,
discourse, and technique (N 264–65/204, 20/4). The entanglement
that we have described here is not that sedimentation of culture
by which the natural sciences forget their own historical formation and believe themselves capable of transparently presenting
nature in itself (Merleau-Ponty 1996a, 43, 76; 2022, 12, 31–32). Nor
is it that mixture of naturalism and artificialism, a mélange of the
human and inhuman, that Merleau-Ponty finds in cybernetics and
neo-Darwinism (N 120/86; Merleau-Ponty 1996a, 42; 2022, 11). The
double game of Anthropocene logic with which we began this chapter may well be the apotheosis of this mélange of naturalism and
artificialism. The entanglement that we are describing is instead
precisely an effort to bring forward "the primordial, nonlexical
meaning always intended by people who speak of 'nature,'" which
is characterized by a "productivity which is not ours, although we

can use it—that is, an originary productivity that continues beneath humanity's artificial creations" (N 19/3, 169/125). Vogel makes a risky choice when he adopts the term *wild* to refer to the unmanaged and unmanageable forces and processes on which any technique or artifice relies, insofar as this term has so often been offered as synonymous with the very independence of nature that he denies—and also then very quickly identified with "wilderness" as a place that excludes human beings.[4] Merleau-Ponty's choice to speak of "wild" being as what precedes and exceeds all culture and reflection seems equally risky from the perspective of phenomenology understood as "correlationism." Wildness in both cases names the nature within us and outside of us that, without being the object of our choice or even of our experience, "precedes us, surrounds us, carries us" (Merleau-Ponty 2008, 51)—and can also resist us.

This account of wildness converges with what we have in earlier chapters, on the basis of certain precedents in the phenomenological tradition, termed *the elements*: that from which the world emerges, by which it is sustained, and into which it ultimately returns.[5] The elements in this sense typically do not register thematically as things or events within the world, even though they condition and structure the world as forces, processes, and materials. Essentially unbuilt, elements make the building of a world possible, just as the silences of language are the wellspring of its meaning. Unlike our artificial creations, they are not exhausted or used up simply by their own endurance (N 169/125). It is this indestructible quality of the elements that historian Carolyn Steedman (2002, 164) captures in her description of dust as neither rubbish nor surplus: "Dust is the opposite thing to Waste, or at least, the opposite principle to Waste. It is about circularity, the impossibility of things disappearing, or going away, or being gone. Nothing *can be* destroyed."[6] In this asubjective circulation, we find what is truly independent of human management and control, an indestructible that fits Nancy's description, quoted earlier, of "a *there is* that would be neither *for* us nor *because* of us. Either that or the 'sensible' world outside the 'sense' given to it by a sentient subject . . . something that neither has its origin nor its end in man" (I 245/85). Our world depends on the elements, but the elements depend neither on our world nor on us; they precede us and outlast us immemorially.

Collapsing Chronologies of the Planetary

In claiming that nature is fictional, Vogel frames his argument entirely within the bookends of human existence. This may be appropriate for targeting claims that nature has somehow been lost or compromised by particular human activities, such as the proposed golden spikes for tracking the onset of the Anthropocene due to agriculture, colonialism, fossil fuel use, nuclear detonations, and so on. Yet, as we noted in the introduction, the Anthropocene is also about imagining the fossils that we are leaving to stratigraphers of the distant future. Vogel never mentions the Anthropocene nor considers the perspective of deep geological time within which human civilization, and even human existence as a distinct form of life, is insignificantly transitory. Even if we granted his argument about the disappearance of nature during the brief human sojourn on the planet, this absence would be a mere eye blink interrupting nature's constant presence for the eons preceding and, presumably, following "us."

On some accounts, the disruptive power of the Anthropocene lay precisely in forcing an intersection between these incongruent temporal scales, what Chakrabarty (2021, 34) has termed the "collapsing of human and geological chronologies." In becoming a geological agent, the human species has gone beyond simply eliminating nature's independence or even taking nature's place during our brief eyeblink on the planet. We have managed instead to transform nature permanently by rewriting the geological archive and thereby have become "immortal, as a trace preserved forever in the rock" (Szerszynski 2012, 180). In short, "the wall between human and natural history has been breached" (Chakrabarty 2021, 45). As the sociologist Bronislaw Szerszynski (2017, 117) puts the point, "this apparent fusion of temporal registers can be seen as an 'Anthropocene moment' as significant as any officially designated start of the Anthropocene geological epoch." For Szerszynski, the clash between human and inhuman registers of time calls for mediation parallel to that provided in other cultural contexts by rituals or monuments. Chakrabarty (2021, 89, 69–70), on the other hand, has identified the "planet" as studied by Earth system science—in distinction from world, earth, and globe, as categories that in one way or another refer to humanity and human history—as the "unhuman backdrop" and "profound otherness" that outstrip all possibility of human experience or phenomenological description. In other words, the planet, as the bearer of geological time, comes to occupy the site of independence formerly granted to nature, reproducing the classic human–nature divide in a temporal register. The problem as Chakrabarty poses it is to "encounter together" planetary and global forms of thinking that are disparate yet intertwined and that refer to "vastly different and incommensurable scales of time" (86). Doing so may allow us to recuperate an understanding of the "human species" that can bring us again into relation with "the history of life on this planet" (40).

Chakrabarty (2021) expects little help from phenomenology with this task of fusing global and planetary thinking or bridging their incommensurable scales of time. He repeatedly dismisses the possibility of anything like a phenomenological approach to geological history or the planetary perspective, because he holds that these are essentially inaccessible to direct human experience (47, 79, 86–87, 191). As it is approached through Earth system science, our planet is "an object of astronomical and geological studies" (70) and one that is necessarily considered as just one planet alongside others (75, 79). Consequently, it is never really "our" planet but rather "a" planet seen from the outside (78), a planet that confronts us with "vast processes of unhuman dimensions" and with "radical otherness" (86–87). In his efforts to articulate what is distinctive about the Anthropocene challenge, Chakrabarty returns repeatedly to the figure of the earth in Husserl and Heidegger, each time concluding that the geological and planetary have displaced the phenomenological account of earth, insofar as the latter continues to bear an essential reference to the human (68–71, 74, 80, 179–80, 183, 195, 205). The strife between earth and world that interests Heidegger may be relevant from the perspective of human dwelling but can say nothing about the astronomical and geological dimensions of the planet—nor about the "history of life" that the planet encompasses (70). And, following Derrida's lead, Chakrabarty concludes that the unity of Husserl's originary earth, the earth that does not move, arises "out of the unity of all humanity" (180). This relation to humanity places "earth," for Chakrabarty, on the side of the worldly and global and over against the planetary. In sum, because the phenomenological earth never severs its natal bond with humanity, it remains on the hither side of the worldly and global rather than broaching the alterity of the planetary.

As I noted in the introduction, Chakrabarty's strategy here parallels the "speculative realist" critique of phenomenology proposed by Quentin Meillassoux, whom Chakrabarty (2021, 87) cites approvingly in this context. We have seen that Meillassoux, in *After Finitude*, criticizes the "correlationism" of phenomenology that, he claims, encloses it within a subjective perspective. He argues that this leaves phenomenology incapable of accounting for (or even accepting the existence of) a time before or after human existence on the planet, and it prevents phenomenology from ever escaping the confines of its subjective prison to encounter the "great outside" of what does not submit to correlation with subjectivity. Chakrabarty apparently accepts this logic while adapting it to his own concepts, so that the "correlation" becomes the global world essentially bound up with human history and the planet becomes the great outside that vastly exceeds our myopic temporal and cognitive perspectives. I discussed my criticisms of Meillassoux's position in chapter 2, and I also reject their creative appropriation by Chakrabarty under the banner of the global and the planetary. Merleau-Ponty sets us on another path by emphasizing that the earth is neither synonymous with world nor the correlate of humanity; earth is, rather, that "nature" that is "given as preceding us and underlying us" (IP 170/127)—the ultimate horizon of what we have called earlier the "unbuilt" or the elements.

Times of Earth and Earthlings

To start, let us recognize that the framing of the issue as a collapse or breaching of human and natural history—understood as two distinct registers, histories, calendars, or chronologies—is a vast oversimplification, no doubt due to Chakrabarty's starting point of identifying the limits of what is counted as "history" by academic historians. Of course, we are neither "inside" human history nor "outside" natural history, so the "breaching" or "collapsing" here strictly concerns only our scholarly constructions of temporal narratives but not our lived experience of time nor the temporalities of nature. Furthermore, the juxtaposition of human history over and against "inhuman" time suggests a simple binarism of chronologies, while in fact we are always enmeshed within innumerable temporal scales, flows, eddies, and percolations—for example, my experience of time at this moment, or this week, or this year; the time of my life and of the lives of those with whom my life overlaps; the known history of my family tree; human written history and unwritten prehistory; the span of organic evolution all the way back to life's earliest common ancestor; geological time encompassing the entire history of the planet; and cosmic time since the big bang. Chakrabarty (2021, 86) does acknowledge that human horizons of time are not reducible to a single, simple calendar, insofar as they encompass "the multiple horizons of existential, intergenerational, and historical time." But neither is natural history reducible to one calendar, and the skein of temporal happenings will not respect the bifurcation of chronologies that Chakrabarty imposes.

My point is that we are moments of passage and becoming for innumerable overlapping and intersecting temporal happenings, and these happenings are neither punctual nor discrete but mutually implicated. In *The Concept of Nature,* Whitehead (2004, 73) notes that "the passage of nature which is only another name for the creative force of existence has no narrow ledge of definite instantaneous present within which to operate. Its operative presence which is now urging nature forward must be sought for throughout the whole, in the remotest past as well as in the narrowest breadth of any present duration. Perhaps also in the unrealized future." It is in Merleau-Ponty's commentary on this text that he proposes to understand Nature as "the Memory of the World" (N 163/120), an idea to which we have returned repeatedly. On this view, our experience of time is corporeal as well as cognitive, and at both levels it is a consequence of the fact that we are ourselves pulses within the passage of nature. Consequently, the "memory of the world"—the entire span of nature's passage—is constitutive of our experience of time. We do not need to build a bridge from lived time to geological time, and any barriers between them have always been breached.

If deep time is not split off from lived and historical time, one implication is that deep time is not a mathematical extrapolation of "clock time" but is essentially historical. Here I am indebted to the account of historical time proposed by Jerome Miller (2020) in the context of what he terms "robust evolution." Clock time, or time as a variable in scientific equations, consists of invariant, standard units that are repeatable. As standard units, any one moment can be substituted for any other, as we have described with Nancy's notion of general equivalence. In historical time, by contrast, past, present, and future are irreducibly heterogenous, and this is why each moment is unique and datable (158). It follows that the future is not simply the next repetition of an invariant temporal atom; it is not reducible to another present. In Miller's words, the future is essentially "*un*like what precedes it. It is *un*precedented" (158). For it to be the future, it must be essentially heterogenous from the present, "always already breaking the present open to possibilities that cannot be assimilated into it" (161). Miller refers to this as the "traumatological" character of historical time, which is its inherent capacity "to *un*do, to rupture" (161). Clock time, on the other hand, is precisely a strategy for managing this world-shattering potential of the future, which it attempts by assimilating this future as merely one more present in a homogenous series of presents. In chapter 8, I discussed how sustainability projects that extrapolate from deep past trends to predict and manage far-future scenarios—such as the planning around the world's first long-term nuclear waste repository in Finland—engage in a comparable effort to manage the risk of the future as such.

What is at risk with every future is the disruption or undoing of what the present carries within itself from the past. That is, the future essentially risks a loss of the world's memory as that memory constitutes every unique and singular present. Extinction, for example, is a standing risk presented by the disruptive future for any form of life. And with that risk comes the possibility of the loss of memory that every form of life embodies. This notion of memory returns us to the question that Chakrabarty has posed concerning our relation to the history of life. Life has often been understood as a kind of organic memory. We noted earlier Elizabeth Grosz's (2008, 6) insight that "life, even the simplest organic cell, carries its past with its present as no material object does." Today the most straightforward way of understanding this notion of organic memory is undoubtedly through the genetics of evolutionary descent. As we noted in chapter 7, this is what evolutionary biologist George Williams (1992, 76) has in mind when he writes that "the generation of diversity by cladogenesis furnishes every population with a unique set of historical legacies. In this sense, an organism is a living record of its own history." I have argued that we can enrich this understanding of organic memory immensely by approaching life in diacritical terms, modeled on language as a system of differences without positive terms. This insight requires us to take relations as more basic than their relata, so that difference precedes and constitutes identity. Biodiacritics offers a more compelling account of what we find significant in the diversity of life than does the received scientific concept of biodiversity.

We complete this account of biodiacritics by understanding each form of life as a memory in a richer sense than mere genetic inheritance. We might take our start from Richard Dawkins's (1993) famous illustration of evolutionary continuity between humans and chimpanzees. Dawkins suggests we imagine holding the hand of our mother, while she holds the hand of her mother and she holds the hand of her mother, in a long, continuous line. Imagine that we allow about a yard for each individual and trace the path of this line into the evolutionary past about three hundred miles. At that point, our ancestor would reach out her other hand to grasp the hand of her other child. And that child would hold the hand of her child, who holds the hand of her child, in a new line that retraces each generation back toward the present. If these two lines form facing each other, then when the second line completes itself in the present day, we will find ourselves linked, through a continuous connection of hands, to our nearest evolutionary relation, the modern chimpanzee, with whom we stand face-to-face. Now, this thought-experiment does an impressive job of helping us picture our evolutionary kinship with our nearest nonhuman relatives, and it can be extended further into the past to illustrate our common ancestry with invertebrates or even plants.[7] But this image is still tied to kinship by descent and filiation. To arrive at a truly biodiacritical understanding, we would need to recognize that each individual along this chain, along every evolutionary line of descent, is what it is only through the myriad relationships that shape its mode of life, that is, with those with which it cooperates or competes, with what it eats and what eats it, with the parasites, microbes, and viruses that colonize it, the trees that provide it shelter, the mycorrhizae that allow those trees to grow, the landscape that offers those trees an opportunity to seed, the climate in which all of these forms of life can flourish, and even with the landforms and hydrology, the soil and the climate, and all of the geological conditions that these relationships require. If we understand biodiacritics in terms of the full network of relationships that make any continuity of life possible, then we must say that every living organism is the diacritical memory of all of these relationships, in pleats and folds that gather the full duration of evolutionary time.

Following this out, the unity of life can be understood as an expressive diacritical network comparable to a language. And every node of organic difference—from genes to organisms to species—exists precisely as the immanently articulated difference from all others, including the patterns and investments through which it has taken form over the course of evolutionary time. To be a living creature, then, is necessarily to be the embodied memory of an entire evolutionary history of expressive divergences. As Donna Haraway (2015, 162) writes, "all critters share a common 'flesh,' laterally, semiotically, and genealogically." When Merleau-Ponty generalizes this diacritical ontology to all beings understood as "flesh," this entails a diacritical account of time as ontological memory, that is, as the concentration of the entire evolutionary history of life into each moment of every organism's life. And this entire condensed history is at stake in every future, because not only death but even extinction is always a possible undoing of this diacritical memory. The future as such is unprecedented because it can wipe away the world's memory, just as it can instead continue to sustain it, as we talk about a musical note that is sustained, or as it can introduce a creative ferment or a swerve that we never saw coming.

Time is therefore historical in a sense that extends to the entire age of the universe and that brings the world-as-memory to bear on each moment as it passes. The uniqueness and singularity of the present are precisely a consequence of the way that the past bears down on it such that it could not be substituted for any other present. But this is also what makes each present vulnerable to the undoing that is its own heterogeneous future. This converges with Jean-Luc Nancy's call to respect the singularity of the present, as we saw in chapter 9, rather than submerging it into a homogenizing equivalence with other "nows."

The historical character of time cannot be represented by a line or counted by a clock, and this is why neither human history nor natural history can be represented by linear chronologies. In fact, as the diacritical account of memory suggests, we endure innumerable temporalities in mutual implication. In chapter 10, we related this to Michel Serres's suggestion that we abandon the linear perspective of time altogether in favor of something more topological—pleated or crumpled time, for example, which allows for the possibility that moments we think of as separated by a thickness of past or future can in fact be in close relation. In his words, time is "an extraordinarily complex mixture, as though it reflected stopping points, ruptures, deep wells, chimneys of thunderous acceleration, rendings, gaps—all sown at random" (Serres and Latour 1995, 57). This concerns less our conscious experience of time than our visceral immersion in the temporal flows that form and re-form us, flows—or interruptions—that condition any possible experience of time. We resonate with these multiple, pleated, and entangled flows of time—across the intersecting scales of the cosmic, geological, organic, cultural, familial, and personal. This means that the deep past—even the geological or cosmic past—reverberates through our bodies and that our explicit awareness of time is formed against the background of this corporeal participation in the time of stones and stars. We might say that, as pulsations within the grand memory of the world, we are also memories, carrying within ourselves the echoes of all the temporal processes that converge on our present moment and open it to the future. Extending this notion of memory, as we have seen, Serres (2003, 55; 2018, 32) proposes that we consider each and every thing to be a memory, an inert or asubjective memory that awaits translation into active remembrance.

In this light, the planetary perspective that Chakrabarty describes with such care is not so much false as it is forgetful, because it takes for granted the perceptual and temporal relationships that every scientist, and every one of us, maintains with the singular earth. In chapter 2, we partially quoted this passage from Merleau-Ponty: "Truth of perception: there is no objectivity without a point of view, in itself; i.e., an observer is necessary, with his 'levels,' his 'soil,' his 'homeland,' his perceptual 'norms,' in short, his 'earth' (which is not fixed in the sense of the pre-Copernicans, but not simply a moving object within a system of relative movements)" (IP 173–74/129). Here Merleau-Ponty is clearly referring to the short fragment "Foundational Investigations on the Phenomenology of

Nature," in which Husserl claims that earth—in the originary sense as earth-ground, as the ground against which all motion and rest become possible—cannot in itself be said to move. This primordial sense of earth has been displaced, of course, by our modern notion of the earth as one relative, moving body among others, that is, precisely as one planet among others. But this new sense is an accomplishment with a history, one that remains essentially conditioned by earth's originary spatiality and temporality. In short, the planetary would be meaningless without the earth as our unique earth-ground. In his late course on "The Possibility of Philosophy Today," Merleau-Ponty (1996a, 45; 2022, 13) writes:

> Show that access to other planets does not relativize the Earth and does not make a *Körper* out of the others, but on the contrary, that such access extends to other planets the function of a pre-objective *Boden*. The other planets become annexes of the Earth or the Earth expands, but one is always someplace.

As I have noted, Chakrabarty (2021) holds that Husserl's account of the earth as experiential ground is challenged by the Anthropocene. Because the unity of the earth, for Husserl, arises "out of the unity of all humanity," it falls short of the inhuman perspective of the planetary (180). Here Chakrabarty is following Derrida's (1962, 80; 1989a, 84) reading that the "unity of humanity" in question is "correlative to the unity of the world as the infinite horizon of experience, and not to the unity of this earth here." Otherwise put, Derrida finds that Husserl's fragment does not present a transcendental account of earth in its own right, as the one earth here, but instead takes the earth as the factical index of the World, which is itself to be understood as a correlate of humanity. Rather than dismissing the contribution of a phenomenological account of earth, then, we might instead conclude that Husserl (along with Heidegger) fails to disentangle earth from world or to offer a genuine account of earth in transcendental terms (see Johnson 2015; Džanić 2020).

But it is also possible to approach Husserl's text from another angle, such as that taken by Merleau-Ponty (1998, 2002) in his late course on "Husserl at the Limits of Phenomenology." Merleau-Ponty finds at least the beginnings of another path here, according to which "the foundation of the unity of history is the uniqueness of the Earth" (83; 68). Rather than the unity of earth being a by-product of the unity of world horizons for transcendental intersubjectivity, the earth shares a mutually implicatory relation with our flesh as the very ground of space and time. Merleau-Ponty admits that Husserl does not follow through on this insight, and perhaps this is why, in his nature lectures, Merleau-Ponty turns from Husserl's earth to Whitehead's account of our temporal implication in the passage of nature. Whitehead (1938, 225, 227) makes explicit our relation of "mutual immanence" with nature and even expresses this relation as a chiasmus: "we are in the world and the world is in us." This describes, not an anthropomorphizing correlation, but instead the lived basis for our engagement with incommensurable and asubjective temporalities. In this case, the unity of humanity and of all earthly life would rest on the uniqueness of the earth, not as a scientific representation, but as the memory that is constitutive of our being from within. The emergent universal history of life that Chakrabarty seeks would then be found in our mutual implication in the unique history of the earth, because that is what makes us all earthlings.

My aim here has been to sketch the beginnings of a phenomenology of deep time, that is, to offer an account of how the multiple, crumpled scales of time play across us as material and living beings. This is certainly a messier picture of our relation to time than Chakrabarty's diptych of global and planetary calendars that are breached by the Anthropocene. I do not see how this distinction between global and planetary enriches our understanding of our relation to deep time, and consequently, I do not see how it can serve to defend the autonomy of Earth system science or deflect those critics who see in it a new Promethianism. Furthermore, I believe the ahistorical interpretation of geological time, as this is approached from the planetary mind-set, is already an effort to assimilate the future as just one more present. Modeled on this homogenous and ahistorical time, sustainability becomes the effort to preserve the world of the present as "we" know it, and as "we" would like it to be, precisely by preventing the arrival of the future as such. From one perspective, the future within historical time is essentially apocalyptical, as the very condition of history. But the management of time and of the planet to prevent the future—especially a future that undoes our present and our past—is an apocalypse *for* history rather than an apocalypse *within* history. In this sense, I believe that the eco-eschatological imaginary of our own future fossils is a recoil from, and a repression of, the genuine future and its power to undo all prediction and management. Is human extinction a genuine possibility? Yes, absolutely, and at every moment. Will the management of the planet by Earth system scientists do anything to change that? No, not at all. Can it make our present much worse? Yes, precisely by framing our relationship with time in a way that liquidates our liability to the past, obscures the singularity of the present, and refuses the unprecedented future. In short, by denying any historical character of planetary time, Chakrabarty creates the very bifurcation that he would like, then, to label the Anthropocene.

Phenomenology suggests a more fruitful path. Husserl describes the world as the horizon of horizons, the ultimate horizon that embraces all possible horizons. But we must then consider the earth as the temporal horizon of horizons, as the ontological memory (and, in equal measures, the ontological forgetting) that embodies all possible geological pasts and futures. Nothing guarantees that we have left our mark as an immortal trace in rock, whether we find in that dream a source of secret pride or a cause for shame. What we can know is that the entire history of the earth expresses itself through every unique moment in time's constellation, that what we have in common is this shared memory, and that every future as future risks its ruin. None of this relieves our responsibilities to nature or to each other; on the contrary, it is only as the confluence of innumerable temporal flows and eddies, as the elemental duration of our bones and the evolutionary memory of our organs, that we can first appreciate our own singular and unique responsibility to the earth and to our fellow earthlings.

Notes

Introduction

1. The proposal to make the Anthropocene a formal unit of geological epoch divisions in the International Geological Time Scale, under consideration by the International Commission on Stratigraphy, has received widespread attention and debate among scholars across disciplines. The term was first proposed by Paul Crutzen and Eugene Stoermer (2000).

2. For an overview of proposed alternatives, see Baskin (2015, 15) and Chakrabarty (2021, esp. chap. 7).

3. For helpful discussion concerning golden spikes, see Szerszynski (2012, 2017).

4. Concerning the interpretation of our traces from the perspective of the distant future, see also Szerszynski (2012) and Zalasiewicz (2017).

5. I return to this issue in chapter 7.

6. Although Chakrabarty does not discuss Meillassoux in detail, he does cite Meillassoux's work approvingly (Chakrabarty 2021, 87).

7. See, e.g., Meillassoux's use of the term *world* in AF (158–60/114–16). We will return to the problem of "world," especially in chapter 9.

8. For an insightful response to speculative realism's criticisms of phenomenology, including the charge of correlationism, see Zahavi (2016).

1. Chronopoiesis

1. On the significance of this phrase for Merleau-Ponty's later ontology, see Carbone (2004).

2. See VI (247/194), N (163/120), and Merleau-Ponty (1996a, 114–15; 2022, 56–57). Merleau-Ponty capitalizes this phrase only in the working note to *The Visible and the Invisible*.

3. Merleau-Ponty cites this phrase at N (154/114): "les bords de la nature sont toujours en guenilles."

4. I make no attempt here to evaluate Merleau-Ponty's appropriation of Whitehead. On Whitehead's philosophy of time, see Mays (1977, chap. 7). On the relation between Merleau-Ponty and Whitehead, see Franck (2005) and Hamrick and Van der Veken (2011).

2. The Elemental Past

1. See, e.g., Étienne Bimbenet's (2011, 136–46) efforts to reconcile phenomenology with the realist perspective.

2. David Wood (2003) calls for such a détente, and the "plexity" of time is key to his account.

3. For an exposition and defense of Husserl's position, see Himanka (2005).

282   Notes to Chapter 2

4. I use involvement and inherence here in the senses developed by James (2009).

5. In Merleau-Ponty's later ontology, "chiasm" names a logic of bidirectional mediation modeled on the reversibility of touch (see Toadvine 2011). We return to this concept in the chapters that follow. Merleau-Ponty (2010) borrows the concept of "institution" from Husserl and develops it as an account of the inauguration of a tradition that opens a field of future trajectories.

6. We will return to this theme of animality as immemorial past in part II.

7. Al-Saji (2008) develops this interpretation of sensibility as generative past.

8. We will take up this theme of apocalyptic imagination in part III.

9. See McNamara (2011), especially the introduction and first two chapters. All of the examples cited in this paragraph are discussed by McNamara.

3. Recursive Reflection and the Music of Nature

1. The example of melody is discussed extensively in Koffka (1935). See also Köhler (1947, 188–89, 198, 254, 261).

2. Merleau-Ponty (2007, 99–100) discusses Köhler's use of the phrase "melodic line" to describe chimpanzee behavior. For Merleau-Ponty's own appropriations of the metaphor of melody to characterize behavior, see SB (111/102, 117/107, 128/118, 131/120, 133/122, 140/130, 168/155, 176/163, 179/166).

3. As attested by the retranslation of Uexküll's (2010) classic essays, Buchanan (2008), and the emergence of biosemiotics as an interdisciplinary field of research.

4. Merleau-Ponty attributes this quote to an unreferenced citation from Buytendijk. For Merleau-Ponty's later reading of Uexküll in his own right, see N (220–34/167–78).

5. On the temporal implication of melody, see SB (96/87, 117/107) and N (228/174). In the latter text, the temporal implication of melody is related to the temporal implication of embryonic development.

6. Such as the remark, at the end of chapter 3 of *The Structure of Behavior*, that "what we call nature is already consciousness of nature, what we call life is already consciousness of life and what we call mental is still an object vis-à-vis consciousness" (SB 199/184). Of course, the final chapter emphasizes that the "consciousness" in question is perceptual rather than intellectual consciousness, the relation between which occupies the book's conclusion and poses the "problem of perception" to be taken up in its sequel (SB 227–28/210–11, 240–41/224). For further discussion on this point, see Toadvine (2009, chap. 1).

7. See, e.g., SB (224–25/208): "for us consciousness experiences its inherence in an organism at each moment; for it is not a question of an inherence in material apparatuses, which as a matter of fact can be only *objects* for consciousness, but of a presence to consciousness of its proper history and of the dialectical stages which it has traversed." This is a point to which we will return in later chapters.

8. For the "problem of perception," see SB (190–91/176, 227/210, 236/219,

240–41/224). Concerning the "outside spectator," see SB (175/162, 199/184). See also Merleau-Ponty (2000, 17) and Toadvine (2009, 47–48).

9. I develop this idea more fully in Toadvine (2017a).

10. It is well known that the parallel between music and myth is central to Lévi-Strauss's later work. The structural parallels between myth and music that are proposed in the "Overture" of the first volume of *Mythologiques, The Raw and the Cooked* from 1964 (1983), are taken up again and defended in the "Finale" of the final volume, *The Naked Man*, in 1971. When Lévi-Strauss, in that same year, pens his few paragraphs about the ambivalent place of music in the final writings of Merleau-Ponty, the choice of music as his point of comparison is significant.

11. Merleau-Ponty cites the French translation by Gabrielle Peiffer and Emmanuel Levinas (Husserl 1996, 73–74). The complete passage reads, "Le début, c'est l'expérience pure et, pour ainsi dire, muette encore, qu'il s'agit d'amener à l'expression pure de son propre sens" (The beginning is the pure and, so to speak, still-mute experience that it is a question of leading to the pure expression of its own sense). The German original may be found in Husserl (1950, 77). The English translation (Husserl 1993, 38–39) renders this passage as follows: "Its beginning is the pure—and, so to speak, still dumb—psychological experience, which now must be made to utter its own sense with no adulteration."

12. I discuss the role of silence in Merleau-Ponty's thought in Toadvine (2008).

13. But note the brief and intriguing remarks concerning contemporary music in his 1959 lectures on the possibility of philosophy, which he promises to expand into a longer analysis (Merleau-Ponty 1996a, 2022).

14. Cf. VI (194/148): "the sonorous existence of my voice is for me as it were poorly exhibited; I have rather an echo of its articulated existence, it vibrates through my head rather than outside."

4. Beyond Biologism

1. Callicott cites here Gary Snyder's (1990) *The Practice of the Wild*, which could just as easily serve as an example of the narrative that we have in mind.

2. See Midgley (2003, 152). Her chapter "Are You an Animal?" (135–41) is also relevant to the role of Darwinism in proposing continuity with other animals.

3. See the "Diagram of Divergence of Taxa" in Darwin (1964, 514).

4. Probably the best-known scientific critic of the geneticist and sociobiological research paradigms is Richard Lewontin, who insists on the irreducible interplay of genes, organisms, and environments in producing biological diversity. For an accessible overview of his position, see Lewontin (2000). Especially noteworthy is Lewontin's description of the "environment" as centered around the organism and composed of those conditions that are relevant to it, which echoes Jakob von Uexküll's descriptions of the *Umwelt* (48–49). Philosophical critiques of the assumptions of sociobiology

284 *Notes to Chapter 4*

include Midgley (1995), especially the introduction to the revised edition (xiii–xxxiii), and Stengers (2009).

5. See, e.g., Mitchell (2009), especially the defense of emergence in chapter 2.

6. See the parallel discussion in FCM (277–83/188–92). See also Derrida's comments on this passage in OS (76–77/48).

7. In addition to Derrida's own remarks on this point (e.g., OS 118–19/74), see Bernasconi (2000).

8. Derrida discusses the nonorganic status of the hand in G (426ff./171ff.). Concerning the senses in which the animal both has and does not have world, see OS (75ff./47ff.). We will return to Heidegger's claims concerning the world-poverty of "the" animal, and to critical responses from Derrida and Nancy, in later chapters.

9. See also Derrida's summary of this political reaction against biologism in A (197/144), where he places Levinas and Lacan in the company of Heidegger on this point.

10. Derrida's use of the masculine here is intentional. See his remarks concerning carnophallogocentrism in A (144/104) and Derrida (1992, 294; 1995, 280).

11. Derrida calls attention to the term *prewired* and its implications in A (168/122–23, 184/134, 168–69n/173n9).

12. Lawlor (2009b) develops this critique of naturalism, and in particular of the efforts to naturalize phenomenology.

13. I take it that this is the point Derrida wishes to convey in insisting, first, that the abyss is between "those who call themselves men and what so-called men, those who name themselves men, call the animal" (A 52/30) and, second, on the historical character of this abyssal rupture. We will return to Agamben's diagnosis of the "anthropological machine" in later chapters.

14. Lawlor occasionally equates the problem of biological continuism with that of "raising" animals "to the level of humans" or of "lowering" humans "to the level of animals" (e.g., Lawlor 2007, 25). But this reinstates a hierarchy based on the association of animals with the irrational and instinctual. What must be recognized—and Lawlor's analyses point in this direction—is that the new logic of the limit undoes this association (the irrational and instinctual belong no more obviously on the "side" of animals than on that of humans) and any hierarchization that might flow from it.

15. See Heidegger (1976, 174; 1998, 262).

16. See Heidegger (1976, 157; 1998, 248).

17. See Heidegger (1976, 157; 1998, 248).

18. Describing the plan for the first volume of *Origin of Truth* in a working note from January 1959, Merleau-Ponty writes, "Our relationship with animality, our 'kinship' (Heidegger) made explicit" (VI 222/168).

19. See also Derrida's discussion of this passage in G (430ff./175ff.) and Lawlor (2007, 49–50).

20. See Lawlor's (2007, 57–60) summary of this argument and the remarks with which Derrida closes *The Animal That Therefore I Am* (A 218–19/159–60).

Notes to Chapter 5 285

21. Lawlor (2009b) grants the possibility that Merleau-Ponty's own descriptions of the *écart* point in the direction of a veritable alteraffection.

22. But note also Merleau-Ponty's remarks concerning the reflexivity of touch and vision (N 285/223), where he describes the incompossible duplicity of the body as a "self torn apart" and points out concerning the mirror that "the gap is larger between the seeing and the seen than between the touching and the touched.—A segment of the invisible is encrusted between the eye and itself as a thing."

23. Lawlor borrows this term from Foucault's *The Birth of the Clinic*. See Lawlor (2007, 5, 37).

24. As Lawlor (2007, 38) says of the pharmakon.

25. Merleau-Ponty borrows this expression from Valéry's (1971, 216–17) "The Graveyard by the Sea." See PP (251/215). I discuss Merleau-Ponty's appropriation of this phrase in Toadvine (2009, esp. 84–85). Derrida's discussion of Lacan's reference to a similar expression from Valéry in A (190–91/139–40) concerning the universe "as a *fault* in the purity of Non-Being" (from "Silhouette of a Serpent"; Valéry 1971, 186–87) invites further comparison of the role this notion of "fault" plays in Merleau-Ponty, Lacan, and Derrida.

26. Concerning the essential technologization of nature, see Lawlor (2009b). We take up this point later, in relation to Jean-Luc Nancy, in chapter 9. Oliver (2009, 209–10, 215, 225, 242–43) also discusses Merleau-Ponty's use of the metaphor of melody at several points.

27. The reconciliation of naturalism with transcendental philosophy is the aim of the last section of *The Structure of Behavior*, "Is There Not a Truth of Naturalism?" (SB 217–41/201–24).

28. Concerning the naturalization of phenomenology, see Roy et al. (1999).

29. See Merleau-Ponty's remarks on science's presupposition of a philosophical perspective in his interview with Madeleine Chapsal, "Merleau-Ponty in Person" (Merleau-Ponty 2007, 382–83).

30. See in particular the fourth sketch, "Two Preliminary Studies" (N 292–318/229–51).

5. The World of the Bee

1. In *The Statesman*, Plato notes that "kings do not arise in cities in the natural course of things in the way the royal bee is born in the beehive—one individual obviously outstanding in body and mind and capable of taking charge of things at once" (Plato 1961, 1072 [301e]). In *History of Animals*, Aristotle notes that honeybees are "thrifty and disposed to lay by for their future sustenance" and refers to the "so-called kings" of the hive (Aristotle 1984, 970–71 [623b22, 623b34]). The gender of the "monarch" was assumed to be masculine until the Dutch biologist Jan Swammerdam (1737, 1758) demonstrated otherwise in *The Book of Nature; or, The History of Insects*. Concerning the thriftiness of bees, Aristotle's remarks echo a fragment from Democritus: "misers have the fate of bees: they work as if they were going to live forever" (fragment 227, in Freeman 1957, 112).

286 *Notes to Chapter 5*

2. As we have seen in the previous chapter, Derrida (A) develops this analysis at length. See also Leonard Lawlor's (2007, esp. 66–67) commentary.

3. Derrida notes the parallel between this passage from *Phaedo* and Socrates's self-description as a gadfly in *Apology*. See Derrida (1981, 119n52).

4. A particularly striking example is Aristotle's description of one bee giving the indication to the hive that it is time to go to sleep (975 [627a25–30]).

5. Maeterlinck cites Vergil's *Georgics* in LB (6/3, 13/7, and 48/26).

6. See also LB (272/143): "whoever brings careful attention to bear will scarcely deny, even though it be not evident, the presence in nature of a will that tends to raise a portion of matter to a subtler and perhaps better condition, and to penetrate its substance little by little with a mystery-laden fluid that we at first term life, then instinct, and finally intelligence; a will that, for an end we know not, organizes, strengthens, and facilitates the existence of all that is."

7. Note also Maeterlinck's invocation of the ocean as a metaphor for nature: "It is the circular ocean, the tideless water, whereon our boldest and most independent thoughts will never be more than mere abject bubbles. We call it Nature today; tomorrow, perhaps, we shall give it another name, softer or more alarming" (LB 207–8/110).

8. See the similar remarks at LB (112/59, 262–63/138–39, and 301–2/157). The digression describing the author's walk with a physiologist, surveying the town from the summit of a plateau in Normandy, extends this motif of the outside spectator with the aim of distinguishing three semblances of truth, the last of which suggests a correspondence between our intellect and the "eternal intellect" that guides the processes of nature. But, for Maeterlinck, this final "semblance" remains speculative and ultimately beyond any certain knowledge (235–46/125–30).

9. The research on which Uexküll's description relies is summarized by Karl von Frisch (1950, 21–24) in lectures prepared for an American audience. This research is also reported in von Frisch (1993, 478–81). See also the brief remarks on bees' perceptions of space and sense of territory in FW (16/57–58, 70/105).

10. As Uexküll puts this, the biologist does not "ask how butyric acid tastes or smells to the tick, but rather, we only register the fact that butyric acid, as biologically significant, becomes a perception mark for the tick" (FW 10/53). Uexküll (1926, 131–32, 135–36, 158–59) elaborates this position, differentiating the task of biology from that of psychology in these terms.

11. That Heidegger reminds the reader of the Kantian basis for this misconception may be a response to Uexküll's own explicitly Kantian inspiration. See, for example, Uexküll (1926, xiii–xvi).

12. Compare especially Scheler's (1949, 2009) contrast between the animal's *Umwelt* and the human world in his last work.

13. Heidegger does not explain why it is preferable to choose an example of an animal whose behavior would be less comparable to our own, nor why insects, in his view, have such an "exemplary function."

14. Heidegger does not attribute this example to Uexküll, but it may be

found in Uexküll (1926, 169). Heidegger's discussion of the example closely parallels Uexküll's own. Swammerdam (1758, 195) also reports a version of this experiment carried out on hornets, which he presents as evidence of their rapacious nature.

15. Concerning "self-preservation," see also FCM (339/232).

16. Mitchell (2009, 46–48) concisely summarizes the implications of this research for evolutionary theory.

17. Ironically, this passage introduces a discussion of the failures of "communal cooperation" between philosophy and science in the university, cooperation that Heidegger's use of scientific sources in this discussion is apparently intended to exhibit.

18. A summary of this research may be found in von Frisch (1950). It was discovered much later that round dances, like the waggle dances discussed later, also include directional information. See Griffin (2001, 195).

19. Griffin (2001, 203–9) summarizes Lindauer's research and subsequent studies concerning communication during swarming.

20. Griffin reports a similar conclusion drawn by Carl Jung (1973, 94), reacting to the discoveries of von Frisch: "This kind of message is no different in principle from information conveyed by a human being. In the latter case we would certainly regard such behavior as a conscious and intentional act and can hardly imagine how anyone could prove in a court of law that it had taken place unconsciously. . . . We are . . . faced with the fact that the ganglionic system apparently achieves exactly the same result as our cerebral cortex. Nor is there any proof that bees are unconscious" (Jung, quoted in Griffin 2001, 210–11).

6. Animal Memories

1. We do, however, find a few interesting paragraphs devoted to a playful cat who is seen "as a sensing and animated Body" but who does not, in this text, manage to look back. See IdII (175–76/185–86).

2. When Husserl introduces the distinction between material and animal nature, he refers us back to the Cartesian contrast between *res extensa* and *res cogitans* (IdII, sec. 12). Yet Descartes (1985, 134) has explicitly denied that any "vegetative or sensitive soul" could be attributed to the animal body, thereby stripping it of any attributes beyond those of mere extension, while reserving the rational soul for the human being alone.

3. This is the conclusion that David Wood draws, noting Husserl's reference to our "animate organism" as the basis for intersubjectivity in *Cartesian Meditations*. See Wood (2004, 140).

4. On the role of generative passivity in Merleau-Ponty's thought, see Beith (2018).

7. Extinction and Memory

1. We will return to this point again in later chapters, especially chapter 9.

2. For a more developed treatment of this critique of biodiversity, see Morar, Toadvine, and Bohannan (2015).

Notes to Chapter 7

3. This is also the typical description for how we should proceed in the case of biodiversity (see, e.g., Maclaurin and Sterelny 2008, 9).

4. For an overview of these developments in the history of ecology, see Worster (1977, 205–20, 291–315; 1993, 156–70).

5. For insightful analyses of Merleau-Ponty's account of expression, see Foti (2013) and Landes (2013).

8. Apocalyptic Turns

1. On the toxicity of the contemporary imagination, see Buell (1998).

2. I revisit this example in chapter 9.

3. The accuracy of Gasquet's portrayal of Cézanne has been an issue of perennial scholarly debate. There is wide agreement, on one hand, that Gasquet presents an "approximate and very personal version of Cézanne's discourse" (Doran 2001, 108) shaped by Gasquet's own philosophical, literary, and political commitments. Yet, despite its faults, some critics conclude that "it is in certain respects the best contemporary account of Cézanne we have" (Kear 2002, 147). See also John Rewald's preface and Richard Shiff's introduction to Gasquet (1991).

4. "It was the things themselves and the faces themselves as he saw them that demanded to be painted in this way, and Cézanne simply said what they *wanted* to say" (CD 27/80); "it is certainly I who have the experience of the landscape, but I am aware in this experience of taking up a factual situation, of gathering together a sense that is scattered throughout the phenomena, and of saying what they themselves want to say" (PP 313/275).

5. I return here to the famous line from Husserl's *Cartesian Meditations* to which Merleau-Ponty repeatedly returns to characterize the aim of phenomenological reduction. See chapter 3, note 11.

6. See "The Philosopher and His Shadow" (S 201–28/159–81). Interestingly, Merleau-Ponty makes no mention of the concept of motivation or of freedom in this later reading of *Ideas II*. It is as if he has taken up themes from the first half of "Cézanne's Doubt" to find their parallel in Husserl but is no longer interested in pursuing (at least in this context) the parallels that had been suggested in the second half of the earlier essay.

7. See also J.-L. Dumas's 1948 report on Merleau-Ponty's lecture "Man and Object" at the Louvre's Pavillon de Marsan (Dumas 2018).

8. Mathias Goy (2018), commenting on Merleau-Ponty's interpretation of Cézanne in "Man and Object," goes so far as to say that Cézanne, in painting faces "like a stone," is "mineralizing" the human being.

9. As Derrida also admits, citing the work of Françoise Dastur, Henri Maldiney, and Jacques Colette (OT 230n1/355n27).

10. Nancy's criticisms are less hesitant, seeing in Merleau-Ponty's account of flesh a figure for the incarnation of spirit into matter that would block our efforts to genuinely think the materiality of the world at its end (C 68–69, 74–75, 86–87, 98–99).

11. We return to this assessment of general equivalence and its relation to global sustainability efforts in chapter 9.

9. The Elements at the End of the World

1. For an insightful discussion of the historical sources and early development of secular eschatological fiction, see Wagar (1982).

2. On the link between apocalypticism and nostalgia in environmental thinking, see Fiskio (2021).

3. McKibben is quoted as attributing this phrase to a conversation with climate scientist James Hansen in Mayer (2011). Hansen's (2012) own published remarks instead use the phrase "game over for the climate."

4. Among the extensive literature currently available on this subject, Collings (2014) stands out for its lucid presentation of the implications of climate change for our present and future.

5. See also Rudwick's (2014) reconstruction of this intellectual history, esp. chapter 5.

6. Benford (1999) provides an interesting account of the influence of science fiction on the work of these research teams, reinforcing my earlier argument concerning the inseparability of fiction and prediction in the eco-eschatological narrative.

7. For a discussion of these efforts in relationship to deep time, see Ialenti (2020).

8. For an overview of ethical factors in setting the discount rate for climate intervention, see Broome (2008).

9. Inspired by this understanding of the world, ecophenomenologists have set out to describe and interpret the built and natural environments in richer terms than metaphysical naturalism allows, attending to the meaningful dimensions and horizonal possibilities opened by our involvement and inherence in what surrounds us. See, e.g., James (2009) and Toadvine (2017b).

10. See esp. Lawlor's chapter 1, "Genesis as the Basic Problem of Phenomenology."

11. See esp. Nancy (2000b, 2008a). Derrida repeatedly calls attention to the distinctiveness of Nancy's approach to ecotechnology understood as the *technē* of the body, which he says "singles out Nancy's thinking among all other modern ideas about the body proper, the flesh, touch, or the untouchable, which is to say, the taking into account of technics and technical ex-appropriation on the very 'phenomenological' threshold of the body proper" (OT 70/56; cf. 113–14/96–97, 131/113, 146–48/127–29, 206/180, 252–53/223, 322–23/286–87). For an insightful reading of Nancy's "The Intruder," see O'Byrne (2002).

12. James (2006, 147–48) links Nancy's ecotechnics with the Derridean themes of arche-writing and *différance*, albeit with essential qualifications.

13. As paradigmatic examples of the environmentalist response to deconstruction, see Wilson (1998, 41, 214–15, 301) and Soulé and Lease (1995). Despite the subtitle of the latter work, only a few passing references to Derrida appear here (usually listed alongside such authors as Rorty, Lacan, and Lyotard), and none of his texts is explicitly cited or discussed. Nancy is not mentioned. Deconstruction's erasure of a pure distinction between the

290 *Notes to Chapter 9*

natural and the technological converges in certain respects with contemporary developments in actor-network theory and environmental critical theory (see, e.g., Latour 2011; Vogel 2015).

14. Nancy mentions "atomic time" in this context (AFEC 52/31).

15. This could be traced back at least to Derrida's discussion of the possibility of the disappearance of truth and of a universal conflagration in his introduction to Husserl's *Origin of Geometry* (Derrida 1962, 91ff.; 1989a, 93ff.). See also Naas (2015, 50–51).

16. Derrida finds such respect already implied by Husserl's recognition that the other can be presented only through analogical appresentation, rather than through direct perception. See R (75–76/161), OT (217–20/190–94), and Naas (2015, 48).

17. In addition to the texts that we discuss here, Derrida (2001) makes this point repeatedly in the memorial essays collected in *The Work of Mourning*. See also Naas (2015, 50ff.).

18. In this respect, as we will see, Derrida's formulations in "Rams" anticipate the discussion of the world as a phantasm in *The Beast and the Sovereign* (e.g., BS2 159–60/104–5). Consequently, we need not conclude, as Geoffrey Bennington (2011, xiii) suggests, that Derrida's claims concerning the absolute end of the world are not to be taken literally: "For if this were simply or literally true there would be no mourning at all, and no survival or living on (and thus no reading) either: so the end of the world must be also, simultaneously, *no end of the world,* and one of the most immediate and most intolerable experiences of the death of the loved other is just this fact that *the world does not end when it ends,* that it simply carries on after its end, has no end, that the end of the world is not the end of the world, that its end in death is also the perspective of an endlessness, an *ad infinitum.*"

19. Although this contrast is not further developed in Derrida's final lectures, it might be fruitfully compared to similar remarks in "No Apocalypse, Not Now" (P 363–86/387–409) and "Autoimmunity: Real and Symbolic Suicides—a Dialogue with Jacques Derrida" (Derrida 2003a). Michael Naas (2015, 54–55, 49) proposes that the second sense of the end of the world, which he describes as the "end . . . of every possible end of the world," should be understood in terms of the world as prosthetic detour necessary for any *autos* or *ipse* to gain a sense of itself, with reference to Derrida's discussion of Robinson Crusoe's reinvention of the wheel at BS2 (137–38/88). This would clearly be related to the notion of ecotechnicity we have developed in conversation with Nancy. But it also seems necessary to understand this second sense of the end of the world in relation to Derrida's remarks elsewhere concerning mondialization as well as the destruction of the archive. Insofar as the total destruction of the archive would mean the end of all possibility of memory, memorialization, or mourning (as Derrida suggests in "No Apocalypse, Not Now"), this would indeed represent the end of every possible end of the world.

20. On the relationship between the monstrosity of the other and ethics, see Derrida (2008b, 108; 2009, 155; BS2 367/266). See also Naas (2015, 56–57)

and Derrida's (1967a, 14; 1976, 5) famous remark concerning the monstrosity of the future in the exergue to *Of Grammatology*.

21. As we noted earlier, Heidegger's theses are that the stone is worldless *(weltlos)*, the animal is poor in world *(weltarm)*, and "man" is world-forming *(weltbildend)*. See FCM (272ff./184ff.).

22. Nancy makes reference to this distinction by Derrida in a subsequent interview (Nancy and Cavalcante Schuback 2013, 40), but without mentioning that Derrida had directed this criticism at him.

23. Matthias Fritsch (2015) proposes a rich interpretation of the role of earth in *The Beast and the Sovereign* in terms of earth's claim on life as its "unpossessable and ungovernable context," such that life must be understood as essentially "interred" or "in-earthed." While Fritsch's reading pursues a path different from the one I develop here, it offers fruitful insights for thinking the relation of earth with habitat and life-death in Derrida's later thought.

24. This point might be fruitfully compared with Jane Bennett's (2010, esp. 10–11) description of mineralization in relation to human "thing-power."

10. Climate Change and the Temporal Sublime

1. This is roughly Naomi Klein's (2014) argument in *This Changes Everything*.

2. Brady (2013) traces some of the early history of the temporal sublime.

3. Such elemental examples of the dynamically sublime are also among the omens for Judgment Day (Kant 1996, 225).

4. In the *Critique of Judgment*, Kant (1987, 315–16) points out that the shape of land and sea as encountered today is the result of chaotic upheavals and disturbances in ancient times, recorded in the "memorials of mighty devastations" studied by the "archeology of nature" (or "theory of the earth"). But Kant does not discuss these "memorials" as having a sublime character due to their antiquity, and they do not predate "man"; the lack of human fossil remains is explained, for Kant, by the fact that "his understanding was able to rescue him (for the most part, at least) from those devastations" (316).

5. See in particular Playfair's (1822, 80–81) description of his 1788 trip with Hutton to Siccar Point, which we summarized in chapter 2.

6. Representative examples include Clingerman and O'Brien (2017), Fagan (2017), Fiskio (2021), Foust and Murphy (2009), Moo (2015), and Skrimshire (2010, 2014).

7. See, e.g., David Wood's (2017, 223) brief remarks on "tipping points."

8. On this point, see Jones (2017, 5) and Skrimshire (2014, 239).

9. See, e.g., speculative fiction author N. K. Jemisin's (2018, 476) insight that "an apocalypse is a relative thing."

10. On the need to break from finality itself, that is, "from aiming, from planning, and projecting a future in general," and instead to work with "other futures," see Nancy (2015, 37). On our ongoing responsibility to "watch out" for the future, see Nancy (2015, 64n4). On the past that is constitutive of our present possibilities, see Wood (2017, 7) on "Constitutive Time."

11. Personal communication with the author.

11. Future Fossils

1. The broken arm example is introduced by Holmes Rolston (2000, 129) to contest claims that environmental restoration is necessarily the creation of an artifactual replica.

2. On the phenomenological basis for the distinction between natural and artificial, see Toadvine (2017a).

3. I am using *built* here to refer strictly to human practices, because it seems that, for Vogel, only humans properly build (as a matter of social practices, which embed norms that presuppose language). But because all organisms construct their environments, we could say that a termite hill is constructed from a termite perspective but not from ours, and that our houses, though built for us, are unbuilt (and often tasty) for termites.

4. As does, e.g., McKibben (2003, 48, 50ff.).

5. For an overview of the phenomenological treatment of geomateriality and the elements, see also Toadvine (2020). McKibben (2003, 48) also mentions the "elemental" character of nature as one reason why we had believed it immune to harm, although he takes climate change as counterevidence of its vulnerability.

6. I am grateful to Fest (2013, 86) for bringing Steedman's treatment of dust to my attention.

7. As H. Peter Steeves has done in an unpublished essay.

Bibliography

Abram, David. 1996. *The Spell of the Sensuous.* New York: Vintage Books.

Agamben, Giorgio. 2002. *L'Aperto: L'Uomo e l'animale.* Torino, Italy: Bollati Boringhieri.

Agamben, Giorgio. 2004. *The Open: Man and Animal.* Translated by Kevin Attell. Stanford, Calif.: Stanford University Press.

Alloa, Emmanuel. 2009. "La chair comme diacritique incarné." *Chiasmi International* 11: 249–61.

Alloa, Emmanuel. 2013. "The Diacritical Nature of Meaning: Merleau-Ponty with Saussure." *Chiasmi International* 15: 167–81.

Al-Saji, Alia. 2008. "'A Past Which Has Never Been Present': Bergsonian Dimensions in Merleau-Ponty's Theory of the Prepersonal." *Research in Phenomenology* 38, no. 1: 41–71.

Anders, Günther. 2007. *Le temps de la fin.* Paris: L'Herne.

Aristotle. 1984. *The Complete Works of Aristotle.* Vol. 1. Edited by J. Barnes. Princeton, N.J.: Princeton University Press.

Aristotle. 1998. *Politics.* Translated by C. D. C. Reeve. Indianapolis, Ind.: Hackett.

Artangel. 2007. "Vatnasafn/Library of Water." https://www.artangel.org.uk/project/library-of-water/.

Atwood, Margaret. 2003. *Oryx and Crake.* New York: Nan A. Talese/Doubleday.

Atwood, Margaret. 2009. *The Year of the Flood.* New York: Nan A. Talese/Doubleday.

Atwood, Margaret. 2013. *MaddAddam.* London: Bloomsbury.

Bachelard, Gaston. 1960. *La poétique de la rêverie.* Paris: Presses Universitaires de France.

Bachelard, Gaston. 1969. *The Poetics of Reverie: Childhood, Language, and the Cosmos.* Translated by Daniel Russell. Boston: Beacon Press.

Baldwin, Thomas. 2004. "Editor's Introduction." In *Merleau-Ponty: Basic Writings,* by Maurice Merleau-Ponty, 1–32. London: Routledge.

Ballard, J. G. (1962) 2014. *The Drowned World.* London: Fourth Estate.

Barbaras, Renaud. 2001. "Merleau-Ponty and Nature." Translated by Paul Milan. *Research in Phenomenology* 31: 22–38.

Barbaras, Renaud. 2004. *The Being of the Phenomenon: Merleau-Ponty's Ontology.* Translated by Ted Toadvine and Leonard Lawlor. Bloomington: Indiana University Press.

Baskin, Jeremy. 2015. "Paradigm Dressed as Epoch: The Ideology of the Anthropocene." *Environmental Values* 24: 9–29.

Bataille, Georges. 1976. "Les conséquences du non-savoir." In *Oeuvres complètes,* vol. 8, 190–98. Paris: Gallimard.

Bataille, Georges. 1986. "Un-knowing and Its Consequences." Translated by Annette Michelson. *October* 36: 80–85.

Bataille, Georges. 2001. "The Consequences of Nonknowledge." Translated by Michelle Kendall and Stuart Kendall. In *The Unfinished System of Nonknowledge,* edited by Stuart Kendall, 111–18. Minneapolis: University of Minnesota Press.

Beith, Don. 2018. *The Birth of Sense: Generative Passivity in Merleau-Ponty's Philosophy.* Athens: Ohio University Press.

Benford, Gregory. 1999. *Deep Time: How Humanity Communicates across Millennia.* New York: HarperCollins.

Benjamin, Andrew. 2017. "The World in Ruins: Heidegger, Poussin, Kiefer." *Journal of Aesthetics and Phenomenology* 4, no. 2: 101–23.

Bennett, Jane. 2010. *Vibrant Matter: A Political Ecology of Things.* Durham, N.C.: Duke University Press.

Bennington, Geoffrey. 2011. *Not Half No End: Militantly Melancholic Essays in Memory of Jacques Derrida.* Edinburgh: University of Edinburgh Press.

Bergson, Henri. 1959. *L'évolution créatrice.* In *Oeuvres,* 487–809. Paris: Presses Universitaires de France.

Bergson, Henri. 1998. *Creative Evolution.* Translated by A. Mitchell. Mineola, N.Y.: Dover.

Bernasconi, Robert. 2000. "Heidegger's Alleged Challenge to Nazi Concepts of Race." In *Appropriating Heidegger,* edited by James Faulconer and Mark Wrathall, 50–67. Cambridge: Cambridge University Press.

Berry, Wendell. 2015. *Our Only World: Ten Essays.* Berkeley: Counterpoint Press.

Bimbenet, Étienne. 2011. *L'Animal que je ne suis plus.* Paris: Gallimard.

Boetzkes, Amanda. 2010. *The Ethics of Earth Art.* Minneapolis: University of Minnesota Press.

Brady, Emily. 2013. *The Sublime in Modern Philosophy: Aesthetics, Ethics, and Nature.* Cambridge: Cambridge University Press.

Brannen, Peter. 2017. *The Ends of the World.* London: Oneworld.

Brannen, Peter. 2019. "The Anthropocene Is a Joke." *The Atlantic,* August 13. https://www.theatlantic.com/science/archive/2019/08/arrogance-anthropocene/595795/.

Brazil, Rachel. 2021. "Marking the Anthropocene." *Chemistry World,* January 29. https://www.chemistryworld.com/features/marking-the-anthropocene/4012969.article.

Broome, John. 2008. "The Ethics of Climate Change." *Scientific American,* June, 69–73.

Brummett, Barry. 1984. "Premillennial Apocalyptic as a Rhetorical Genre." *Central States Speech Journal* 35, no. 2: 84–93.

Brunschvicg, Léon. 1964. *La modalité du jugement.* 3rd ed. Paris: Presses Universitaires de France.

Buchanan, Brett. 2008. *Onto-ethologies: The Animal Environments of Uexküll, Heidegger, Merleau-Ponty, and Deleuze.* Albany: State University of New York Press.

Buell, Frederick. 2010. "A Short History of Environmental Apocalypse." In *Future Ethics: Climate Change and Apocalyptic Imagination,* edited by Stefan Skrimshire, 13–36. London: Bloomsbury.

Buell, Lawrence. 1998. "Toxic Discourse." *Critical Inquiry* 24, no. 3: 639–65.

Buffon, Georges. 1778. *Histoire naturelle des époques de la nature.* Paris: De l'Imprimerie Royale.

Calarco, Matthew. 2008. *Zoographies: The Question of the Animal from Heidegger to Derrida.* New York: Columbia University Press.

Callicott, J. Baird. 1998. "The Wilderness Idea Revisited: The Sustainable Development Alternative." In *The Great New Wilderness Debate,* edited by J. Baird Callicott and Michael Nelson, 337–66. Athens: University of Georgia Press.

Carbone, Mauro. 2004. *The Thinking of the Sensible: Merleau-Ponty's A-Philosophy.* Evanston, Ill.: Northwestern University Press.

Carson, Rachel. 1962. *Silent Spring.* Boston: Houghton Mifflin.

Cavalieri, Paola. 2009. *The Death of the Animal: A Dialogue.* New York: Columbia University Press.

Chakrabarty, Dipesh. 2009. "The Climate of History: Four Theses." *Critical Inquiry* 35: 197–222.

Chakrabarty, Dipesh. 2021. *The Climate of History in a Planetary Age.* Chicago: University of Chicago Press.

Claudel, Paul. 1929. *Art poétique.* Paris: Mercure de France.

Claudel, Paul. 1948. *Poetic Art.* Translated by Renée Spodheim. New York: Philosophical Library.

Clingerman, Forrest, and Kevin J. O'Brien. 2017. "Is Climate Change a New Kind of Problem? The Role of Theology and Imagination in Climate Ethics." *WIREs Climate Change* 8, no. 5: 1–10.

Cohen, Jeffrey. 2015. *Stone: An Ecology of the Inhuman.* Minneapolis: University of Minnesota Press.

Colebrook, Claire. 2014. "Archiviolithic: The Anthropocene and the Hetero-Archive." *Derrida Today* 7, no. 1: 21–43.

Colebrook, Claire. 2017. "Anti-Catastrophic Time." *New Formations* 92: 102–19.

Collings, David A. 2014. *Stolen Future, Broken Present: The Human Significance of Climate Change.* Ann Arbor, Mich.: Open Humanities Library.

Cooper, Keith. 2017. "Looking for LUCA, the Last Universal Common Ancestor." *Astrobiology at NASA*, March 30. https://astrobiology .nasa.gov/news/looking-for-luca-the-last-universal-common -ancestor/.

Corcoran, Patricia L., Charles J. Moore, and Kelly Jazvac. 2014. "An Anthropogenic Marker Horizon in the Future Rock Record." *GSA Today* 24, no. 6: 4–8.

Critchley, Simon. 2001. *Continental Philosophy: A Very Short Introduction.* New York: Oxford University Press.

Crosby, Alfred. 1997. *The Measure of Reality: Quantification and Western Society, 1250–1600.* Cambridge: Cambridge University Press.

Crutzen, Paul, and Christian Schwägerl. 2011. "Living in the Anthropocene: Toward a New Global Ethos." *Yale Environment 360,* January 24. https://e360.yale.edu/features/living_in_the _anthropocene_toward_a_new_global_ethos.

Crutzen, Paul, and Eugene Stoermer. 2000. "The 'Anthropocene.'" *Global Change Newsletter* 41: 17–18; reprinted at IGBP, http://www .igbp.net/news/opinion/opinion/haveweenteredtheanthropocene .5.d8b4c3c12bf3be638a8000578.html.

Cuvier, Georges. 1812. *Recherches sur les ossemens fossiles de quadrupèdes.* Vol. 1. Paris: Deterville.

Darwin, Charles. 1964. *On the Origin of Species: A Facsimile of the First Edition.* Cambridge, Mass.: Harvard University Press.

Dawkins, Richard. 1993. "Gaps in the Mind." In *The Great Ape Project,* edited by Paola Cavalieri and Peter Singer, 81–87. New York: St. Martin's Griffin.

Deleuze, Gilles. 1968. *Différence et répétition.* Paris: Presses Universitaires de France.

Deleuze, Gilles. 1994. *Difference and Repetition.* Translated by Paul Patton. New York: Columbia University Press.

Deleuze, Gilles, and Félix Guattari. 1980. *Mille Plateaux.* Paris: Éditions de Minuit.

Deleuze, Gilles, and Félix Guattari. 1987. *A Thousand Plateaus.* Translated by Brian Massumi. Minneapolis: University of Minnesota Press.

Deleuze, Gilles, and Félix Guattari. 1991. *Qu'est-ce que la philosophie?* Paris: Éditions de Minuit.

Deleuze, Gilles, and Félix Guattari. 1994. *What Is Philosophy?* Translated by Hugh Tomlinson and Graham Burchell. New York: Columbia University Press.

Deleuze, Gilles. 2002. *Francis Bacon: Logique de la sensation.* Paris: Éditions du Seuil.

Deleuze, Gilles. 2003. *Francis Bacon: The Logic of Sensation.* Translated by Daniel Smith. Minneapolis: University of Minnesota Press.

Derrida, Jacques. 1962. Introduction to *L'Origine de la géométrie,* by Edmund Husserl. Paris: Presses Universitaires de France.

Derrida, Jacques. 1967a. *De la Grammatologie.* Paris: Éditions de Minuit.

Derrida, Jacques. 1967b. *La voix et le phénomène.* Paris: Presses Universitaires de France.

Derrida, Jacques. 1976. *Of Grammatology.* Translated by Gayatri Spivak. Baltimore: The Johns Hopkins University Press.

Derrida, Jacques. 1981. "Plato's Pharmacy." In *Dissemination,* translated by B. Johnson, 61–171. Chicago: University of Chicago Press.

Derrida, Jacques. 1987a. *De l'esprit.* Paris: Éditions Galilée.

Derrida, Jacques. 1987b. "*Geschlecht* II: Heidegger's Hand." Translated by John P. Leavey Jr. In *Deconstruction and Philosophy,* edited by John Sallis, 161–96. Chicago: University of Chicago Press.

Derrida, Jacques. 1987c. *Psyché: Inventions de l'autre, tome I.* Paris: Éditions Galilée.

Derrida, Jacques. 1989a. *Edmund Husserl's Origin of Geometry: An Introduction.* Translated by John Leavey Jr. Lincoln: University of Nebraska Press.

Derrida, Jacques. 1989b. *Of Spirit.* Translated by Geoff Bennington and Rachel Bowlby. Chicago: University of Chicago Press.

Derrida, Jacques. 1992. *Points de suspension.* Paris: Éditions Galilée.

Derrida, Jacques. 1995. *Points . . . Interviews, 1974–1994.* Edited by Elisabeth Weber. Stanford, Calif.: Stanford University Press.

Derrida, Jacques. 2000. *Le toucher, Jean-Luc Nancy.* Paris: Éditions Galilée.

Derrida, Jacques. 2001. *The Work of Mourning.* Edited by Pascale-Anne Brault and Michael Naas. Chicago: University of Chicago Press.

Derrida, Jacques. 2002. *Without Alibi.* Edited by Peggy Kamuf. Stanford, Calif.: Stanford University Press.

Derrida, Jacques. 2003a. "Autoimmunity: Real and Symbolic Suicides—a Dialogue with Jacques Derrida." In *Philosophy in a Time of Terror,* by Giovanna Borradori, 85–136. Chicago: University of Chicago Press.

Derrida, Jacques. 2003b. *Béliers.* Paris: Éditions Galilée.

Derrida, Jacques. 2003c. *Chaque fois unique, la fin du monde.* Paris: Éditions Galilée.

Derrida, Jacques. 2003d. *Voyous.* Paris: Éditions Galilée.

Derrida, Jacques. 2005a. *On Touching—Jean-Luc Nancy.* Translated by Christine Irizarry. Stanford, Calif.: Stanford University Press.

Derrida, Jacques. 2005b. *Rogues.* Translated by Pascale-Anne Brault and Michael Nass. Stanford, Calif.: Stanford University Press.

Derrida, Jacques. 2005c. *Sovereignties in Question: The Poetics of Paul Celan.* Edited by Thomas Dutoit and Outi Pasanen. New York: Fordham University Press.

Derrida, Jacques. 2006. *L'Animal que donc je suis.* Paris: Éditions Galilée.

Derrida, Jacques. 2007. *Psyche: Inventions of the Other, Volume I.* Edited by Peggy Kamuf and Elizabeth Rottenberg. Stanford, Calif.: Stanford University Press.

Derrida, Jacques. 2008a. *The Animal That Therefore I Am.* Translated by D. Wills. New York: Fordham University Press.

Derrida, Jacques. 2008b. *Séminaire: La bête et le souverain, Volume I (2001–2002).* Paris: Éditions Galilée.

Derrida, Jacques. 2009. *The Beast and the Sovereign, Volume I.* Translated by Geoffrey Bennington. Chicago: University of Chicago Press.

Derrida, Jacques. 2010. *Séminaire: La bête et le souverain, Volume II (2002–2003)*. Paris: Éditions Galilée.

Derrida, Jacques. 2011a. *The Beast and the Sovereign, Volume II*. Translated by Geoffrey Bennington. Chicago: University of Chicago Press.

Derrida, Jacques. 2011b. *Voice and Phenomenon*. Translated by Leonard Lawlor. Evanston, Ill.: Northwestern University Press.

Derrida, Jacques. 2015. *Séminaire: La peine de mort, Volume II (2000–2001)*. Paris: Éditions Galilée.

Derrida, Jacques. 2017. *The Death Penalty, Volume II*. Translated by Elizabeth Rottenberg. Chicago: University of Chicago Press.

Descartes, Rene. 1985. "Discourse on the Method." In *The Philosophical Writings of Descartes, Volume I*, edited by John Cottingham, Robert Stoothoff, and Dugald Murdoch, 111–51. Cambridge: Cambridge University Press.

de Waal, Frans. 1999. "Anthropomorphism and Anthropodenial: Consistency in Our Thinking about Humans and Other Animals." *Philosophical Topics* 27: 255–80.

Doran, Michael, ed. 2001. *Conversations with Cézanne*. Translated by Julie Cochran. Berkeley: University of California Press.

Dumas, J.-L. 2018. "Man and Object." Translated by Marie-Eve Morin. *Chiasmi International* 20: 89–95.

Džanić, Denis. 2020. "The Earth and Pregivenness in Transcendental Phenomenology." *Research in Phenomenology* 50: 31–52.

Ellsworth, Elizabeth, and Jamie Kruse, eds. 2012. *Making the Geologic Now: Responses to Material Conditions of Contemporary Life*. Brooklyn, N.Y.: Punctum Books.

Environmental Protection Agency. 2005. "Public Health and Environmental Radiation Protection Standards for Yucca Mountain, Nevada; Proposed Rule." *Federal Register* 70, no. 161. https://www.gpo.gov/fdsys/pkg/FR-2005-08-22/pdf/05-16193.pdf.

Fagan, Madeleine. 2017. "Who's Afraid of the Ecological Apocalypse? Climate Change and the Production of the Ethical Subject." *British Journal of Politics and International Relations* 19, no. 2: 225–44.

Fest, Bradley J. 2013. "Apocalypse Networks: Representing the Nuclear Archive." In *The Silence of Fallout: Nuclear Criticism in a Post–Cold War World*, edited by Michael J. Blouin, Morgan Shipley, and Jack Taylor, 81–103. Newcastle upon Tyne, U.K.: Cambridge Scholars.

Bibliography

Fink, Eugen. 1933. "Die phänomenologische Philosophie Edmund Husserls in der gegenwärtigen Kritik." *Kant-Studien* 38: 319–83.

Fink, Eugen. 1970. "The Phenomenological Philosophy of Edmund Husserl and Contemporary Criticism." In *The Phenomenology of Husserl,* edited by R. O. Elveton, 73–147. Chicago: Quadrangle Books.

Fiskio, Janet. 2021. *Climate Change, Literature, and Environmental Justice.* Cambridge: Cambridge University Press.

Fóti, Véronique. 2013. *Tracing Expression in Merleau-Ponty: Aesthetics, Philosophy of Biology, and Ontology.* Evanston, Ill.: Northwestern University Press.

Foucault, Michel. 1973. *The Order of Things: An Archaeology of the Human Sciences.* New York: Vintage Books.

Foust, Christina R., and William O'Shannon Murphy. 2009. "Revealing and Reframing Apocalyptic Tragedy in Global Warming Discourse." *Environmental Communication* 3, no. 2: 151–67.

Franck, Robert. 2005. "Whitehead et la phénoménologie: Une lecture croisée du dernier Merleau-Ponty et du Whitehead de *Process and Reality.*" *Chiasmi International* 7: 341–69.

Freeman, Kathleen, trans. 1957. *Ancilla to the Pre-Socratic Philosophers.* Cambridge, Mass.: Harvard University Press.

Fritsch, Matthias. 2015. "Interment: Earth and Lifedeath in Derrida." Unpublished lecture presented at the 2015 Collegium Phaeonomenologicum.

Frost, Robert. 1923. "Fire and Ice." In *New Hampshire,* 80. New York: Henry Holt.

Ganopolski, A., R. Winkelmann, and H. Schellnhuber. 2016. "Critical Insolation–CO_2 Relation for Diagnosing Past and Future Glacial Inception." *Nature* 529: 200–203.

Gasquet, Joachim. 1926. *Cézanne.* Paris: Bernheim-Jeune.

Gasquet, Joachim. 1991. *Joachim Gasquet's Cézanne: A Memoir with Conversations.* Translated by Christopher Pemberton. London: Thames and Hudson.

Gillett, Nathan, Vivek K. Arora, Kirsten Zickfeld, Shawn J. Marshall, and William J. Merryfield. 2011. "Ongoing Climate Change Following a Complete Cessation of Carbon Dioxide Emissions." *Nature Geoscience* 4 (February): 83–87.

Goy, Mathias. 2018. "Merleau-Ponty: The Legacy of His Oeuvre." Translated by Ted Toadvine. *Chiasmi International* 20: 43–59.

Gratton, Peter. 2012. "The Speculative Challenge and Nancy's Post-deconstructive Realism." In *Jean-Luc Nancy and Plural Thinking: Expositions of World, Ontology, Politics, and Sense,* edited by Peter Gratton and Marie-Eve Morin, 109–25. Albany: State University of New York Press.

Greenpeace International. 2009. "Horsemen of the Apocalypse Descend on Copenhagen." *Scoop Independent News,* December 16. http://www.scoop.co.nz/stories/WO0912/S00466.htm.

Griffin, Donald. 2001. *Animal Minds: Beyond Cognition to Consciousness.* Chicago: University of Chicago Press.

Gross, Lawrence W. 2014. *Anishinaabe Ways of Knowing and Being.* New York: Routledge.

Grosz, Elizabeth. 2008. *Chaos, Territory, Art.* New York: Columbia University Press.

Hadot, Pierre. 2006. *The Veil of Isis: An Essay on the History of the Idea of Nature.* Translated by Michael Chase. Cambridge, Mass.: Belknap Press of Harvard University Press.

Halák, Jan. 2022. "Mathematics Embodied: Merleau-Ponty on Geometry and Algebra as Fields of Motor Enaction." *Synthese* 200: Article 34.

Hamilton, William D. 1964. "The Genetical Evolution of Social Behavior I and II." *Journal of Theoretical Biology* 7: 1–32.

Hamrick, William, and Jan Van der Veken. 2011. *Nature and Logos: A Whiteheadian Key to Merleau-Ponty's Fundamental Thought.* Albany: State University of New York Press.

Hansen, James. 2012. "Game Over for the Climate." *New York Times,* May 9. http://www.nytimes.com/2012/05/10/opinion/game-over -for-the-climate.html.

Haraway, Donna. 2015. "Anthropocene, Capitalocene, Plantationo-cene, Chthulucene: Making Kin." *Environmental Humanities* 6: 159–65.

Harman, Graham. 2005. *Guerrilla Metaphysics: Phenomenology and the Carpentry of Things.* Chicago: Open Court.

Hass, Marjorie, and Lawrence Hass. 2000. "Merleau-Ponty and the Origin of Geometry." In *Chiasms: Merleau-Ponty's Notion of Flesh,* edited by Fred Evans and Leonard Lawlor, 177–87. Albany: State University of New York Press.

Heidegger, Martin. 1961. *Nietzsche, Erster Band.* Pfullingen, Germany: Günther Neske.

302 *Bibliography*

Heidegger, Martin. 1962. *Being and Time.* Translated by John Macquarrie and Edward Robinson. San Francisco: Harper and Row.

Heidegger, Martin. 1963. *Sein und Zeit.* Tübingen, Germany: Max Niemeyer.

Heidegger, Martin. 1968. *What Is Called Thinking?* Translated by J. Glenn Gray. New York: Harper and Row.

Heidegger, Martin. 1971. *Was heisst Denken?* 3rd ed. Tübingen, Germany: Niemeyer.

Heidegger, Martin. 1976. "Brief über den 'Humanismus.'" In *Wegmarken,* 313–64. Frankfurt am Main, Germany: Vittorio Klostermann.

Heidegger, Martin. 1977. *Holzwege.* Frankfurt am Main, Germany: Vittorio Klostermann.

Heidegger, Martin. 1982. *Nietzsche.* Vol. 3. Translated by Joan Stambaugh, David Farrell Krell, and Frank A. Capuzzi. San Francisco: Harper and Row.

Heidegger, Martin. 1983. *Die Grundbegriffe der Metaphysik: Welt—Endlichkeit—Einsamkeit.* Frankfurt am Main, Germany: Vittorio Klostermann.

Heidegger, Martin. 1989. *Nietzsche.* Vol. 1. Pfullingen, Germany: Günther Neske.

Heidegger, Martin. 1991. *Nietzsche.* Vol. III. Translated by Joan Stambaugh, David Farrell Krell, and Frank Capuzzi. San Francisco: HarperCollins.

Heidegger, Martin. 1993. *Basic Writings.* Rev. ed. Edited by David Farrell Krell. San Francisco: HarperCollins.

Heidegger, Martin. 1995. *The Fundamental Concepts of Metaphysics: World, Finitude, Solitude.* Translated by W. McNeill and N. Walker. Bloomington: Indiana University Press.

Heidegger, Martin. 1998. "Letter on 'Humanism.'" In *Pathmarks,* edited by William McNeill, 239–76. Cambridge: Cambridge University Press.

Herr, Lucien. 1894. "Hegel." In *La Grande Encyclopédie,* vol. 19. Paris: H. Lamirault et Cie.

Hettinger, Ned, and Bill Throop. 1999. "Refocusing Ecocentrism: De-emphasizing Stability and Defending Wildness." *Environmental Ethics* 21: 3–21.

Himanka, Juha. 2005. "Husserl's Argumentation for the Pre-Copernican View of the Earth." *Review of Metaphysics* 58: 621–44.

Holmes, Arthur. 1913. *The Age of the Earth*. London: Harper.

Horne, Gerald. 2018. *The Apocalypse of Settler Colonialism: The Roots of Slavery, White Supremacy, and Capitalism in Seventeenth-Century North America and the Caribbean.* New York: Monthly Review Press.

Hulme, Mike. 2010. "Four Meanings of Climate Change." In *Future Ethics: Climate Change and Apocalyptic Imagination,* edited by Stefan Skrimshire, 37–58. London: Continuum.

Human Interference Task Force. 1984. "Reducing the Likelihood of Future Human Activities That Could Affect Geologic High-Level Waste Repositories." U.S. Department of Energy. http://www.osti .gov/scitech/servlets/purl/6799619.

Hume, David. 2007. *A Treatise of Human Nature.* Vol. 1. Edited by David Fate Norton and Mary J. Norton. Oxford: Oxford University Press.

Husserl, Edmund. 1928. *Logische Untersuchungen.* Second book, first part, 4th ed. Halle, Germany: Max Niemeyer.

Husserl, Edmund. 1940. "Grundlegende Untersuchungen zum phänomenologischen Ursprung der Räumlichkeit der Natur." In *Philosophical Essays in Memory of Edmund Husserl,* edited by Marvin Farber, 305–25. Cambridge, Mass.: Harvard University Press.

Husserl, Edmund. 1950. *Cartesianische Meditationen,* Husserliana I. Edited by Stephan Strasser. The Hague: Martinus Nijhoff.

Husserl, Edmund. 1952. *Ideen II.* Husserliana IV. The Hague: Martinus Nijhoff.

Husserl, Edmund. 1962. *Die Krisis der Europäischen Wissenschaften und die Transzendentale Phänomenologie.* Husserliana VI. The Hague: Martinus Nijhoff.

Husserl, Edmund. 1970. *The Crisis of European Sciences and Transcendental Phenomenology.* Translated by David Carr. Evanston, Ill.: Northwestern University Press.

Husserl, Edmund. 1976. *Ideen I.* Husserliana III.1. The Hague: Martinus Nijhoff.

Husserl, Edmund. 1982. *Ideas I.* Translated by Fred Kersten. The Hague: Martinus Nijhoff.

Husserl, Edmund. 1989. *Ideas II.* Translated by R. Rojcewicz and André Schuwer. Dordrecht, Netherlands: Kluwer.

Husserl, Edmund. 1993. *Cartesian Meditations.* Translated by Dorion Cairns. Dordrecht, Netherlands: Kluwer.

Husserl, Edmund. 1996. *Méditations cartésiennes.* Translated by Gabrielle Peiffer and Emmanuel Levinas. Paris: Vrin.

304 *Bibliography*

Husserl, Edmund. 2001. *Logical Investigations*. Vol. 1. Translated by
J. N. Findlay. London: Routledge.

Husserl, Edmund. 2002. "Foundational Investigations of the Phe-
nomenological Origin of the Spatiality of Nature: The Originary
Ark, the Earth, Does Not Move." Translated by Fred Kersten and
Leonard Lawlor. In *Husserl at the Limits of Phenomenology*, by Maurice
Merleau-Ponty, edited by Leonard Lawlor and Bettina Bergo, 117–31.
Evanston, Ill.: Northwestern University Press.

Hutton, James. 1788. *Theory of the Earth*. Edinburgh: Royal Society of
Edinburgh.

Ialenti, Vincent. 2014. "Adjudicating Deep Time: Revisiting the
United States' High-Level Nuclear Waste Repository Project at
Yucca Mountain." *Science and Technology Studies* 27, no. 2: 27–48.

Ialenti, Vincent. 2020. *Deep Time Reckoning*. Cambridge, Mass.: MIT
Press.

James, Ian. 2006. *The Fragmentary Demand: An Introduction to the
Philosophy of Jean-Luc Nancy*. Stanford, Calif.: Stanford University
Press.

James, Simon. 2009. *The Presence of Nature: A Study in Phenomenology
and Environmental Philosophy*. Hampshire, U.K.: Palgrave Macmillan.

Jemisin, N. K. 2018. "An Apocalypse Is a Relative Thing: An
Interview with N. K. Jemisin." *ASAP/Journal* 3, no. 3: 467–77.

Johnson, Andrew Tyler. 2015. "A Critique of the Husserlian and
Heideggerian Concepts of Earth: Toward a Transcendental Earth
That Accords with the Experience of Life." *Journal of the British
Society for Phenomenology* 45, no. 3: 220–38.

Johnson, Galen. 2010. *The Retrieval of the Beautiful*. Evanston, Ill.:
Northwestern University Press.

Jones, Ben. 2017. "The Challenges of Ideal Theory and the Appeal of
Secular Apocalyptic Thought." *European Journal of Political Theory*.

Jung, Carl. 1973. *Synchronicity: A Causal Connecting Principle*. Princeton,
N.J.: Princeton University Press.

Kant, Immanuel. (1790) 1987. *The Critique of Judgment*. Translated by
Werner S. Pluhar. Indianapolis, Ind.: Hackett.

Kant, Immanuel. 1996. "The End of All Things." In *Religion and
Rational Theology*, translated by Allen W. Wood and George
di Giovanni, 219–31. Cambridge: Cambridge University Press.

Kant, Immanuel. (1764) 2007. "Observations on the Sublime and
the Beautiful." In *Anthropology, History, and Education*, edited

by Robert B. Louden and Günter Zöller, 18–62. Cambridge: Cambridge University Press.

Katz, Eric. 2000. "The Big Lie: The Human Restoration of Nature." In *Environmental Restoration: Ethics, Theory, and Practice*, edited by William Throop, 83–93. Amherst, N.Y.: Humanity Books.

Kear, Jonathan. 2002. "Le sang Provençal: Joachim Gasquet's Cézanne." *Journal of European Studies* 32: 135–50.

Kearney, Richard. 2011. "What Is Diacritical Hermeneutics?" *Journal of Applied Hermeneutics*, December. https://doi.org/10.11575/jah.v0i0.53187.

Kearney, Richard. 2013. "Écrire la chair: L'Expression diacritique chez Merleau-Ponty." *Chiasmi International* 15: 183–96.

Kearney, Richard. 2015. "The Wager of Carnal Hermeneutics." In *Carnal Hermeneutics*, edited by Richard Kearney and Brian Treanor, 15–56. New York: Fordham University Press.

Killingsworth, M. Jimmie, and Jacqueline S. Palmer. 1996. "Millennial Ecology: The Apocalyptic Narrative from Silent Spring to Global Warming." In *Green Culture: Environmental Rhetoric in Contemporary America*, edited by Carl G. Herndl and Stuart C. Brown, 21–45. Madison: University of Wisconsin Press.

Klein, Naomi. 2007. *The Shock Doctrine: The Rise of Disaster Capitalism.* New York: Henry Holt.

Klein, Naomi. 2014. *This Changes Everything: Capitalism vs. the Climate.* New York: Simon and Schuster.

Koffka, Kurt. 1935. *Principles of Gestalt Psychology.* New York: Harcourt, Brace, and World.

Köhler, Wolfgang. 1947. *Gestalt Psychology.* New York: Liveright.

Koricheva, Julia, and Helena Siipi. 2004. "The Phenomenon of Biodiversity." In *Philosophy and Biodiversity*, edited by Marrku Oksanen and Juhani Pietarinen, 27–53. Cambridge: Cambridge University Press.

Krug, Andrew Z., and David Jablonski. 2012. "Long-Term Origination Rates Are Reset Only at Mass Extinctions." *Geology* 40, no. 8: 731–34. https://doi.org/10.1130/G33091.1.

Landes, Donald. 2013. *Merleau-Ponty and the Paradoxes of Expression.* London: Bloomsbury.

Latour, Bruno. 2011. "Love Your Monsters: Why We Must Care for Our Technologies as We Do Our Children." *Breakthrough Journal* 2 (Fall): 21–28.

306 Bibliography

Lawlor, Leonard. 2002. *Derrida and Husserl: The Basic Problem of Phenomenology.* Bloomington: Indiana University Press.

Lawlor, Leonard. 2003. *The Challenge of Bergsonism.* London: Continuum.

Lawlor, Leonard. 2007. *This Is Not Sufficient: An Essay on Animality and Human Nature in Derrida.* New York: Columbia University Press.

Lawlor, Leonard. 2009a. "Auto-affection and Becoming (Part I): Who Are We?" *Environmental Philosophy* 6, no. 1: 1–19.

Lawlor, Leonard. 2009b. "Becoming and Auto-affection, Part 2: Who Are We?" *Graduate Faculty Philosophy Journal* 30, no. 2: 219–37.

Leach, Jeremy, and John Fitch. 1995. "Nature, Music, and Algorithmic Composition." *Computer Music Journal* 19, no. 2: 23–33.

Leopold, Aldo. 1968. *A Sand County Almanac.* London: Oxford University Press.

Levinas, Emmanuel. 1947. *De l'existence à l'existant.* Paris: Fontaine.

Levinas, Emmanuel. 1969. *Totality and Infinity.* Translated by Alphonso Lingis. Pittsburgh, Pa.: Duquesne University Press.

Levinas, Emmanuel. 1971. *Totalité et infini.* 4th ed. The Hague: Martinus Nijhoff.

Levinas, Emmanuel. 1990. "Simulacra: The End of the World." Translated by David Allison. In *Writing the Future,* edited by David Wood, 11–14. London: Routledge.

Levinas, Emmanuel. 2001. *Existence and Existents.* Translated by Alphonso Lingis. Pittsburgh, Pa.: Duquesne University Press.

Lévi-Strauss, Claude. 1976. *Structural Anthropology.* Vol. 2. Translated by Monique Layton. Chicago: University of Chicago Press.

Lévi-Strauss, Claude. 1983. *The Raw and the Cooked.* Translated by John Weightman and Doreen Weightman. Chicago: University of Chicago Press.

Lévi-Strauss, Claude. 2006. "On Merleau-Ponty." Translated by Christine Gross. In *Merleau-Ponty: Critical Assessments,* vol. 1, edited by Ted Toadvine, 215–20. London: Routledge.

Lewontin, Richard. 2000. *The Triple Helix: Gene, Organism, and Environment.* Cambridge, Mass.: Harvard University Press.

Lindauer, Martin. 1971. *Communication among Social Bees.* 2nd ed. Cambridge, Mass.: Harvard University Press.

Llewelyn, John. 2004. *Seeing through God: A Geophenomenology.* Bloomington: Indiana University Press.

Longrich, Nicholas. 2019. "Were Other Humans the First Victims of the Sixth Mass Extinction?" *The Conversation,* November 21.

https://theconversation.com/were-other-humans-the-first-victims -of-the-sixth-mass-extinction-126638.

Maclaurin, James, and Kim Sterelny. 2008. *What Is Biodiversity?* Chicago: University of Chicago Press.

Madison, Gary Brent. 1981. *The Phenomenology of Merleau-Ponty.* Athens: Ohio University Press.

Maeterlinck, Maurice. 1905. *La vie des abeilles.* Paris: Bibliothèque Charpentier.

Maeterlinck, Maurice. 2006. *The Life of the Bee.* Translated by Alfred Sutro. Mineola, N.Y.: Dover.

Maier, Donald. 2012. *What's So Good about Biodiversity? A Call for Better Reasoning about Nature's Value.* Dordrecht, Netherlands: Springer.

Mayer, Jane. 2011. "Taking It to the Streets." *New Yorker,* November 28. http://www.newyorker.com/magazine/2011/11/28/taking-it-to-the -streets.

Mays, Wolfe. 1977. *Whitehead's Philosophy of Science and Metaphysics: An Introduction to His Thought.* The Hague: Martinus Nijhoff.

McKibben, Bill. 2003. *The End of Nature.* Rev. ed. London: Bloomsbury.

McNamara, Kenneth. 2011. *The Star-Crossed Stone.* Chicago: University of Chicago Press.

McNeill, William. 1999. "Life beyond the Organism: Animal Being in Heidegger's Freiburg Lectures, 1929–30." In *Animal Others: On Ethics, Ontology, and Animal Life,* edited by H. Peter Steeves, 197–248. Albany: State University of New York Press.

Meillassoux, Quentin. 2006. *Après la finitude.* Paris: Éditions du Seuil.

Meillassoux, Quentin. 2008. *After Finitude: An Essay on the Necessity of Contingency.* Translated by Ray Brassier. London: Continuum.

Merleau-Ponty, Maurice. 1942. *La structure du comportement.* Paris: Presses Universitaires de France.

Merleau-Ponty, Maurice. 1945. *Phénoménologie de la perception.* Reprinted, 2005; Paris: Gallimard.

Merleau-Ponty, Maurice. 1947. "Le primat de la perception et ses conséquences philosophiques." *Bulletin de la société française de philosophie* 49: 119–53.

Merleau-Ponty, Maurice. 1960. *Signes.* Paris: Gallimard.

Merleau-Ponty, Maurice. 1963. *The Structure of Behavior.* Translated by Alden Fisher. Boston: Beacon Press.

Merleau-Ponty, Maurice. 1964a. *L'Œil et l'esprit.* Paris: Gallimard.

308 *Bibliography*

Merleau-Ponty, Maurice. 1964b. *Signs*. Translated by Richard McCleary. Evanston, Ill.: Northwestern University Press.

Merleau-Ponty, Maurice. 1964c. *Le visible et l'invisible*. Paris: Gallimard.

Merleau-Ponty, Maurice. 1968a. *Résumés de cours, Collège de France 1952–1960*. Paris: Gallimard.

Merleau-Ponty, Maurice. 1968b. *The Visible and the Invisible*. Translated by Alphonso Lingis. Evanston, Ill.: Northwestern University Press.

Merleau-Ponty, Maurice. 1969. *La prose du monde*. Paris: Gallimard.

Merleau-Ponty, Maurice. 1973. *The Prose of the World*. Translated by John O'Neill. Evanston, Ill.: Northwestern University Press.

Merleau-Ponty, Maurice. 1988. "Themes from the Lectures at the Collège de France, 1952–1960." Translated by John O'Neill. In *In Praise of Philosophy and Other Essays*, 71–199. Evanston, Ill.: Northwestern University Press.

Merleau-Ponty, Maurice. 1995. *La nature, notes, cours du Collège de France*. Paris: Éditions du Seuil.

Merleau-Ponty, Maurice. 1996a. *Notes de cours, 1958–1961*. Paris: Gallimard.

Merleau-Ponty, Maurice. 1996b. *Sens et non-sens*. Paris: Gallimard.

Merleau-Ponty, Maurice. 1998. *Notes de cours sur "L'Origine de la géométrie" de Husserl*. Edited by Renaud Barbaras. Paris: Presses Universitaires de France.

Merleau-Ponty, Maurice. 2000. *Parcours deux 1951–1961*. Lagrasse, France: Verdier.

Merleau-Ponty, Maurice. 2001. "Two Unpublished Notes on Music." Translated by Leonard Lawlor. *Chiasmi International* 3: 17–18.

Merleau-Ponty, Maurice. 2002. *Husserl at the Limits of Phenomenology*. Edited by Leonard Lawlor, with Bettina Bergo. Evanston, Ill.: Northwestern University Press.

Merleau-Ponty, Maurice. 2003a. *L'Institution, la passivité*. Tours, France: Belin.

Merleau-Ponty, Maurice. 2003b. *Nature: Course Notes from the Collège de France*. Translated by Robert Vallier. Evanston, Ill.: Northwestern University Press.

Merleau-Ponty, Maurice. 2007. *The Merleau-Ponty Reader*. Edited by Ted Toadvine and Leonard Lawlor. Evanston, Ill.: Northwestern University Press.

Merleau-Ponty, Maurice. 2008. "La nature ou le monde du silence (pages d'introduction)." In *Maurice Merleau-Ponty,* edited by Emmanuel de Saint Aubert, 41–53. Paris: Hermann Éditeurs.

Merleau-Ponty, Maurice. 2010. *Institution and Passivity.* Translated by Leonard Lawlor and Heath Massey. Evanston, Ill.: Northwestern University Press.

Merleau-Ponty, Maurice. 2011. *Le monde sensible et le monde de l'expression.* Geneva: Mētis Presses.

Merleau-Ponty, Maurice. 2012. *Phenomenology of Perception.* Translated by Donald Landes. London: Routledge.

Merleau-Ponty, Maurice. 2020. *The Sensible World and the World of Expression.* Translated by Bryan Smyth. Evanston, Ill.: Northwestern University Press.

Merleau-Ponty, Maurice. 2022. *The Possibility of Philosophy.* Translated by Keith Whitmoyer. Evanston, Ill.: Northwestern University Press.

Midgley, Mary. 1995. *Beast and Man: The Roots of Human Nature.* Rev. ed. London: Routledge.

Midgley, Mary. 2003. *The Myths We Live By.* London: Routledge.

Mill, John Stuart. 1874. *Three Essays on Religion.* New York: Henry Holt.

Miller, Jerome. 2020. "Robust Evolution in Historical Time." *International Philosophical Quarterly* 60, no. 2: 153–72.

Mitchell, Sandra. 2009. *Unsimple Truths: Science, Complexity, and Policy.* Chicago: University of Chicago Press.

Moo, Jonathan. 2015. "Climate Change and the Apocalyptic Imagination: Science, Faith, and Ecological Responsibility." *Zygon* 50, no. 4: 937–48.

Mooney, Chris. 2014. "Finally, Neil deGrasse Tyson and 'Cosmos' Take on Climate Change." *Mother Jones,* May 5. http://www.motherjones.com/environment/2014/05/neil-tyson-cosmos-global-warming-earth-carbon.

Morar, Nicolae, Ted Toadvine, and Brendan Bohannan. 2015. "Biodiversity at Twenty-Five Years: Revolution or Red Herring?" *Ethics, Policy, and Environment* 18, no. 1: 16–29.

Morin, Marie-Eve. 2012. *Jean-Luc Nancy.* Cambridge: Polity Press.

Morris, David. 2005. "Animals and Humans, Thinking and Nature." *Phenomenology and the Cognitive Sciences* 4: 49–72.

Morris, David. 2018. *Merleau-Ponty's Developmental Ontology.* Evanston, Ill.: Northwestern University Press.

310 *Bibliography*

Naas, Michael. 2015. *The End of the World and Other Teachable Moments: Jacques Derrida's Final Seminar.* New York: Fordham University Press.

Naess, Arne. 1989. *Ecology, Community and Lifestyle.* Translated and edited by David Rothenberg. Cambridge: Cambridge University Press.

Nancy, Jean-Luc. 1990. *Une pensée finie.* Paris: Éditions Galilée.

Nancy, Jean-Luc. 1992. "L'Indestructible." *Cahiers Intersignes,* nos. 4–5: 237–49.

Nancy, Jean-Luc. 1993a. *The Birth to Presence.* Translated by Brian Holmes et al. Stanford, Calif.: Stanford University Press.

Nancy, Jean-Luc. 1993b. *Le sens du monde.* Paris: Éditions Galilée.

Nancy, Jean-Luc. 1994. *Les muses.* Paris: Éditions Galilée.

Nancy, Jean-Luc. 1996a. *Être singulier pluriel.* Paris: Éditions Galilée.

Nancy, Jean-Luc. 1996b. *The Muses.* Translated by Peggy Kamuf. Stanford, Calif.: Stanford University Press.

Nancy, Jean-Luc. 1997. *The Sense of the World.* Translated by Jeffrey Librett. Minneapolis: University of Minnesota Press.

Nancy, Jean-Luc. 2000a. *Being Singular Plural.* Translated by Robert Richardson and Anne O'Byrne. Stanford, Calif.: Stanford University Press.

Nancy, Jean-Luc. 2000b. *L'Intrus.* Paris: Éditions Galilée.

Nancy, Jean-Luc. 2002. *La création du monde ou la mondialisation.* Paris: Éditions Galilée.

Nancy, Jean-Luc. 2003a. *A Finite Thinking.* Edited by Simon Sparks. Stanford, Calif.: Stanford University Press.

Nancy, Jean-Luc. 2003b. *Noli me tangere.* Paris: Bayard.

Nancy, Jean-Luc. 2007. *The Creation of the World or Globalization.* Translated by François Raffoul and David Pettigrew. Albany: State University of New York Press.

Nancy, Jean-Luc. 2008a. *Corpus.* Bilingual ed. Translated by Richard Rand. New York: Fordham University Press.

Nancy, Jean-Luc. 2008b. *Noli me tangere: On the Raising of the Body.* Translated by Sarah Clift, Pascale-Anne Brault, and Michael Naas. New York: Fordham University Press.

Nancy, Jean-Luc. 2012. *L'Équivalence des catastrophes (Après Fukushima).* Paris: Éditions Galilée.

Nancy, Jean-Luc. 2015. *After Fukushima: The Equivalence of Catastrophes.* Translated by Charlotte Mandell. New York: Fordham University Press.

Nancy, Jean-Luc. 2017. *The Possibility of a World: Conversations with Pierre-Philippe Jandin*. Translated by Travis Holloway and Flor Méchain. New York: Fordham University Press.

Nancy, Jean-Luc, and Marcia Sá Cavalcante Schuback, eds. 2013. *Being with the Without*. Stockholm: Axl Books.

Nelson, Stephanie. 1998. *God and the Land: The Metaphysics of Farming in Hesiod and Vergil*. New York: Oxford University Press.

Nieh, James. 1993. "The Stop Signal of Honey Bees: Reconsidering Its Message." *Behavioral Ecology and Sociobiology* 33: 51–56.

Nordhaus, Ted, and Michael Shellenberger. 2007. *Break Through: From the Death of Environmentalism to the Politics of Possibility*. Boston: Houghton Mifflin Harcourt.

Norton, Bryan. 2008. "Biodiversity: Its Meaning and Value." In *A Companion to the Philosophy of Biology*, edited by Sahotra Sarkar and Anya Plutynski, 368–89. Malden, Mass.: Blackwell.

O'Byrne, Anne. 2002. "The Politics of Intrusion." *New Centennial Review* 2, no. 3: 169–87.

O'Byrne, Anne. 2012. "Nancy's Materialist Ontology." In *Jean-Luc Nancy and Plural Thinking: Expositions of World, Ontology, Politics, and Sense*, edited by Peter Gratton and Marie-Eve Morin, 79–93. Albany: State University of New York Press.

Oliver, Kelly. 2009. *Animal Lessons: How They Teach Us to Be Human*. New York: Columbia University Press.

Oliver, Kelly. 2015. *Earth and World: Philosophy after the Apollo Missions*. New York: Columbia University Press.

Pascal, Blaise. 2004. *Pensées*. Translated by Roger Ariew. Indianapolis, Ind.: Hackett.

PBS. 2018. "Climate Change Is 'Most Important Issue We Face,' UN Chief Says." December 3. https://www.pbs.org/newshour/world/climate-change-is-most-important-issue-we-face-un-chief-says.

Peterson, Michael. 2018. "Responsibility and the Non(bio)degradable." In *Eco-deconstruction: Derrida and Environmental Philosophy*, edited by Matthias Fritsch, Philippe Lynes, and David Wood, 249–60. New York: Fordham University Press.

Plath, Sylvia. 1965. *Ariel*. New York: Harper and Row.

Plato. 1961. *The Collected Dialogues of Plato*. Edited by E. Hamilton and H. Cairns. New York: Random House.

Playfair, John. 1822. "Biographical Account of the Late James Hutton, M.D." In *The Works of John Playfair*, vol. 4. Edinburgh: Archibald

Constable. Reprinted from *Transactions of the Royal Society of Edinburgh* 5 (1805): 71–73.

Rádl, Emanuel. 1903. *Untersuchungen über den Phototropismus der Tiere.* Leipzig, Germany: Wilhelm Engelmann.

Ricoeur, Paul. 1967. *Husserl: An Analysis of His Phenomenology.* Translated by Edward Ballard and Lester Embree. Evanston, Ill.: Northwestern University Press.

Rilke, Ranier Maria. 1989. *Duino Elegies.* Bilingual ed. Translated by Stephen Cohn. Evanston, Ill.: Northwestern University Press.

Rogozinski, Jacob. 2008. "The Chiasm and the Remainder (How Does Touching Touch Itself?)." In *Rethinking Facticity,* edited by François Raffoul and Eric Sean Nelson, 229–52. Albany: State University of New York Press.

Rolston, Holmes, III. 1988. *Environmental Ethics: Duties to and Values in the Natural World.* Philadelphia: Temple University Press.

Rolston, Holmes, III. 2000. "Restoration." In *Environmental Restoration: Ethics, Theory, and Practice,* edited by William Throop, 127–32. Amherst, N.Y.: Humanity Books.

Roy, Jean-Michel, Jean Petitot, Francisco J. Varela, and Bernard Pachoud. 1999. "Beyond the Gap: An Introduction to Naturalizing Phenomenology." In *Naturalizing Phenomenology: Issues in Contemporary Phenomenology and Cognitive Science,* edited by Jean Petitot, Francisco J. Varela, Bernard Pachoud, and Jean-Michel Roy, 1–80. Stanford, Calif.: Stanford University Press.

Rudwick, Martin. 2014. *Earth's Deep History: How It Was Discovered and Why It Matters.* Chicago: University of Chicago Press.

Sallis, John. 1994. *Stone.* Bloomington: Indiana University Press.

Sallis, John. 1998. "Levinas and the Elemental." *Research in Phenomenology* 28, no. 1: 152–59.

Sallis, John. 2000. *Force of Imagination: The Sense of the Elemental.* Bloomington: Indiana University Press.

Sallis, John. 2012. *Logic of Imagination: The Expanse of the Elemental.* Bloomington: Indiana University Press.

Sartre, Jean-Paul. 1943. *L'Être et le néant.* Paris: Gallimard.

Sartre, Jean-Paul. 1965. *Situations.* Translated by Benita Eisler. New York: George Braziller.

Sartre, Jean-Paul. 1990. *Situations philosophiques.* Paris: Gallimard.

Sartre, Jean-Paul. 1994. *Being and Nothingness.* Translated by Hazel Barnes. Avenel, N.J.: Gramercy Books.

Scheler, Max. 1949. *Die Stellung des Menschen im Kosmos.* Munich, Germany: Nymphenburger.

Scheler, Max. 1954. *The Nature of Sympathy.* Translated by P. Heath. London: Routledge and Kegan Paul.

Scheler, Max. 2009. *The Human Place in the Cosmos.* Translated by M. Frings. Evanston, Ill.: Northwestern University Press.

Serres, Michel. 2003. *L'Incandescent.* Paris: Éditions Le Pommier.

Serres, Michel. 2018. *The Incandescent.* Translated by Randolph Burks. London: Bloomsbury.

Serres, Michel, and Bruno Latour. 1995. *Conversations on Science, Culture, and Time.* Translated by Roxanne Lapidus. Ann Arbor: University of Michigan Press.

Shelley, Mary. 1998. *The Last Man.* Edited by Morton D. Paley. Oxford: Oxford Paperbacks.

Skrimshire, Stefan, ed. 2010. *Future Ethics: Climate Change and Apocalyptic Imagination.* London: Continuum.

Skrimshire, Stefan. 2014. "Climate Change and Apocalyptic Faith." *WIREs Climate Change* 5, no. 2: 233–46.

Skrimshire, Stefan. 2017. "Anthropocene Fever: Memory and the Planetary Archive." In *Religion in the Anthropocene,* edited by Celia Deane-Drummond, Sigurd Bergmann, and Markus Vogt, 138–54. Eugene, Oreg.: Cascade Books.

Skrimshire, Stefan. 2018. "Confessing Anthropocene." *Environmental Humanities* 10, no. 1: 310–29.

Snyder, Gary. 1990. *The Practice of the Wild.* San Francisco: North Point Press.

Sober, Elliott. 2005. "Comparative Psychology Meets Evolutionary Biology: Morgan's Canon and Cladistic Parsimony." In *Thinking with Animals: New Perspectives on Anthropomorphism,* edited by Lorraine Daston and Gregg Mitman, 85–99. New York: Columbia University Press.

Solomon, Susan, Gian-Kasper Plattner, Reto Knutti, and Pierre Friedlingstein. 2009. "Irreversible Climate Change due to Carbon Dioxide Emissions." *Proceedings of the National Academy of Sciences of the United States of America* 106, no. 6: 1704–9.

Soulé, Michael E., and Gary Lease, eds. 1995. *Reinventing Nature? Responses to Postmodern Deconstruction.* Washington, D.C.: Island Press.

Srivastava, Diane, and Mark Vellend. 2005. "Biodiversity–Ecosystem

Function Research: Is It Relevant to Conservation?" *Annual Review of Ecology, Evolution, and Systematics* 36: 267–94.

Steedman, Carolyn. 2002. *Dust: The Archive and Cultural History.* New Brunswick, N.J.: Rutgers University Press.

Stengers, Isabelle. 2009. "Toward a Speculative Approach to Biological Evolution." Translated by Taylor Hammer. *Environmental Philosophy* 6, no. 1: 77–112.

Swammerdam, Jan. 1737. *Bybel der Natuure, of Historie der Insecten/Biblia Naturae; sive Historia Insectorum.* Edited by Herman Boerhaave, with facing-page translation into Latin by Hieronimus David Gaubius. Leiden, Netherlands: Isaak Severinus, Boudewyn vander Aa, and Pieter vander Aa.

Swammerdam, Jan. 1758. *The Book of Nature; or, The History of Insects.* Translated by Thomas Floyd. Revised with notes by John Hill. London: C. G. Seyffert.

Szerszynski, Bronislaw. 2012. "The End of the End of Nature: The Anthropocene and the Fate of the Human." *Oxford Literary Review* 34, no. 2: 165–84.

Szerszynski, Bronislaw. 2017. "The Anthropocene Monument: On Relating Geological and Human Time." *European Journal of Social Theory* 20, no. 1: 111–31.

Takacs, David. 1996. *The Idea of Biodiversity: Philosophies of Paradise.* Baltimore: The Johns Hopkins University Press.

Thompson, Allen. 2009. "Responsibility for the End of Nature; or, How I Learned to Stop Worrying and Love Global Warming." *Ethics and the Environment* 14, no. 1: 79–99.

Tilley, Christopher. 2004. *The Materiality of Stone: Explorations in Landscape Phenomenology.* Oxford: Berg.

Tilman, David. 2012. "Biodiversity and Environmental Sustainability amid Human Domination of Global Ecosystems." *Daedalus* 141, no. 3: 108–20.

Toadvine, Ted. 2008. "The Reconversion of Silence and Speech." *Tijdschrift voor Filosofie* 70: 457–77.

Toadvine, Ted. 2009. *Merleau-Ponty's Philosophy of Nature.* Evanston, Ill.: Northwestern University Press.

Toadvine, Ted. 2011. "The Chiasm." In *Routledge Companion to Phenomenology,* edited by Sebastian Luft and Søren Overgaard, 336–47. London: Routledge.

Toadvine, Ted. 2017a. "Naturalism, Estrangement, and Resistance: On the Lived Senses of Nature." In *Ontologies of Nature: Continental Perspectives and Environmental Reorientations,* edited by Gerard Kuperus and Marjolein Oele, 181–98. Cham, Switzerland: Springer International.

Toadvine, Ted. 2017b. "Phenomenology and Environmental Ethics." In *Oxford Handbook of Environmental Ethics,* edited by Stephen Gardiner and Allen Thompson, 174–85. Oxford: Oxford University Press.

Toadvine, Ted. 2020. "Geomateriality." In *50 Concepts for a Critical Phenomenology,* edited by Gail Weiss, Ann V. Murphy, and Gayle Salamon, 149–54. Evanston, Ill.: Northwestern University Press.

Uexküll, Jakob von. 1926. *Theoretical Biology.* Translated by D. L. Mackinnon. New York: Harcourt, Brace.

Uexküll, Jakob von. 1956. *Streifzüge durch die Umwelten von Tieren und Menschen.* Hamburg, Germany: Rowohlt Taschenbuch.

Uexküll, Jakob von. 2010. *A Foray into the Worlds of Animals and Humans.* Translated by Joseph O'Neil. Minneapolis: University of Minnesota Press.

United Nations. n.d. "Climate Change." https://web.archive.org/web/20190525005813/https://www.un.org/en/sections/issues-depth/climate-change/.

Valéry, Paul. 1971. *Poems.* Translated by David Paul. The Collected Works of Paul Valéry 1. London: Routledge and Kegan Paul.

van Dooren, Thom. 2014. *Flight Ways: Life and Loss at the Edge of Extinction.* New York: Columbia University Press.

Virgil. 1916. *Virgil.* Vol. 1. Translated by H. Rushton Fairclough. New York: G. P. Putnam's.

Vogel, Steven. 2015. *Thinking Like a Mall: Environmental Philosophy after the End of Nature.* Cambridge, Mass.: MIT Press.

von Frisch, Karl. 1950. *Bees: Their Vision, Chemical Senses, and Language.* Ithaca, N.Y.: Cornell University Press.

von Frisch, Karl. 1993. *The Dance Language and Orientation of Bees.* Translated by L. Chadwick. Cambridge, Mass.: Harvard University Press.

von Haller, Albrecht. 2002. "Unvollkommenes Gedicht über die Ewigkeit/Uncompleted Poem on Eternity." Translated by Arnulf Zweig. *Philosophical Forum* 33, no. 3: 304–11.

Vrahimis, Andreas. 2012. "Was There a Sun before Men Existed? A. J. Ayer and French Philosophy in the Fifties." *Journal for the History of Analytical Philosophy* 1, no. 9.

Wagar, W. Warren. 1982. *Terminal Visions: The Literature of Last Things.* Bloomington: Indiana University Press.

Weiss, Madeline C., Filipa L. Sousa, Natalia Mrnjavac, Sinje Neukirchen, Mayo Roettger, Shijulal Nelson-Sathi, and William F. Martin. 2016. "The Physiology and Habitat of the Last Universal Common Ancestor." *Nature Microbiology* 1, no. 16116.

Welton, Donn. 2003. "World as Horizon." In *The New Husserl: A Critical Reader,* edited by Donn Welton, 223–32. Bloomington: Indiana University Press.

Whitehead, Alfred North. 1938. *Modes of Thought.* New York: Macmillan.

Whitehead, Alfred North. 2004. *The Concept of Nature.* Mineola, N.Y.: Dover.

Whyte, Kyle Powys. 2018. "Indigenous Science (Fiction) for the Anthropocene: Ancestral Dystopias and Fantasies of Climate Change Crises." *Environment and Planning E: Nature and Space* 1, no. 1–2: 224–42.

Williams, George C. 1992. *Natural Selection: Domains, Levels, and Challenges.* Oxford: Oxford University Press.

Wilson, Edward O. 1975. *Sociobiology: The New Synthesis.* Cambridge, Mass.: Belknap Press.

Wilson, Edward O. 1998. *Consilience: The Unity of Knowledge.* New York: Alfred Knopf.

Wolfe, Cary. 2009. "On a Certain Blindness in Human Beings." In *The Death of the Animal: A Dialogue,* by Paola Cavalieri, 123–33. New York: Columbia University Press.

Wood, David. 2003. "What Is Eco-phenomenology?" In *Eco-phenomenology: Back to the Earth Itself,* edited by Charles Brown and Ted Toadvine, 211–33. Albany: State University of New York Press.

Wood, David. 2004. "Thinking with Cats." In *Animal Philosophy: Ethics and Identity,* edited by Peter Atterton and Matthew Calarco, 129–44. London: Continuum.

Wood, David. 2006. "On the Way to Econstruction." *Environmental Philosophy* 3: 35–46.

Wood, David. 2007. *Time after Time.* Bloomington: Indiana University Press.

Wood, David. 2017. "Temporal Phronesis in the Anthropocene." *Research in Phenomenology* 47, no. 2: 220–27.

World Bank. 2018. "Nearly Half the World Lives on Less than $5.50 a Day." October 17. https://www.worldbank.org/en/news/press-release/2018/10/17/nearly-half-the-world-lives-on-less-than-550-a-day.

Worster, Donald. 1977. *Nature's Economy: A History of Ecological Ideas.* Cambridge: Cambridge University Press.

Worster, Donald. 1993. *The Wealth of Nature: Environmental History and the Ecological Imagination.* Oxford: Oxford University Press.

Zahavi, Dan. 2016. "The End of What? Phenomenology vs. Speculative Realism." *International Journal of Philosophical Studies* 24, no. 3: 289–309.

Zalasiewicz, Jan. 2017. "The Extraordinary Strata of the Anthropocene." In *Environmental Humanities: Voices from the Anthropocene,* edited by Serpil Oppermann and Serenella Iovino, 115–31. London: Rowman and Littlefield.

Publication History

Previous versions of the chapters in this book were published in the following publications.

Portions of chapter 1 are adapted from "Natural Time and Immemorial Nature," *Philosophy Today* 53, SPEP Suppl. (2009): 214–21, https://doi.org/10.5840/philtoday200953Supplement46.

Portions of chapter 2 are adapted from "The Elemental Past," *Research in Phenomenology* 44, no. 2 (2014): 262–79, https://doi.org/10.1163/15691640-12341288; reprinted with permission of Brill; permission conveyed through Copyright Clearance Center, Inc.

Portions of chapter 4 are adapted from "Life beyond Biologism," *Research in Phenomenology* 40, no. 2 (2010): 243–66, https://doi.org/10.1163/156916410X509940; reprinted with permission of Brill; permission conveyed through Copyright Clearance Center, Inc.

Portions of chapter 5 are adapted from "The Entomological Difference: On the Intuitions of Hymenoptera," *Poligrafi: Journal for Interdisciplinary Study of Religion* 16, no. 61–62 (2011): 185–214.

Portions of chapter 6 are adapted from "The Time of Animal Voices," *Environmental Philosophy* 11, no. 1 (2014): 109–24, https://doi.org/10.5840/envirophil20142241.

Portions of chapter 7 are adapted from "Biodiversity and the Diacritics of Life," in *Carnal Hermeneutics*, edited by Richard Kearney and Brian Treanor, 235–48 (New York: Fordham University Press, 2015), https://doi.org/10.1515/9780823265916-016.

Portions of chapter 8 are adapted from "Apocalyptic Imagination and the Silence of the Elements," in *Ecopsychology, Phenomenology, and the Environment: The Experience of Nature,* edited by Douglas A. Vakoch and Fernando Castrillón, 211–21 (New York: Springer, 2014).

Portions of chapter 8 are adapted from "Nature's Wandering Hands: Painting at the End of the World," *Klēsis: Revue Philosophique* 25 (2013): 109–23.

Portions of chapter 9 are adapted from "Thinking after the World: Deconstruction and Last Things," in *Eco-Deconstruction: Derrida and*

Environmental Philosophy, edited by Matthias Fritsch, Philippe Lynes, and David Wood, 21–47 (New York: Fordham University Press, 2018); reprinted with permission of Fordham University Press; permission conveyed through Copyright Clearance Center, Inc.

Portions of chapter 10 are adapted from "Climate Collapse, Judgment Day, and the Temporal Sublime," *Puncta: Journal of Critical Phenomenology* 4, no. 2 (2021): 127–43.

Portions of chapter 10 are adapted from "Climate Apocalypticism and the Temporal Sublime," in *Environmental Ethics: Cross-Cultural Explorations,* edited by Monika Kirloskar-Steinbach and Mădălina Diaconu, 115–31 (Freiburg, Germany: Karl Alber, 2020).

Portions of chapter 11 are adapted from "Ecophenomenology after the End of Nature," in *Transforming Politics with Merleau-Ponty: Thinking beyond the State,* edited by Jérôme Melançon, 127–44 (Lanham, Md.: Rowman and Littlefield, 2021); reprinted with permission of Rowman & Littlefield Publishing Group, Inc.; permission conveyed through Copyright Clearance Center, Inc.

Portions of chapter 11 are adapted from "Anthropocene Time and the Memory of the World," *Chiasmi International* 24 (2022): 171–90.

Index

Abram, David, 186

Agamben, Giorgio, 20, 65, 97, 137, 139, 140–41, 155

Alloa, Emmanuel, 158

Al-Saji, Alia, 148

alteraffection, 19, 22, 25, 66, 83, 87, 91–92, 101–3, 106, 107, 108, 150, 155–56, 179, 196, 212–13

Ambrosino, Georges, 43

Anders, Günther, 215–16

animal: becoming-, 19, 20, 69, 112–13, 120, 134–35, 139, 145, 148–50; human relation with non-human, 19–20, 71, 73, 87–109, 113–14, 124–30, 133, 137–51, 224, 226, 275; poverty in world of, 19, 93–94, 101, 103, 113, 122–23, 126, 127, 134, 227. *See also* animality; bees; insects

animality, 123; as dimension of humans, 19–20, 58–59, 73, 137–51, 166; inter-, 6, 19; phenomenology of, 7, 19–20, 137–39, 141, 144, 155–56

Anning, Mary, 1, 2, 4

Anthropocene, 6, 7, 8–13, 24, 242, 250, 258–60, 261, 265, 268, 270, 271, 278, 279, 280, 281n1 (chap. 1)

anthropocentrism, 7, 10, 45, 87–88, 94, 97, 107, 198

apocalypse, 52, 176, 196, 216, 217, 218, 234; climate change as, 235–40, 242–48, 250, 253–55; fantasies of environmental, 6, 7, 11, 21, 206–8, 239, 250 (*see also* eco-eschatology); impossible future as, 46, 60; phenomenology and, 21, 178–79, 211–13; religion and, 242–45, 247–48; speculative fiction and,

201–8; time and, 23–24, 245–55, 279. *See also* eco-eschatology; world: end of the

Aristotle, 55, 64, 112, 113–14, 117

art, 21–22, 107–8, 109, 133–34, 167, 179–89, 191, 192, 193–94, 253–55. *See also* music; painting

atomic bomb, 9. *See also* nuclear; war

Attenborough, David, 235

Atwood, Margaret, 153

Augustine, 29, 41

autoaffection, 19, 20, 22, 25, 30, 47, 77, 87, 90, 91, 98, 100–102, 106, 108, 149, 155–56, 163, 179, 192–93, 195–96, 212–13, 217. *See also* sensible–sentient relation

Ayer, A. J., 17, 43–44, 47, 49

Bachelard, Gaston, 21, 175–76, 178, 183, 185, 187, 192, 194

Bacon, Francis, 183, 184

Baldwin, Thomas, 45, 46–47, 49, 52

Ballard, J. G., 153

Barbaras, Renaud, 30, 72, 76

Baskin, Jeremy, 8, 13, 259

Bataille, Georges, 17, 43–44, 47, 49, 59

bees, 19–20, 111–36, 264; communication of, 113–14, 129–33; hive in comparison with human society, 111–14; world of, 19, 113, 121–30, 132

Benjamin, Andrew, 238

Bennington, Geoffrey, 290n18

Bergson, Henri, 13, 19, 29, 41, 106, 112, 116–20, 125, 126, 134–35, 170, 255

Berry, Wendell, 252

biodiacritics, 7, 21, 157–59, 163–71, 275–76

322 *Index*

biodiversity, 6, 7, 20–21, 156–57, 167–69, 201, 274–75
biologism, 91, 92–98, 100, 102, 103
biologistic continuism, 19, 89, 90–91, 95–98, 100, 104
biology. *See* science: biology
biosemiotics, 65
Boethius, 64
Boetzkes, Amanda, 193
Brannen, Peter, 10
Brazil, Rachel, 10
Brunschvicg, Léon, 48
Buell, Frederick, 244–45
Buffon, Georges, 231
built environment, 24, 261–68, 292n3
Buytendijk, Frederik, 137

Calarco, Matthew, 87–88, 89, 90, 95, 96, 104
Callicott, J. Baird, 88, 263
Callison, Candis, 250
capitalism, 12–13, 213, 215, 216, 244–45, 250, 260
Carson, Rachel, 153, 201, 241, 243, 248, 257
Celan, Paul, 220–22, 224–25
Cézanne, Paul, 21, 179–88, 192, 193
Chakrabarty, Dipesh, 11–13, 15–16, 24–25, 260–61, 270–74, 277–80
chiasm, 20, 22, 53, 54, 76–78, 82, 139–40, 145, 179, 182, 192–93, 195, 197, 279, 282n5 (chap. 2)
Claudel, Paul, 17, 32, 38–40, 42, 49, 62, 63, 64
Clements, Frederic, 165
climate change, 5, 6, 9, 11, 13, 23, 153, 155, 177, 201, 202, 203, 204, 214, 235–40, 242–47, 250–55, 257, 259, 260, 265; economic discount rates and, 205, 216
Cohen, Jeffrey, 228, 230
Colebrook, Claire, 10, 237
Collings, David, 237–38
colonialism, 8, 12, 153, 236, 250, 253, 270
Copernicus, Nicolaus, 47

correlationism, 13–15, 18, 30–31, 45, 49, 51–52, 53–54, 56, 60, 78, 187, 189, 198, 230, 269, 272, 279
Cowles, Henry, 165
Crutzen, Paul, 11, 259
Cuvier, Georges, 204, 241

Darwin, Charles, 88, 89, 90, 99, 104, 111, 130, 138, 166, 167
Dawkins, Richard, 89, 104, 275
death, 16, 33, 34, 60, 62, 101–3, 115, 139, 144, 178, 185–86, 189, 231, 232, 242, 276; as end of the world, 22, 171, 219–29; life and, 19, 91, 102, 107, 154–56, 158, 170–71, 186, 187, 199, 207, 212, 223, 227, 228–29, 232
deconstruction, 6, 206–7, 209, 212–14, 289n13; eco-, 208
deep time: Anthropocene and, 10–13, 270–80; apocalyptic narratives and, 239–42; cosmic, 7, 273, 277; distinct rhythms of, 53; elements and, 189–90, 231–32; evolutionary, 4, 7, 15, 16–17, 24, 260, 273, 275–76; future and, 5, 8, 11, 18, 23, 25, 42, 203–6, 231, 241, 249, 251–52; geological, 4, 7, 9, 16–17, 23, 24, 49–53, 149, 239, 246, 251, 257, 260, 271, 273, 277, 279; as historical, 273–74; human history and, 12–13, 24, 46, 259–61, 270–80; human lived time and, 4, 5, 6, 11, 13, 15–17, 52–53, 56, 206, 251–55, 272, 273, 277; phenomenology of, 5–7, 13, 15–18, 21, 25, 44, 46, 54–60, 279–80; present and, 198–99, 206, 251–55; scientific discovery of, 4–5, 49–53, 241; stone and, 231–32
Deleuze, Gilles, 20, 69, 106, 108, 134–35, 139, 145, 148–49, 183, 184, 188
Derrida, Jacques, 209, 213, 271, 278; death, 102, 155, 171, 207, 212, 219–28; end of the world, 22–23, 171, 202, 207, 212–14, 219–28, 242; fossils, 4; hetero-affection, 91, 101; human–animal relation, 19,

89–97, 100–101, 104–5, 109, 112, 127, 135, 224, 226, 228–29; life, 228; Merleau-Ponty and, 22, 47–48, 179, 195–96
Descartes, René, 88, 138
desire, 91, 103, 106, 119, 135, 149
de Waal, Frans, 89, 104, 138
diacritical difference, 80–81, 157–65, 168–70, 275–77. *See also* biodiacritics

earth, 189, 222, 226, 228: age of, 51–52; art, 193; as future ruins, 237; -ground, 47, 278; Heidegger on, 15, 63, 271–72, 278; Husserl on, 15, 47, 48, 271–72, 277–80; as not moving, 48–49; phenomenology of, 15–16, 22, 24–25, 47–49, 53, 261, 271–72, 277–80; planet distinct from, 16, 24–25, 270–72; strangeness of, 183, 190; transcendental, 47, 56, 278; unity of, 8, 278
Earth: planetary perspective on, 5, 12–13, 15–16, 24–25, 203, 208, 258–59, 260–61, 270–72, 277–78, 279–80; systems, 8, 16, 258; system science, 11, 16, 260, 270–71, 279, 280
écart, 18, 66, 77–78, 82, 91, 99–103, 146, 151, 163, 192, 195
eco-eschatology, 8, 23, 154, 202–3, 205–6, 208, 212, 230, 232–33, 280. *See also* apocalypse: fantasies of environmental
ecology. *See* science: ecology
ecotechnical, 22, 206, 213–19, 248, 249, 262, 289n11
Ehrlich, Paul, 243
elementals, 56, 190–91
elements, 46, 175, 176, 183, 186–88, 190–91, 193, 199, 206, 207, 210, 226–34, 240, 261, 269, 272; Levinas on, 18, 22, 59–60, 179, 183, 187, 188–91; worldlessness of, 59–60, 188–91, 227. *See also* materiality: geo-
Ellsworth, Elizabeth, 258

enslavement, 250
environmentalism, 6, 8, 11, 20, 88, 156, 159, 201–6, 213–14, 239, 242–45, 248, 250, 257, 260, 262, 263, 265, 266
environmental justice, 236, 243
eternity, 21, 60, 175, 180, 184–85, 198, 240–41, 246, 248
ethics: animal kinship and, 138; bees and, 111; biodiversity and, 156–57; climate change and, 177–78; end of the world and, 22, 203, 208, 220, 221–23; environmental, 159, 263; future generations and, 204–5, 232, 248; geomateriality and, 258; of human entanglement in temporal scales, 5, 248–55, 257, 280; land, 165; music and, 81–82; nature as guide for, 262, 265
evolution, 5, 7, 105–6, 108, 119, 154, 166, 169–70; as expressive, 105–7, 166–67; of eyes, 166, 169; and human–animal continuity, 87–90, 98, 99, 275; phenomenology and, 19, 92, 103; sexual selection in, 19, 91–92, 106–7, 149, 167. *See also* deep time: evolutionary; memory: evolutionary; time: evolutionary
expression, 73, 169: evolution as, 105–7, 166–67; mathematics as, 15. *See also* art; language; life: as expressive; Merleau-Ponty, Maurice: expression
extinction, 7, 9, 11, 20, 153–55, 169–71, 274, 276; human, 7, 52, 60, 153–54, 203–4, 243, 249, 251, 280; mass events of, 5, 257

Fink, Eugen, 208–9
Fiskio, Jay, 254
Fitch, John, 64
flesh, 108, 154, 184, 276. *See also* Merleau-Ponty, Maurice: flesh
fossils, 4, 61–62, 204, 232; ammonite, 1–4; arche-, 49, 51, 53, 56; collecting in Lyme Regis, 1–4; future human, 8, 9–10, 231, 257, 270, 280;

324 *Index*

phenomenology and, 18, 54–57, 59. *See also* science: paleontology
Foust, Christina, 245–46
Fritsch, Matthias, 291n23
Frost, Robert, 230
Fukushima nuclear accident, 22, 215, 249
future, 12, 17, 29, 39, 41, 60, 62, 87, 118, 153, 170, 176, 192, 206, 208, 212, 223, 231, 237, 240–41, 244, 247, 248, 254–55, 273, 277; climate change and, 237–39, 242; deep time and, 5, 8, 11, 18, 23, 25, 42, 203–6, 231, 241, 249, 251–52; economic discounting of, 205, 216; generations, 177–78, 204–5; impossible, 32, 46, 60, 61; as incommensurable, 198, 199; management of, 23–25, 198, 206, 207, 214, 216, 218, 239–40, 242, 249–50, 252–53, 257, 274, 279–80; ruins of, 237–39, 254; speculative projections of, 6–8, 10–11, 201–6; sustainability and, 198–99, 204–7, 214, 216, 218, 236; as unprecedented, 25, 217, 274, 276, 280. *See also* fossils: future human

Galileo, 14–15
Gasquet, Joachim, 179–81, 187, 288n3 (chap. 8)
general equivalence, 198–99, 206–7, 214, 215–18, 239, 248–55, 274, 276
geology. *See* science: geology
glaciers, 254–55
globalization, 12, 206, 213, 215, 260
Greenland Analogue Project, 205, 274
Greenpeace, 242
Griffin, Donald, 130–33
Gross, Lawrence, 250
Grosz, Elizabeth, 19, 91–92, 106–8, 149, 167, 170, 274
Guattari, Félix, 20, 69, 108, 134–35, 139, 145, 148–49

Hadot, Pierre, 63
Haraway, Donna, 276
Harman, Graham, 45

Hegel, G. W. F., 36, 93, 185
Heidegger, Martin, 60, 65, 209, 255; animals, 19, 90, 93–96, 98–99, 101, 104–5, 106, 112, 113, 122–30, 138, 141, 155; biologism, 92–96; earth, 15, 63, 271–72, 278; life, 98, 141, 163–64; stone, 55, 122, 133–34, 197–98, 227–30; time, 13, 48; world, 212, 220, 224, 227–30
Heraclitus, 63
Herr, Lucien, 36–37, 42, 185
Hettinger, Ned, 165
Holmes, Arthur, 52
Holocene, 5, 9
Homo heidelbergensis, 61
Horn, Roni, 24, 193, 240, 253–55
Horne, Gerald, 250
Hulme, Mike, 243–45
Human Interference Task Force, 176–77, 204–5
humanism, 91, 94–95, 218; post-, 65
humanity: animality of, 19–20, 58–59, 73, 137–51; Anthropocene and, 242, 258–61; climate change and, 236–37; construction of nature by, 260–69; geological scale of impacts, 5, 258; geomateriality of, 198, 251–52, 258, 280; nature displaced by, 258–60; as a species, 7, 12–13, 15, 24, 51, 52, 88, 204, 270, 271; unity of, 25, 259, 271–72, 278. *See also* extinction: human; fossils: future human
Hume, David, 240, 241, 251
Husserl, Edmund, 45, 81, 142, 144, 181, 212, 255; animals, 137–38, 155; earth, 15, 47, 48, 271–72, 277–80; fossils, 54; lifeworld, 47; mathematization of nature, 15; time, 13; touching–touched relation, 76–77, 145, 181–82, 195; world annihilation, 21, 178, 206, 207, 210–12, 221–22
Hutton, James, 50–51, 53, 241

imagination: apocalyptic, 176–79, 185, 186, 187, 190, 192, 194, 199; cosmic, 21, 175–79, 185, 187, 194;

eco-eschatological, 23, 60, 153–54, 206, 212, 230, 280
immemorial past. *See* Merleau-Ponty, Maurice: immemorial past; time: immemorial
insects, 111, 127, 134, 266: fossilized, 4. *See also* bees
instinct, 19, 91, 96, 106, 107, 112, 116–20, 125–26, 128, 132, 135, 243
Isadore of Seville, 64

James, Simon, 63–64
Jones, Ben, 247
Judgment Day, 23, 239, 241, 244, 245–50, 253
Jung, Carl, 287n20

Kafka, Franz, 111
Kant, Immanuel, 13, 14, 65, 124, 208, 240–41, 247–48, 251, 291n4
Katz, Eric, 266
Kearney, Richard, 157–58, 161
Kepler, Johannes, 64
Klein, Naomi, 245
Koffka, Kurt, 65
Köhler, Wolfgang, 65, 69, 137
Kripke, Saul, 47
Kruse, Jamie, 258

Lacan, Jacques, 104–5, 111
language, 47, 49, 82–83, 112, 115, 224, 269; of bees, 130–31; diacritical difference and, 80, 158–62, 164, 166, 275–76; extinction of, 170; life compared with, 7, 21, 157, 167, 276; music and, 83; species and, 170
Laplace, Pierre, 44, 47, 49, 54
Lascaux, 61
Lawlor, Leonard, 83, 95–97, 100, 101–3, 107, 150, 209
Leach, Jeremy, 64
Leopold, Aldo, 88, 165
Levinas, Emmanuel, 18, 21–22, 59–60, 138, 179, 183, 187, 188–91, 194, 206, 211–12, 230
Lévi-Strauss, Claude, 18, 66, 78–81, 83, 283n10
Lewontin, Richard, 283n4

Library of Water, 24, 240, 253–55
life, 13, 93, 97–98, 112, 116–17, 119, 122, 125, 125–26, 129, 134, 139, 159, 164, 228; as autoaffection, 19, 90, 100, 155–56, 217; bare, 20, 139, 155; death and, 19, 91, 102, 107, 154–56, 158, 170–71, 186, 187, 199, 207, 212, 223, 227, 228–29, 232; as diacritical, 158–59, 163–64, 275, 276 (*see also* biodiacritics); as expressive, 105–8, 166–67, 169; as gestalt, 57–58, 67–73, 141–43, 144–45, 146–47; hospitality toward, 164; language and, 7, 21, 157, 167, 276; last universal common ancestor of, 7, 273; as memory, 7, 21, 57–58, 149, 159, 169–70, 274–76; music and, 65–74, 103, 148–49; nonorganic, 107–9; saying no to, 139, 141, 144; temporality of, 38, 87, 232; universal history of, 24–25, 271, 274–76, 279; valuing differences of, 157, 159
lifeworld, 46, 47, 56, 220, 258, 264
Lindauer, Martin, 132
Llewelyn, John, 232
Lyme Regis, 1–2, 3

Madison, Gary, 58
Maeterlinck, Maurice, 19, 112, 117–20
Maier, Donald, 156–57
Malraux, André, 82
Mandelbrot, Benoit, 73
Marx, Karl, 215, 247
materialism, 188, 205; new, 6; radical, 213, 226
materiality, 15, 18, 23, 54, 57–58, 60, 108, 188, 189, 190–91, 194, 196–99, 207, 210, 214, 227–29, 232–34, 251, 261; geo-, 4, 6, 17, 23, 24, 25, 198, 206, 230–32, 257–58, 261. *See also* elements; materialism; stone
McKibben, Bill, 24, 202, 259, 260, 261, 262, 263, 267
McNamara, Kenneth, 61
McNeil, William, 124, 134
Meillassoux, Quentin, 13–15, 16, 18, 44, 45, 49, 51–54, 56, 60, 198, 272

326 Index

memory, 29, 35, 37, 41, 67, 74, 78, 143, 169, 251, 254, 255; corporeal, 170; diacritical, 276, 277; evolutionary, 6–7, 20–21, 73, 143, 149, 154, 170, 251, 274–76, 280; geological, 199, 207, 231, 232; involuntary, 149; life as, 7, 21, 57–58, 149, 159, 169–70, 274–76; ontological, 7, 21, 25, 72, 276–77, 279–80; organic, 73, 106, 154, 274–75; of the world, 17, 18, 25, 31, 32, 42, 46, 53, 54, 63, 66, 87, 261, 273, 274, 276, 277

Merleau-Ponty, Maurice, 43, 233; alterity of things, 63; anonymous and personal selves, 17, 31–36, 58–59, 79–80, 140, 147–48, 184; art, 21, 179–88; Derrida and, 22, 47–48, 179, 195–96; desire, 106, 107; diacritical difference, 158–64, 276; earth, 48, 272, 277–79; elements, 186–87, 188; embodiment, 29–36, 58, 76, 99, 178; ethics, 81–82; expression, 32, 81–82, 105, 160–61, 181; flesh, 18, 21, 29, 38, 49, 66, 78, 91, 98, 99–103, 107–8, 158, 162, 179, 182, 276, 279, 288n10; foundation of mathematical truth, 15; human–animal relation, 19, 20, 71, 73, 91, 97, 98–99, 105–7, 137, 138–48, 150, 155; immemorial past, 17–18, 30, 31–32, 34, 36–37, 41–42, 54, 58–59, 80–81, 140, 148, 184–87, 192, 195; institution, 53; language, 80, 158–62; life, 57–58, 65, 66–70, 73–75, 83, 87, 103, 108, 139, 141–45, 164–65, 167; music, 65, 66, 67–74, 78–83, 99, 103, 143; naturalism, 104, 268; natural time, 6–7, 17, 29–42, 46–49, 53; nature, 40–41, 46, 53, 58, 71–72, 75, 103, 105, 180–81, 186, 268–69, 272, 273; ontology, 18, 29, 47–48, 57–58, 66, 69–76, 78–79, 87, 100, 143, 162–63, 179, 182, 269, 276; perception, 3, 41, 48, 158, 161–62; radical reflection, 31–32, 36, 41–42, 74–76, 181, 191–92, 195; silence, 62, 80–81, 83, 98, 161, 162;

symbolic behavior, 70–71; *there is*, 188–89; touching–touched relation, 21–22, 76–78, 82, 99–100, 102, 145–46, 179–82, 192–93, 195–96; transcendental philosophy, 57, 104, 142; world prior to humanity, 44–49, 55–56. *See also* chiasm; *écart*

Messiaen, Olivier, 149

Mill, John Stuart, 261–62, 267–68

Miller, Jerome, 17, 273–74

Morin, Marie-Eve, 196, 226

Morris, David, 129, 163

mourning, 186, 207, 222, 223, 231, 232

Munch, Edvard, 177

Murphy, William, 245–46

music: life and, 65–74, 103, 148–49; myth and, 283n10; nature and, 64–75, 79, 109, 194–95; ontology and, 18, 67–74, 78–83, 143. See also *musica universalis*

musica universalis, 18, 64, 65, 66, 67

Naas, Michael, 225, 290n19

Naess, Arne, 143, 165

Nancy, Jean-Luc, 22, 23–24, 196–99, 206, 207–8, 212–19, 224, 225–26, 229, 230, 232, 233–34, 239, 248–49, 252, 262, 269, 274, 276

naturalism, 19, 44, 45, 46–47, 56, 72, 90–91, 94, 96–98, 100, 102, 103, 104, 107, 138, 142, 144, 180, 181, 208, 238

nature, 109, 120, 124; art and, 167, 180–86, 193–94; autoaffection and, 195–96; autonomy of, 63–64, 75, 78, 186, 189–90, 259–73; auto-productivity of, 105–8, 167, 268–69, 273; built environment and, 24, 261–68, 292n3; end of, 24, 259, 262; at the first day, 32, 36–40, 42, 185; historicity of, 38; human relation with, 258–64; mathematization of, 14, 16; music and, 64–75, 79, 109, 194–95; philosophy of, 214; self-concealment of, 63, 66, 74,

75, 78, 102; social construction of, 260–69; technology and, 213–14, 217 (*see also* ecotechnical). *See also* Merleau-Ponty, Maurice: nature; time: natural

Nazism, 92, 96

Neanderthals, 61, 257

Nelson, Stephanie, 115–16

Nietzsche, Friedrich, 93–94, 164

Nordhaus, Ted, 243

Novotny, Fritz, 186

nuclear: apocalypticism, 243; destruction, 8, 22, 153–54, 202–3, 211, 215, 217, 249; semiotics, 176–77, 204–5; war, 202–3, 211, 214, 223, 239, 241, 242; waste, 21, 176–77, 204–5, 216, 231, 274. *See also* Fukushima nuclear accident

Odum, Eugene, 165

O'Leary, Stephen, 245

Oliver, Kelly, 8, 91, 98–100, 101, 103, 105, 106, 109

ontological difference, 101, 109, 163, 190

ontology: diacritical, 162–63; gestalt, 18, 57–58, 65–76, 78, 87, 143, 144, 162; object-oriented, 14, 45, 49. *See also* memory: ontological; Merleau-Ponty, Maurice: ontology; music: ontology and; ontological difference; science: ontology and

painting, 21–22, 79, 81–82, 179–89, 193. *See also* Bacon, Francis; Cézanne, Paul; Munch, Edvard

Paley, William, 166

Pascal, Blaise, 59–60, 62

past that has never been present. *See* time: immemorial

perception: body-world dialogue of, 3; diacritical difference and, 161–62; sensation and, 21, 33, 179, 182–84, 186–88, 189, 194; temporal dimensions of, 3. *See also* Merleau-Ponty, Maurice: perception

phenomenology: alteraffection and, 108, 155, 212–13; animality and, 7, 19–20, 137–39, 141, 144, 155–56; apian, 113, 133–36; apocalypse and, 21, 178–79, 211–13; biodiversity and, 21; critical, 238; deep time and, 5–7, 13, 15–18, 21, 25, 44, 46, 54–60, 279–80; earth in, 15–16, 22, 24–25, 47–49, 53, 261, 271–72, 277–80; eco-, 206–7, 213, 289n9; elements in, 269; evolution and, 19, 92, 103; fossils and, 18, 54–57, 59; intentionality, 31, 104, 108, 155, 178, 187; mathematization of nature and, 14–15; motivation, 182; *musica universalis* and, 64–65; naturalism and, 19, 44–45, 56, 90–91, 103, 104; naturalizing, 104; natural time and, 29, 46; nature's self-concealment in, 63–64; reduction, 21, 142, 178, 179, 181; science and, 14–15, 45, 47, 49–55, 93, 104, 109, 271; stone and, 232; transcendental, 45, 46, 57, 92, 97–98, 208, 212, 221, 279; transcendental ego, 142, 144; wildness in, 268–69; world in, 22, 206, 208–14, 227, 280

philosophy: analytic–Continental divide in, 17, 43–44, 45; climate change and, 238; of consciousness, 45, 47–48, 56; environmental, 216; intuition and, 112, 116–17, 119–20, 126, 134; of nature, 214; transcendental, 57, 90, 97–98, 104, 108, 208, 212 (*see also* phenomenology: transcendental)

planetary thinking, 12–13, 15–16, 24, 259–61, 271–72, 277, 278, 279–80

Plath, Sylvia, 135–36

Plato, 19, 88, 90–91, 97, 111, 113

Playfair, John, 50–51, 241

Pliny the Elder, 1

poiesis, 18, 32, 39, 63, 64, 225

posthumanism, 65

present. *See* time: present

Proust, Marcel, 66, 79, 80, 149

328 *Index*

Putnam, Hilary, 47
Pythagoreans, 64

Quine, W. V. O., 47

racism, 92, 96, 236
Rádl, Emanuel, 127–28
realism, 47; environmental, 64;
postdeconstructive, 213; specula-
tive, 6, 13–14, 44, 45, 49, 56, 198,
272
Ricoeur, Paul, 142
Rilke, Rainer Maria, 150
Rogozinski, Jacob, 192–93
Rolston, Holmes, 154, 263
Rose, Neil, 10
Routley, Richard, 263

Sallis, John, 48–49, 150–51, 183,
190–91, 231–32
Sartre, Jean-Paul, 29, 40–41, 138,
182, 189
Saussure, Ferdinand de, 158, 159
Scheler, Max, 20, 112, 125–26, 128–29,
134, 138, 139, 141, 144
Schwägerl, Christian, 11, 259
science, 9, 11, 103, 109, 116–17, 119, 134,
218, 268; biologism and, 92–93; biology, 20–21, 65, 92–93, 103, 105–6,
122–23, 127, 163–64, 204; deep time
and, 4–5, 49–55, 60, 204, 241;
Earth system, 11, 16, 260, 270–71,
279, 280; ecology, 159, 165, 213, 214,
217; emergent properties in, 92;
geology, 8–11, 16, 24, 49–55, 230,
241; ontology and, 93, 98, 104, 123,
163–64; paleontology, 1, 4, 9, 204,
241; phenomenology and, 14–15,
45, 47, 49–55, 93, 104, 109, 271;
sociobiology, 92, 105, 107, 283n4;
technicization of, 14–15, 47
sensation, 128, 180–81; anonymous,
21, 33, 148, 179, 182–88, 189, 193–94;
as diacritical, 162; double, 76–77,
99, 181–82; intensification of,
91–92, 107–8
sensible–sentient relation, 76, 78,
195; of sight, 101–2, 108, 150–51; of

touch, 21–22, 76–78, 82, 99–102,
108, 145–46, 151, 179–82, 192–93,
195–96, 213. *See also* voice, reflexivity of
Serres, Michel, 251, 252, 255, 277
sexual selection. *See* evolution:
sexual selection in
Shellenberger, Michael, 243
Shelley, Mary, 201, 203–4, 241
silence, 18, 59–60, 62, 67, 80–81, 83,
87, 98, 103, 161, 183–84, 187, 189,
193, 269
Skrimshire, Stefan, 9, 244
Snyder, Gary, 88
social Darwinism, 92
sociobiology. *See* science:
sociobiology
Socrates, 113
speculative fiction, 201–8, 244–45
Srivastava, Diane, 156
Steedman, Carolyn, 269
stone, 54–55, 98, 122, 133–34, 186–87,
189, 197–99, 207, 225, 227–33, 277
sublime, 190, 230; temporal, 23,
50–51, 239, 240–42, 248, 249–50,
251
sustainability, 199, 204–5, 207, 214,
249, 279
Szerszynski, Bronislaw, 270

Taylor, Paul, 263
technology, 8, 22, 154, 213–19, 258,
265–69. *See also* ecotechnical
there is, 59–60, 188–89, 190–91, 214,
231, 233, 269
Throop, Bill, 165
Tilley, Christopher, 231
Tilman, David, 156
time: ancestral, 14–15, 18, 45, 49,
51–53, 60; apocalyptic image of,
23–24, 239–55; comic and tragic
modes of, 239, 245–47; creativity of, 37–40, 42; death and, 62;
elemental, 6, 18, 46, 55, 59, 183,
194, 254–55; embodied, 6, 20, 35,
42, 46, 58–59, 79–80, 261, 276; entangled durations of, 4, 53, 251–55,
272–73, 277, 279–80; evolutionary,

7, 18, 19, 55, 154, 273–76; general equivalence of, 198–99, 216, 248–55, 274; as historical, 273–74, 276–77, 279–80; human experience of, 6, 13, 33–35, 272; immemorial, 6, 17–18, 20, 22, 25, 30, 31–32, 34, 36, 41–42, 53–55, 58–60, 73–74, 80, 137, 147, 149–50, 159, 170, 176, 179, 191, 231–32, 251, 269; incommensurable scales of, 12–13, 46, 60–61, 194, 251–55, 260–61, 271, 272–73, 277; justice and, 216, 239–40, 248–55; music and, 68, 79; natural, 6–7, 17, 29–42, 46; perceptual scales of, 3–4; present, 198–99, 203–4, 208, 218–19, 238, 240, 251–55, 276; serial order of, 6, 52, 198, 245–46, 252, 273–74, 276–77; spiraling, 24, 240, 253–55; subjective bias in philosophical theories of, 13; sublime and, 23, 50–51, 239, 240–42, 248, 249–50, 251; sun and, 48–49. *See also* deep time; eternity; future; Judgment Day; perception: temporal dimensions of

touching–touched relation. *See* sensible–sentient relation: of touch

Turrell, James, 193

Tyson, Neil deGrasse, 204

Uexküll, Jakob von, 18, 19, 65–66, 67–70, 112, 113, 121–24, 127–30, 137, 143

Umwelt, 19, 69, 70, 113, 121–24, 130

unbuilt, 24, 261, 264–68, 269, 272, 292n3

Valéry, Paul, 158

van Dooren, Thom, 154

Vellend, Mark, 156

Vergil, 19, 112, 114–17, 120, 126, 127

Vienna Circle, 47

Vinteuil, 66, 79, 80

Vogel, Steven, 24, 260–70

voice, reflexivity of, 67, 82–83, 149–50

von Frisch, Karl, 121, 130–32

von Haller, Albrecht, 240–41

Vrahimis, Andreas, 43

Wagar, W. Warren, 201

war, 8, 201, 202–3, 211, 214, 223, 241, 242

Welton, Donn, 22, 206, 209–11

Wentworth, Charles, 230

Whitehead, A. N., 17, 31, 32, 40–42, 53, 63, 273, 279

white supremacy, 250

Whyte, Kyle Powys, 24, 240, 250, 253–55

wilderness, 214, 269

Wilderness Act, 88

wildness, 24, 88, 261, 266–69

Williams, George, 166, 169–70, 274–75

Wilson, Edward O., 92, 111

Wood, David, 89, 104, 134, 138, 206

world, 128; absolute Outside as, 14, 52; beginning of the, 183, 184–85, 187, 208–9, 210, 212, 220; in common, 220–26, 232; ecotechnical and, 217–18; elements and, 191, 199, 207, 226–27, 258; end of the, 18, 22–23, 52, 60, 153–54, 170–71, 177–79, 183, 184, 188, 193–94, 196–99, 201–34, 237, 238, 243, 249; memory of the, 17, 18, 25, 31, 32, 42, 46, 53, 54, 63, 66, 87, 261, 273, 274, 276, 277; as phantasm, 22–23, 207, 220, 224–25, 232; phenomenological concept of, 22, 206, 208–14, 227, 280; planet distinct from, 16, 208, 270–72; sense of, 196–99, 207–8, 213–14, 217–19, 226–27, 233, 249; stone and, 227–233; unity of, 8, 187, 209–12, 224. *See also* animal: poverty in world of; bees: world of; lifeworld; *Umwelt*

World Trade Center, 206, 209–11

Xenophanes, 55

Zeno, 159

(continued from page ii)

54 *Postcinematic Vision: The Coevolution of Moving-Image Media and the Spectator*
Roger F. Cook

53 *Bleak Joys: Aesthetics of Ecology and Impossibility*
Matthew Fuller and Olga Goriunova

52 *Variations on Media Thinking*
Siegfried Zielinski

51 *Aesthesis and Perceptronium: On the Entanglement of Sensation, Cognition, and Matter*
Alexander Wilson

50 *Anthropocene Poetics: Deep Time, Sacrifice Zones, and Extinction*
David Farrier

49 *Metaphysical Experiments: Physics and the Invention of the Universe*
Bjørn Ekeberg

48 *Dialogues on the Human Ape*
Laurent Dubreuil and Sue Savage-Rumbaugh

47 *Elements of a Philosophy of Technology: On the Evolutionary History of Culture*
Ernst Kapp

46 *Biology in the Grid: Graphic Design and the Envisioning of Life*
Phillip Thurtle

45 *Neurotechnology and the End of Finitude*
Michael Haworth

44 *Life: A Modern Invention*
Davide Tarizzo

43 *Bioaesthetics: Making Sense of Life in Science and the Arts*
Carsten Strathausen

42 *Creaturely Love: How Desire Makes Us More and Less Than Human*
Dominic Pettman

41 *Matters of Care: Speculative Ethics in More Than Human Worlds*
María Puig de la Bellacasa

40 *Of Sheep, Oranges, and Yeast: A Multispecies Impression*
Julian Yates

39 *Fuel: A Speculative Dictionary*
Karen Pinkus

38 *What Would Animals Say If We Asked the Right Questions?*
Vinciane Despret

37 *Manifestly Haraway*
Donna J. Haraway

36 *Neofinalism*
Raymond Ruyer

35 *Inanimation: Theories of Inorganic Life*
David Wills

34 *All Thoughts Are Equal: Laruelle and Nonhuman Philosophy*
John Ó Maoilearca

33 *Necromedia*
Marcel O'Gorman

32 *The Intellective Space: Thinking beyond Cognition*
Laurent Dubreuil

31 *Laruelle: Against the Digital*
Alexander R. Galloway

30 *The Universe of Things: On Speculative Realism*
Steven Shaviro

29 *Neocybernetics and Narrative*
Bruce Clarke

28 *Cinders*
Jacques Derrida

27 *Hyperobjects: Philosophy and Ecology after the End of the World*
Timothy Morton

26 *Humanesis: Sound and Technological Posthumanism*
David Cecchetto

25 *Artist Animal*
Steve Baker

24 *Without Offending Humans: A Critique of Animal Rights*
Élisabeth de Fontenay

23 *Vampyroteuthis Infernalis: A Treatise, with a Report by the Institut Scientifique de Recherche Paranaturaliste*
Vilém Flusser and Louis Bec

22 *Body Drift: Butler, Hayles, Haraway*
Arthur Kroker

21 *HumAnimal: Race, Law, Language*
Kalpana Rahita Seshadri

20 *Alien Phenomenology, or What It's Like to Be a Thing*
Ian Bogost

19 *CIFERAE: A Bestiary in Five Fingers*
Tom Tyler

18 *Improper Life: Technology and Biopolitics from Heidegger to Agamben*
Timothy C. Campbell

17 *Surface Encounters: Thinking with Animals and Art*
Ron Broglio

16 *Against Ecological Sovereignty: Ethics, Biopolitics, and Saving the Natural World*
Mick Smith

15 *Animal Stories: Narrating across Species Lines*
Susan McHugh

14 *Human Error: Species-Being and Media Machines*
Dominic Pettman

13 *Junkware*
Thierry Bardini

12 *A Foray into the Worlds of Animals and Humans,* with *A Theory of Meaning*
Jakob von Uexküll

11 *Insect Media: An Archaeology of Animals and Technology*
Jussi Parikka

10 *Cosmopolitics II*
Isabelle Stengers

9 *Cosmopolitics I*
Isabelle Stengers

8 *What Is Posthumanism?*
Cary Wolfe

7 *Political Affect: Connecting the Social and the Somatic*
John Protevi

6 *Animal Capital: Rendering Life in Biopolitical Times*
Nicole Shukin

5 *Dorsality: Thinking Back through Technology and Politics*
David Wills

4 *Bíos: Biopolitics and Philosophy*
Roberto Esposito

3 *When Species Meet*
Donna J. Haraway

2 *The Poetics of DNA*
Judith Roof

1 *The Parasite*
Michel Serres

Ted Toadvine is the Nancy Tuana Director of the Rock Ethics Institute and associate professor of philosophy at The Pennsylvania State University. He is author of *Merleau-Ponty's Philosophy of Nature* and editor or translator of six books, including *The Merleau-Ponty Reader* and *Eco-Phenomenology: Back to the Earth Itself.*